D0428126

Investing in People

RURAL STUDIES SERIES
of the
Rural Sociological Society

Series Editor

Forrest A. Deseran, *Louisiana State University*

Editorial Board

Lionel J. Beaulieu, *University of Florida*
Richard S. Krannich, *Utah State University*
Dudley L. Poston, *Texas A&M University*
C. Matthew Snipp, *University of Wisconsin–Madison*
Deborah M. Tootle, *USDA ERS ARED*
DeeAnn Wenk, *University of Oklahoma*

Rural Studies Series

Investing in People: The Human Capital Needs of Rural America, Lionel J. Beaulieu and David Mulkey

Against All Odds: Rural Community in the Information Age, John C. Allen and Don A. Dillman

Rural Data, People, and Policy: Information Systems for the 21st Century, edited by James A. Christenson, Richard C. Maurer, and Nancy L. Strang

Economic Adaptation: Alternatives for Nonmetropolitan Areas, edited by David L. Barkley

Persistent Poverty in Rural America, Rural Sociological Society Task Force on Persistent Rural Poverty

Rural Policies for the 1990s, edited by Cornelia B. Flora and James A. Christenson

Research, Realpolitik, and Development in Korea: The State and the Green Revolution, Larry L. Burmeister

Investing in People

The Human Capital Needs of Rural America

EDITED BY

Lionel J. Beaulieu
and David Mulkey

Westview Press

BOULDER • SAN FRANCISCO • OXFORD

Rural Studies Series, Sponsored by the Rural Sociological Society

All rights reserved. No part of this publication may be reproduced or transmitted in any form or by any means, electronic or mechanical, including photocopy, recording, or any information storage and retrieval system, without permission in writing from the publisher.

Copyright © 1995 by Westview Press, Inc.

Published in 1995 in the United States of America by Westview Press, Inc., 5500 Central Avenue, Boulder, Colorado 80301-2877, and in the United Kingdom by Westview Press, 12 Hid's Copse Road, Cumnor Hill, Oxford OX2 9JJ

Library of Congress Cataloging-in-Publication Data
Investing in people : the human capital needs of rural America /
    edited by Lionel J. Beaulieu and David Mulkey.
      p.   cm. — (Rural studies series)
    Includes bibliographical references and index.
    ISBN 0-8133-8503-2
    1. Rural development—United States.   2. Human capital—United
States.   3. United States—Rural conditions.   I. Beaulieu, Lionel
J.   II. Mulkey, W. David.   III. Series: Rural studies series of the
Rural Sociological Society.
HN90.C6I58   1995
307.1'412'0973—dc20

92-13025
CIP

Printed and bound in the United States of America

The paper used in this publication meets the requirements
of the American National Standard for Permanence of Paper
for Printed Library Materials Z39.48-1984.

10   9   8   7   6   5   4   3   2   1

To the late Ken Wilkinson, who, in addition to making a significant contribution to this book, instilled in those of us who were fortunate enough to have known him, a spirit of caring for the people and communities of rural America.

Contents

Acknowledgments   xi
List of Contributors   xiii

PART ONE
From Concept to Reality

1   Human Capital in Rural America: A Review of Theoretical
    Perspectives
    Lionel J. Beaulieu and David Mulkey   3

2   Current Status of Human Capital in the Rural U.S.
    Molly Sizer Killian and Lionel J. Beaulieu   23

PART TWO
Forces Shaping the Future of Rural America

3   Economic Forces Shaping the Future of Rural America
    Glen C. Pulver   49

4   Social Forces Shaping the Future of Rural Areas
    Kenneth P. Wilkinson   65

5   Paradigm Gridlock and the Two Faces of Technology
    Drew Hyman, Larry Gamm and John Shingler   85

PART THREE
Aspects of Human Resources Conditions Across Rural America

6   Human Capital and Nonmetropolitan Poverty
    Leif Jensen and Diane K. McLaughlin   111

7   The Educational Attainments of American Indians
    C. Matthew Snipp   139

8   Down and Out in Rural America: The Status of Blacks
    and Hispanics in the 1980s
    Thomas A. Lyson   167

9   Gender Differences in Human Capital in Rural America
    Jill L. Findeis   183

10 Adapting to Economic Change: The Case of Displaced Workers
    Paul Swaim   213

11 Migration and the Loss of Human Resources in Rural America
    Daniel T. Lichter, Diane K. McLaughlin and Gretchen T. Cornwell   235

PART FOUR
Strategies for Strengthening the Human Capital Resources
of Rural America

12 Capacity Building: Reexamining the Role of the Rural School
    Daryl Hobbs   259

13 The Influence of Health and Health Care on Rural Economic
    Development
    W. Bruce Vogel and Raymond T. Coward   285

14 Family and Household Effects on the Educational Attainment
    of Young Adults
    DeeAnn Wenk and Constance L. Hardesty   313

15 The Labor Market and Human Capital Investment
    *Judith I. Stallmann, Ari Mwachofi, Jan L. Flora
    and Thomas G. Johnson*   333

16 Community Agency and Disaffection: Enhancing Collective
    Resources
    A. E. Luloff and L. E. Swanson   351

17 Human Capital as a Rural Development Strategy: Promise or
    False Hope?
    David Mulkey and Lionel J. Beaulieu   373

    Index   381

Acknowledgments

The idea of devoting an entire volume to human resources issues in rural America was conceived in the late 1980s, at a time when rural communities across the U.S. were suffering the pains associated with a significant restructuring of their economies. A host of reports being released by various public agencies and private organizations were suggesting that America's workforce simply did not possess the knowledge and skills needed to effectively compete in the "new economy." Since the rural labor force was less likely to be as educated or well-trained as workers residing in urban areas, it was feared that rural areas would suffer the lion's share of the social and economic woes resulting from this transformation.

As a way to begin the process of systematically assessing the human resources issues in the rural U.S., we approached the directors of the respective Regional Rural Development Centers to seek their assistance. Each director agreed to send and provide financial support for a small number of individuals from their region to take part in a weekend "think" session that we (i.e., Beaulieu and Mulkey) organized in Atlanta, GA. The list of participants included Jan Bokemeier (Michigan State University), Peggy Cook (ERS/ARED), Don Dillman (Washington State University), Jill Findeis (Penn State University), Glen Pulver (University of Wisconsin), Sue Raftery (formally with Auburn University), and Bonnie Teater (Southern Rural Development Center). During the course of that weekend, participants engaged in a lively and stimulating discussion of the human capital issues in rural America. It was from these discussions that the outline of this book and list of potential chapter authors took shape. The completed volume preserves much of what was debated and decided at that Atlanta meeting. To our colleagues who gave unselfishly of their precious time to be part of our Atlanta work session, we express our sincere thanks.

Appreciation is extended to the four center directors who believed in what we were trying to accomplish with this edited volume. These individuals are Doss Brodnax (Southern Rural Development Center, Mississippi State University), Daryl Heasley (Northeast Regional Center for Rural Development, Penn State University), Pete Korsching (North Central Regional Center for Rural Development, Iowa State University), and Russ Youmans (Western Rural Development Center, Oregon State University).

Producing a manuscript of this nature cannot be realized without the involvement of a variety of very talented individuals. Eileen Beckett, from *re: formats*, worked tirelessly on various working drafts of each chapter and sought to ensure that the final document would be produced in accordance with Westview Press guidelines. Her dedication to and positive spirit in approaching this monumental task is very much appreciated. We also are grateful to Mike Garner, graduate research assistant, who spent many hours redesigning several of the figures contained in this book.

Moreover, several of our social science colleagues were called upon to critically review and comment on each of our book chapters. There is little doubt that the many revisions made as a consequence of their input resulted in a much-improved product. To them, we extend our deepest appreciation for their professionalism and friendship.

Lionel J. (Bo) Beaulieu
David Mulkey

Contributors

Lionel J. Beaulieu is Professor of Rural Sociology, Institute of Food and Agricultural Sciences, University of Florida.

Gretchen T. Cornwell is a Research Associate in the Population Research Institute, Penn State University.

Raymond T. Coward is Professor and Associate Director of the Institute of Health Policy Research, University of Florida.

Jill L. Findeis serves as Associate Professor in Penn State University's Department of Agricultural Economics and Rural Sociology.

Jan L. Flora is Professor in the Department of Sociology, Iowa State University.

Larry Gamm is Associate Professor of Health Policy and Administration at Penn State University.

Constance L. Hardesty is Assistant Professor in the Department of Sociology, Social Work, and Criminology at Morehead State University, Kentucky.

Daryl Hobbs is Professor of Rural Sociology and Director of the Office of Social and Economic Data Analysis, University of Missouri at Columbia.

Drew Hyman is Professor of Public Policy and Community Systems, Department of Agricultural Economics and Rural Sociology, Penn State University.

Leif Jensen is Assistant Professor in the Department of Agricultural Economics and Rural Sociology at Penn State University.

Thomas G. Johnson is Professor in the Department of Agricultural and Applied Economics, Virginia Polytechnic Institute and State University.

Molly Sizer Killian is Coordinator of the Rural Policy Research Institute, Department of Agricultural Economics and Rural Sociology, University of Arkansas.

Daniel T. Lichter is Professor of Sociology in the Department of Sociology, Penn State University.

A. E. Luloff is Professor of Rural Sociology, Department of Agricultural Economics and Rural Sociology, Penn State University.

Thomas A. Lyson is Professor in the Department of Rural Sociology, Cornell University.

Diane K. McLaughlin is a Research Associate in the Population Research Institute, Penn State University.

David Mulkey is Professor of Regional Economics, Food and Resources Economics Department, University of Florida.

Ari Mwachofi is a Doctoral Candidate in the Department of Agricultural and Applied Economics, Virginia Polytechnic Institute and State University.

Glen C. Pulver is Professor Emeritus, Department of Agricultural Economics, University of Wisconsin, Madison.

John Shingler is Project Manager of the Consumer Services Information System Project, Penn State University.

C. Matthew Snipp is Professor in the Department of Rural Sociology and Director of American Indian Studies, University of Wisconsin, Madison.

Judith I. Stallmann is Assistant Professor in the Department of Agricultural and Applied Economics, Virginia Polytechnic Institute and State University.

Paul Swaim is Leader of the Rural Labor Section, Human Resources and Industry Branch, Economic Research Service, U.S. Department of Agriculture, Washington, D.C.

L. E. Swanson is Professor in the Department of Sociology, University of Kentucky.

W. Bruce Vogel is Associate Professor in the Department of Health Services Administration and a faculty affiliate in the Institute of Health Policy Research, University of Florida.

DeeAnn Wenk is Assistant Professor in the Department of Sociology, University of Oklahoma.

Kenneth P. Wilkinson served as Professor of Rural Sociology at Penn State University. Dr. Wilkinson passed away in the Fall of 1993.

PART ONE

From Concept to Reality

1

Human Capital in Rural America: A Review of Theoretical Perspectives

Lionel J. Beaulieu
David Mulkey

Over the course of the last three decades, the social sciences literature has given a significant amount of attention to the set of factors that might prove important in explaining why some people are better able than others to command the knowledge and skills needed to participant actively in the labor force. Why is it that rural areas consistently do more poorly than urban areas on educational attainment, earned wages, and employment status of its populace? Are rural residents more likely to possess certain individual or family characteristics that predispose them to a life of economic hardships vis a vis their urban counterparts? Or, are the forces that constrain the economic well-being of rural people less a matter of their human resource attributes and more a matter of a broader set of structural characteristics associated with rural areas that effectively condition the type of economic success people residing in these localities are likely to enjoy over the long term? These are but a sampling of the difficult questions that social scientists have devoted their energies to over the past several years.

As a product of these efforts, a significant number of theoretical frameworks have been advanced. Some have been focused principally on the characteristics that individuals bring to the marketplace, the so-called supply side of the equation. Others, on the other hand, have given attention to the demand side—the set of social structural factors that affect the type of jobs available in local areas (Granovetter 1981). Our intent, in this chapter, is to offer a brief overview of these conceptual models, particularly those that are incorporated in one or more of the chapters contained in this volume. While not attempting to be all inclusive, the hope in this chapter is to offer readers a vehicle for quickly familiarizing themselves with key elements associated with these major theoretical approaches.

Education as an Investment:
The Human Capital Framework

Rooted in the seminal work of Theodore Schultz (1961), and followed by those of Becker (1962) and Mincer ((1962), this perspective argues that variations in worker skills, productivity, and earnings are a consequence of different embodiments of human capital (Rumberger 1981). Central to the notion of human capital theory is the belief that individuals can, by forego-ing present earnings, significantly enhance the quality of their labor skills and augment their future job-related earnings (Riley 1979). As England (1992) notes, these improvements can be achieved through three major avenues: (1) formal schooling; (2) formal or informal on-the-job training activities that have utility to a variety of firms or industries; and (3) on-the-job training efforts that are firm/industry specific and have applica-tion only to the particular enterprises providing the training.[1]

The linkage between human capital investments and earnings is visually presented in Figure 1.1. As Marshall and Briggs (1989:190) argue, the fundamental assumption of human capital theory is that investments made by an individual, be they in the form of education and/or on-the-job

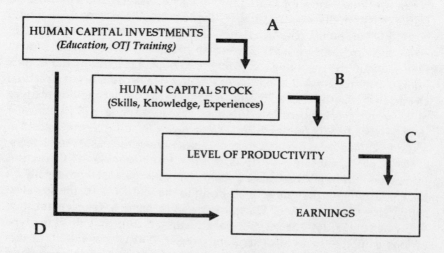

FIGURE 1.1. The Connection Between Human Capital Investments and Work-Related Earnings.

training, serve to enhance his/her human capital stock (i.e., the cognitive skills, knowledge, and experiences that one possesses). With this improved stock, it is purported that the person's productivity is enhanced. Because earnings are closely tied to productivity, an individual with greater human capital is expected to be more productive and, as a result, garner higher earning than a person with less human capital.

While Figure 1.1 offers a conceptualization of human capital theory, the ability of human capital theorists to fully subject these purported causal relationships to empirical scrutiny has been lacking. Marshall and Briggs (1989) suggest a number of reasons why this is so. For one, data needed to directly test the theory are limited. As an example, **Path A** in Figure 1.1 indicates that educational investments improve one's knowledge, skills, and experiences. A commonly used measure of educational investment embraced by human capital theorists is years of schooling completed (McCrackin 1984). Years of schooling reflects a measure of the quantity of time that a person has spent in school, but says nothing about the quality of the education that a person may have received while in school. It could be argued that the knowledge, skills, and experiences that one acquires is as much a product of the quality of the education received as it is the duration of time spent in school. But, educational quality is not a concept that is easily measurable. Similarly, links between variables represented in **Paths B** and **C** require access to sound information on worker productivity, data that are very difficult to secure.

Because of various measurement problems and the difficulty associated with acquiring data on many of the key elements incorporated in their model, human capital theorists have had to rely heavily on indirect examinations of their thesis. In essence, relationships implied in **Paths A, B,** and **C** have gone virtually untested and have had to be inferred by human capital proponents. Consequently, relationships denoted in **Path D** have been the central focus of most empirical analyses that they have conducted (Marshall and Briggs 1989). The general flavor of these studies is that human capital investments are positively associated with individuals' work-related earnings (Becker 1975: Mincer 1974: Schultz 1961).

While human capital theory has garnered its share of supporters, it has been the subject of much criticism. Concerns have tended to develop along two major lines: (1) the relative inattention given as to why some persons are better able than others to invest in their human capital; and (2) the simplistic linkage that human capital theorists contend exist between investments and work-related earnings. We briefly turn to the first of these lines of criticisms.

Human capital theory assumes that individuals rationally decide whether or not to invest in their human capital after undergoing careful analysis of the expected costs of, and future returns from, such investments

(Cohn 1975: Rumberger 1981).[2] Accordingly, disparities existing among individuals, be they in terms of income levels or occupational status, are viewed as end-products of prior human capital investment decisions reached by these individuals (Smith 1993). Realizing economic success, therefore, is a burden that rest squarely on the shoulders of individuals (Falk and Lyson 1988).

Some critics contend, however, that investment decisions of this nature are an outgrowth of a pre-existing set of productivity-enhancement attributes that place some people in a more favorable position to follow through on such investments (Marshall and Briggs 1989). Family background characteristics, for example, have much to say about why some persons are more likely than others to invest in schooling or other human capital investment activities (McCrackin 1984: Smith 1993). Further, the communities or neighborhoods in which individuals reside may prove important given that they represent the social context in which residents' educational aspirations are often fostered (Semyonov 1981).

There is little doubt, however, that the lion's share of attention in the literature has centered around the second line of criticisms. Horan et al. (1980) note that human capital proponents assume a marketplace that is open, homogeneous, and equally accessible to all individuals. This assumption leads human capital theorists to believe that an individual's competitive position in the marketplace, and the financial rewards that he or she receives, are tied directly to the resources that the person brings to that marketplace. But critics suggest that the linkage between human capital investments and economic rewards is far from direct. One opposing viewpoint intimates that schooling does not directly lead to higher income. Rather, formal education is used as a screening mechanism for selecting persons who are likely to be the best candidates for productivity-enhancing job training (Marshall and Briggs 1989; Spence 1974; Thurow 1975). Another perspective contends that the structure of jobs, and the rewards associated with such positions, differ across various structural contexts (Fligstein et al. 1983; Granovetter 1981). Due to the manner in which the economy or labor market is organized, rates of return to human capital are greater in some economies or labor markets than in others (Horan et al. 1980; Rumberger 1981; Snipp et al. 1993). The collective message contained within the second line of criticisms is that the linkage between human capital investments and earnings cannot be fully understood without a careful study of the social structural and institutional forces facilitating or impeding economic opportunities for labor force participants (Fligstein et al 1983; Summers et al. 1993).

The alternative frameworks developed in response to the two distinct streams of criticisms of human capital theory are the subject of the remainder of this chapter.

Family and Community as Contributors
to Human Capital Development

One of the significant criticisms advanced against human capital theorists, as noted earlier, is their tendency to be insensitive to forces beyond the individual that may impinge on his/her capacity to invest in himself/herself (McCrackin 1984). It has been suggested, for example, that individuals' abilities and levels of schooling are significantly shaped by important family characteristics (Rumberger 1983). The line of thought that best exemplifies this perspective is the work conducted under the banner of status attainment research (see for example, Blau and Duncan (1967) and Sewell et al. (1969)). This well developed theoretical framework contends that a family's socioeconomic status (SES) plays a substantial role in shaping a persons's success in school and in influencing his/her early occupational choices. In essence, SES serves to condition the environment of support for aspirations and achievement in that individuals from higher SES families are more often socialized to place a high value on educational achievement (Blau and Duncan 1967; Smith 1993; Wagenaar 1987).

The clear message from the social status research is that a family's location within the social stratification system represents a dominant factor in models of educational/occupational attainment, and in the earnings that one garners once in the marketplace (Blau and Duncan 1967; Granovetter 1981; Smith 1993). Findings emerging from this research have been subjected to several replications and the outcomes of such efforts have reaffirmed the significant role of family SES in explaining educational and occupational aspirations and attainment (Campbell 1983).

Extending Status Attainment Research

An important variation and expansion of the status attainment research is proffered in works by James S. Coleman and his associates (for example, Coleman 1990; Coleman and Hoffer 1987; Coleman et al. 1982). Coleman (1988b) concurs that family background plays a central role in the academic success and aspirations of children, as noted in the status attainment literature. He argues, however, that the influence of family background can be actually disaggregated into three important components; families provide *financial capital, human capital,* and *social capital* to their children. *Financial capital* constitutes the wealth and income which the family possesses, resources that can facilitate the child's access to activities that might enhance achievement. The notion of *human capital* represents the educational level of the parents, a measure that offers some clue of the cognitive environment to which the child might be exposed and which might contribute to learning. *Social capital* reflects the nature of the relations that exist between the child and parents, or between the child and other members of the family (Coleman 1988a: S109). It represents the norms, the social networks, and the relationships between adults and children that are of value to the child while growing up (Coleman 1990: 334).

What is of particular interest is the argument advanced by Coleman that social capital is on par with human capital in terms of its importance in stimulating the emergence of skilled and capable individuals. Using family as the reference point, he states that the human capital attributes embedded in parents (such as their educational or occupational status) have a more limiting impact on the educational growth of their child when they fail to be complemented by social capital, represented by quality interactions and relations between parents and child (Coleman 1988b: 384). He notes that despite the human capital enhancements that parents have achieved over the course of the last several years, the academic performance and success of students has not kept pace with these human capital improvements. The reason, argues Coleman, is that the social capital of the family, denoted by the presence of parents in the home and by strong parent child interactions on matters of academic, social and personal concerns, has slowly eroded. And, it is this weakening of the family's social capital that has jeopardized the human capital stock of today's youth (Coleman 1990: 336).

The Role of the Community

Majoribanks (1972:324) offers the view that family constitutes only one part of the "total network of forces" impacting educational and occupational aspirations of individuals. The social environment represented by the community constitutes another vital factor impacting aspirations and attainment. The importance of community can be traced, in fact, to the status attainment research where the impact of the community on the social stratification process has been given treatment. Such studies have found that greater opportunities to enhance one's status are likely to be found in larger-sized, more complex communities (Lane 1968). Similarly, educational and occupational aspirations tend to be higher among urban and small town students than students residing in rural areas (Cobb et al. 1989; Sewell 1964). Rural students, for example, are more inclined than urban or suburban students to feel satisfied with less education and to report lower levels of occupational aspirations (Hansen and MacIntyre 1989).

A variety of studies note that size of community is associated with other important contextual attributes of a locality, such as level of industrialization, economic composition, and occupational structure—all factors which can affect a student's educational and career aspirations (Blau and Duncan 1967; Lane 1968; Semyonov 1981). These findings tend to lend support to the assertion by Wagenaar (1987:174) that community structural variables are valuable in that they help situate "individual level correlates within a larger context, thereby showing how individual decisions can be affected substantially by social structure."

But, achievement and aspirations are influenced by more than the structural characteristics of a community. Coleman suggests that communities can help youth be successful in school by investing in relationships with them through the process of interpersonal interaction. He finds, for example, that children from single-parent families are more like their two-parent counterparts in both achievement and in continuation in school when the schools are in communities with extensive social capital (Coleman 1991: 10). Social capital at the community level exists in the norms, social networks, and interactions between adults and children that serve to facilitate or support educational attainment. It is represented by the genuine concern and interest that adult members of the community have in the activities of another person's child. Signs of its presence include the enforcement of norms deemed important to the family or community, adults providing a listening ear to youngsters experiencing problems which they are hesitant to discuss with their parents, monitoring of students' activities by non-family adult members of the community, and providing a variety of community sponsored programs for youth that can serve to provide them with positive, productive environments for using their time and energy (Coleman et al. 1987).

Figure 1.2 attempts to bring synthesis to the set of pre-existing factors that weigh heavily on a person's human capital investment decisions and future employment-related opportunities and earnings. It suggests that family attributes, viewed in terms of the financial, human, and social capital endowments present in the home, have a potent impact on a person's

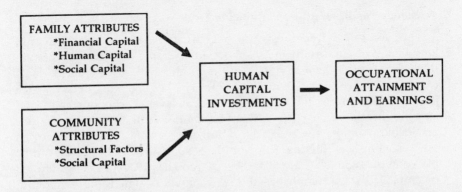

FIGURE 1.2. Factors Influencing the Human Capital Investment Activities of Individuals.

investment decisions and subsequent occupational and income attainment. At the same time, the community milieu in which the person resides plays a vital role. So, the structural characteristics of an individual's community, coupled with the strength of the social capital present in that locality, shape the social context affecting the person's human capital investment decisions (Semyonov 1981).

Exploring the Other Side of the Coin: Factors Affecting Labor Demand

The introduction of family and community attributes in Figure 1.2 is designed to offer a more comprehensive view of the factors affecting human capital investment decisions (and subsequent work-related earnings) by individuals. Without a doubt, the focus remains on the supply side—the set of traits that individuals bring to the marketplace. This singular focus on supply, however, has spurred concern among several social sciences researchers who have argued for the importance of articulating factors that affect the demand for workers. From this latter perspective, it is believed that the structural features of the job market, and the ability of that market to fully avail itself of the human capital qualities that workers bring to the marketplace, are forces that ultimately determine the economic well-being that individuals are likely to enjoy over their life course (Granovetter 1981; Sorensen 1983).

Three alternative perspectives are offered as frameworks for under-standing the role of social structural features in shaping or mediating the effects of individual human capital resources on income (Fligstein et al. 1983). These are the *screening/job competition model*, the *dual economy perspective*, and the *dual labor markets theory*.

Screening Hypothesis/Job Competition Model

The screening hypothesis suggest that employers, lacking full knowledge of the productivity of potential employees, rely on certain devices that offer them a "signal" of the productivity level of individuals (Arrow 1973; Spence 1974; Stiglitz 1975). The key signaling device which job candidates invest in is education. That is, level of schooling is utilized as a certification device by workers to communicate to employers their productive abilities. These signals, in turn, are read and used by employers for "screening" or "filtering" job candidates so that the right person can be placed in the right job (Layard and Psacharopoulas 1974). Earnings offered by employers are generally based on the amount of signals (i.e., schooling) that workers possess (Rumberger 1981; Spence 1973).

A critical distinguishing point between the screening hypothesis and

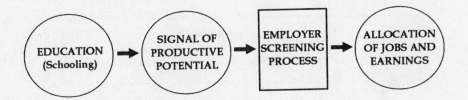

FIGURE 1.3. The Screening Hypothesis Framework.

human capital theory, however, is that "screening" advocates do not contend that education intrinsically enhances an individual's productivity (as do human capital theorists). Rather, schooling simply "certifies that those who have successfully completed a given level (of education) possess certain qualities (skills, ability or family background) that should be rewarded" (Goodman 1979: 270). Education, then, is used by employees to identify pre-existing differences in talents among potential employees (Layard and Psacharopoulos 1974).

A simple diagram of the screening hypothesis is offered in Figure 1.3. It shows that one of the key elements of this thesis is the existence of a filtering mechanism that operates for the purpose of efficiently allocating workers to jobs where they have the greatest comparative advantage (McCrackin 1984). Earnings received by workers is viewed as an outgrowth of the allocative (or screening) process carried out by the employer.

Closely aligned to the screening hypothesis is a framework introduced by Thurow (1975) under the rubric of "job competition model." This perspective suggests that there is an array of job opportunities that exists in the labor market and attached to these job positions are certain wages (Sakamoto 1988). These jobs are ranked on the basis of their desirability, from best to worst. Better jobs have attractive training ladders associated with them, while less desirable positions are accompanied by limited training slots (see Figure 1.4).

Workers' access to these jobs is dependent upon their location in the labor queue. The ranking of individuals in this queue is based upon the costs associated with training them to perform activities attached to different jobs in the economy. Persons who are expected to require the lowest training costs are ranked at the top of the labor queue, while individuals with the highest training costs are placed at the low end of the job queue. Background characteristics of potential employees serve as the key ingredients in ranking workers on the basis of their expected training costs. Educational attainment and performance are viewed as the most critical of

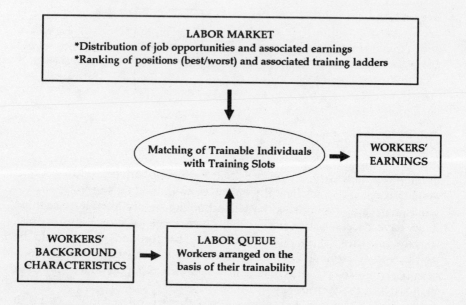

FIGURE 1.4. Key Elements of the Job Competition Model.

these background characteristics. However, other background factors such as age, sex, race, innate abilities, and dependability, can enter into the equation as well. The assumption is that workers who possess the more favorable background qualities require lower training costs and thus, should be ranked higher in the labor queue (Thurow 1975).

As Figure 1.4 suggests, a matching process occurs where individuals who are ranked higher in the labor queue are selected to fill the jobs that have better career lines and earning power (Sakamoto 1988), while persons having the least attractive background credentials are placed in the worst jobs. The intent of this matching process is to efficiently allocate employees to those slots that will minimize the training costs borne by the employer (McCrackin 1984). Depending upon the rate at which these jobs are accepted by workers, the employer will move down the labor queue until all available jobs (or training slots) have been filled (Thurow 1975). In the end, the earnings that employees receive are tied directly to the training ladders that they have been placed in.

Worthy of note is the role that discrimination plays in the labor queue ranking. Thurow (1975) contends that the process of positioning people in the labor queue commences with a careful review of objective attributes associated with potential employees, such as level of schooling, relevant experiences, and psychological tests. In the event that several individuals are found to have little difference in training costs as a result of this process, subjective factors enter into the picture. These subjective preferences become the deciding factors as to the labor queue ranking of individuals. If an employer is adverse to hiring women or minorities, regardless of how strong the objective background characteristics of these workers might be, such individuals will be placed at a lower position in the labor queue.

Dual Economy Theory

Proponents of the dual economy theory state that because of the historical manner in which production and distribution has developed in the United States, the economy can be said to consists of two distinct sectors—one being the core sector and the second the periphery (Averitt 1968; Beck et al. 1978; Horan et al. 1980). The underlying factor which serves to distinguish these sectors is the manner in which firms/industries situated within them are organized (Wallace and Kalleberg 1981). The core sector is founded on the basis of a high degree of monopolistic elements, while the periphery sector is based on competitive capitalism. This basic distinction "produces fundamentally different market situations with different principles governing the organization of production" (Horan et al. 1980: 282).

Drawing upon the works of Horan et al. (1980) and Bluestone et al. (1973), the set of features that can be used for distinguishing the two economic sectors are presented in Table 1.1. The core sector tends to be comprised of large firms that have significant social, economic and political power (Wallace and Kalleberg 1981). They are inclined to be highly concentrated, capital intensive, and high profit-oriented. Core sector employees are likely to be very skilled, highly productive, and unionized. Because internal labor markets and on-the-job training are readily accessible, worker wages tend to be high and employee turnover low.

The second industrial segment, namely, the periphery sector, is comprised of firms who are in a constant struggle to survive. They lack the size, financial resources, or political might to be a major economic force. Such industries tend to be labor intensive and have poor profit margins. Workers associated with this sector possess limited job skills and have minimal access to internal labor markets or on-the-job training programs. Consequently, both worker productivity and wages tend to be low. High worker turnover is commonplace.

From the perspective of dual economy advocates, wages that an individual is able to garner have much less to do with the human capital

TABLE 1.1. Distinguishing Elements of the Core and Periphery Economic Sectors (Bluestone et al. 1973: Horan et al. 1980).

CORE SECTOR	PERIPHERY SECTOR
Oligopolistic Capitalism	Competitive Capitalism
* Economic activities are concentrated	* Low amount of economic concentration
* Small number of firms	* Intensive market competition
* Significant market power in products and labor markets	* Limited capacity to exercise market power in products or labor markets
Large-scale firms	Small-sized firms
Diversified products	Limited product line
High profits	Low profits
Capital-intensive	Labor intensive
High productivity	Poor productivity
Well-developed internal labor markets	Minimal internal labor markets
Significant presence of unionization	Lack of unionization
High-level of job skills required	Low job skill requirements
Excellent wages and working conditions	Low wages and poor-working environment
High investment in on-the-job training	Minimal on-the-job training
Low turnover in workers	High worker turnover

attributes that he or she may possess, and more to do with the economic sector in which he or she is employed. That is, rates of return to human capital are inclined to be much greater in firms situated in the core than in the periphery sectors of the economy (Kalleberg et al. 1981: Tolbert et al. 1980).

Dual Labor Markets Perspective

A conceptual framework that closely parallels the dual economy thesis is that of segmented (dual) labor markets. Dual labor market theorists are principally concerned with segmentation existing in labor markets and are less interested in the historical bases of such segmentation, as is the case with dual economy proponents (Tolbert et al. 1980). An underlying difference between these two approaches is that one focuses on segmentation among firms (i.e., dual economy) and the other on segmentation associated with jobs (i.e., dual labor markets).

The central thesis of dual labor market advocates is that jobs are situated in primary and secondary labor markets (Doeringer and Piore 1971; Piore

1970). Jobs existing in one sector have a distinct set of characteristics relative to the other sector. A synopsis of some of the distinguishing features of the two labor market segments are offered in Table 1.2. Prominent features of the primary sector are that internal labor markets are pervasive; employment is stable and jobs secure; wages are high; working conditions are good; workers are punctual and dependable; investment in employee training is extensive; and worker turnover is low. While primary sector jobs generally have entry level requirements associated with them, once hired, the existence of internal labor markets accords workers the opportunity for upward mobility.

Secondary labor market jobs offer workers few, if any, opportunities for advancement given that internal labor markets are rarely present. Further, employment is unstable and jobs insecure. Requirements for gaining entry into these positions are virtually non-existent. Both wages paid and work conditions tend to be poor. Few, if any, job training programs are extended to workers, so employee commitment to the job is low. As a consequence, worker turnover, absenteeism and tardiness are extensive (Althauser and Kalleberg 1981).

Both Gordon (1972) and Rumberger (1981) note that mobility between primary and secondary labor markets is generally difficult. Because of limited training, irregular work histories, inadequate job experience, or place of residence, secondary sector workers lack the credentials to gain entre into primary market jobs. Unfortunately, the historic concentration of women and minorities in secondary sector jobs often restricts their

TABLE 1.2. Distinguishing Attributes of Primary and Secondary Labor Markets (Althauser and Kalleberg 1981; Doeringer and Piore 1971).

PRIMARY	*SECONDARY*
Series of internal labor markets are present	Absence of internal labor markets
Stable employment and job security	Unstable employment; jobs are insecure
Job ladders which facilitate upward mobility	Limited opportunities for advancement
Entry requirements	Limited job entry requirements
Considerable training provided	Limited amount of training offered
High wages	Low wages
Punctual, dependable workers	Frequent cases of worker absenteeism and tardiness
Good working conditions	Poor working conditions
Low turnover	High turnover

movement into the kind of "good jobs" that are commonplace in the primary labor market (Rumberger 1981)

As with dual economy advocates, dual labor market proponents assert that human capital investments are likely to pay higher dividends to those persons gaining access to and advancing within internal labor markets (Marshall and Briggs 1989). Returns to education and training are significantly lower for those employed in the secondary sector given the "dead end" nature of these jobs (Falk and Lyson 1988).

Concluding Comments and Overview of This Volume

This chapter has presented a series of paradigms that offer a roadmap of how one might want to proceed in examining the complex set of human resources issues impacting rural America. Our primary intent has been to provide a theoretical context for several of the chapters that follow. While no attempt has been made to give full treatment to the frameworks considered, our hope has been to present a fair and accurate snapshot of these key theoretical perspectives.

The following chapters present a comprehensive examination of one of the overarching issues that is likely to influence the face of rural America as it approaches the 21st century—the quality and capacity of its human capital resources. Chapters are organized thematically into four major sections:

Part One: From Concept to Reality

In addition to the theoretical groundwork presented in this first chapter, this section provides an overview of existing human resource conditions in rural America (by Killian and Beaulieu). These authors explore whether a mismatch exists in the supply of and demand for qualified workers in rural areas. They conclude that one of the serious problems existing in rural America today is the failure to create good jobs that effectively utilize the existing human capital resources of the locality.

Part Two: Forces Shaping the Future of Rural America

A central aspect of this section is to give focus to key economic, social, and technological changes that are likely to shape the future viability of rural areas. Pulver (Chapter 3) examines the major structural shifts taking place in the U.S. and global economies and outlines how these changes are likely to impact the long-term economic health of the rural U.S. In Chapter 4, Wilkinson contends that rural communities are being confronted by a host of social problems and issues that are likely to go unresolved unless a strengthening of the community can be realized. Such strengthening requires an improved capacity of local people to act collectively in the pursuit of commonly held goals. Hyman, Gamm and Shingler (Chapter 5) describe the potential negative consequences of modern technology on rural communities. But, they offer a framework that is intended to ensure that technology can be used to create sustainable rural communities.

Part Three: Aspects of Human Resources Conditions Across Rural America

The uneven impacts of human capital deficits on various segments of rural America serve as the major focus of this portion of our volume. Jensen and McLaughlin (Chapter 6) undertake an ambitious examination of poverty and its links to human capital endowments. They offer substantive evidence of the deleterious economic outcomes associated with human capital deficits of rural people. The nation's most rural minority, American Indians, serves as the focus of Chapter 7 prepared by Snipp. The educational gains and shortfalls experienced by this population are described. He suggests that the economic disadvantages facing American Indians are likely to persist given the lingering barriers to educational achievement existing for this populace. The changing social and economic status of rural blacks and Hispanics during the period of the 1980s is presented in Chapter 8 by Lyson. Also given treatment are the likely prospects that await these rural minorities during the decade of the 1990s. Findeis (Chapter 9) explores gender-related differences that might exist in rural labor markets in the U.S. She argues that the challenge for many rural communities is how to more effectively utilize the human capital resources that women bring to the rural marketplace. The nature and extent of worker displacement in rural labor markets is presented by Swaim in Chapter 10. He offers empirical evidence of the significant explanatory power that human capital deficiencies and labor market conditions provide to the worker displacement problem in rural America. Lichter, McLaughlin, and Cornwell document import shifts that have taken place in the flow of human resources between metro and nonmetro areas during the period of the mid-1970s to late 1980s (Chapter 11). They note that migration has, over this period of time, resulted in a noticeable depletion in the human capital stock of rural areas.

Part Four: Strategies for Strengthening the Human Capital Resources of Rural America

The host of investments necessary to strengthen rural America's human capital in the years ahead serves as the substantive focus of the final portion of this book. In Chapter 12, Hobbs offers his views on the role that human capital can play in the pursuit of more effective rural economic development strategies. In so doing, he articulates the integral role that rural schools can perform in this development process. Vogel and Coward (Chapter 13) provide a comparative analysis of the health care conditions, resources, and use patterns existing between metro and nonmetro area residents. Also outlined are the important contributions that the rural health care sector provides to the economic vitality of rural communities. The chapter prepared by Wenk and Hardesty (Chapter 14) gives focus to the influences of family and household characteristics on educational success of young adults. They find that structural attributes of the family/household have a profound impact on educational attainment. They suggest that an effective mechanism for increasing human educational resources is to attend to difficulties created by family and household circumstances. Stallmann, Mwachofi, Flora, and Johnson (Chapter 15) contend that local labor markets create incentives for human capital investment. Drawing from data collected in Virginia, the authors find that the mix of jobs found in local labor markets has an important impact on the human capital investment decisions of individuals. They encourage rural communities to pursue economic development efforts that are designed to increase the demand for highly skilled labor. In Chapter 16, Luloff and Swanson note that no matter what the socioeconomic assets (or weaknesses) of a community, its ability to effectively mobilize these resources depends on the presence of "community agency"—the capacity of local residents to work in concert in addressing local needs. They underscore the importance of finding strategies to remove barriers to the effective emergence of community agency. The concluding chapter (Chapter 17), prepared by the editors of this volume, offers a synthesis of key points and policy suggestions that have been presented by chapter authors. The intent is to articulate those strategies that might help bring improvement to the social and economic well-being of rural communities and their residents.

Notes

1. Becker (1962) asserts that general on-the-job training improves workers' knowledge and skills that can be applied not only to their current positions, but to jobs in other firms. Because general training enhances workers' competitive stance in the marketplace, it is rare for employers to pay the costs of general training activities since they may not be able to fully capture the returns on such investments. Specific training, on the other hand, provides workers with skills that are relevant only to their present employer. Consequently, firms employing such workers are more inclined to bear the costs of such training.

2. As Marshall and Briggs (1989: 180) state, human capital investments consist of direct and indirect costs. Direct expenditures represent out-of-pocket costs, such as tuition and fees, that individuals must pay to attend college. Indirect costs are

the earnings that are forgone during the period in which these human capital investments are being made. Attending college, for example, is time-intensive and does not allow individuals to easily engage in other activities. Thus, an indirect cost of college attendance is the value of time that it takes from other activities.

References

Althauser, Robert P., and Arne L. Kalleberg. 1981. "Firms, occupations, and the structure of labor markets: A conceptual analysis." Pp. 119-49 in Ivar Berg (ed.), *Sociological Perspectives on Labor Markets.* New York, NY: Academic Press.

Arrow, Kenneth J. 1973. "Higher education as a filter." *Journal of Public Econ.* 2 (July): 193-216.

Averitt, R.T. 1968. *The Dual Economy.* New York, NY: Norton.

Beck, E. M., P. Horan, and C. Tolbert. 1978. "Stratification in a dual economy." *American Sociological Review* 43 (October): 704-20.

Becker, Gary S. 1962. "Investment in human capital: A theoretical analysis." *The Journal of Political Economy* 70 (5-2): 9-49.

Becker, Gary S. 1975. *Human Capital.* Second Edition. New York, NY: National Bureau of Economic Research.

Blau, P. M., and O. D. Duncan. 1967. *The American Occupational Structure.* New York, NY: Wiley and Sons.

Bluestone, Barry, W. M. Murphy, and M. Stevenson. 1973. *Low Wages and the Working Poor.* Ann Arbor, MI: Institute of Labor and Industrial Relations, University of Michigan.

Campbell, Rex T. 1983. "Status attainment research: End of the beginning or beginning of the end?" *Sociology of Education* 56: 47-62.

Cobb, R. A., W. G. McIntyre, and P. A. Pratt. 1989. "Vocational and educational aspirations of high school students: A problem of rural America." *Research in Rural Education* 6 (2): 11-15.

Cohn, Elchanan. 1975. *The Economics of Education.* Cambridge, MA: Ballinger.

Coleman, James S. 1991. "Parental involvement in education." *Policy Perspective Series* (June).

Coleman, James S. 1990. *Equality of Achievement in Education.* Boulder, CO: Westview Press.

Coleman, James S. 1988a. "Social capital in the creation of human capital." *American Journal of Sociology* 94 (Suppl.): 95-120.

Coleman, James S. 1988b. "The creation and destruction of social capital: Implications for the law?" *Notre Dame Journal of Law, Ethics and Public Policy* 3: 375-404.

Coleman, James S., and T. Hoffer. 1987. *Public and Private High Schools: The Impact of Communities.* New York, NY: Basic Books.

Coleman, James S., T. Hoffer, and S. Kilgore. 1982. *High School Achievement.* New York, NY: Basic Books.

Doeringer, P., and M. Piore. 1971. *Internal Labor Markets and Manpower Analysis.* Lexington, MA: Heath.

England, Paula. 1992. *Comparable Worth: Theories and Evidence.* New York, NY: Aldine de Gruyter.

Falk, William W., and Thomas A. Lyson. 1988. *HIgh Tech, Low Tech, No Tech: Recent Industrial and Occupational Change in the South.* Albany, NY: State University of New York Press.

Fligstein, Neil, Alexander Hicks, and S. Philip Morgan. 1983. "Toward a theory of income determination." *Work and Occupations* 10 (3): 289-306.

Goodman, Jerry D. 1979. "The economic returns of education: An assessment of alternative models." *Social Science Quarterly* 60 (September): 269-82.

Gordon, D. M. 1972. *Theories of Poverty and Underemployment.* Lexington, MA: Heath.

Granovetter, Mark. 1981. "Toward a sociological theory of income differences." Pp. 11-47 in Ivar "Berg (ed.), *Sociological Perspectives on Labor Markets.* New York, NY: Academic Press.

Hansen, Thomas D., and Walter G. McIntyre. 1989. "Family structure variables as predictors of educational and vocational aspirations of high school seniors." *Research in Rural Education* 6 (2): 39-49.

Horan, Patrick M., E. M. Beck, and Charles M. Tolbert II. 1980. "The market homogeneity assumption: On the theoretical foundations of empirical knowledge." *Social Science Quarterly* 61: 278-92.

Kalleberg, Arne L., M. Wallace, and R. P. Althauser. 1981. "Economic segmentation, worker power, and income inequality." *American Journal of Sociology* 87: 651-83.

Lane, A. 1968. "Occupational mobility in six cities." *American Sociological Review* 33: 740-49.

Layard, Richard, and George Psacharopoulos. 1974. "The screening hypothesis and the returns to education." *Journal of Political Economy* 82 (5): 985-98.

Marshall, Ray, and Vernon M. Briggs, Jr. 1989. *Labor Economics: Theory, Institutions, and Public Policy.* Homewood, IL: Richard D. Irwin, Inc.

Majoribanks, Kevin. 1972. "Ethnic and environmental influences on mental abilities." *American Journal of Sociology* 78 (2): 323-37.

McCrackin, Bobbie. 1984. "Education contributions to productivity and economic growth." *Economic Review* (November): 8-23.

Mincer, Jacob. 1974. *Schooling, Experience, and Earnings.* New York, NY: National Bureau of Economic Research.

Mincer, Jacob. 1962. "On-the-job training: Costs, returns, and some implications." *Journal of Political Economy*, Supplement, 70 (October): 50-79.

Riley, John G. 1979. "Testing the educational screening hypothesis." *Journal of Political Economy* 87 (5) part 2: S227-52.

Rumberger, Russell W. 1983. "Dropping out of high school: The influence of race, sex, and family background." *American Educational Research Journal* 20: 199-220.

Rumberger, Russell W. 1981. *Overeducation in the U.S. Labor Market.* New York, NY: Praeger Publishers.

Sakamoto, Arthur. 1988. "Labor market structure, human capital, and earnings inequality in metropolitan areas." *Social Forces* 67 (1): 86-107.

Schultz, Theodore W. 1961. "Investment in human capital." *American Economic Review* LI (March): 1-17.

Semyonov, M. 1981. "Effects of community on status attainment." *Sociological Quarterly* 29: 24-38.

Sewell, W. H. 1964. "Community of residence and college plans." *American Sociological Review* 22: 359-72.

Sewell, W. H., A. O. Haller, and A. Portes. 1969. "The educational and early occupational attainment process." *American Sociological Review* 34 (1): 82-92.

Smith, Mark H. 1993. *Family Characteristics, Social Capital, and College Attendance*. Unpublished dissertation. Department of Sociology, University of Florida.

Snipp, Matthew, Hayward D. Horton, Leif Jensen, Joane Nagel, and Refugio Rochin. 1993. "Persistent rural poverty and racial and ethnic minorities." Pp. 173-99 in *Persistent Poverty in Rural America*. Boulder, CO: Westview Press—Rural Studies Series.

Sorensen, Aage B. 1983. "Sociological research on the labor market: Conceptual and methodological issues." *Work and Occupations* 10 (3): 261-86.

Spence, Michael. 1974. *Market Signaling*. Cambridge, MA: Harvard University Press.

Spence, Michael. 1973. "Job market signaling." *Quarterly Journal of Economics* 87 (August): 355-74.

Stiglitz, J. 1975. "The theory of 'screening', education and the distribution of income." *American Economic Review* 65 (June): 283-300.

Summers, Gene F., Leonard E. Bloomquist, Frederick Buttel, Patricia Garrett, Nina Glasgow, Craig Humphrey, Daniel T. Lichter, Thomas Lyson, Matthew Snipp, and Ann Tickamyer. 1993. "Introduction." Pp. 1-19 in *Persistent Poverty in Rural America*. Boulder, CO: Westview Press—Rural Studies Series.

Tolbert, Charles, P.M. Horan, and E. M. Beck. 1980. "The structure of economic segmentation: A dual economy approach." *American Journal of Sociology* 85 (5): 1095-117.

Thurow, Lester C. 1975. *Generating Inequality: Mechanisms of Distribution in the U.S. Economy*. New York, NY: Basic Books, Inc.

Wagenaar, Theodore C. 1987. "What do we know about dropping out of high school?" *Research in the Sociology of Education and Socialization* 7: 161-90.

Wallace, Michael, and Arne L. Kalleberg. 1981. "Economic organization of firms and labor market consequences: Toward a specification of dual economy theory." Pp. 77-117 in Ivar Berg, ed., *Sociological Perspectives on Labor Markets*. New York, NY: Academic Press.

2

Current Status of Human Capital in the Rural U.S.

Molly Sizer Killian
Lionel J. Beaulieu

An important debate among rural social scientists centers on the match (or lack thereof) between the types of skills that rural workers bring to the labor market and the types of skills that rural employers need for the production of goods and services. Although based on national demographic and economic trends, William Johnston and Arnold Packer's widely read 1987 report, *Workforce 2000: Work and Workers in the 21st Century* helped bring this issue to the forefront of the rural development research agenda. Johnston and Packer's study predicts an impending shortage of qualified workers to fill the expanding number of jobs that require college degrees and/or sophisticated analytical, mathematical, and verbal skills. Rural advocates of the *Workforce 2000* predictions believe that this education/skills mismatch is a major contributor to many of the problems facing rural America today.

Other rural researchers interpret the labor force and labor market trends differently. According to these dissenters, the social and economic problems in rural areas are not primarily due to an inadequate supply of well-educated, highly skilled rural workers. Instead, rural problems of chronic poverty, high unemployment, and population decline are said to be rooted in a persistent spatial division of labor between large metropolitan economic systems and smaller, more dependent rural economies. This spatial division of labor erects barriers to the creation and retention of good jobs demanding higher level skills in rural areas.

The central thrust of this chapter is to assess the relative merits of these opposing perspectives. We do so by delving more deeply into the arguments being advanced by both camps and offering key points about each perspective. Next, using some of the most recent data available, we describe the current status of and trends in the human capital resources of rural areas (vis a vis urban areas) as reflected in levels of education among adults and status dropout rates among younger residents.[1] Having considered these supply issues, we subsequently perform a series of empirical analyses to estimate the match between the human capital invested in rural workers and the human capital required to perform their jobs.[2] Finally, we offer concluding comments regarding the supply/demand debate and lay out selected implications for rural America.

The Supply/Demand Debate: An Overview

Empirical support for the *Workforce 2000* position derives primarily from national, aggregate analyses which compare average educational levels in the rapidly growing job categories with average educational levels achieved by people in the most rapidly growing population categories. The report's authors suggest that, due to the significant transformations taking place in today's global economy, the overall demand for more sophisticated, knowledge-intensive and multi-skilled workers is intensifying. This increased demand is said to derive from two sources. First, the assertion is made that the new jobs being created in today's economy tend to require greater skills, thus shifting the distribution of job requirements upward. The major source for new jobs is the rapidly expanding service sector, and many jobs in this sector require workers to manipulate and transform information rather than physical objects. Second, it is argued that there is a content shift taking place in the skill requirements within many current jobs (especially in manufacturing), such that jobs that were once filled by relatively unskilled workers are now demanding persons who possess more complex, technically and cognitively-oriented skills.

In his summary of the *Workforce 2000* argument, Sidor (1992) notes that a number of business leaders (e.g., chairmen of the boards of BellSouth Corporation and Xerox, the CEO of Helene Curtis), analysts from think tanks and not-for-profit associations (e.g., National Alliance of Businesses, Hudson Institute, National Council for Urban Economic Development), and government researchers (e.g., Department of Labor and the Office of Technology Assessment), embrace the notion that "the future is now." These individuals argue that a human capital supply deficit already exists and is seriously undermining the capacity of American employers to compete effectively in the global marketplace. They further suggest that unless the U.S. seeks to quickly upgrade the skills and educational levels of today's workers, our country's human capital deficiencies will only grow worse.

It is in the context of these purported changes outlined by proponents of the *Workforce 2000* perspective that concerns with the economic health of rural America are raised. Given that levels of educational attainment are lower in rural than in urban areas (e.g., Pollard and O'Hare 1990; Rosenfeld et al. 1988), it is argued that the human capital crisis is, and will continue to be, worse in nonmetropolitan areas of the country unless dramatic steps are taken to improve the skills and training of rural workers.

Workforce 2000 Under Fire

In their Economic Policy Institute report titled, *The Myth of the Coming Labor Shortage*, Mishel and Teixeira (1991) argue that the human capital deficit may not be as great as claimed by *Workforce 2000* proponents. In fact, they state "there is no evidence that large-scale job enrichment is taking place" (Mishel and Teixeira 1991:1). Moreover, they predict that the rate of growth in job skill requirements associated with an upgrading of occupations may actually slow down in the 1990s. Similarly, McGranahan and Ghelfi (1991:48) find that "the overall rate of increase in educational requirements resulting from shifts toward high-education jobs was somewhat lower in the 1980s than in the 1970s."

Additional evidence is accumulating that what little skills upgrading may have occurred in recent years has been confined primarily to urban localities and has not extended very far into rural areas. It is to this issue that we now turn.

The Spatial Division of Labor: Urban and Rural Differences

The view that labor force requirements in urban and rural areas have developed along different streams is based on observations of a spatial division of labor in which the numbers and types of jobs carried out in some locales are distinctly different from the numbers and types of jobs undertaken in others.[3]

Advocates of the spatial division of labor viewpoint suggest that urban labor markets tend to attract employers needing workers with strong analytical, creative, and organizational skills. These workers must be capable of performing complex, technically sophisticated tasks. Rural labor markets, on the other hand, are inclined to attract employers seeking cheaper labor to perform relatively routine, simple and repetitive tasks.

Rural areas have long been dependent on the agriculture, mining, and manufacturing sectors for jobs, sectors which have suffered a steady loss of employment over the past few decades. During the period of the 1980s, these traditionally rural industries added few, if any new jobs, to the economy (see Figure 2.1). Moreover, within all economic sectors, a significant spatial division of labor exists: management decisions frequently

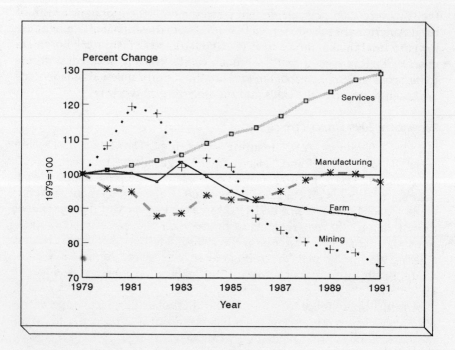

FIGURE 2.1. Change in Nonmetro Employment 1979-1991
Source: Regional Economic Information Systems, Bureau of Economic Analysis, U.S. Department of Commerce (various years).

locate the lower skilled, routine production jobs in rural areas and the more highly skilled professional, managerial, and technical jobs in urban locales.

Even in the producer services industries (usually considered to be among the more desirable and fastest growing service jobs), there is a spatial division of labor which does not favor rural areas. For example, Porterfield and Killian (forthcoming) examined the rate at which producer services were centralizing (i.e., becoming more concentrated in metropolitan areas) or decentralizing (i.e., moving out into the rural periphery). The decentralizing producer services (e.g., photofinishing labs, equipment rental, etc.) tend to offer low wages and temporary or part-time employment, whereas the centralizing producer services (e.g., legal services, accounting, auditing and bookkeeping) typically consist of highly professional and well-paying jobs.

Both direct and indirect evidence help substantiate the spatial division of labor argument. Empirically-based studies, for example, offer direct testimony that the demand for human capital tends to be considerably lower in rural than in urban areas (McGranahan and Ghelfi 1992; Teixeira and Mishel 1992). Rural employers seem more likely to demand lower wages and fewer regulations than they are to insist on higher education or skills levels. This is indicated by findings that rural employment growth rates were more responsive to lower local earnings per job than they were to higher average educational levels (Killian and Parker 1991).

Studies showing that weak rural demand for high levels of education have a dampening effect on the supply of educated workers, offer indirect support for the spatial division of labor argument. Unless rural employers have job openings for college graduates, the better educated workers tend to leave rural labor markets to seek better job options in urban areas (e.g., McGranahan 1992; Voth et al. 1993). This substantial erosion in the human resources in rural areas is documented by Lichter et al. in Chapter 11 of this volume. Comparing data secured from the 1976 and 1988 March annual demographic supplements of the Current Population Survey (CPS), the authors present evidence that a significant flow has occurred in the migration of young, talented people from nonmetro to metro areas of the county. They attribute these migration flows to the lack of good jobs for these individuals to secure in their rural localities. When faced with limited employment opportunities and low returns to education in their own local labor market, it is no wonder that some rural families (and communities) end up placing little value on the pursuit of additional education (Smith 1988; Stallmann et al. in Chapter 15 of this volume).

Examining the Human Resource Attributes
of Rural America

The historical disparity in the median levels of education among residents of metropolitan and nonmetropolitan areas is well known. In recent years, however, clearcut distinctions between these two areas have begun to dissipate. For example, in 1970, the median school years completed by persons 25 years of age and above stood at 12.2 years in the metro U.S. and at 11 years in the nonmetro areas of the country (a 10.9 percent difference). In 1980, the median education between metro/nonmetro residents underwent substantial convergence, with median school years completed standing at 12.6 years for metro adults and 12.3 years among nonmetro people. Recent data show that the metro/nonmetro gap in median education continues to close.

While useful in providing policy makers, educators, and social scientists with a general sense of the educational status of various sub-populations, median educational attainment can mask important differences in the human resource attributes possessed by these groups. Some of the more meaningful measures for gauging the relative educational resources in a population are represented by the distribution of educational attainment among adults, and by the rate of high school completion among young people. A current view of how rural America fares on these measures, vis a vis the urban areas of the U.S., is the central theme of this section of our chapter.

As shown in Table 2.1, over one-half of all nonmetropolitan residents aged 25 years and over lacked a high school education in 1971. In the metropolitan areas of the country, the figure reached the 40 percent mark. While the relative size of this less educated group decreased by similar percentage points over the course of the next two decades (20.2 percentage points in metro vs. 22.2 percentage points in nonmetro areas), the rate of decline was faster in metro than in nonmetro localities (- 50.6 percent vs. - 44 percent).[4]

As a result of these changes, the rural/urban gap at the lower end of the distribution grew slightly (see Figure 2.2).[5] That is, in 1971, the relative size of the lowest educational category was 21 percent smaller in metro areas than it was in nonmetro areas. By 1991, the metro low educational group was 30 percent smaller than that of the nonmetro grouping.

Among individuals who have completed a high school education or more, the performance of nonmetropolitan areas actually outshone that of metropolitan localities. Nonmetro areas realized their greatest gains relative to metro areas in the middle of the distribution. The percentage of the metro population with a high school degree scarcely changed between 1971 and 1991, whereas the portion of the nonmetro population achieving this educational status increased by 28 percent. The difference in growth rates was large enough for nonmetro areas to actually reverse the gap among the middle educational group. In 1971, for example, the percent of adults 25 years of age or above with a high school education stood at 35.1 percent among metro residents and 33.1 percent among nonmetro individuals. By 1991, this figure had barely increased among the metro group, but had accelerated to 42.5 percent among the nonmetro adult population.

Even at the upper end of the distribution, nonmetro areas achieved some small gains. The size of the best educated group (4 + years of college) grew slightly faster in nonmetro than in metro areas (77 percent vs. 72 percent) and the relative size of the gap between these two geographic locales declined slightly.

Despite these nonmetropolitan gains in educational attainment over two decades (as noted in Table 2.1), the proportion of adults 25 years of age and above with a baccalaureate degree or more stood at less than 14 percent among rural residents (10 percentage points lower than that found in urban areas). Thus, the pool of highly educated persons, the so-called best and brightest, continues to be proportionally smaller in nonmetro than in metro areas of the U.S.[6]

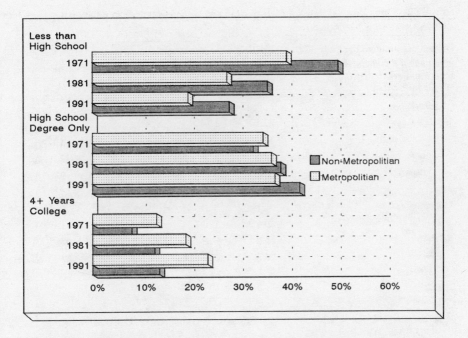

FIGURE 2.2. Percentage of Persons 25 Years and Over By Years of School Completed and Residence 1971, 1981, and 1991

TABLE 2.1. Distribution of Educational Attainments of Metropolitan and Nonmetropolitan Population, 1971-1991

Percent of population aged 25 and older with:	1971	1981	1991	Percent Change 1971-1991
Metropolitan				
Less than High School	39.9	27.7	19.7	-50.6
High School	35.1	36.8	37.5	6.8
More than High School	25.0	35.5	42.9	71.6
Nonmetropolitan				
Less than High School	50.4	36.0	28.2	-44.0
High School	33.1	38.7	42.5	28.4
More than High School	16.6	25.3	29.3	76.5

Source: U.S. Bureau of the Census, Current Population Reports, Series P-20. *Educational Attainment in the United States* (various years). U.S. Government Printing Office, Washington, D.C.

TABLE 2.2.. Status Dropout Rates of Metropolitan and Nonmetropolitan Population by Ethnic Categories, 1981-1991.

Percent of population aged 16 - 24 who have not completed high school and are not currently enrolled in school:	1981	1986	1991	Percent Change 1981-1991
Metropolitan				
Total	13.1	12.0	12.8	-2.3
White	12.3	11.8	12.8	4.1
Black	17.5	13.9	14.5	-17.1
Hispanic	32.6	30.0	35.6	9.2
Nonmetropolitan				
Total	16.4	13.1	11.3	-31.1
White	15.0	12.8	11.4	-24.0
Black	21.7	15.1	9.3	-57.1
Hispanic	36.4	31.6	29.1	-20.1

Source: U.S. Bureau of Census, Current Population Reports, P20-469. *School Improvement— Social and Economic Characteristics of Students,* October (various years). U.S. Government Printing Office , Washington D.C.

Reviewing Status Dropout Rates

Trends in the status dropout rate among residents 16 to 24 years of age offer additional positive news for nonmetropolitan areas. Status dropout rates measure the proportion of people in the 16 to 24 age cohort who have not completed high school and are not currently enrolled in school (as of October of that given year). These rates are important in that they reflect the extent of the dropout problem in the population (Kaufman et al. 1992:v).

Over the course of the 1981-86 period, status dropout rates declined in both metro and nonmetro areas. In metropolitan America, the dropout rates dipped from 13.1 to 12 percent among persons 16-to-24 years of age. In nonmetro areas, the figures declined from 16.4 to 13.1 percent. Interestingly, over the span of the next five years (1986 to 1991), the status dropout rates among young people in metro areas took a decidedly different path from those living in nonmetro locales. Nonmetropolitan residents 16-to-24 years of age continued to show improvements in their high school completion rates. That is, status dropout rates continued to decrease in nonmetro areas (from 13.1 to 11.3 percent between 1986 and 1991), but edged upwards among metro youngsters (from 12.0 to 12.8 percent). Most important, the dip in the nonmetro status dropout rates touched all three broad racial/ethnic categories, with the most spectacular reductions occurring among nonmetro blacks. Not only did nonmetro blacks slash their dropout rates by more than one-half over a 10 year period, they actually had a status dropout rate in 1991 that was lower than that experienced by nonmetro whites (9.3 percent vs. 11.4 percent).[7]

The data presented to this point suggest that while rural educational levels continue to lag behind those of their urban counterparts, the trends have been positive:

Rural educational levels have steadily improved over the course of the last twenty years;
The gap in the educational levels between rural and urban residents has narrowed appreciably, particularly in the middle and upper parts of the distribution;
Status dropout rates have declined steadily in rural areas during the 1980s.

Despite these gains, the question still remains as to whether the supply of human capital in rural areas is sufficient to meet the needs of the local labor market. Unfortunately, our capacity to address this issue is constrained somewhat by the limited availability of up-to-date secondary data that are capable of exploring this key matter. While not as current as we would wish, data provided from workers in the 1985 *Panel Study of Income Dynamics* (PSID) is useful in helping provide some understanding of the *supply of* and *demand for* human capital in metro and nonmetro areas of the country. It is to an analysis of these data base that this chapter now turns.

The Demand for Human Capital:
Is There a Mismatch With Supply?

The 1985 survey data from the PSID offers unique insights into the question of a match between the human capital skills supplied by workers and the human capital skills needed on their jobs. The dataset contains interview data on the educational experience, work history, and current job characteristics of a sample of 11,255 (unweighted N) adults. We selected only those 8,427 persons in the sample who were 18 years or older in 1985, who worked during the previous year (i.e., total wage and other labor income in 1984 was greater than zero and annual hours worked in 1984 were greater than zero), and who were currently employed or temporarily laid off, on sick leave or maternity leave. Our analyses are weighted to be representative of the population in 1985.

Answers to two questions posed to workers in the 1985 PSID sample are used to measure the supply of human capital:

*What is the highest educational degree you have completed? (ED-AT-
TAINED)*
*How many months have you spent in your current position/work situation?
(EXP-ATTAINED).*

The demand for human capital is tapped using workers' responses to
the following questions:[8]

*How much formal education is required these days to get a job like yours?
(ED-REQUIRED)*
*On a job like yours, how long would it take the average new person to become
fully trained and qualified? (EXP-REQUIRED)*

To facilitate the presentation of results, we collapsed replies to the
questions on educational attainment and educational requirements into
three categories: *less than a high school diploma, high school diploma,* and *more
than a high school diploma.* Similarly, we classified the two on-the-job experience variables (EXP-ATTAINED and EXP-REQUIRED) into three
groupings: *less than one year of on-the-job experience, one to two years of
on-the-job experience,* and *three or more years of on-the-job experience.*

We then combined each set of worker attainment and job requirement
variables to create two additional variables measuring the specific match
between a worker's educational and experience qualifications and the
educational and experience requirements of his/her job. The educational
match variable (ED-MATCH) is coded into three categories: *under-educated,*
where the worker's educational attainment is less than the educational
requirements of his/her job; *educationally matched,* where the worker is
appropriately educated for his/her job, and *over-educated,* where the
worker's level of education is higher than that required by his/her job. The
experience match variable (EXP-MATCH) follows a parallel construction
with the three categories of *under-experienced, experientially matched,* and
over-experienced.[9]

Comparisons between the overall distribution of the education supplied
by nonmetro and metro workers (ED-ATTAINED) with the distribution of
the education demanded by their jobs (ED-REQUIRED) are presented in
Figure 2.3. The data show that while 40 percent of the nonmetro workers
possess more than a high school education, only 29 percent of the nonmetro
jobs command that much schooling. In metro areas, 55 percent of the
workers, compared to only 41 percent of the jobs, fall into the highest
educational category.

In contrast, more than 48 percent of the nonmetro jobs require a high
school diploma, but only 42 percent of nonmetro workers with this educational credential are available to fill these jobs. The discrepancy between

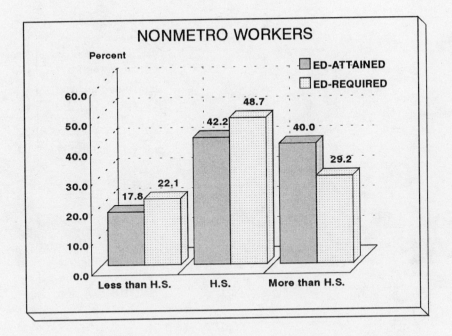

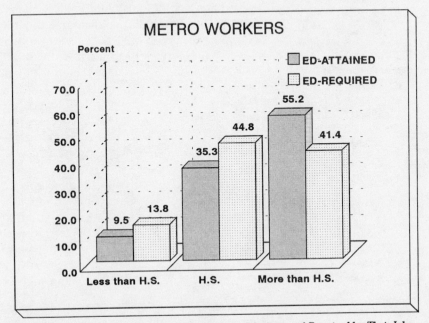

FIGURE 2.3. Distribution of Education Supplied by Workers and Required by Their Jobs

34

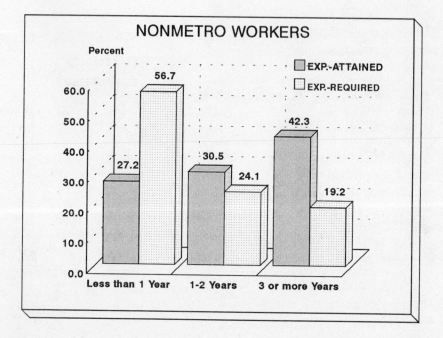

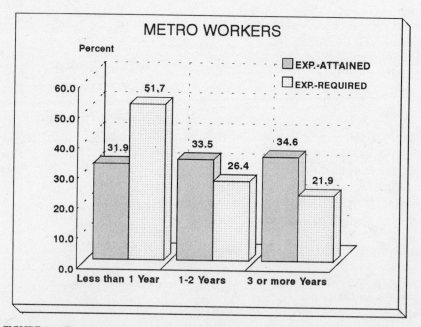

FIGURE 2.4. Distribution of On-the Job Work Experience Attained and Required by Nonmetro/Metro Workers

the demand for and supply of high school educated persons is quite similar in metro areas: 45 percent of metro jobs require a high school education, while only 35 percent of the metro workers are high school educated. The match between supply and demand for workers with less than a high school degree is much closer in both metro and nonmetro areas, although in both locations, there are slightly more jobs needing less education than there are workers.

In Figure 2.4, we compare the supply of and demand for on-the-job (OTJ) work experience (EXP-ATTAINED and EXP-REQUIRED). Again, we find that the distribution of workers across the three experience categories differs significantly from the distribution of jobs. Over 40 percent of nonmetro workers have worked on their job for three or more years, but less than 20 percent of nonmetro jobs require that much OTJ experience. In metro areas, the difference is smaller with 35 percent of workers, compared to 22 percent of jobs, falling into the highest experience category. The contrasts between the supply of and demand for workers with less than one year of experience is even larger, with 27 percent of nonmetro workers available to fill the 57 percent of nonmetro jobs that fall in this least experienced category, and 32 percent of metro inexperienced workers available to fill 52 percent of metro jobs.

In sum, these distributional analyses show that, in both metro and nonmetro areas, there is a considerable oversupply of workers with higher levels of human capital and a substantial undersupply of workers with lower levels of human capital. These analyses, however, have only examined the overall distribution of workers and jobs. In the next step, we examine the specific match between the educational attainments and OTJ experience of individual workers and the human capital requirements of their own jobs (ED-MATCH and EXP-MATCH).

In terms of educational matches between individual workers and their present jobs (Figure 2.5), we find that 12.4 percent of nonmetro workers are under-educated for their jobs—that is, their educational attainment is less than the educational requirements of their position. Relatively fewer metro workers face an educational deficit in their jobs—10.4 percent of metro workers have fewer years of schooling than their jobs require. Contrary to popular assumptions, educational mismatches due to over-education are more than twice as prevalent as those due to under-education. Be it nonmetro or metro areas, approximately 24 percent of the working population are in jobs that do not fully utilize their educational accomplishments.[10]

Figure 2.6 presents the OTJ experience match between individual workers and their present jobs. We find that over 17 percent of nonmetro workers are under-experienced for their jobs—that is, their OTJ experience is less than the experience requirements of their jobs. On-the-job deficiencies are greater for metro workers where 22.6 percent of metro workers have

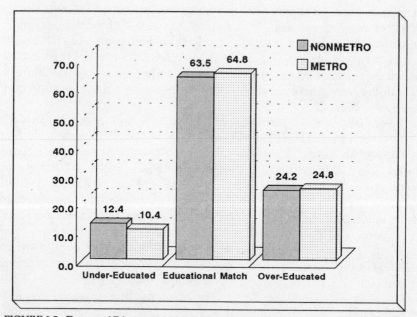

FIGURE 2.5. Degree of Educational Match Between Worker Attainments and Present Job Requirements

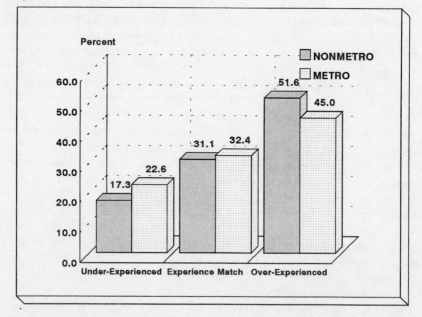

FIGURE 2.6. Degree of On-the-Job Experience Match Between Years Worked and Present Job Requirements

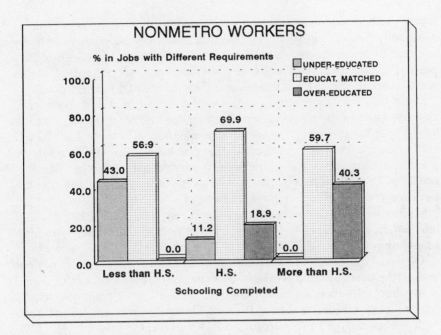

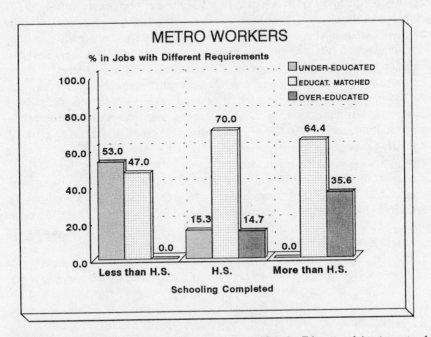

FIGURE 2.7. Educational Match Between Workers and Jobs by Educational Attainments of Workers

fewer years of experience than their jobs require. Counter to what is commonly believed, mismatches resulting from over-experience are likely to occur at twice the rate as those due to under-experience. Over fifty percent (51.6 percent) of nonmetro workers and 45 percent of metro workers are in jobs that do not make full use of their OTJ experience.

As a final step, we briefly examine the educational and experience characteristics of those workers who are under-or over-qualified for their jobs. By disaggregating the working population into three educational categories, we find (not surprisingly) that problems of under-education are greatest among persons with the poorest educational credentials (see Figure 2.7). Thus, in nonmetro areas, 43 percent of nonmetro workers who have not completed high school are in need of additional investments in schooling in order to meet the educational requirements of their present job. On the other hand, only 11.2 percent of nonmetro workers with high school diplomas (or GED's) are facing an educational deficit.[11]

Obviously, problems of over-education are more likely to be prevalent among the best educated workers. Nonmetro workers with better than a high school education are more than twice as likely to be employed in jobs requiring less education than is the case for rural workers holding only a high school degree (40.3 percent and 18.9 percent, respectively). Mismatches resulting from over-education tend to be more acute among well-educated nonmetro workers than for the well-educated workers living in the metro areas of the U.S. (40.3 percent compared to 35.6 percent).

In Figure 2.8, we separate the working population into the three experience categories. Again, we find that mismatches are greatest among the more experienced workers: only 15 percent of nonmetro workers with one to two years of experience are in jobs with matching requirements, and 23 percent of nonmetro workers with three or more years of experience are appropriately matched to the requirements of their jobs. About 61 percent of the less experienced workers appear to occupy jobs that require the kind of minimal experience which they possess.

Mismatches due to over-experience are much more prevalent than are mismatches due to under-experience among workers. Approximately three-fourths of the most experienced workers (those with three or more years of OTJ experience) are gainfully employed in jobs that require less experience than these individuals currently possess. This situation is essentially the same for workers residing in either nonmetro or metro areas (76.7 percent for nonmetro workers and 74.7 percent for metro employees).

In sum, our examination of the supply and demand for human capital using the PSID data suggests that, at least in 1985, nonmetro areas were not taking full advantage of the human capital already invested in their workers, be it in the form of educational attainment or years of job-related experiences:

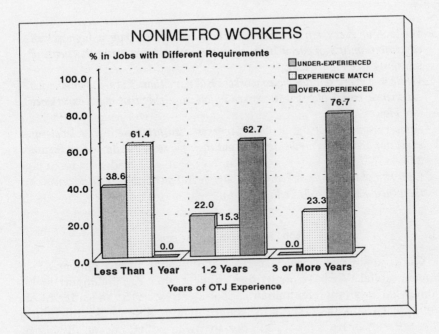

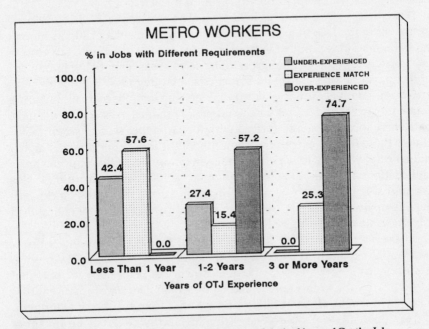

FIGURE 2.8. Experience Match Between Workers and Jobs by Years of On-the-Job Experience

While 4 of every ten nonmetro workers had better than a high school education, only 3 of every 10 workers were in jobs requiring that level of schooling (see Figure 2.3);

While 4 of every ten nonmetro workers had more than 3 years of on-the-job experience, only 2 of every 10 worked in jobs requiring that much experience (see Figure 2.4);

Almost a quarter of the nonmetro workers had attained higher levels of education than were needed to carry out their job responsibilities (see Figure 2.5);

Over half of the rural workers in our sample had more job-related experiences than their job required (see Figure 2.6).

Discussion/Implications

Our focus in this chapter has been on the labor market dimensions of human capital. We have not tried to examine other, equally important, but somewhat less tangible, human capital attributes such as leadership or entrepreneurial skills. Within the context of struggling rural communities, these resources are at least as important as schooling and on-the-job experience, albeit somewhat more difficult to measure.

Nonetheless, these findings lend credence to the spatial division of labor argument that a lack of jobs which adequately utilize the available human capital is a serious problem in rural America today. Nonmetro job growth is considerably slower than growth in metro areas, especially among the higher paying professional and managerial job categories. Nonmetro areas are losing relatively lower skill, routine production jobs as manufacturing firms restructure and/or relocate to off-shore production sites. For the most part, these jobs are being replaced with lower paying service sector jobs.[12] Unless these trends reverse, the migration of the more educated and highly skilled rural workers to superior employment opportunities in urban areas will continue to drain rural areas of human capital. Thus, according to this demand-side perspective, rural development efforts that focus on expanding and upgrading the job structure in nonmetro areas are more critical than are efforts to invest in more human capital.

At the same time, these findings suggest that there may indeed be a substantial need for improved human capital resources in rural America. According to Thurow's (1975) job queue theory of labor markets, potential workers are ranked in a queue according to their human capital endowments, and employers start filling job vacancies from the top of that queue. For example, if two people—one with a high school degree and the other with a college degree—apply for the same job, the employer is more likely to hire the better educated applicant, even if the job only requires a high school education. In this sense, as long as there is an over-supply of well educated workers in nonmetro areas, those workers with only a high school diploma are likely to be competing with college educated workers for the same jobs. Thus, in order for the nonmetro worker with a high school degree to successfully compete for jobs, that worker must improve his or her stock of human capital, even though those jobs only formally require a high school education.

What the future will bring is unclear. Most of the data presented here are cross-sectional and cannot be used to predict trends. Moreover, in today's rapidly changing international economy, the data from 1985 are already seriously outdated. It is possible that the current trends in international trade may result in significant shifts in the spatial division of labor within the United States. Such shifts could result in a higher demand for better educated, more highly skilled workers in rural areas.

Finally, regardless of future trends, the educational improvements described earlier in this chapter are remarkable, especially given the current evidence of a weak demand for education in rural areas. To their immense credit, the populations in rural areas appear to have taken the call for more and better education very seriously. However, without a more equitable spatial division of labor, there is little likelihood that the remarkable achievements made in rural America will be translated into significant economic gains for these areas.

Notes

1. For purposes of this chapter, the terms urban and rural are used interchangeably with those of metropolitan and nonmetropolitan. The Office of Management and Budget's standard definitions of metro and nonmetro areas are used in all analyses.

2. As is all too often the case, lack of data about the demand for human capital at the local level restricts our ability to truly represent labor market processes. The following analyses must be viewed, therefore, as illustrative: representing what the supply of and demand for human capital would be, if the national labor market were in fact divided into only an urban and a rural segment.

3. For simplicity's sake, we summarize the spatial division of labor perspective as if the national labor market was divided into only two segments: rural and urban. This summary is subject to the same criticisms of earlier segmentation theories which divided the national economy into only two sectors: a core and a periphery. Ultimately, any questions about the match (or lack thereof) between the supply of and demand for human capital must be answered at the level of the local labor market, where real workers are matched up with real jobs.

4. The change variables in Tables 1 and 2 are computed as:

((Size of Category T_2 - Size of Category T_1) / Size of Category T_1) * 100.

5. The "metro-nonmetro gap" in the size of educational categories is computed as: ((Size of Category$_M$ - Size of Category$_{NM}$) / Size of Category$_{NM}$) * 100

6. More detailed information on the educational attainment of metro and nonmetro residents is presented in the chapter appendix.

7. It is important to acknowledge that the size of the population 16-24 years of age has declined considerably over the 1981-91 time period in nonmetropolitan areas, but has remained relatively stable in metropolitan localities. This suggest that modest numerical shifts in the number of dropouts in nonmetro areas is likely to result in a more significant change in the nonmetro status dropout rate than would be the case if this numerical shift occurred in metro areas.

8. Two caveats must be made about using these data to represent the demand for human capital. First, these reports of the sampled respondents on characteristics of their jobs do not constitute a random sample of jobs. And second, workers' perceptions of the education and experience requirements of their jobs may differ from employers' expectations. However, given the lack of comparable data on the characteristics of metro and nonmetro jobs and the workers in those jobs, we must sacrifice some degree of statistical accuracy in order to be able to say something about the structure of human capital requirements in nonmetro jobs.

9. Strictly speaking, the experientially matched category may contain some mismatches. For example, a job may require 10 years of experience and be filled by a worker with only 8 years of OTJ experience, or by one with 12 years. In both cases, the experience required and the experience attained are greater than 3 years and the workers would thus be placed into the experientially matched category. Since our concern is at the lower end of the skills continuum, we chose to confine our analysis to only the first 3 years of experience. Additional cutoff points of 4 and 5 years yielded essentially the same results.

10. This pattern of over-education mismatches being twice the size of under-education mismatches holds for all regions of the country, although the incidence of either type of mismatch is smallest in the Northeast and largest in the West.

11. The mismatch for less educated workers in metro areas is even greater—53 percent of metro workers with less than 12 years of schooling are under-educated for their jobs. However, since metro areas have relatively fewer workers in the lower educational categories, the overall number of metro workers with educational shortfalls is not as large.

12. Over 90 percent of the new jobs created in nonmetro areas during the 1980s were in the service sector (see *Rural Conditions and Trends*, Vol. 4, No.3).

References

Johnston, William B., and Arnold E. Packer. 1987. *Workforce 2000: Work and Workers for the 21st Century*. Indianapolis, IN: Hudson Institute.

Kaufman, Phillip, Marilyn M. McMillen, and Denise Bradby. 1992. *Dropout Rates in the United States: 1991*. U.S. Department of Education, Office of Educational Research and Improvement. National Center for Education Statistics NCES 92-129 (September).

Killian, Molly Sizer, and Timothy S. Parker. 1991. "Education and local employment growth in a changing economy." Chapter 4 in *Education and Rural Economic Strategies for the 1990's.* Agriculture and Rural Economy Division, Economic Research Service, U.S. Department of Agriculture. ERS Staff Report No. AGES 9153: 40-92.

Lichter, Daniel T., Diane K. McLaughlin, and Gretchen T. Cornwell. 1994. "Migration intentions and the loss of human resources in rural America." In Lionel J. Beaulieu and David Mulkey (eds.), *Investing in People: The Human Capital Needs of Rural America.* Boulder: Westview Press—Rural Studies Series.

McGranahan, David A. 1991. "Introduction." Chapter 1 in *Education and Rural Economic Strategies for the 1990's.* Agriculture and Rural Economy Division, Economic Research Service, U.S. Department of Agriculture. ERS Staff Report No. AGES 9153: 1-12.

McGranahan, David A., and Linda M. Ghelfi. 1991. "The education crisis and rural stagnation in the 1980's." Chapter 3 in *Education and Rural Economic Strategies for the 1990's.* Agriculture and Rural Economy Division, Economic Research Service, U.S. Department of Agriculture. ERS Staff Report No. AGES 9153: 40-92.

Mishel, Lawrence, and Ruy A. Teixeira. 1991. *The Myth of the Coming Labor Shortage: Jobs, Skills, and Incomes of America's Workforce 2000.* Washington, DC: Economic Policy Institute.

Pollard, Kevin M., and William P. O'Hare. 1990. *Beyond High School: The Experience of Rural and Urban Youth in the 1980's.* Washington, DC: Population Reference Bureau (March).

Porterfield, Shirley L., and Molly Sizer Killian. 1994. "Producer services and rural economic development." *Rural Development Perspectives* (forthcoming).

Rosenfeld, Stuart A., Emil E. Malizia, and Marybeth Dugan. 1988. *Reviving the Rural Factory: Automation and Work in the South.* Research Triangle Park, NC: The Southern Technology Council.

Sidor, John. 1991. *Put Up or Give Way: States, Economic Competitiveness, and Poverty.* Washington, DC: Council of State Community Development Agencies.

Smith, Eldon D. 1988. "Reflections on human resources in the strategy of rural economic development." Staff Paper 256. Department of Agricultural Economics, University of Kentucky, Lexington.

Stallmann, Judith, Ari Mwachofi, Jan L. Flora, and Thomas G. Johnson. 1994. "The labor market and human capital investment." In Lionel J. Beaulieu and David Mulkey (eds.), *Investing in People: The Human Capital Needs of Rural America.* Boulder, CO: Westview Press—Rural Studies Series.

Teixeira, Ruy A., and Lawrence Mishel. 1991. "Upgrading workers' skills not sufficient to jump-start rural economy." *Rural Development Perspectives* 7(June-September): 19-24.

Thurow, Lester C. 1975. *Generating Inequality: Mechanisms of Distribution in the U.S. Economy.* New York, NY: Basic Books.

Voth, Donald E., Molly Sizer Killian, and Frank L. Farmer. 1994. "Selective migration and the 'educational brain drain' from the Lower Mississippi Delta Region in 1975-1980." *Southern Rural Sociology* 10 (1): 131-146.

TABLE A-2.1. Years of School Completed by Persons 25 Years Old and Over by Region and Type of Residence, 1990

Region and Type of Residence	Overall	Race / Ethnicity		
		White	Black	Hispanic
NORTHEAST REGION				
Overall				
8 years or less	9.8	8.5	11.0	25.6
1 to 3 years of high school	14.7	13.1	23.7	22.8
High school degree	32.3	33.1	30.1	24.0
1 to 3 years of college	21.2	21.3	22.7	17.4
4+ years of college	22.0	23.9	12.5	10.2
Total Population (in thousands)	33,815	28,551	3,232	1,992
Metropolitan Status				
8 years or less	9.8	8.4	11.0	25.7
1 to 3 years of high school	14.7	12.9	23.7	22.8
High school degree	31.6	32.3	30.1	23.9
1 to 3 years of college	21.3	21.5	22.7	17.4
4+ years of college	22.6	24.9	12.5	10.2
Total Population (in thousands)	30,653	25,454	3,232	1,967
Nonmetropolitan Status				
8 years or less	9.5	9.4	10.9	16.7
1 to 3 years of high school	14.9	14.7	26.3	21.4
High school degree	39.5	39.8	28.5	25.4
1 to 3 years of college	20.2	20.1	24.0	22.2
4+ years of college	15.8	15.9	10.3	14.3
Total Population (in thousands)	3,162	3,097	40	25
MIDWEST REGION				
Overall				
8 years or less	9.2	8.6	10.5	28.6
1 to 3 years of high school	13.8	12.7	24.2	18.5
High school degree	34.1	35.0	27.9	23.6
1 to 3 years of college	24.8	24.7	27.0	19.2
4+ years of college	18.1	19.0	10.4	10.1
Total Population (in thousands)	37,689	33,752	3,148	789
Metropolitan Status				
8 years or less	8.0	7.0	10.4	28.8
1 to 3 years of high school	13.7	12.3	24.1	18.4
High school degree	31.9	32.7	27.8	23.1
1 to 3 years of college	25.9	25.9	27.1	19.2
4+ years of college	15.8	15.9	10.3	14.3
Total Population (in thousands)	26,997	23,288	3,008	701

TABLE A-2.1. Continued

Region and Type of Residence	Overall	Race / Ethnicity White	Black	Hispanic
MIDWEST REGION				
Nonmetropolitan Status				
8 years or less	12.4	12.2	14.0	26.3
1 to 3 years of high school	14.0	13.8	25.1	19.0
High school degree	39.7	39.9	30.1	27.9
1 to 3 years of college	21.9	21.9	23.6	19.4
4+ years of college	12.0	12.2	7.2	7.3
Total Population (in thousands)	10,692	10,464	140	88
SOUTH				
Overall				
8 years of less	13.2	11.0	16.9	31.8
1 to 3 years or high school	16.2	14.6	23.3	17.3
High school degree	28.7	29.6	27.2	21.0
1 to 3 years of college	23.4	24.4	20.3	19.1
4+ years of college	18.5	20.4	12.3	10.8
Total Population (in thousands)	55,940	43,478	8,909	3,553
Metropolitan Status				
8 years or less	11.1	8.6	13.5	30.3
1 to 3 years of high school	14.8	13.1	21.9	17.2
High school degree	27.5	28.2	26.9	21.0
1 to 3 years of college	25.3	26.3	22.9	20.0
4+ years of college	21.3	23.8	14.8	11.5
Total Population (in thousands)	40,119	30,509	6,498	3,112
Nonmetropolitan Status				
8 years or less	18.8	16.7	25.8	43.0
1 to 3 years of high school	19.6	18.2	27.2	17.9
High school degree	31.7	32.7	28.0	21.0
1 to 3 years of college	18.6	19.8	13.2	12.7
4+ years of college	11.3	12.5	5.8	5.4
Total Population (in thousands)	15,821	12,969	2,411	441
WEST				
Overall				
8 years or less	10.5	6.5	7.0	32.4
1 to 3 years of high school	12.8	11.2	16.8	19.9
High school degree	24.9	25.7	24.6	20.6
1 to 3 years of college	30.6	32.3	36.8	19.7
4+ years of college	21.2	24.2	14.8	7.4
Total Population (in thousands)	31,844	25,394	1,594	4,856

TABLE A-2.1. Continued

Region and Type of Residence	Overall	Race / Ethnicity		
		White	Black	Hispanic
WEST				
Metropolitan Status				
8 years or less	10.6	6.3	7.0	32.6
1 to 3 years of high school	12.6	10.8	16.6	20.0
High school degree	23.8	24.6	24.6	20.1
1 to 3 years of college	30.8	32.6	36.9	19.8
4+ years of college	22.1	25.6	14.9	7.5
Total Population (in thousands)	27,100	21,155	1,549	4,396
Nonmetropolitan Status				
8 years of less	9.8	7.5	7.0	32.6
1 to 3 years or high school	13.8	13.2	21.7	18.8
High school degree	30.0	31.6	25.4	25.8
1 to 3 years of college	29.3	30.4	33.9	18.6
4+ years of college	16.1	17.3	9.8	6.0
Total Population (in thousands)	4,744	4,239	45	460

Source: U.S. Bureau of Census, Current Population Report, Series P-20. *Educational Attainment in the United States* (various years). U.S. Government Printing Office, Washington D.C.

PART TWO

Forces Shaping the Future of Rural America

3

Economic Forces Shaping the Future of Rural America

Glen C. Pulver

Rural America is economically diverse. It is no longer dependent primarily on agriculture and natural resource based industries for its livelihood. It is a complex of specialized subregions—some primarily dependent on farming, some on manufacturing, and others on a variety of income sources. Many have economies very similar to urban regions.

Today, only one in three jobs in nonmetropolitan America is connected in any way to agriculture, either as farmers, input providers, or product processors or distributors. Most of the remainder are found in manufacturing and service-producing sectors. In most rural regions of the United States, economic crises are driven as much by job losses in manufacturing and mining as by farm income and land value losses. In contrast to previous times, an economic policy focused solely on increasing incomes in a single industry such as farming or forestry will do little to improve rural incomes.

The economic well-being of most rural regions depends on a wide array of industries, firm sizes, and income sources. Consequently, the shifting forces that influence the broader United States economy will have a profound effect on both rural and urban areas. Policies addressing past rural conditions and opportunities will have limited future success. As the economic environment changes, the size and shape of the components of rural development policy also changes (Brown et al. 1988; Joint Economic Committee 1986; Pigg 1991; United States General Accounting Office 1993).

Rural Economic Diversity

Farming has not been the dominant employer or income sources in rural America for some time. Over the past half century, farming has accounted for a relatively small and declining proportion of U.S. personal income. The number of U.S. farm operations was highest in 1916 (Lacy and Bogie 1986).

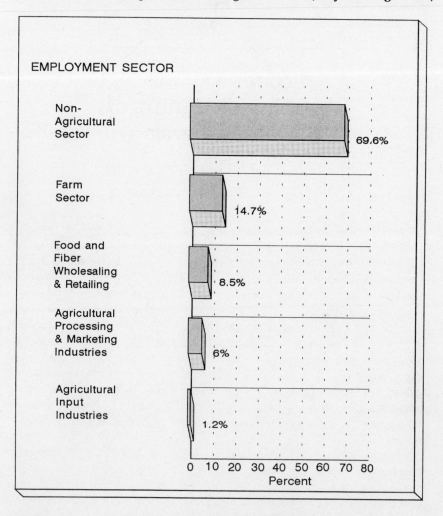

FIGURE 3.1   Agriculturally Related Employment in the Nonmetro Economy, 1982.

Source: Fred K. Hines, Bernal L. Green & Mindy Petrulis 1986. "Vulnerability to farm problems varies by region," in *Rural Development Perspectives* 2 (June): 12.

By 1929, only 8.8 percent of total U.S. personal income came from farming. Farm earnings (net farm income adjusted for inventory valuation and capital consumption) reached nearly 10 percent of U.S. personal income in the late 1940s, but fell to less than 2 percent in the 1980s (Bureau of Economic Analysis 1984; 1988).

Farm earnings, alone, do not reflect the total importance of agriculture to the economy. Many people supply inputs to farmers and process agricultural products. Only 14.7 percent of the workers in nonmetropolitan counties are on the farm, 1.2 percent are in farm supplies, 6 percent in processing industries, and 8.5 percent in retailing and wholesaling of food and fiber (see figure 3.1).

Although farming represents a declining share of total personal income in rural areas, this does not imply that the income of farm families is lower. As a matter of fact, the average farm household income has been roughly equivalent to that of all U.S. households in recent years (Deavers 1990). It is important to note that many farm families' incomes come from nonfarm sources. Currently, over 50 percent of the farmers in nonmetropolitan counties work off the farm (Parker and Whitener 1989). Farm families with annual gross sales of less than $40,000 are almost totally dependent upon nonfarm income. Much of this nonfarm income has little connection to agriculture (Deavers 1990).

In addition to rural America's dependence on the nonfarm sector, there is great variability in income sources across nonmetropolitan regions. Only 21.7 percent of the nonmetropolitan counties in the United States receive

TABLE 3.1   Nonmetropolitan Counties by Type: 1986

	Number	Percent
Farming	512	21.7
Federal Lands	243	10.3
Government	347	14.7
Manufacturing	553	23.5
Mining	124	5.3
Poverty	239	10.1
Retirement	480	20.4
Unclassified	519	22.0

Total number of nonmetropolitan counties in 48 contiguous U.S. states - 2357. Counties may be classified in more than one type thus the columns total more than 2357 and 100 percent.
Source: Hady, Thomas, F. and Peggy J. Ross. 1990. "Nonmetro Counties Less Dependent on Farming, Manufacturing, and Mining." *Rural Development Perspectives.* U.S.D.A., E.R.S., A.R.E.D. (June-September).

20 percent or more of labor and proprietor income from farming. A slightly higher percentage (23.5 percent) receive 30 percent or more of total labor and proprietor income from manufacturing. Approximately one in five counties is experiencing a net in-migration of people 60 years of age and older, a rate that has exceeded expectations by some 15 percent. Such counties have been classified as retirement destination counties (Table 3.1). Since 1983, over half of the population growth in nonmetropolitan areas has occurred in retirement destination counties. These areas are also often prime recreation and tourism locations (Deavers and Long 1989). The combination of natural resource conditions and amenities such as health care facilities, educational institutions, and cultural activities appear to attract both retirement and tourism.

Rural areas currently experiencing the most severe economic problems are those outside easy daily commuting distances from growing urban areas. These remote regions have been the most dependent upon farming, forestry, and mining. Although they experienced job growth in manufacturing during the 1970s, they are once again lagging behind urban areas. As a result, these rural counties are less likely to provide alternative employment opportunities for families leaving farming or those seeking temporary or supplementary income. In some situations, these remote regions are experiencing growth in tourism, but passive income received by the elderly is often the major income source (Henry et al. 1987).

The employment opportunities of rural families living within easy commuting distances of cities of 15,000 or more people are generally better than those in more remote regions. This is especially true if the urban centers are experiencing economic growth. If, however, the cities are economically stagnant, then the surrounding rural areas suffer as much as remote regions (Gilmer, Keil and Mack 1989).

The economic development options of small towns near urban centers are drastically different than those farther away. Because of relatively easy access to critical industrial location factors provided by proximity to cities, the industrial opportunities of such rural communities are much the same as nearby cities. Remoteness limits access, thus narrowing opportunities. Many of the poorest rural counties are relatively remote and contain a high percentage of racial minorities (United States General Accounting Office 1993).

The great variation in economic dependency and regional remoteness in rural America presents a major problem in establishing an effective rural development policy. Actions that focus on improving farm incomes may be of major assistance in certain regions, but of little assistance elsewhere. Policies targeted at expanding manufacturing or forestry-based industries will benefit some regions, but prove insufficient elsewhere. To prove successful, national and state rural development policy must be comprehensive, covering a wide range of economic options, yet be flexible enough to respond to unique conditions in specific communities.

Major Economic Changes

Rural development policymakers must not only recognize the diversity of rural areas, but also respond to continuing major long run structural changes in the United States and global economies. Four changes are having a powerful influence on both rural and urban America:

* most job growth is in the services-producing sector;
* the population of much of the developed world is aging;
* small businesses are the primary generators of net new jobs; and
* nearly all businesses are affected directly by the global economy.

These shifts must be all considered carefully when assessing the future of rural areas.

Growth in the Services Sector

Although the economic future of much of rural America remains closely tied to the success of resource extraction and other goods-producing industries, little or no net job growth can be anticipated in this sector. The number of farm proprietors and employees has declined steadily for over 50 years. Employment in mining and forestry has also declined in recent years. While there has been some expansion in high-technology manufacturing, the number of people employed in manufacturing in the U.S. is now about the same as 10 years ago. Continued intensive international competition and technological change is likely to lead to fewer U.S. workers in farming, forestry, manufacturing, and mining in the years ahead. Thus, goods-producing industrial sectors, which historically were perceived as the primary generators of job growth, no longer drive economic expansion. They may produce more output, but few net new jobs.

Most future employment growth in the United States will be in the services-producing sector. The Bureau of Labor Statistics projects an additional 21 million jobs will be generated in the services-producing sector in the United States between 1986 and 2000. This sector is expected to account for four out of every five jobs at the end of the period. The top 20 producers of net new jobs during the period are projected to be services industries. Nineteen of the top 20 industries, in terms of rates of employment growth, are in this sector. In terms of industrial output, 15 of the fastest growing 20 industries are services-producers (Personick 1987).

There is some question as to whether services-producing industries, especially the higher wage producer services, can be expected to locate and grow in rural areas at the same pace as in urban areas. At the present time, they represent a lower percentage of workers in nonmetropolitan counties than in metropolitan counties (Porterfield 1990). In addition, employment in services-producing industries is growing more slowly in nonmetropolitan areas (2.9 percent per year) than in metropolitan areas (3.6 percent) (Economic Research Service 1990).

There appear to be no major limitations to employment growth in rural counties closest to metropolitan areas. The location and job growth patterns of services industries in counties adjacent to metropolitan areas are similar to their urban neighbors. This is not the case in more remote rural areas. Nonetheless, some services industries have exhibited consistent growth potential in communities distant from urban areas (Pulver 1986; Pulver and Lien 1989). Trucking, eating and drinking places, and nursing and personal care services are examples of industries which seem to do well in remote rural regions. The future is bright for rural areas that can effectively attract services-producing industries that expect rapid growth and provide higher paying wages. For those that are unable to do so, long term economic decline is all but assured.

Some high-technology industries are also expected to grow rapidly on a national scale. While studies of the factors important to industrial location have focused on traditional goods-producing sectors, some insights have been gained regarding the services-producing sectors and the new high-technology manufacturers (Ady 1986; Premus 1986; Smith and Pulver 1981). It appears that the factors which are important to the location and growth of services-producers and high-technology manufacturing are, with few exceptions, the same as those for traditional manufacturing. Most critical among the location variables are access to knowledge, capital, telecommunications, transportation, and a high quality living environment. Locational requirements are not necessarily the same for all specific industries. For instance, high-technology manufacturers and producer services generally demand a more highly educated workforce than traditional manufacturers. However, the average education and training requirements of the high-tech industries which tend to locate in rural areas differ little from those of low-tech firms (Porterfield and Pulver 1991; Smith and Barkley 1988). Obviously, communities which do not provide access to those variables critical to the location of growth industries will encounter development problems.

Aging of the Population

The baby boom which peaked in the U.S. in 1960, is now providing the impetus for a rapidly aging America. In 1960 there were approximately 16 million Americans 65 years or older. The number will more than double by the year 2000 (see Figure 3.2). This is the fastest growing age group.

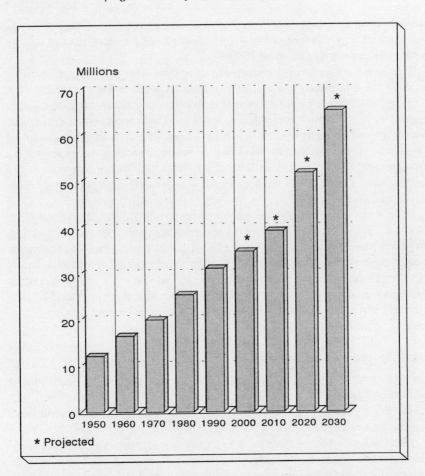

FIGURE 3.2 Growth of the Mature Market: The Increase in the U.S. Population Over 65.

Source: U.S. Department of Commerce, Bureau of the Census, *Historical Statistics of the U.S.* and *Current Population Reports*, Series P-25, Nos. 519,917, 1022, and unpublished data.

Today people of retirement age control over one in three dollars of personal income (Hoppe and Ghelfi 1990). People over 65 years of age now have the highest discretionary income (income after housing and taxes). A population once thought to be a negative economic influence now provides community vitality.

The number of nonmetropolitan retirement destination counties in the United States continues to grow. Retirement counties are defined as those with at least 15 percent net in-migration of the elderly. Not only does the population of these counties grow faster than those of other nonmetropolitan counties, so do their economies, as measured by per capita income and employment. Many of these counties are in relatively remote regions (Reeder and Glasgow 1990).

The more mature rural retirement counties—those with one-sixth or more of their population as elderly—seem to perform best economically. They exhibit higher population and employment growth rates and show greater stability during economic cycles than other retirement counties and nonmetropolitan counties as a whole. Furthermore, concentrations of elderly do not significantly raise health costs of local governments. An increase in the number of retirees also has a positive influence on the employment shares of the services sector (Reeder and Glasgow 1990; Smith, Willis and Weber 1986).

People of retirement age have become an important base for community economic well-being. Therefore, as the number of people reaching retirement age continues to grow in the U.S., it is imperative that rural regions garner their share. This is especially true for remote rural regions. Many rural areas have attractive natural beauty, but their community leaders must pay particular attention to health care, education, cultural opportunities, and other amenities if these regions are to be competitive retirement destinations.

Small Business as Job Generators

It has long been recognized that the largest source of employment growth in the U.S. has been the expansion of existing firms. The often repeated "80 percent of net new jobs come from the growth of existing firms" may be an understatement.

What is less well recognized is the growing importance of small businesses in the generation of new jobs. Through most of the 1980s, a large percentage of net new job growth in the U.S. was produced by firms with less than 500 employees (The State of Small Business 1987). Between 1982 and 1986, nearly three out of four net new jobs were generated by companies with fewer than 20 employees (Cognetics 1987). Although some large firms continued to generate jobs as a result of rapid growth during the period, nearly as many jobs were cut by large firms through reductions in employment.

Part of the growing importance of small business is explained by the increasing economic influence of services-producing firms, many of which are relatively small in size. This is particularly true of the retail sector and other consumer services. At the same time, part of the decline in employment in large firms is explained by increased efficiency in production processes, especially in manufacturing. Robotics and other computer-aided technological innovations have reduced labor requirements per unit of output. Industrial activity (both manufacturing and services) once dominated by large scale, low-technology, standardized production has now shifted toward small scale, high-technology production activities (Barkley 1988).

The sustained economic progress of the U.S. is dependent on the continued development of new products and services by small young firms and old corporate giants (Vaughan et al. 1985). The birth and growth of small firms is of special importance to the economic vitality of rural areas. Jobs lost in farming, forestry, and mining and traditional rural manufacturing must be replaced by jobs generated by other basic employers. Few rural regions have major employers to take up the slack, thus the heavy dependence on new business start-ups. Unfortunately, the rate of small business employment growth in rural areas is less than that in urban counties. This is particularly true for high-technology industries (Miller 1989).

The creation of an entrepreneurial environment, which stimulates the formation and growth of small businesses in rural communities, is essential. An entrepreneurial environment exists in a community when there are development opportunities, available role models, accessible funds, rewards for risk taking, and an absence of barriers such as severe permitting restrictions (Pulver 1987; Vaughan et al. 1985). The lack of economic diversity within specific rural communities creates difficulty; sensitivity to broad development opportunities may be less. There are fewer role models, especially within industrial subsectors. Lenders have more difficulty in assessing the economic viability of loan applications for non-familiar businesses and less opportunity to spread risk across sectors. Community leaders often have little tolerance of business failure and thus, discourage entrepreneurship. All of those limitations must be addressed if rural areas are to compete with urban areas for small businesses in the future.

Global Competition

Few areas of the U.S. have escaped the direct impact of the globalization of the economy. Most U.S. firms must now compete head to head with their foreign counterparts. The success or failure of entire industries or individual businesses is dependent not only on their comparative production efficiency, but on variables outside of their control such as trade balances, exchange rates, protective tariffs, and other trade restrictions. A minor change in national monetary or fiscal policy may drive some U.S. firms out of business.

Small town retailers must be sensitive to the comparative dependability and price of foreign made goods versus those produced in the U.S. Their shelves are often stocked with foreign made products. If domestically produced goods cannot compete in price or service, they are quickly replaced by those from other parts of the world. Retailers who fail to respond are soon out-of-business.

Farmers, large and small, must not only worry about the prospects of drought in the U.S., but in other parts of the world. They must also be sensitive to the impact of foreign exchange rates on the prices of U.S. farm products. If the value of the dollar rises dramatically against other currencies, it becomes increasingly difficult to export U.S. farm products.

Historically, rural areas were often attractive locations for small scale manufacturing because they offered lower cost land and cheaper labor than urban areas. Today, those advantages are being lost and U.S. firms are seeking foreign locations. The down-sizing of manufacturing plants and the growth in small businesses has reduced the space requirements per establishment, thereby reducing the importance of land costs as a factor in plant siting. Furthermore, the internationalization of corporate ownership and production processes has allowed firms to reach across national boundaries for even cheaper labor than that offered by rural America. Rural regions are no longer the most cost effective location for many industries that use relatively standardized production systems.

U.S. industrial competitiveness appears strongest in products (both goods and services) requiring sophisticated technology and highly skilled labor. Industries with these requirements tend to favor urban proximity. Rural leaders must find a way to overcome these limitations (Deavers 1990).

Foreign investment in the U.S. has the potential to increase the economic well-being of the regions in which the investments are made. This is especially true if the investment is not merely a change in ownership, but results in new facilities. Until now, however, foreign investment in the U.S. has occurred primarily in urban areas and has consisted mostly of buyouts, which add few jobs. Through 1987, only about 10 percent of the foreign investment in the U.S. was in nonmetropolitan counties. To the economic development advantage of rural areas, however, a much higher share of these investments were employment creating (38 percent), as compared to investments in urban areas (17 percent) (Glasmeier and Glickman 1990).

Rural areas that hope to participate in the global economy must provide ready access to those factors which allow private businesses to compete effectively. This will include access to a well educated workforce with excellent communication and computational skills, the latest in telecommunications equipment, first rate transportation, capital sources familiar with international business needs, and a living environment which will attract and keep competent employees. All of these factors are particularly important to the location and growth of producer services and high technology manufacturing.

The capacity to produce competitively in the global economy will not be sufficient. Participation in the world marketplace will require increased language competency and a sensitivity to cultural diversity. Small rural school systems may not have the size or fiscal capacity to offer a wide spectrum of language courses, but all systems have the capacity to create greater understanding of and appreciation for the religious, ethnic and cultural differences which exist across nations. Closed, nationalistic perspectives will have little place in future global markets.

Economic Development Literacy

These four powerful economic forces will play out in different ways in various rural regions. Every rural community represents a unique combination of goals, resources, and opportunities. No single economic development approach will be effective in all cases. Communities in remote rural regions may be unsuccessful in attracting rapidly growing producer services industries as a whole, but may be able to nurture the start-up and growth of businesses created by local entrepreneurs. Other rural communities may have unique natural environments which can serve as the basis for the development of retirement centers or tourism. Still others may be experiencing substantial urban pressures and thus, have decided the primary need is to manage growth more wisely.

Since goals, resources and opportunities differ among rural areas, development policies and strategies must be specific to communities and regions. Local leaders must choose a combination of strategies, including efforts aimed at increasing the efficiency of existing businesses, attracting new basic employers, helping new business start-ups, capturing existing dollars, and acquiring assistance from broader units of government.

Choices have been complicated by the jungle of economic development programs created by state and national governments and by private businesses and organizations. Policymakers must be aware of the full array of external assistance, and must know how to tap into that which is useful. Rural leaders must fashion effective policy out of this complex maze of local goals, internal resources, external resources, and realistic opportunities. This must be accomplished within an environment of continuous economic change.

In small towns and big cities alike, very specialized knowledge is required to develop effective economic policy. Policymakers must understand employment trends; market possibilities; structural changes in the local, national, and global economy; industrial location factors; consumer spending patterns; sources of financing; impacts of actions on groups such as minorities, women, and the poor; and the environmental consequences of change. They need to understand the division of responsibilities among local, state, and national governments; the role of the private sector; mechanisms for providing and financing services; and the importance of volunteers. They need to possess personal leadership and organization skills and know how to use effective community development processes.

In rural areas, local government officials, community organizations, and private business people are at a disadvantage as compared to their urban counterparts. Because of their smaller populations and more specialized industrial structure, rural areas have a narrower knowledge base and are farther from specialized knowledge sources. For example, it is difficult for private business people, government officials, and local organizational lenders from rural locations to access state and federal agency staff located in capital cities. In addition, legal, accounting, financing, engineering, and other business specialists are usually found in larger cities. Rural areas have a smaller base with which to finance a local staff capable of providing economic analysis and counsel on a continuing basis. As a consequence, the serious development efforts of well-intentioned local leaders in rural areas are often misinformed and end in failure and frustration (Somersan 1989).

Implications for Human Resource Development

The powerful economic forces which are driving change throughout the entire U.S. economy necessitate important shifts in rural development policy. Historic rural policy has emphasized improving prices, expanding markets, and increasing production in farming, forestry, and other natural-resource based industries. But, targets must be shifted to recognize the premium on highly developed human capital generated by the current shifts in economic forces.

If rural areas are to attract high technology manufacturing and producers services, their fundamental educational systems must produce a workforce with excellent basic communication and computational skills, plus an ability to respond to the rapid technological changes associated with these industries. Retirement destination communities must provide access to excellent health care and cultural, educational, and recreational amenities. A positive entrepreneurial climate demands creativity and the acceptance of risk as well as supportive business, financial, and technical institutions. A new business idea may be produced by chance or result from stress. A positive entrepreneurial environment which is supportive of the new idea requires community intent.

Rural areas hoping to be competitive in the global economy, must provide a competitive setting, including internationally literate public and private leadership. Success in dealing with these powerful economic forces may be more closely linked to the quality of human resources than anything else. Sound elementary, secondary, higher, and continuing education; first rate health care; supportive social systems; and other elements essential to high quality human resources are fundamental to an adequate rural response to economic change.

Perhaps the single most important human resource development initiative which could be undertaken to improve the economic well-being of rural America would be the provision of educational and technical assistance in community economic development policy to national, state, and local leaders. Such assistance would help people understand critical changes in global economic forces, analyze their specific economic problems and opportunities, and build comprehensive policies offering real hope of goal achievement. This educational and technical assistance is especially critical for local leaders in rural communities who, for the most part, lack the same access to critical knowledge enjoyed by their urban counterparts. Recipients of this assistance would include local government officials, business leaders, bankers, educators, industrial developers, planners, health care providers, community organizations, prospective entrepreneurs, and others interested in economic development. The result would be a stronger citizenry with the capacity to make informed decisions regarding the future of their communities and thus, an economically healthier rural America.

References

Ady, Robert M. 1986. "Criteria used for facility location." Pp.72-84 in Norman Walzer and David L. Chicoine (eds.), *Financing Economic Development in the 1980s*. New York, NY: Praeger.

Barkley, D. L. 1988. "The decentralization of high-technology manufacturing to nonmetropolitan areas." *Growth and Change* 19 (1): 13 - 30.

Brown, David L., J. Norman Reid, Herman Bluestone, David A. McGranahan, and Sara M. Mazie. 1988. *Rural Economic Development in the 1980's*. Economic Research Service. U.S. Department of Agriculture. Washington, D.C.

Bureau of Economic Analysis. 1984. *State Personal Income: 1929-82*. U.S. Department of Commerce, Washington, D.C. (February).

Bureau of Economic Analysis. 1988. *Survey of Current Business: 1987*. U.S. Department of Commerce, Washington, D.C.

Cognetics, Inc. 1987. *Inc. Magazine*. (September).

Deavers, Kenneth. 1990. "Rural vision—rural reality." *Benjamin H. Hibbard Memorial Lecture Series*. Department of Agricultural Economics. University of Wisconsin-Madison. Madison, WI.

Deavers, Kenneth L., and Richard W. Long. 1989. "Rural policy after the renaissance: Western Europe and American perspectives." *Increasing Understanding of Public Problems and Policies—1988*. Farm Foundation. Oak Brook, IL.

Economic Research Service. 1990. "Nonmetro job growth in cyclical industries increased during 1987." *Rural Conditions and Trends* 1 (Spring): 10-11.

Gilmer, Robert W., Stanley R. Keil, and Richard S. Mack. 1989. "The service sector in a hierarchy of rural places: Potential for export activity." *Land Economics* 65 (August): 217-28.

Glasmeier, Amy, and Norman Glickman. 1990. "Foreign investment boosts rural economies." *Rural Development Perspectives* 6 (June-September): 19-25.

Henry, Mark, Mark Drabenstott, and Lynn Gibson. 1987. "Rural growth slows down." *Rural Development Perspectives* 3 (June): 25-30.

Hoppe, Robert A., and Linda M. Ghelfi. 1990. "Nonmetro areas depend on transfers." *Rural Development Perspectives* 6 (February-May): 22-24.

Lacy, A. Wayne, and Donald W. Bogie. 1986. "America's farm population: Historical changes and recent trends." Pp. 98-113 in *New Dimensions In Rural Policy: Building Upon Our Heritage.* Joint Economic Committee, Congress of the United States, Washington, D.C.

Miller, James P. 1989. "The product cycle and high technology industry in metropolitan areas, 1976-1980." *The Review of Regional Studies* 19: 1.

Parker, Timothy, and Leslie A. Whitener. 1989. "Farmers and their search for off-farm employment." *Rural Development Perspectives* 5 (February): 27-33.

Personick, V. A. 1987. "Projections 2000, industry output and employment through the end of the century." *Monthly Labor Review* 110: 9.

Porterfield, Shirley. 1990. "Service sector offers more jobs, lower pay." *Rural Development Perspectives.* Economic Research Service. U.S. Department of Agriculture. Washington, D.C. 6: 3.

Pigg, Kenneth E. 1991. *The Future of Rural America.* . Boulder, CO: Westview Press.

Porterfield, Shirley L., and Glen C. Pulver. 1991. "Services producers: Exports, imports and locations." *International Regional Science Review* 14: 1.

Premus, Robert. 1986. "Attracting high-tech industry and jobs: An assessment of state practices." Pp. 55-71 in Norman Walzer and David L. Chicoine (eds.), *Financing Economic Development in the 1980s.* New York, NY: Praeger.

Pulver, Glen C. 1986. "Service-producing industries in economic development." Pp. 209-15 in Robert P. Wolenky and Edward J. Miller (eds.), *The Small City and Regional Community.* The University of Wisconsin-Stevens Point. Stevens Point, WI.

Pulver, Glen C. 1987. "Fitting entrepreneurs into community development strategies." *Proceedings of the National Rural Entrepreneurship Symposium.* Southern Rural Development Center. Series No. 97.

Pulver, Glen C., and Bentley C. Lien. 1989. "Rural location prospects of exportable services-producing industries." Department of Agricultural Economics. University of Wisconsin-Madison. Madison, WI.

Reeder, Richard J., and Nina L. Glasgow. 1990. "Nonmetro retirement counties' strengths and weaknesses." *Rural Development Perspectives* 6 (February-May): 12-17.

Rural Development Profile of Rural Areas. 1993. United State General Accounting Office, Washington D.C. (April).

Smith, Gary W., David B. Willis, and Bruce A. Weber. 1986. *Transfer Payments, the*

Aging Population, and the Changing Structure of the Oregon and Washington Economies. Western Rural Development Center. No. 30.

Smith, Stephen M., and David L. Barkley. 1988. "Labor force characteristics of 'high tech' vs. 'low tech' manufacturing in nonmetropolitan counties in the West." *Journal of the Community Development Society* 19 (1): 21-36.

Smith, Stephen M., and Glen C. Pulver. 1981. "Nonmanufacturing business as a growth alternative in nonmetropolitan areas." *Journal of the Community Development Society* 12 (1): 33-48.

Somersan, Ayse. 1989. *Testimony to the Subcommittee Conservation, Credit and Rural Development of the Committee on Agriculture.* U.S. House of Representatives, Washington, D.C.

Subcommittee on Agriculture and Transportation. 1986. *New Dimensions In Rural Policy: Building Upon Our Heritage.* Joint Economic Committee. Congress of the United States. U.S. Government Printing Office. Washington, D.C.

The State of Small Businesses: A Report of the President. 1987. U.S. Government Printing Office. Washington, D.C.

Vaughan, Roger, Robert Pollard, and Barbara Dyer. 1985. *The Wealth of States.* CSPA, Washington, D.C.

4

Social Forces Shaping the Future of Rural Areas

Kenneth P. Wilkinson

The future of the rural community is being molded in large part by a wave of technological, economic, and political changes that could either reduce the social and economic disadvantages associated with remote location and small-scale social organizations or leave rural communities even further behind in the future than they have been in the past. Hopeful signs for the future such as new communications technologies to reduce the friction of rural space and efforts in many nations and states to establish rural development as a goal of government policy appear prominently among these changes, but as yet few of the potential benefits have been realized in rural areas. Instead, recent reports from the countryside (Davidson 1990; Fitchen 1991; Flora and Christenson 1991; Luloff and Swanson 1990; Pigg 1991) continue to give a less than rosy view of the conditions of rural community life. In fact, it appears that developments in the changing world order could do as much harm as good to highly vulnerable rural communities (Catelli 1992). In such a setting of change and uncertainty, the rural social sciences, as advocates for rural well-being, are challenged to find ways of using new developments to help solve rural community problems.

A useful analysis of social forces shaping the future should focus, above all, on how well the needs of people who live in rural areas are served by the means available to pursue social goals. Such an analysis should begin with the awareness that rural populations around the world have many unmet needs. Jobs and income lead the list of obvious rural deficits. Without adequate economic resources, communities tend to wither and often die. Services, public infrastructure, planning expertise, and other pressing needs also appear among the issues to be addressed by rural development initiatives. While these economic and service deficits are worthy objects of ameliorative action, they must be recognized as only surface manifestations of a more fundamental underlying problem of contemporary rural life, namely the problem of community deterioration. What rural communities need most is denoted by the term "community" itself. Rural communities too rarely, in fact, are "communities." Instead, rural places tend to be locations where particular problems and issues appear instead of social units where effective collective actions occur. It is not enough to solve particular problems; what is needed is to improve the overall capacity of the community to cope with changes affecting local life. More than anything, rural communities need to be able to "act" (Luloff, 1990), that is to organize and carry out projects on their own behalf by deciding among alternative scenarios of the future and undertaking collective actions to pursue the goals they select. This ability depends on social relationships that organize and energize the collective life of a local population. The idea that "community" needs to be encouraged in local social interaction addresses the central requirement for a better future in rural areas. Community development, which refers to the development of community in a local population, is what is needed to build the capacity of people in rural areas to shape their own future well-being.

A Critical Approach to Rural Community Development

The assertion that social science can and should serve the normative goal of reducing rural deficits and thus of increasing rural well-being expresses the first principle of a critical approach in rural sociology—a commitment to an analysis that cuts to the roots of inequality and injustice and searches for alternatives to practices that stifle the natural well-being of human communities. Critical approaches in the sociology of development (Bottomore 1984), particularly in the sociology of rural development (Buttel and Newby 1980; Long 1977), have much to contribute to the study of rural conditions and changes, although the usefulness of the body of literature known specifically as critical theory has been limited somewhat in the past by its narrow emphasis on capitalist development and rigorous adherence to the Marxian interpretation of social change. A broader concern for freedom, justice, and community empowerment is needed in the search for the sources of problems that restrict social well-being. Indeed any approach that seeks to understand social life for purposes of promoting these goals—freedom, justice and community empowerment—can be, and should be, not only normative, but critical as well, with or without a focus on the issues that dominate a Marxian analysis.

Contemporary post-Marxian critical approaches (e.g. Habermas 1984) support such an effort in that they seek to liberate naturally occurring affirmative tendencies in human communication and social interaction from distortions and suppression wrought by contemporary economic and political trends. From this broader viewpoint, the "natural" condition of human affairs is seen to be pretty much the same as that envisioned by Marx, namely a condition of communal solidarity based on the implicit mutuality of all human beings. The foundation of a critical approach is the observation that human interaction always depends upon and supports the recognition of an underlying solidarity among people, a shared recognition that, whatever their differences, people have equal status as human beings. This commonality might be denied by popular culture and perverted into hatred or disregard; but the fact remains that at some level people can respond to other people as people. Otherwise they could not communicate with one another, and without communication people could not survive as people. The implicit mutual recognition of common equality supports a mutual commitment to the requirements of human discourse, which include the necessity of seeing oneself from another person's perspective and thus of seeking to understand the meaning of the other's actions. This commitment creates a bond that is the basis, not only of community, but of society as well. Without this shared commitment to the fundamental rules of interpersonal communication, society would be impossible. Thus, the basis of community is present as an underlying reality in all human interaction, even among people who share little else, and even in settings where its expression is suppressed or dwarfed by cleavages that prevent authentic social interaction.

Ubiquitous potential, however, gives no assurance that community will develop. In the Marxian view, historical inequities in control of vital resources have prevented the full development and realization of this natural condition of community among people, notwithstanding (according to Marx) a dialectic that propels society, fitfully but inevitably, towards the classless, communal existence that this natural tendency demands. The basic idea is that community, which is essential for the full realization of human well-being, must be pursued in struggle against powerful impediments to its emergence, even though the potential for community, given in the basis of all social life, is always present. A critical approach, then, searches for barriers to the expression of naturally occurring affirmative tendencies in human interaction, and it does so explicitly for the purpose of removing those barriers.

Although the term community has many meanings, when it is defined from the perspective of interaction theory in sociology (Kaufman 1959; Wilkinson 1991), it refers explicitly to naturally occurring affirmative tendencies in local social interaction. The foundation of this theory is the observation that people who share a local territory and meet their daily needs together create and maintain community—a generalized, multi-interest network of locality-oriented relationships among neighbors—simply as a matter of course. They do so because that is what people, being people, do. They form and maintain interpersonal bonds with one another as they go about the daily business of living together. Community occurs because it is natural for it to occur, and when it occurs it contributes to social well-being.

This is so because the community is such an important point of contact between the individual and society (Wilkinson 1979). It is the setting for emergence of the self in face-to-face relationships and for expression of universal human needs for association and collective action. Also, as a field of locality-oriented collective actions, the community serves as a medium wherein the individual can be involved directly in group efforts to improve local living conditions. The degree to which community is maintained in a local setting, therefore, is an indicator of the degree to which social life is supportive of the well-being of people. People who live together in local societies that meet their daily needs tend, as a matter of course, to experience community in their relationships with one another; and, if extant conditions prevent them from having this experience, they will search for alternative ways of finding it (Cernic and Longmire 1988).

Critical questions suggested by this conception of the community and social well-being point to the conditions under which community as a natural tendency occurs and how community might be suppressed. Specification of the conditions for community, as the term is used here, begins with three necessary elements (see Wilkinson 1991), namely: (a) a locality or place where people meet their daily needs together; (b) a more or less complete local society; and (c) the opportunity for the local residents to express mutual locality-oriented interests in collective actions. Given these conditions, community emerges. Where they are not present, community is blocked and social well-being is at risk.

Critical questions for analysis and guidelines for praxis follow from these observations when they are applied to a particular setting, such as a rural settlement. Are the residents, in fact, able to meet their daily needs together in the locality, or must they go elsewhere, separately, to do so? Is the local society complete; that is, does it include a full complement of the groups, roles, agencies, services and institutions people use for meeting their needs together and for pursuing their mutual interests? Or is the local settlement only part of a community, such as a residential neighborhood attached to some larger center? Can the people work together to solve problems and pursue community goals or is the field of local public affairs characterized more by apathy than by activism, or more by turbulent power struggles among self-seeking special interest groups than by truly collective action? To conduct a critical analysis, other questions also must be raised:

Why are people prevented from meeting their needs together? Why is the local society incomplete? What prevents people from working together on community issues? What can be done, and by whom, to remove these barriers to community and social well-being? The answers, if grounded in empirical research, could provide both a diagnosis and a prescription for rural areas based on the simple axiom that community, a natural part of social life, is essential to social well-being.

The Community in Rural Areas

It has become obvious to many journalists, policy makers, and social scientists that something is seriously wrong with the community in the small town and country settlements that make up rural America. Osha Gray Davidson, in a book about the Midwest, entitled *Broken Heartland*, gives (1990: 157-58) the following report:

> *Conditions in America's rural communities are far worse than is generally recognized. Contrary to national assumptions of rural tranquility, many small towns—even those white picket-fenced hamlets in our fabled Heartland—today warrant the label "ghetto." No other word so vividly, and yet so accurately, conveys the air of ruin and desolation that now hangs over our rural communities.*

And, Davidson continues (1990:158):

> *The word "ghetto" speaks of the rising poverty rates, the chronic unemployment, and the recent spread of low-wage, dead-end jobs. It speaks of the relentless deterioration of health-care systems, schools, roads, buildings, and of the emergence of homelessness, hunger, and poverty. It speaks, too, of the inevitable outmigration of the best and brightest youths. Above all the word "ghetto" speaks of the bitter stew of resentment, anger, and despair that simmers silently in those left behind. The hard and ugly truth is not only that we have failed to solve the problems of our urban ghettos, but that we have replicated them in miniature a thousand times across the American countryside.*

The deterioration described by Davidson in the Midwest is portrayed in equally compelling detail in recent discussions of rural community life in other regions (Beaulieu 1988; Fitchen 1991; Luloff and Swanson 1990).

The farm crisis of the 1980s, which drew national attention to rural problems, was only one acute episode in what now can be recognized as a chronic rural problem in the United States. Moreover, the essence of this rural problem is not to be found in any single sector, such as agriculture, nor is its solution merely a matter of applying new and promising technologies. Instead, the picture now unfolding of the prevailing situation in rural areas is best described as a crisis of community, and, that being the case, the only hope for its solution must lie in a concerted effort to restore the conditions that give rise to community development. Rural settlements often suffer deficits in jobs and income, and this reduces the prospects for people to meet their needs together in the local setting. Services and organizational structures tend to be less well developed in areas with low population density, especially in those with limited access to larger centers; and this reduces the prospects of maintaining a complete and vital local society. Limited local resources and uneven access to outside resources contribute in many rural settlements to extreme inequalities among local population segments; and these inequalities, along with economic deficits and paucity of services and organizations, undermine local capacity for collective action and self-help. The upshot is a community problem; the potential for community to emerge in local social interaction is thwarted, and well-being is depressed. The results include a process of pulling apart rather than together in community affairs, a loss of capacity to provide mutual assistance, and ultimately, an end to involvement in activities that can truly be called community life. Sadly, this is what one finds all too often today in rural American settlements.

That communities are in trouble in the countryside is relatively easy to see, and the proposition that community is essential for social well-being gives a strong argument for tracing many of the apparent symptoms of rural malaise and distress to the barriers that block the emergence of community in rural settlements. But why do these barriers exist? Are they inevitable? What about currently emerging trends in technology and in political and economic organization; will these help the rural situation or do they threaten to weaken further the economic and social infrastructure of rural community life? What can be done and by whom to protect and restore the community in rural life? These are key questions for a critical analysis of the community in rural America.

The Concept of the Social Cost of Rural Space

Part of the answer to these questions for rural areas must rest upon a realistic appraisal of the roots of rural disadvantage in an increasingly urban world. There are competing theoretical views to consider in making this appraisal. Theories of human ecology offer one explanation with the proposition that the overall adaptive capacity of a community increases with the extent of differentiation of specialized capacities within its structure, which tends to increase with urbanization. This suggests that rural communities face a downward drift in well-being by virtue of the fact that they are rural and that not much can be done to alter the direction of this drift. Rural communities, therefore, must either urbanize, decline or be subsidized by urban communities. Theories of political economy, taking a more critical view, argue that rural settlements suffer not so much from inherent ecological disadvantages as from vulnerability to exploitation at the hands of urban-based investors who control the flow of capital and other vital resources into and out of rural communities. Rural communities can organize to resist exploitation and to capture "spin-offs" of development, but without sustained outside support for their efforts the possibility of success in retaining local control while meeting local needs for jobs and income is limited at best. These arguments from human ecology and political economy might be posed as competing explanations, but in fact they have much in common.

Specifically, both human ecology and political economy recognize that rural communities, as a class, are in serious trouble; that the reasons for the trouble are to a large extent beyond the control of local actors; and that intervention into the ordinary business-as-usual workings of the national ecology/economy would be necessary to improve rural well-being in any fundamental or lasting way. Thus the competing explanations can be put together, for practical purposes, under a general concept such as Carl Kraenzel's notion of the "social cost of space" (1955). Such a concept recognizes that rural community viability is endangered both by geography and by the way modern economic processes use and take advantage of geography. It also recognizes that rural revitalization cannot consist merely of encouraging people in rural communities to make wise and informed choices about the use of their resources. Instead, the idea that rural space has social cost says that without a lot of help from the outside— substantial help involving direct intervention into the free operation of human ecological and economic processes—rural community development might be a lost cause.

The Cost of Space in Rural America

Does this pessimistic outlook in theory give a fair appraisal of the actual situation in rural America? In American society, the social cost of space always has been high, although years ago other characteristics of rural communities might have offset this cost somewhat. Access to the essential resources for meeting the daily needs of people, the first requisite for maintaining a community and ensuring social well-being anywhere, anytime, is limited in many parts of rural America by distance and by low population density.

As Sorokin and Zimmerman (1929) observed early in the twentieth century, relative isolation in small settlements need not be a source of social distress if the effects of limited access can be offset by the warmth and security of close-knit family and community networks in a more or less self-sufficient local economy. Observers today give a quite different view of the effects of remoteness (Bly 1980). As local residents of almost all communities have become increasingly dependent on the larger society for meeting many daily needs, and as the ability of local institutions and groups in rural areas to hold the commitments of residents has declined, physical isolation has become more closely associated with social isolation than with social cohesion. Isolation is cited, for example, among likely explanations for the finding that rural populations have not only high rates of poverty and other material deficits but also high rates of suicide, homicide, and mental distress (Wilkinson 1984). Whatever might have been the situation in the past, the social cost of space in rural America now is high, and this cost is not subsiding with the passage of time.

A number of interrelated changes in the past have raised the social cost of rural space. Urbanization is the most obvious of these in the American case. Over the entire course of American history, people and communities in rural areas have been under the influence of urbanization. In particular, until recently, rapid economic growth has been concentrated in large cities. Displaced by advances in agricultural technology early in the twentieth century, rural workers and their families migrated to cities by the hundreds of thousands to take advantage of industrial job opportunities. As the national economy became predominantly industrial and culture became predominantly urban, small communities in remote areas found themselves at a disadvantage in meeting the needs of residents. A small, localized economy could no longer be self-sufficient. Large numbers of users are needed to justify and sustain modern community services and facilities. Residents of small communities now must commute, often over great distances and to multiple centers, for jobs and services; or they have to make do with the lesser resources available in the rural locale.

An unstable economic base, as shown by recent trends in traditional rural industries such as agriculture and mining and in the manufacturing industries that have developed in rural areas, is part of the cost of space in rural America. Another part is the limited range of services that can be supported in small dispersed settlements. In addition, as Kraenzel (1980) observes, rural isolation depresses the ability of a local population to organize for effective collective action, in contrast to the image of close-knit rural communities acting for the common good in times past.

An even greater part of the cost, according to Kraenzel's (1980) analysis, is the tendency for profit-seeking firms to move into and out of rural areas, taking with them the benefits of development but leaving behind many of the externalities to be endured by the rural community. Rural dependency on increasingly mobile outside investments no doubt has contributed, as argued by Kraenzel, to spatial inequalities. As the outside investments come and go in search of profits, so do the jobs and income available to rural workers. Concentration of a single sector of a manufacturing process in a rural site or domination of a rural labor market by a single installation of a multi-site firm increases rural vulnerability to shifts and cycles in the larger economy. Lovejoy and Krannich (1982), assessing the consequences of boom and bust cycles associated with highly mobile investments in natural resource-based industries, find little cause for hoping that rural economic development will contribute to rural community well-being if prevailing patterns of development continue. Similarly, Marchak (1983: 368), examining the effects of large multi-national firms on economic stability and social well-being in timber dependent communities, concludes that while such firms have the ability to weather shifting economic currents and thus could provide security of local employment, they will not necessarily do the latter. Instead, decisions by firms that affect rural well-being often are made with little apparent regard for rural well-being. The goal of firm decision-making, of course, is to maximize profits and this often means hastening the flow of capital from rural operations and converting rural resources as quickly and efficiently as possible into profits for the benefit of investors who rarely reside in the rural community. The point is not that profit seeking is improper, but that in the spatial context of rural America the simple pursuit of profits by outside firms can work to the disadvantage of local communities.

In the specific case of rural America, these two sources of rural disadvantage identified under the general concept of the social cost of space have had clear and often devastating effects on rural community life. Small size, limited access, and related ecological characteristics pose problems for community organization and make it difficult for local residents to interact effectively as a community. Urban concentration of control over increasingly mobile resources puts rural areas, as peripheries, at the mercy of decisions which have the manifest function of favoring, not rural community well-being, but the extraction of profits from the rural area by outside investors. The history of the community in rural America is quite well summed up by the concept of the social cost of space.

Trends Molding the Future

Against this background of persisting rural problems, contemporary trends shaping the future of rural America must be evaluated critically as to their effects on the prospects for rural community development and well-being. The changes now influencing community life in rural and urban settlements alike are impressive, to say the least. Perhaps a new era is at hand in trends that will reduce or mitigate against the ecological and economic foundations of the social cost of space. Alternatively, perhaps the social cost of space will increase as these trends unfold. The future of the rural community will be affected crucially either way.

Much has been written recently about the economic and demographic implications of such macro-trends as the globalization of society, the restructuring of the American economy, and the changing spatial structure of the American countryside (Brown and Deavers 1989; Flora and Christenson 1991; Pigg 1991; Wilkinson 1991). From these discussions, important questions can be framed about the future of rural America; and among the questions, two issues in particular are suggested that bear directly on the prospects for rural community development. One issue relates to technology and infrastructure for fast and efficient long-distance communications (Dillman 1991). Clearly a revolution is underway in this field. A critical analysis must ask whether the new developments will make it easier or more difficult for people in rural areas to meet their needs together in local social interaction. The other issue relates to contemporary efforts to incorporate community development into a national rural development policy. The issue here has two parts: What are the prospects for a national rural development policy; and, if a national rural development policy is forthcoming, what will the policy offer for rural community development?

The Communications Revolution

There can be little doubt that changes now taking place in long-distance communications will affect rural community life in dramatic ways, for better or for worse (Dillman 1991). What is in considerable doubt is whether the results will be the "twilight" of spatial inequality, as argued optimistically by some, including Harland Cleveland (1985), or the final collapse of community, as foreseen by others, including Manuel Castells (1989). Already, according to human ecologists (Hawley 1978), new communications technologies are undermining the old central place hierarchy and producing a more diffuse pattern of growth of population centers. Indeed, most of the likely impacts of the new field of "telematics" (which represents the convergence of telecommunications, broadcast media, and computerization) are still to come (Dillman 1991; Office of Technology Assessment 1991).

One reason these changes are of such importance is that their currency is information, the stuff of modern economic and political development.

The major technological developments and their potential for speeding the flow and increasing the volume of information exchanges are well-known and need only brief mention here. Fiber-optic cables, which carry up to two billion bits of information a second, exceed the conventional copper telephone cables in capacity by a factor of up to 30,000 times, at an installation cost per household of only about four times the cost of conventional lines (Ramirez 1991). In combination with digital switches, which make possible advanced telephone services and computer-to-computer applications, fiber-optic cables are channels of access to information and vehicles for participation in what has become a global network for exchange of goods, services, and ideas. Essential to full participation in this network are a number of specific services that currently are far from universally available, especially in rural areas, in addition to fiber-optic cables and digital switching. These include (see Parker et al. 1989) voice telephone service itself, which is still limited and often very expensive to provide and maintain in the rural areas of some regions of the United States, single-party telephone access, reliable transmission of facsimile documents, access to competitive long-distance carriers, local access to value-added data networks, 911 emergency service with automatic number identification, cellular telephone service, touchtone and custom calling services such as call forwarding, call waiting and three-way calling. Communications infrastructure also includes cable television, which like telephone services, can be the basis of interactive transmission. The range of applications, as Dillman (1991) observes, is endless, and these applications not only could affect, but are now affecting businesses as diverse as farms, pharmacies, travel agencies, and investment firms, along with voluntary organizations, governments, schools, and, libraries. Given the importance of information in meeting the needs of people and communities, this revolution has become a key element in the matrix of forces that will determine and constrain social well-being for the years ahead.

What will be the effects on rural-urban inequalities? An essay by Cleveland (1985) in the journal, *Public Administration Review*, argues that the sudden and pervasive dominance of information as a resource is demolishing established assumptions about the hierarchies that structure modern societies. Information, he notes, has several qualities that differ sharply from characteristics of resources that have been the basis of social organization in the past. In particular, he notes, information is expandable, substitutable, transportable, diffusive, and sharable; moreover, it is not subject to the laws of thermodynamics. Instead, the ultimate use of information is to organize things and people, and its unique qualities as a resource mean that it organizes them in new and potentially liberating ways. Thus, about the past, he says (1985:187):

the inherent characteristics of physical resources ("natural" and man-made) made possible the development of hierarchies of power based on control (of new weapons, of energy sources, of trade routes, of markets, and especially of knowledge), hierarchies of influence based on secrecy, hierarchies of class based on ownership, hierarchies of privilege based on early access to valuable resources, and hierarchies of politics based on geography. With the ascendance of information as the basic resource for the future, he says (1985: 187), "secrets are harder to keep, and ownership, early arrival, and geography are of dwindling significance in getting access to the knowledge and wisdom which are the really valuable legal tender of our time." With the "passing of remoteness" as a basis of inequality, he says (1985: 195) the prospect is raised for community structure to rest more on the creative efforts of people that on the advantages or disadvantages of location.

Cleveland's optimism is quite encouraging to those who seek to reduce the social cost of rural space, but a question remains as to whether in fact spatially rooted inequalities will yield to the new technology. Castells, in a book entitled *The Informational City* (1989), provides a critical counterpoint to Cleveland's analysis. Technology, he reminds us, does not develop in a vacuum, but in the context of the structure of class and power relationships that define the capitalist mode of production. In agreement with Cleveland's analysis, Castells observes that the ascendance of information as a basic resource is associated with a fundamental restructuring of society. Castells' critical analysis, however, disagrees with the assessment that hierarchies are crumbling in the face of the liberating qualities of information and information technology. Quite to the contrary, he maintains, the accelerated development of information technologies is part of the quest for a new model of socio-economic organization in the wake of the global political and economic crisis of the 1970s. The new information-based model will serve the same goals as served by earlier models, namely (1989: 23):

to enhance the rate of profit for private capital, the engine of investment, and thus of growth; to find new markets, both through deepening the existing ones and by incorporating new regions of the world into an integrated capitalist economy; to control the circulation process; and to assure the social reproduction and the economic regulation of the system through mechanisms that would not contradict those established to achieve the preceding goals of higher profit rates, expanding demand, and inflation control.

The new model of capitalism that began to emerge in response to the crisis of the 1970s, he says, has three major features, namely: (a) the appropriation of higher profits through higher productivity, lower wages, reduced social benefits, less protective working conditions, decentralization of production to regions characterized by lower wages and more relaxed regulation of business activities, and dramatic expansion of the informal economy; (b) increased state activism in support of capitalist development; and (c) accelerated internationalization of all economic processes, to increase profitability and to open up markets through the expansion of the system.

In brief, Castells argues that the "informational mode of development," born of the technological revolution in telecommunications, represents and contributes to the overpowering of labor by capital. Organizationally, he says, this leads to concentration, not to decentralization of knowledge-generation and decision-making processes. It also leads to down-grading of the power of such groups as organized labor, that have agendas other than profit making, and to transforming localities from communities into mere localities where labor and other resources can be sought and used to produce profits. Thus, from Castells' viewpoint, the information society is producing, not an end to hierarchies, but an increase in inequality, especially in rural-urban inequality.

Between the perspectives set forth respectively by Cleveland and Castells has emerged a body of literature by rural sociologists outlining specific impediments to realization of the potential benefits of modern communications technologies in rural areas (see Dillman 1985; 1991; Swanson 1990). In a nutshell, these appraisals observe that the factors that have constrained rural economic and community development in the past will continue to pose formidable barriers to the utilization of telecommunications technologies to increase rural well-being in the future. These constraining factors include low educational levels, limited capital resources, cultural biases in favor of traditional economic activities, inadequate economic and social infrastructure, and other factors associated with the friction of space. These might be reduced but cannot be eliminated by the new technologies.

Cautions need to be noted in evaluating the idea that new space-shrinking technologies will close the gap between urban and rural settlements in modern societies. Most rural areas are already far behind in gaining access to the new information technologies. Rural communities typically lack the specialized leadership and organizations that would be needed to take full advantage of new and highly specialized technologies. Rural acceptance of the new social patterns associated with new information technologies is likely to lag behind their acceptance in more urbanized settings. Nothing inherent to the new technologies assures increased social and economic equality; indeed, it is just as likely the new technologies will reinforce old patterns of metropolitan exploitation of rural resources. Thus policy, not technology, must determine the outcomes of the communications revolution for rural communities.

Community Development and
Rural Development Policy

Since the 1930s, rural policy in the United States has been mainly farm policy, although there has been something of a movement since the early 1950s to establish a rural development policy at the federal level. In 1979, the Carter Administration issued a rural development policy statement, the first by a federal administration, and the Congress passed the Rural Development Policy Act in 1980 requiring all subsequent administrations to have an explicit rural development policy and to report regularly to the Congress on efforts and accomplishments under its policy. In compliance, the Reagan Administration, in a document entitled "Better Country," set forth a policy of reduced federal involvement in addressing rural problems. What rural citizens need, the policy said, is to get government off their backs. The Bush Administration, in January 1990, established a somewhat more proactive policy emphasizing research, extension, and other educational and information tools to assist local authorities and entrepreneurs. The Clinton Administration, in 1993, proposed a broad program of rural initiatives, many concerned with strengthening community capacity for decision-making and collective action.

The rhetoric of these policy pronouncements and the steps underway to implement them are noteworthy, but the route to an effective national policy for coping with the social cost of rural space still is not clearly in view. There remains, among other issues, a crucial lack of consensus as to the justifications for having a rural policy. Recent documents in the national rural development movement ignore some highly divisive issues that are nowhere near resolution in the nation's political arena. A key question is yet to be answered: *Why should an urban society use tax resources to address rural problems and thus, to subsidize rural America with what would amount to transfer payments?* Until such issues are addressed, little consensus is likely to be reached on specific aspects of rural policy.

In addition, criticisms of the emphasis on science and education as rural development instruments need to be addressed. One is that the new federal initiatives tend to address local symptoms of rural problems but not the underlying structural causes of the problems. The aim of helping local actors solve their problems certainly is an admirable one, but a singular emphasis on this aim assumes that with good information (the products of research and education), local actors *can* solve their problems. The fact is, unless impediments to community development are removed, many local problems cannot be solved by local actors, especially in rural areas. Notwithstanding, the potential for community development that is given in human experience, simply handing the responsibility over to local actors carries no assurance that they will be able to carry out that responsibility. Efforts are needed first to allow community capacity for action to develop. A second criticism points to the absence of federal resolve and action to stand behind the research and extension thrusts that, thus far, constitute the core of federally supported rural development efforts. Science and education *instead* of action will fall short of meeting the larger goal of empowering local communities to act on their own behalf. A third criticism is that the new initiatives have little to say and promise to do little about the glaring inequalities among local population segments that hamper self-help efforts in rural localities. The fourth criticism is an old criticism of the land-grant system applied to its new rural agenda: system rhetoric claims integration of research and extension as its keystone, but in fact this integration exists more as system rhetoric than as fact. The research and extension bureaucracies that will implement rural development still have few real mechanisms for undertaking joint or integrated projects. A fifth criticism is that farm organizations and other major clientele groupings of the land-grant system tend to be lukewarm at best to the idea that agricultural research and extension should take rural development as a major focus (Swanson 1989). Still, there is a basis of optimism in the fact that structures which could address fundamental rural problems are being proposed and discussed in the national policy arena.

More or less clearcut policy choices on a number of rural development questions have come into focus as the debate about rural policy objectives has unfolded (Brown and Deavers 1989; Drabenstott et al. 1987; Swanson 1989; Tweeten 1988). Should policy emphasize development of particular economic sectors, such as manufacturing and services, which might benefit rural and urban residents alike, or should the emphasis be on development problems of particular territorial units, such as rural regions or communities, irrespective of the sectors involved? Whether the approach is sectoral or territorial, should the strategy be one of stimulating development so as to overcome existing problems, or would it be better to help people make a transition out of a hopeless situation to employment in some other sector or to residence in another territorial location where development might be more feasible? Should assistance be targeted to needy individuals, or would it be better to work with groups and communities? Should organizations and institutions that serve primarily agricultural interests continue to play the leading roles in rural development, or should the leadership come from outside the agricultural establishment? Good arguments can be made on both sides of each of these questions, and political factors can figure prominently in the choices taken.

One way to cut through the debate and give at least some direction to the inevitable political maneuvering is to accept an overriding paradigm in which rural development is but a means and social well-being is the end.

This is a wholly acceptable notion from most perspectives, at least in the abstract, although it is one that invites controversy about the precise meaning of "social well-being." The proposition that community is a key to social well-being (Wilkinson 1979) provides a useful perspective for side-stepping such controversy. Recognizing and keeping in mind that rural development itself is not the ultimate goal of rural policy but is only one means by which to pursue the goal of enhanced social well-being would go a long way toward resolving much of the current debate. As an instrument or tool, rather than as a valued end in its own right, rural development is more easily modified and deployed to fit the needs of particular groupings and is far less likely to become associated with some singular ideological or political posture. Rural development, therefore, could be something to use as a means where appropriate rather than something to be promoted no matter what. When used in this spirit, rural development is likely to contribute explicitly to community development and thus to social well-being in rural areas.

Conclusion

The technological revolution in communications and the national debate about rural policy have emerged together at a time of heightened concern among social scientists and others about the deterioration of community life and social well-being in rural America. What is needed now to harness and focus the energy of the information and rural policy movements is the recognition that communications technology and rural development are means for the realization of human goals, not ends in themselves. If these means of achieving goals are applied the way means usually are applied in today's world, the beneficiaries are not likely to be rural communities; rather, both the communications revolution and some forms of rural development could contribute dramatically to the final demise of the rural community as a viable social form. On the other hand, if rural community development becomes the goal to which these tools are applied, the potential for improving the well-being of rural populations is substantial.

Essential steps in the process of community development are suggested in the extensive literature on community action and self-help (Wilkinson 1991). The first is to create the opportunity for people to participate, not simply as recipients or clients of the actions of others, but as the main players in the process of identifying and tackling community problems. Second, even with opportunities provided, rural community development faces the formidable task of overcoming the legacy of hegemony in rural-urban power relations and the pervasive quiescence of disadvantaged rural groupings (such as farm workers, small farmers, minorities, women, the poor, the elderly, and others) to the wishes and even the perspectives of more powerful groups. Overcoming rural quiescence requires education as well as opportunity. Third, there is the problem of rural organization. Traditionally, rural life is not highly organized, at least not formally; new modes of organization are required to break out of entrenched patterns of patronage and exclusion and to focus collective efforts on problems common to all local groupings. Mobilization of resources—local ones, such as people, ideas, materials, and money, but also resources outside the locality —is a fourth essential step. Informed decision-making is the fifth step (and here is where information institutions such as extension and libraries can help best); rural participants in community decision-making need assistance in gaining access to the information and to the analytical paradigms necessary for making sound decisions about community goals and action strategies. Finally, the most important step is action itself: community action builds the capacity for subsequent community actions as it creates networks, roles, and a pool of shared experience. Community development, as a process of local capacity building, can be self-sustaining if all these steps are possible. The most important policy choice for the future of rural America is to decide whether this self-sustaining process, or the demise of the rural community, will be the legacy of the information society and the rural development movement.

References

Beaulieu, Lionel J. 1988. "The rural South in crisis: An introduction." Pp. 1-12 in Lionel J. Beaulieu (ed.). *The Rural South in Crisis: Challenges for the Future.* Boulder, CO: Westview Press.

Bly, Carol. 1980. *Letters from the Country.* New York, NY: Harper and Row.

Bottomore, T. B. 1984. *The Frankfurt School.* London, England: Tavistock Publications.

Brown, David L., and Kenneth L. Deavers. 1989. "The changing context of rural economic policy in the United States." *Research in Rural Sociology and Development* 4: 255-275.

Buttel, Frederick H., and Howard Newby (eds.). 1980. *The Rural Sociology of the Advanced Societies: Critical Perspectives.* Montclair, NJ: Allanheld, Osmun.

Castells, Manuel. 1989. *The Informational City.* Oxford, England: Basil Blackwell.

Catelli, Giampaolo. 1992. "Rural society in the changing world order." Presidential Address, Eighth World Congress for Rural Sociology. The Pennsylvania State University, University Park, PA (August).

Cernea, Michael M. 1985. *Putting People First: Sociological Variables in Rural Development.* New York, NY: Oxford University Press.

Cernic, David, and Linda Longmire. 1988. "Introduction." Pp. xii-xx in David Cernic and Linda Longmire (eds.). *The Search for Community.* New York, NY: University Press of America.

Cleveland, Harlan. 1985. "The twilight of hierarchy: Speculations on the global information society." *Public Administration Review* 45 (January/February): 185-195.

Davidson, Osha Gray. 1990. *Broken Heartland: The Rise of America's Rural Ghetto.* New York: Doubleday.

Dillman, Don A. 1985. "The social impacts of information technologies in rural North America." *Rural Sociology* 50 (1):1-26.

Dillman, Don A. 1991. "Telematics and rural development." Pp. 292-306 in Cornelia B. Flora, and James A. Christenson (eds.). *Rural Policies for the 1990s.* Boulder, Colorado: Westview Press.

Drabenstott, Mark, Mark Henry, and Lynn Gibson. 1987. "The rural economic policy choice." *Economic Review* (January): 41-58.

Fitchen, Janet M. 1991. *Endangered Spaces, Enduring Places: Change, Identity, and Survival in Rural America.* Boulder, Colorado: Westview Press.

Flora, Cornelia B., and James A. Christenson. 1991. "Critical times for rural America: The challenge for rural policy in the 1990s." Pp. 1-7 in Cornelia B. Flora and James A. Christenson (eds.). *Rural Policies for the 1990s.* Boulder, Colorado: Westview Press.

Habermas, Jurgen. 1984. *Reason and the Rationalization of Society. The Theory of Communicative Action.* Volume 1. Boston: Beacon Press.

Hawley, Amos H. 1950. *Human Ecology: A Theory of Community Structure.* New York: The Ronald Press Company.

Hawley, Amos H. 1978. "Urbanization as a process." Pp. 3-26 in David Street and Associates (eds.). *Handbook of Contemporary Urban Life.* San Francisco: Josey-Bass.

Kaufman, Harold F. 1959. "Toward an interactional conception of the community." *Social Forces* 39 (1): 8-17.

Kraenzel, Carl F. 1955. *The Great Plains in Transition.* Norman: University of Oklahoma Press.

Kraenzel, Carl F. 1980. *The Social Cost of Space in the Yonland.* Bozeman, Montana: Big Sky Books.

Long, Norman. 1977. *An Introduction to the Sociology of Rural Development.* London: Tavistock Books.

Lovejoy, Stephen B. and Richard S. Krannich. 1982. "Rural industrial development and domestic dependency relations: Toward an integrated perspective." *Rural Sociology* 47 (3): 475-95.

Luloff, A. E. 1990. "Community and social change: How do small communities act?" Pp. 214-227 in A. E. Luloff and Louis M. Swanson (eds.). *American Rural Communities.* Boulder, Colorado: Westview Press.

Luloff, A. E. and Louis M. Swanson. 1990. "Introduction." Pp. 1-6 in A. E. Luloff and Louis M. Swanson (eds.). *American Rural Communities.* Boulder, Colorado: Westview Press.

Marchak, Patricia. 1983. *Green Gold: The Forest Industry in British Columbia.* Vancouver: University of British Columbia Press.

Office of Technology Assessment. 1991. *Rural America at the Crossroads: Networking for the Future.* Washington, D.C.: Congress of the United States.

Parker, Edwin B., Heather E. Hudson, Don A. Dillman, and Andrew D. Roscoe. 1989.

Rural America in the Information Age. Lanhorn, Maryland: University Press of America.

Pigg, Kenneth E. 1991. "Introduction: The future of rural America." Pp. 1-13 in Kenneth E. Pigg (ed.). *The Future of Rural America: Anticipating Policies for Constructive Change.* Boulder, Colorado: Westview Press.

Ramirez, Anthony. 1991. "Some doubts on rewiring of Japan." New York Times, November 9.

Sorokin, Pitirim A. and Carl C. Zimmerman, 1929. *Principles of Rural-Urban Sociology.* New York: Henry Holt and Company.

Swanson, Louis E. 1989. "The rural development dilemma." *Resources* (Summer): 14-16.

Swanson, Louis E. 1990. "Non-technical barriers to the use of telecommunications technologies for rural development." (Draft) Report to the Office of Technology Assessment, United States Congress.

Tweeten, Luther G. 1988. "Elements of a sound rural development policy." *Research in Domestic and International Agribusiness Management* 9: 103-111.

Wilkinson, Kenneth P. 1979. "Social well-being and community." *Journal of the Community Development Society.* 10 (1): 5-16.

Wilkinson, Kenneth P. 1984. "Rurality and patterns of social disruption." *Rural Sociology* 49 (1): 23-36.

Wilkinson, Kenneth P. 1991. *The Community in Rural America.* Westport, Connecticut: Greenwood Press.

5

Paradigm Gridlock and the Two Faces of Technology

Drew Hyman
Larry Gamm
John Shingler

Modern technology presents a Januslike visage to rural America. One face promises to bring high quality education, health, community services, and infrastructure to rural communities. The other face threatens to decimate rural communities or replace them with urban sprawl. Attention to the challenges of technology sets the stage for consideration of their implications for human capital. This chapter first discusses the plight of rural communities and the threat posed to them by the two dominant paradigms in use today. We then suggest a paradigm for sustainable rural communities as an opportunity for positive action. The final sections explore specific areas of public policy and the implications of technology for creating sustainable rural communities.

Advocates of increased reliance on technology to solve problems promise space-age benefits for rural communities. Computers can provide expert systems to schedule planting and harvesting, optimize nutrient and pesticide applications, and plant/animal combinations. Linkages to national weather, marketing, and a myriad of other services promise to create a "national neighborhood" wherein rural residents have access to the same services and processes as their urban counterparts. "Electronic cottages" have the potential for creating home or farm businesses, jobs linked to larger firms, and a wide range of education and training opportunities. But technology does not act without human guidance and control; and the current infrastructure, resources, and training necessary to make these promises a reality are targeted primarily to areas of high population density. Rural areas may be left even farther behind than they are now.

The directions these systems take in the future are guided by our ideas of the possible and of the future—our mental technology. We suggest that America's mental technology is caught in a conceptual traffic jam. Our policy and planning processes are trapped in a gridlock between two outmoded visions of rural development, and our current paradigm-in-use, industrial agriculture, incorporates diseconomies of scale and leads to the deterioration of rural communities and rural populations. Without clear directions for policy and research, happenstance and political influence will decide the outcome for rural communities.

Technological Visions of a Developed Rural America: Paradigm Gridlock

The mental images that guide human creativity and action are the most fundamental aspects of technology. Without an image, an idea or a pattern toward which to build, no purposive change can occur. This is true for science, engineering, education, agriculture, the arts, and other areas of human endeavor. David Goldsworthy (1988) puts it this way:

> *All development theories, policies, plans and strategies consciously or unconsciously express preferred notions of what development is. These preferences in turn reflect values. . . .These contrasting sets of beliefs and moral attitudes lie at the heart of the different ideological thought-worlds and their visions of the developed society; indeed, for many people the 'developed' society is virtually interchangeable with the 'good' society.*

At the same time, we contend that our paradigms for rural development are woefully inadequate for dealing with coexistence in a high-tech urbanized environment. Paradigm gridlock constrains creativity and directs action into indiscriminate patterns. Our reasoning begins with the fact that "rural development" itself is an internally inconsistent concept. Dictionary definitions of "rural" portray rustic, pastoral, agriculture-based settings for the production of food and fiber. "Development" denotes growth, concentration, urbanization, and industrialization. Given these images, how can an area be both rural and developed? This inconsistency in terms unwittingly contributes to conceptual confusion, contentious policies, and an inability to create a consensus for action. Furthermore, we believe that both the "rural" and the "development" visions of society are inadequate for today. Contemporary society faces not only "paradigm gridlock," but also "paradigm obsolescence."

Vision and values are inextricably intertwined as the fundamental bases for policy and action (Hyman and Miller 1985). The agrarian and industrial paradigms are the visions of rural America that guide policies today. The *agrarian paradigm* views rural areas as farm-dominated. What's good for farmers is good for rural America. This traditional perspective comes from a historical vision of self-sufficient family farmers. A variety of field crops and vegetables provide for most of the needs of the people and animals on the farm, and the surpluses go to market. Animal manure is recycled as fertilizer. Crops are rotated from year to year. Rural communities exist to provide markets and supplies for farmers. While this paradigm may still apply to many small farmers, some "organic" farmers, and the Amish, it does not suffice for feeding an industrialized nation and exporting to other countries. It is not a paradigm to guide development policies for the almost one in four Americans who live in rural areas and are not farmers. What is needed is a paradigm for rural communities that includes farms, not a paradigm for rural farms per se.

The dominant contemporary alternative, the *industrial/urbanization paradigm*, would "develop" rural areas by replacing farms with factories and farm jobs with factory jobs. The assumption is, what's good for industry is good for the U.S.A. The industrialization of rural areas is seen as the answer to rising unemployment and associated malaise in rural communities. The intention is to create manufacturing and industrial opportunities in rural areas. Industrial parks, economic enterprise zones, business incubators, and specialized job training are emphasized. This paradigm, too, provides unsuitable images of rural communities because it would replace farms and towns with factories and cities. Once we bring the city to the country, rural is gone forever.

A hybrid of the two, *industrial agriculture*, is a natural extension of industrialization to the food and fiber system. The logic follows the same pattern: bigger is better, hi-tech is hi-profit. This perspective views rural areas as large-scale, hi-tech, hi-production areas to be exploited. Agricultural production and marketing processes are standardized, centralized, specialized, routinized, and bureaucratized. This vision characterizes the rural America that has emerged from a century of farm policies. Its success is the success of American agriculture. But it is not without its down side.

Large-scale industrial agriculture relies heavily on capital and machines. To employ powerful technologies, farm owners must borrow large sums of money, pay interest on loans, rent or borrow more land and machines, etc. This leveraging, in turn, leads to increased susceptibility to variations in financial markets. A priority on profit rather than product tends to emphasize specialized, high-yield crops in selected high-profit areas only. Studies show that conservation practices are less common, poverty increases, and social conditions in the local community tend to deteriorate where large farms and absentee ownership dominate (Strange 1988). Small and medium sized farm units provide better support for local business establishments and retail trade, building trades, equipment suppliers, schools, hospitals, parks and recreation, and even newspapers, churches, and civic organizations. In many ways, industrial agriculture characterizes our present predicament—the forces which enable two percent of the workforce to feed the nation, also fuel the general deterioration of our rural families and communities. This mingling of the two historical paradigms is deficient if we are to have viable rural families and communities in the 21st century.

Toward an Appropriate Paradigm for
Sustainable Community Systems

The agrarian and industrial paradigms are sociologically rooted in the positivistic organicism of Toennies and Durkheim. Toennies viewed inter-dependence as the basis of society. He articulated two forms of society, Gemeinschaft and Gesellschaft. Gemeinschaft, rooted in superstition and mutual fear of the irrational, "being based upon consensus of wills--rests on harmony and is developed and ennobled by folkways, mores, and religion" (Etzioni 1964). People are tied to each other and to the land by the natural drive to survive. Gesellschaft is social order which, being based upon a union of rational wills, rests on convention and agreement, is safeguarded by political legislation, and finds its ideological justification in public opinion. Gesellschaft is based on specialization and division-of-labor which isolates families from others. Peace and commerce are main-tained through conventions and the underlying mutual fear. Government protects this civilization through legislation and politics (Etzioni 1964:64-65).

Both of these visions see society as imperatively coordinated: there is a central authority that exercises overall direction and control. Society is an identifiable, tangible entity, a collectivity that has interests, goals, values, and decision making in and of itself. Despite the claim of some that a worldwide conspiracy or cabal exists, we have a difficult time identifying a global controlling entity. Highly industrialized nations that participate in multinational trade and cultural interactions are similar. No centralized totalitarian control of all facets of life exists. Control is divided among nations, multinational corporations, a variety of regional and sub-national groups and organizations, and similar patterns at the local levels. Societal direction and control are key elements in a new paradigm.

A modern perspective views direction and control of the community as an interactional field of individuals, organizations and institutions, not as a single collectivity with a "head." From this perspective, the overall system is neither centrally controlled nor random and chaotic. An interactional system is characterized by a variety of systemic interconnections among relatively independent units. Warren (1978) notes that the actions of the parts are negotiated among the parts rather than being directed by a central controlling unit. The shared values and norms flow from a common macro-culture which guides decision making and action. The community does not act, its parts do (Warren 1978:410). Simultaneously, the community is ever changing, fluctuating, and capable of taking on manifold forms. The world community, and local communities for that matter, are seen as a series of simultaneous games where the interactions of some have greater or lesser effects on the others. The parts retain considerable separate identity and individual autonomy in full recognition of their interdependence with others. This perspective embodies the structural underpinnings of a new paradigm which we will call "teleological society."[1] The new paradigm has recent roots in the writings of contemporary futurists.

Two Visions of a Hi-Tech Future

Three decades ago many writers saw the portents of a super-industrial civilization emerging. In *The Programmed Society*, Alain Touraine (1971) envisaged a highly technological society wherein human behavior was programmed from cradle to grave. Super-bureaucratization, super-synchronization, super-surveillance and super-control were characteristics of the emerging society. The dangers of uncontrolled growth were addressed in the Club of Rome's publication, *The Limits to Growth;* they predicted that if industrial growth continues at present rates, some combination of population increase, industrial pollution, depletion of non-renewable resources, and depletion of arable land will bring about an inevitable collapse of world society sometime in the mid-21st Century. The bleak futures predicted in *Brave New World*, and *1984*, appeared on the horizon (Meadows, et al. 1972). Alvin Toffler's *Future Shock* (1970) embraces the apprehensions of this era that a super-industrial future would exhaust both the human and natural resources of the earth.

The futurists were not all pessimistic, however. McLuhan, in *Understanding Media* (1964), spoke of an emerging "global Village". E.F. Schumacher, in *Small is Beautiful* (1973), predicted a more quality and whole product-oriented appropriate technology. Writers such as Alfred Kahn, Amitai Etzioni, and Alvin Toffler envision a more enlightened civilization emerging in the 21st Century.

These two antithetical visions of the future are encapsulated in the six "civilizations" identified by Toffler as characteristic of the "Second Wave" of civilization, industrial society: standardization, centralization, specialization, synchronization, concentration, and maximization (see Toffler 1980, Chapter 4). A super-industrial society will reify these characteristics making individuals and organizations insignificant cogs in a vast global industrial machine.

Toffler's discussion of the "Third Wave" of civilization and the projections of other futurists allow us to construct a more positive alternative. We call the new paradigm "teleological society" because of a primary concern with permanence, sustainibility and the "ends" of social action in terms of quality-of-life. Teleological society differs radically from super-industrial society. Teleological society is characterized by mutual respect and well-being. It emphasizes the "ends" of social processes. Quality and flexibility are its hallmark compared to quantity and standardization for its industrial alternative. Teleological society stresses individualization through customization, diversity, and flexibility in contrast to industrial society's other-determined tendency for standardization, punctuality, and sameness. Dispersion of production and decentralization of power and control are the norm in both public and private sectors, and in economy and government. Localities gain increased decisional autonomy, discretion, within broad societal norms. Decision making moves toward the periphery, being more dispersed throughout society, rather than being concentrated in large centralized structures.

Human capital experiences major redirection. Education and employment tend toward generalization and preparation of multi-skilled individuals. People are trained in understanding and problem solving that can be applied to a number of fields. Serial careers become the norm. Rather than industrial synchronization of both individuals and organizations to the dictates of a central control, teleological society allows individual discretion that is in harmony with societal values. The standard for success is optimization marked by appropriate scale, rather than the bigger-is-better, most-is-best maximization principle.

The teleological paradigm eliminates the contradiction between "rural" and "development." It foresees the "development" of communities that retain the size and ambience of "rural" while providing for the amenities of modernism. It is also clear that the choice is ours as a society. We can continue development toward a super-industrial future; or we can move in the direction of what we label teleological society. Let us consider some specific possibilities for the future.

Technology, Community Systems and Human Capital

The threat invoked by technology is a dehumanizing super-industrial future; however, unlimited opportunities for developing sustainable rural communities are inherent in the teleological paradigm. The following sections present brief discussions of current and emerging technology and the threats and opportunities technology presents for human capital in the areas of energy, telecommunications, robotics and biotechnology, health and human services, education and training, culture and infotainment, governance and decision making, economic development, and land use.

Contemporary technology promises to unleash novel changes on rural communities that are the converse of those wrought by previous waves of innovation. Former technological changes such as the construction of hydroelectric power, pipelines, telegraph and telephone lines, railroads and highways redefined the rural landscape to carry food, raw materials, people, and communications from the country to the cities. As a result, local rural jobs generated were often high-risk, low-skill and low-pay—jobs that encouraged the best and brightest to migrate. Today, appropriate technology and information technologies create the potential to reverse the flow to rural America, through the promise of higher skilled, long term jobs based on local businesses. Further, the speed with which information age technology can be substituted for capital, labor, and other aspects of economic development is increasing. If rural areas can successfully acquire new technologies, sustainable communities based on the teleological paradigm are quite probable.

Dillman (1989) and Wilkinson (1987) point out that current technology can either help reverse the decline of rural communities by reducing the social costs of space, or accelerate the decline as the benefits of this technology are adopted more quickly and aggressively by urban-based organizations. We note, too, that contemporary technology has the potential to overcome the costs of distance and space associated with rural areas. The prospects for rural enhancement are almost endless. Nevertheless, most of the technologies reviewed below are now generally more fully exploited in non-rural areas. The technologies, along with some rural applications, are reviewed with an eye to encouraging wider application in rural settings.

Energy: Are We Fueling
Rural Exploitation or Rural Development?

While raw materials for the nation's energy are provided by rural areas (at considerable environmental cost using today's technology), the benefits of energy generally accrue elsewhere. Whether it be from coal, petroleum or water, the raw materials for electricity and petro-chemical fuels are extracted from rural areas for use in urban areas. Despite this fact, most of the energy-related jobs, especially the higher-skilled jobs in the value-added stream, are not in rural areas. Similarly, the large refining and processing plants, research and development, and engineering functions of energy corporations contribute more value to urban areas. Super-industrial society would continue this pattern: exploitation of the natural and human resources of rural areas.

The teleological paradigm, however, offers a different outlook: alternative energy and appropriate applications. Available and emerging technologies could provide feasible systems for using alternative energy sources both as supplements and replacements for fossil fuels. Advances have been made in the field of petroleum-substitution technology (methanol, syncrude from shale oil, coal liquification, and waste pyrolysis). Energy can also be derived from agricultural and forestry waste products. Smaller, more efficient, and cleaner units can enhance rural areas. These sources of energy have the potential to provide both locally-produced sources of energy, and income from cogeneration arrangements with major energy companies for supply to urban areas.

Some energy production methods are especially appropriate for rural areas. Rural areas, for example, are particularly suited for the production of solar and wind power. More than half of the states in the U.S. may have areas with sufficient wind patterns to produce energy on a constant basis. Ethanol plants are appropriate for rural areas because they use organic materials such as wood and corn. An assessment of a proposed ethanol plant in rural Florida in 1981 focused on three areas of impact: economic, infrastructure, and environment. The proposed plant would provide 113 jobs and generate 180 additional positions in supplementary enterprises. All but three of the positions were to be filled from the local population. Positive impacts included an increase in per capita income and increased retail sales. Construction and housing repairs were also predicted. Using natural, renewable resources such as tree trunks and corn stalks could reduce the environmental impact, thus recycling heretofore discarded byproducts of the farming and timber industries. An old railway spur was to be converted into a truck route to allow the heavy traffic generated by the plant to bypass local communities. The pollutants produced by the plant would be organic and not emitted at harmful levels. Such a plant appears almost ideally suited for rural areas.

Rural areas also require significant amounts of energy, because modern agriculture and extractive industries draw considerably on the nation's energy supply. Rural areas need reliable and readily available power that new technologies may be able to provide. For example, advances in plasma technology in the electric industry produce greater energy than fossil fuels, more rapid heat transfer and controllability, and reduce pollutants and increase productivity in industry. Plasma technology offers promise for revitalizing older industries, particularly those that cannot meet environmental standards. The electric industry is also adopting more efficient equipment, made possible by advances in computerized software. Refrigeration, lighting, and other aspects of production can now be controlled through "smart" machines. Electric vehicles offer a solution to noise and environmental pollution. Electric heat pumps for homes offer better control of residential air and temperature at lower costs (Balhiser 1989).

Technology thus offers the promise of ample energy that is less exploitative and less polluting than existing sources.

Current trends and projections to the year 2000 are attuned to teleological society. Utilities are diversifying, turning to nonutility generators for their capacity needs, and large base-load generating units (that form the backbone of present utility systems) are notably absent from capacity plans for the future (Perrault 1990). Installations using wind and solar power are increasingly common. These developments represent evidence of those features called for by the teleological paradigm, namely, smaller and more appropriately sized units, diversification and flexibility, and decentralization.

Telecommunications and Information Technologies: Control or Freedom?

Telecommunications technology is undeniably a fundamental feature driving the emerging rural society. Parker (1989) notes that "as rural economic activities and social services become more information intensive, they rely more heavily on access to high quality telecommunication facilities." Sources in the popular media estimate that as much as half of the total U.S. labor force may be performing some work in home offices by the year 2000 (O'Malley 1991). It is essential, therefore, that rural communities develop the skills to use new information technologies to produce quality goods and services in a competitive marketplace. Modern telecommunications expand options from simple voice communications to include interactive voice, video and data transmission. Super-industrial society will use these technologies for increased control of the periphery by the center. Teleological society can produce applications that increase individual choice, control, participation, diversity, and free exchange of information and ideas.

The lexicon of the emerging information technology is varied, rich and seemingly endless. Satellites, earth stations, microwave, minicomputers, interactive television, fiberoptics, cellular communications, compressed video, and digital switching are integral to the rise of information industries. All have a strong impact on the publishing trade, libraries, word processing, data processing, and professional services in the communications and knowledge fields. All can be operated from rural communities, provided the telecommunications infrastructure is available. Telecommunications technologies also offer great opportunities for rural government, centers of administration, health and human services, education, and law enforcement. Further, there are direct impacts on traditional rural activities. Livestock can be fed and monitored by computers which determine their diet, milking, and slaughter times. Planning, planting, cultivating, harvesting, and marketing of crops can be attuned to the most recent information on seed or livestock varieties and weather and market conditions (Molitor 1981). Expert systems can provide for on-farm integrated pest management that is attuned to specific soil, plant, weather, season, and pest conditions.

The issues affecting rural America's survival in the information age also reflect on our national ability to compete in the global economy. Voice activated machines, super computers, vivid graphics, holograms, better home appliances, and picture telephones and videotext systems are all now available in Japan, Germany and France. According to Hanley (1989), all true technological and social innovation is occurring in these countries. A federal effort to develop a modern system is necessary if any is to enjoy widespread success in the United States. The National Council on Public Works Improvement says "The quality of America's infrastructure is barely adequate to fulfill current requirements, and insufficient to meet the demands of future economic growth and development" (Hanley 1989).

If information *is* power, then information technology *shares* power. Telecommunications can be an equalizer of urban and rural. Telecommunications and information technologies also proffer some interesting implications for the social and economic structure of the rural society. Advances in technology have transformed telecommunications from a simple basic home service into a tool for economic growth. Hi-tech telecommunications is a basic ingredient of the infrastructure, which is as necessary as roads. According to Parker et al. (1989: 8), telecommunications "give rural residents an equal opportunity to participate in the national economy and determine their own destiny." At the same time, the fiber-optic networks essential to many of the new applications are being installed first and primarily in urban areas—a repeat of patterns that have already disadvantaged rural communities. Thus, the way information technology is mobilized may precipitate a significant break in the rural dependency of the past, or it may impose new forms of dependency.

Robotics and Biotechnology:
Of Clocks and Clones

The specter of super-industrial society looms most clearly when technologies replace people, plants and animals with man-made, computerized processes and machines. Robotic machines that assemble automobiles and appliances (and thus replace human workers) are commonplace today. Human workers also have been replaced on the farm by machines that feed, water, and milk a dairy herd. Similar agricultural processes exist for other livestock. Automated planting, watering and harvesting are growing technologies. Biotechnical manufacturing of food and fiber is also an emerging field. Cloned beefsteaks grown in nutrient tanks could provide consistent, high-quality protein without breeding, feeding, and caring for cattle. (Cloned egg production could eliminate the chicken-egg debate.) Similar processes for other products eliminate the plant or animal as intermediary between raw nutrients and the dinner table. Robotics and biotechnology can eliminate the need for most farmers.

These processes could free humankind from the drudgery of backbreaking, manual labor. Evidence is emerging, however, that many of these applications are being developed in urbanized areas, depriving rural communities of the jobs and value-added economic benefits that these technologies could provide. Robotics and biotechnology, however, could make a crucial difference for rural communities. Under the teleological paradigm, such technologies can be organized and structured to provide employment, services, and amenities for an educated, enlightened rural population.

Hi-Tech Health and Human Services

Super-industrial society would continue the present trend toward more expensive and centralized health and human service systems resulting in inferior and more distant care for lower-income citizens in rural areas. In contrast, teleological society would use technology to provide appropriately dispersed, hi-tech care regardless of location. Current technologies have the capability to assure high-quality health and human services in rural America. Geographical distances should pose few problems for the systems of the future. New methods will enable health and emergency services to make home visits and to monitor the health of rural families. Even today, tele-medicine enables some care providers to consult with distant specialists and with patients situated in remote locations.

Technological advances promise to make small hospitals appropriate for many types of care if linked to high-tech service facilities for expensive or infrequently used procedures. Small rural hospitals and nursing homes, ambulatory care and outpatient facilities, child care and protection, social service and other human service agencies are frequently characterized by relatively small numbers of specialized professional personnel. Communication technology facilitates the sharing of expertise to strengthen quality health care. Second opinions and consultations with specialists are enhanced by the ability to transmit digitalized records, test results, and images. Support for appropriate diagnoses and interventions is realized through the transmission of computerized clinical information associated with utilization review and quality assurance activities. Interactive video also promises to make client-professional and professional-professional links immediate and personal.

The potentialities for human capital are significant. If other professionals are not available for consultation, computer-based expert systems have an important back-up role to play in professional decision making in rural facilities. Physicians and nurses, for example, working alone or with very little professional support near at hand can draw upon the "packaged expertise" of dozens of professionals via reliance upon expert systems. Such systems, moreover, offer more than advice in difficult situations; they can improve quality control through real-time alerts and reduce malpractice exposure through documentation of the decision process (Warner 1987). At the same time, however, there are increasing numbers of court cases in which economic damages, injuries and death have been linked to computer systems, including expert system failures. The fault can rest with poor design of the software or with misuse of the software by professionals in the field (Baram 1987).

Typical of the teleological paradigm pattern, personnel in rural hospitals may be called upon to play a wider variety of roles than their counterparts in larger urban facilities. The need for cross-training, updating, and continuing education for physicians, nurses and other clinical personnel can be met, in part, by effective use of telecommunications, computer-based simulation, and interactive video-disk technology. Other applications of technology in health and human services involve organization, management support, and information systems. Rural hospitals and rural human service providers may join "remote integrated networks" of larger organizations to identify and register patients by computer links with appropriate experts, specialists, and hospitals. The same arrangement might aid in recruiting and retaining professionals in rural areas (Anderson 1986:50). Some expert systems are already dedicated to management of health care facilities and "managed patient care" (Adkins and Smith 1987:53). Applications in the broader human services field could end the fragmentation that typically exists.

Shared computer services could equip rural facilities with state-of-the-art software for accounting, management information, and decision support functions. Computer supported cost accounting systems may be as critical, even more critical, to the small volume rural program as it is to the large urban facility. Another option is the creation of a network or consortium of small rural facilities. The network would enable the members to join forces for the development and use of technology appropriate to their needs.

There are significant gains to be had in maintaining the skills of human capital for health and human services as well. Satellite/telephone-based, interactive, computer supported instruction is increasingly used for educational programs for both clinical and administrative personnel, even for graduate education programs in management. The use of satellite programming has been identified, along with computer-assisted instruction, by hospital educational directors as a high priority for education program development (Ulschak and Atchison 1986). Another variation on the same technologies enables rural hospitals to limit storage capacity while insuring sufficient inventory using remote "real-time" inventory monitoring and ordering services. The availability of technology as described above may make the difference between existence and dissolution for rural health and human service programs whose financial conditions are otherwise precarious.

Community-based and in-home care, too, can benefit from technology. For example, improvements in anesthesia and surgical techniques have increased the number of surgical procedures that can be performed on an outpatient basis in suitably equipped, free-standing rural health clinics. Similarly, technological improvements in intravenous therapy, respiratory therapy, infection control, and other areas support shifting larger segments of treatment to home care. These advances place greater reliance upon access to affordable formal home health services; they also introduce the need for training for in-home care support for family, friends, and local providers.

Cellular telephone technology, now available to over two-thirds of the U.S. population and diffusing rapidly to the remaining portion, offers significant support to the rural care-giver. Similar to the effect of the first telephone exchanges at the corner pharmacy on practice efficiency of the country doctor, cellular technology serves the professional-on-the-move. For the circuit-riding physician, the home-health nurse, and emergency medical personnel, cellular telephones reduce the "down-time" normally associated with travel. Information on patients can be transmitted to and from professionals in-transit, schedules can be modified, and practice efficiency can be enhanced.

The linking of cellular telephone technology with other technologies offers additional benefits. The recently developed portable cellular cardiograph can transmit heart data from the ambulance to a distant emergency room (Notebaert 1988). Variations on this technology allow the distant licensed professional to actually initiate defibrillation with the assistance of on-site emergency medical personnel. Applications in other service areas—day care, emergency housing, mental health, crisis services—offer additional hope.

The availability of technology as described above may make the difference between existence and dissolution for rural health and human service programs and hospitals whose financial conditions are otherwise precarious. At the same time, small rural hospitals are being closed or absorbed into larger city-based hospitals at a record rate. Thus, the trend toward consolidation in larger units is more characteristic of the industrial society paradigm, and runs counter to the promises inherent in the teleological model.

Education and Training

Rural education and training would be dramatically different for super-industrial and teleological societies. Super-industrial society would see the population of rural America as being increasingly populated by unskilled or low-skilled workers and their supervisors. The corporate absentee landlords of the industrial agriculture paradigm would reside primarily in metropolitan areas, receiving high quality education and training. Rural areas would also have to deal with new waves of unskilled immigrants speaking different languages—with the best and brightest creamed off for metropolitan education. Rural educational systems would emphasize the basics, technical education, and screening for metro-educational institutions. The teleological paradigm envisions high-tech, high-quality rural education with the full range of subjects available for both masses and elites.

New information technologies offer unprecedented opportunities for rural education. No longer is it necessary to co-locate teacher and student. Interactive systems allow people access to education and training when and where they want it. Remote locations can now receive the benefits of direct interactive contact with highly-qualified instructors from thousands of miles away. Such capabilities are especially important where specialized training, specific skills, and new applications are involved. Not only can we develop systems for equivalent education for young people, we can also meet the challenge of continually educating adults and workers.

Workers and non-workers alike must have the capabilities to use the new technologies if the values of equal educational opportunity are to be realized (Norat and Minc 1980). There is, therefore, a very strong need to make the new technologies available to the average adult citizen. New technologies will give workers a chance to develop new career skills. Smith's (1989) study of the urban office setting suggests this opportunity is especially important as new developments displace workers, making their skills and experience obsolete. His observations are applicable to rural businesses and any place where a new technology is adopted. Businesses must find people who both understand the new technology, its uses and how to use it, and can teach it to others. Thus, for jobs lost by the adoption of new technologies, there will also be jobs created. A comprehensive and well coordinated job training policy can minimize the jobs lost while optimizing the human capital for jobs created.

The classroom environment in even the most isolated rural schools can be enhanced by satellite communication of the highest quality educational programs. As human capital concerns become more pressing, reliance upon more costly two-way interactive televideo communication will become available to schools, permitting the most talented teachers and educational resource specialists to interact with individual students in distant locations. Advanced communications will enable the teacher in any given specialty in a rural facility to participate in networks with counterparts from any number of schools. Such technology will permit teachers in isolated areas to experience something akin to the collegial, specialized professional support which larger schools have been able to provide. Teachers will be encouraged and enabled to continually assess and upgrade their knowledge in their field—and to live and work in rural areas. Reliance upon community residents and institutions with particular areas of expertise or resources, respectively, can strengthen and energize classes. To the extent that these resources can be made available inexpensively to the school and teachers, significant upgrading and equalization of learning environments across schools might be attained. These efforts, along with courses and activities which stress local issues and conditions, might help to retain young people in the community.

If rural communities and organizations are to compete successfully with their urban counterparts in the information and advanced technology age, a greater degree of interorganizational exchange and coordination will be required. Considered individually, rural schools, rural hospitals, and rural human services agencies are lean with respect to professional staff and other resources. If one considers the total technological expertise and technologies in place in these organizations, however, one might well be impressed by their resources. For instance, the resources of these multiple organizations might be fruitfully brought to bear in the science, industrial arts, or social science classroom or through field trips to enrich the educational experience. Courses and support groups dealing with parenting in the two-wage-earner family can draw upon the technological expertise of staff of several organizations and benefit both workers and their employers. Education and planning related to service technologies, management support technologies, and information systems technologies can be shared among many organizations. Such efforts can be devoted to sharing technology where possible, or simply assisting individual organizations to adopt the appropriate technologies.

Culture and Infotainment

Infotainment, sometimes called edutainment, involves using computing and communications technology to inform or educate while entertaining. Modern technology promises multimedia and hypermedia presentations that combine two or more media—such as video and audio, text, graphics, and interactive communication. The combination of sound, video, computer-generated animation as well as actual scenes promise to make theater and musical presentations available to people in remote locations. Moreover, distant audiences can communicate with each other thus enhancing their involvement and understanding.

Human interactions can be enhanced as well. Interactive audio already makes telephone reassurance, group discussions, chat lines, and a variety of other previously "proximity-dependent" interactions available to people thousands of miles apart. Interactive video and other multimedia technologies promise to expand the horizons of people worldwide.

Governance, Decision Making and Social Control

A teleological society would use the new technologies differently than would a super-industrial society. For instance, a super-industrial society would use the new technologies to increase surveillance and control of citizens; whereas a teleological society would use new technologies to broaden opportunities for participation in political and social arenas. Such applications are certainly important for rural citizens, who often find that the distance and density of their communities effectively excludes them from state and national politics. It is more difficult for rural Americans to attend speeches, rallies, and other forms of political participation that are historically urban centered. The increased local control and decentralization of both economic and political units of the teleological paradigm places greater responsibility at local levels. Modern technology can increase the capacity of local governments and local industries to manage their communities and companies (Tydemann 1982). Decision support and expert systems can enhance the capacity of smaller units to manage the planning and governance of local organizations. Improvements in decision making technologies can thus strengthen the managerial capacities of rural governments and organizations.

Economic Development: Rural Businesses and Industry

Economic development often benefits only a few existing or new businesses while imposing increased costs on the broader community in the form of infrastructure, services, education, pollution, etc. Growth in the community fits the super-industrial model of growth—large firms develop and prosper with little regard for their impact on the community and its residents. Development of the community is the hallmark of sustainable community systems. In a teleological society, each organization is free to seek the optimum level of production that is consistent with its responsibilities to and impact on the broader community.

New technologies can contribute to efficiency and productivity in the workplace. Rural businesses can get price and market information at the same time as urban counterparts. Telecommunication and transportation technologies assist in reducing down-time, reducing inventory, increasing the timely delivery of products to the market, reducing travel costs, increasing energy savings, and promoting decentralization. Analysts predict that there will be a surplus of benefits over costs to customers of new systems, and the benefits of the new technologies will accrue to both parties of the transaction.

The advantages of new technologies are not limited to small businesses. They are also applicable to more traditional forms of rural economies. Farmers can use desktop computers and other computerized equipment to improve productivity. Other technologies promise to increase the possibilities of value-added activities on the farm. A downturn in traditional mining, timber, and agriculture increases the need for rural communities to diversify into small businesses. Telecommunications allow rural areas to overcome the cost of rural space and to develop home-based, farm-based or community-based businesses or to operate dispersed units of larger corporations. Rural businesses can provide software, consulting, telemarketing, tele-shopping, and data processing services to customers from all over the country. Faxes, modems, low cost long distance, the replacement of electromechanical switches with computer controlled digital switches, and fiber optics make it possible for rural businesses to compete with urban counterparts while retaining the rural character of their environment.

Again, the prospects are not without drawbacks. The breakup of the Bell/AT&T system may have unwittingly initiated a trend away from universal service as "competition" leads providers to favor more lucrative markets in high-density areas. The result is either lack of service or exorbitantly higher prices in less densely populated areas. A super-industrial model will continue the emphasis on more and better service to high density areas; a teleological model will move toward optimizing the delivery of service to all geographic areas.

New Technologies and Land Use

As exploitation of nonrenewable resources and pollution are hallmarks of an industrial society, replacement and recycling will be integral to a teleological society. Technological advances have made recycling more efficient and more attractive. Nearly all the literature assumes that the information age will benefit the land and environment. A shift away from natural resource based industries to a service sector and information technology based society will alter resource requirements and lessen society's ecological impacts (Spreng and Weinberg 1980). Most of the literature takes this assumption at face value and does not subject it to critical analysis. Some authors are overly optimistic. According to Dillman (1985:11), Kahn writes that information technologies will "free us from ecological constraints and thus guarantee limitless progress." No-till, low-input, sustainable agricultural practices are more benevolent to the land. Advances in the mining sector offer new ways of revitalizing older mines, and advances in soil technology offer methods of reclaiming land from old mine sites.

Technology is only part of the issue. Human values and preferences are equally crucial. For example, the current indifference to most "ordinary" land (and rural space) and reverence for only specially selected, unique areas, is a result of the natural resource intensive industrial age. Because rural areas are often considered isolated, one myth is that rural people in the industrial society are closer to the land, more bound to natural rhythms, and more aware of time and place. Indeed, this is probably true to some degree. Will the introduction of information technologies into rural communities disrupt this? If farmers become connected to global information and technologies, and if rural people are now indoors, working on telemarketing and similar businesses, connected instantly with areas all over the world, will they lose their dependence on locality? If so, will appreciation for the land become replaced by indifference? It is possible that the true environmental impacts of the information age in rural society is more cerebral than physical, more detrimental to people's senses than to the land itself. Of all the information age authors, only Miles (1988) comes close to sharing this concern. Among his predictions is, "a growing mismatch between individual mental models of the social world and the nature and meaning of one's actions within it".

Rudel (1984) explains that the most effective means of controlling land use has historically been through zoning laws. However, communities without zoning tend to be rural (Clawson 1981), and sentiment against zoning is highly concentrated in rural places (Geisler 1979). Ironically, anti-planning sentiments are especially high in sensitive land areas. Studies indicate, however, that a connection exists between land use conversion and land use control procedures. Therefore, as diffusion brings new technologies to rural areas, and with them new land uses, then land use controls in rural communities might not be far behind (Rudel 1984).

The needs of modern settlements have always been dictated by economic pursuits. Transportation and communications have always been integral parts of the economically oriented structure of settlements. When transportation and communications are inexpensive, people tend to move to the periphery, where land is cheaper. When energy becomes scarce, the effect is to centralize. Only inexpensive energy and communications will break this tendency. New technologies can increase the flow of information and energy, even across great distance—what Max Weber called "proximity without propinquity."

Some Caveats About Reality

The introduction of new technologies into rural areas (or anywhere for that matter) brings new problems as well as new opportunities. These new problems are not just physical or economic in nature; they are also psychological and spiritual, striking at the roots of human capital. First of all, new technologies, especially in the telecommunications field, often pose threats to the sense of self, one's relationship to the land, and, ultimately, the sense of community. If technology allows people to transcend the limitations of distance and time, it will make them less dependent on the people, the land and the seasons right outside the door. Lopez (1989) notes that as people become less dependent, they become less sensitive. With this decreased sensitivity comes the increased danger that they are less aware. The land becomes more susceptible to exploitation by outside interests, or can become "packaged" to serve the images of outside visitors, or can just become "dead" from neglect.

In many cases, it is possible that the diffusion of a new technology will be accompanied by the diffusion of new technological problems, and that a lag in the diffusion of the skills and knowledge necessary to identify and correct the problems will defeat efforts to vitalize rural areas through technological change. Take, for example, the issue of technical support functions. Simply put, if a system "crashes," if the new fiber optics are severed or stop functioning, someone must locate and correct the problem. In the city, this person can come from across the hall or across town. In rural areas, it is likely that the person must first *get* there from some distant location. Hence, there is a time lag and increased costs in fixing things when they stop functioning. The solution is that local people must be trained in the skills necessary to detect and fix problems should they occur. In essence, the adoption of the new technologies in rural areas is not a discrete issue: you just do not install the technology and train the people and secure a repair person and you are in business. Real development is an unending, ongoing process, constantly adjusting and adapting to changes in the external and internal environments. The real challenge might not be in getting the technology to the people or in training the people to use it, but in keeping up with the changes in potential problems and upgrades once the systems are in place and functioning.

We see the core issue of human capital for rural areas as the core issue for education in a teleological model of society. People must be educated with problem solving and resource utilization skills. They must be multi-disciplinary and multi-skilled. And most of all, they must be flexible, ever open to new directions as existing knowledge and skills become obsolete-just as their equipment and software become outmoded.

The Challenge: An Enlightened Vision of Rural Development

Rural policy and rural development are bound up in a predicament driven by global changes, and these changes have serious implications for the existence of rural America. Citizens and policymakers must cope with the reality that most people in rural areas are not farmers. The majority of agricultural production comes from a minority of farm units, and the average rural citizen enjoys lower levels of both the necessities of life and the amenities of living in America. Our review of contemporary technology and its implications for rural areas is intentionally asymmetric, designed to counterpoise the threats and opportunities we see in the current political economy. At the same time, our presentation is generally optimistic, hoping that the potentialities available in current and emerging technologies will be realized.

The implications for rural families and rural communities are clear and dramatic. Just as clearly, existing research, funding, and policies are inadequate. The challenge of today is to embrace a new vision to guide rural development into the 21st Century. Emergent policies must deal with the full range of community life including health, social, educational, cultural, recreation, infrastructure, economic, and housing systems. Continued improvement in agricultural production for the nation and the world is essential. Attention must also be given to the proper role of forestry, mining, and manufacturing. Production units must be optimal size, consistent with the character and ambience of rural communities and the natural environment.

Considering the desire of Americans for freedom, diversity, and choice, we can expect a variety of communities to emerge. Not all of our present communities will survive. Nor do they need to become ghost towns. Several existing political units may cooperate to form "cluster communities" that combine resources and amenities. We may need to establish "development centers" or "sustainable community confederations" that are capable of providing the community systems and amenities expected in modern America while retaining their rural character. Rather than development as unbounded industrial and economic growth they will focus on "quality of life," "livability for people" and "viability of community systems." We believe that modern technology can make "rural development" possible while respecting agriculture, open spaces, the natural environment, and above all, people.

The Januslike visage of rural America is ours to see and ours to change.

On the up side we foresee hi-tech electronic villages, recreation and retirement communities, artistic and cultural communities, industrial service and bedroom centers, diversified agribusiness and food processing hubs, and resort villages, all developed in harmony with agriculture and the environment. On the down side, urban sprawl, re-industrialized smokestack communities, lo-tech, low-wage manufacturing centers, one-industry dominant areas, and urban refuse dumps are just as possible. There is also the possibility that if technology allows us to transcend the limitations of distance then geography, weather, and the seasons become irrelevant. The ties of people to the land are weakened along with the foundations of the local community. From this perspective, the technological transformation of rural areas will destroy forever their true nature and ambience.

The way we individually and collectively respond to contemporary technological change in each aspect of society will determine the face of the future for the nation and the global community. In the past, community and economic development tended to produce development *in* communities; the benefits of change went to a few and frequently led to increased costs for others. The sustainable community systems approach addresses development *of* communities where the costs of doing business and the costs of business are comparable. We can end paradigm gridlock and the contradictions in the term "rural development" by insisting on a teleological paradigm for sustainable rural community systems.

Notes

1. We choose the term "teleological society" because the term implies a primary concern for ends or results. "Teleology" comes from the greek telos (an end) and logia (a word). Webster defines teleology as a study of final causes, the fact or quality of being directed toward a definite end or having an ultimate purpose, especially as attributed to natural processes. This seems appropriate to describe a society based on values of creating sustainable communities based on mutual respect for humans, communities, and the natural and built environments.

References

Anderson, Howard JK. 1986. "Physician computer network moves into new markets after Michigan tests." *Modern Healthcare* 16 (November 21): 50.

Adkins, Bobby, and Stephen D. Smith. 1987. "An information revolution: The transition to expert systems." *Computers in Healthcare* 8 (January 7): 53.

Balzhiser, Richard E. 1989. "Technology as a key to business strategy." *Public Utilities Fortnightly.* (April 13).

Baram, Michael. 1987. "Expert systems' liability exposures grow." *National Underwriter* 91 (October 19): 17-18.

Clawson, Marion. 1981. "Land use trends." Pp. 645-67 in Amos Hawley and Sara

Mills Mazie (eds.) *Non-Metropolitan America in Transition.* Chapel Hill, NC: University of North Carolina Press.

Dillman, Don A. 1985. "The social impacts of information technologies in rural North America." *Rural Sociology* 50 (Spring): 1-26.

Dillman, Don A., Donald M. Beck, and John C. Allen. 1989. "Rural barriers to job creation remain, even in today's information age." *Rural Development Perspectives* (February): 21-27.

Etzioni, Amitai, and Eva Etzioni. 1964. *Social Change.* New York, NY: Basic Books, Inc..

Geisler, Charles C. 1979. "A sociological interpretation of land use planning in a capitalist society." Ph.D Dissertation, University of Wisconsin, Madison, cited in Rudel, 1984.

Goldsworthy, David. 1988. "Thinking politically about development." *Development and Change* 19: 505-30.

Hanley, Patrick. 1989. "The telecommunication infrastructure could speed the arrival of the information age." *Public Utilities Fortnightly* (August): 22-30.

Hyman, Drew, and Joe Miller. 1985. *Community Systems and Human Services: An Ecological Approach to Policy, Planning and Management* Kendall-Hunt Publishing Co.

Lopez, Barry. 1989. "The American geographies." *Orion Nature Quarterly* (Fall).

McLuhan, Marshall. 1964. *Understanding Media.* New York, NY: McGraw Hill Book Company.

Meadow, Donella H., Dennis L. Meadows, Jorgen Randers, and William W. Behrens III. 1972. *The Limits to Growth.* New York, NY: Universe Books.

Miles, Ian. 1988. "The electronic cottage: Myth or near myth?" *Futures* (August): 355-66.

Molitor, Graham T. T. 1981. "The information society: The path to post-industrial growth." *The Futurist* (April): 23-30.

Norat, Simon, and Alain Minc. 1980. "Computing society." *Society* (Jan/Feb): 25-30.

Notebaert, Richard C. 1988. "Portable phones for a mobile society." *Telecommunication Products and Technology* 8 (April): 31-33.

O'Malley, Christopher. 1991. "High-tech tools for the home office." *Popular Science* (May): 87-93.

Parker, Edwin B., Heather E. Hudson, Don A. Dillman, and Andrew D. Roscoe. 1989. *Rural America in the Information Age: Telecommunications Policy for Rural Development.* Lanham, MD: The Aspen Institute and University Press of America.

Perrault, G.A. 1990. "Downsizing generation: Utility plans for the 1990s." *Public Utilities Fortnightly* 126 (September 27): 15-18.

Rudel, Thomas K. 1984. "The quiet revolution in municipal land use control: Competing explanations." *Journal of Environmental Management* 10 (July): 125-37.

Schumacher, E. F. 1973. *Small is Beautiful.* New York, NY: Harper & Row, Publishers.

Smith, Michael R. 1989. "Technologizing office work." *Social Science and Public Policy* (May/June): 65-72.

Spreng, Daniel T., and Alvin M. Weinberg. 1980. "Time and decentralization." *Daedalus* 109 (Winter): 137-43.

Strange, Marty. 1988. *FAMILY FARMING: A New Economic Vision* Lincoln, NB: University of Nebraska Press, and Institute for Food and Development Policy.

Toffler, Alvin. 1970. *Future Shock*. New York, NY: Random House.

Toffler, Alvin. 1980. *The Third Wave*. New York, NY: William Morrow & Co., Inc.

Touraine, Alain. 1971. *The Post-Industrial Society: Tomorrow's Social History: Classes, Conflicts and Culture in the Programmed Society*. L.F.X. Mayhew, tr., New York, NY: Random House.

Tydeman, John. 1982. "Videotext: Ushering in the electronic household." *The Futurist* (February): 54-61.

Ulshak, Francis L., and Tom Atchison. 1986. "Hospital education programs show strength, potential for future growth." *Modern Healthcare* 16 (November 7): 142, 144.

Warner, Homer. 1987. "Expert systems: AI Solutions." *Computers in Healthcare* (July): 50-55.

Warren, Robert. 1978. *The Community in America* Third Edition Chicago, IL: Rand McNally College Publishing Company.

Wilkinson, Kenneth P. 1987. "Socioeconomic trends changing rural America." Pp. 3-15 in *Increasing Understanding of Public Problems and Policies*. Oak Brook, IL: Farm Foundation.

PART THREE

Aspects of Human Resources Conditions Across Rural America

6

Human Capital
and Nonmetropolitan Poverty

Leif Jensen
Diane K. McLaughlin

Poverty often is found near the top of the national policy agenda, but the intensity of academic and political concern seems to ebb and flow. During the 1980s, popular and scholarly research on the urban underclass rivetted national attention on the plight of the inner city poor (Auletta 1982; Wilson 1987). This concern was revived in the Spring of 1992 amidst intensive media coverage of widescale rioting in Los Angeles.

Though not denying the seriousness of urban poverty, rural social scientists often point out the little known fact that poverty is as severe in the countryside as it is in urban places (Deavers and Hoppe 1992; Jensen and Tienda 1989). Original computations from the U.S. Census Bureau's 1990 Current Population Survey (CPS) show that the poverty rate in nonmetropolitan (nonmetro) areas is higher than that in metro areas (15.9 percent and 12.1 percent, respectively), and is almost as high as that in central cities of metro areas (18.7 percent). Moreover, when key race/ethnic groups are considered separately, poverty rates are consistently highest in nonmetro America.[1]

A commonly invoked explanation for high poverty rates among certain demographic groups, e.g. nonmetro residents, is that they lack human capital relative to other groups. Low levels of education, training and labor force experience, it is argued, increase poverty risks by reducing wages and employment stability (Thurow 1969). The purpose of this chapter is to evaluate the role of human capital in accounting for geographic differences in poverty risks.

We open with a brief review of the theoretical and empirical links between poverty and human capital—paying particular attention to the implications of nonmetro residence. Using data on household heads from the 1988 wave of the *Panel Study of Income Dynamics*, we examine the extent of variation in educational attainment and labor force experience among poor and nonpoor household heads in metro and nonmetro counties. We then determine the differences in poverty rates among metro and nonmetro household heads with given levels of human capital endowments. These descriptive data reveal the link between human capital attainment, residence and poverty. Because many other attributes of household heads in metro and nonmetro areas vary, we then examine the relationship between human capital and poverty, controlling for these other characteristics. We use logistic regression models of household poverty to ascertain (1) the extent to which observed differences in human capital attainment in metro and nonmetro counties account for higher reported poverty rates in nonmetro areas, and (2) the effect of human capital on the risk of being poor when other factors related to poverty are considered. Because prior research has found strong links between levels of human capital and poverty, it is important to understand the process of human capital attainment, particularly education. We present models of educational attainment that identify factors affecting high school completion. In the concluding section, we draw on our findings and those of other studies to formulate policy recommendations.

Poverty and Human Capital: Theoretical Issues

Human capital theory was developed by economists in an attempt to explain why wages differed across individuals (Granovetter 1981). It moved neoclassical economics away from the notion that labor is provided in comparable "units." Human capital theory carried the economic idea of the "rational actor" to the decisions individuals make in investing in attributes that make them more valuable to employers. Those investing in human capital delay current returns (foregone earnings) in exchange for greater returns in the future. Thus, investment in human capital is only rational if the returns to that investment are greater than the foregone earnings.

Investment in education, training, and work experience are the most readily recognized forms of human capital, but also included are native ability, willingness to extend job search to obtain a higher return on investments, investment in health care, and geographic mobility in search of higher returns (Kalleberg and Sorenson 1979). All of these investments, but especially education and on-the-job work experience, increase the productivity of workers and their value to employers, thus increasing their wage or salary (Ehrenberg and Smith 1982; Thurow 1969). The higher returns (earnings) to those with higher levels of education and work experience found in empirical studies (Blaug 1976) tend to verify the rationality of investment in education and the value of obtaining work experience. Persons with the lowest incomes generally are those with lower levels of education and/or training, or are people who, for various reasons, do not participate fully in the labor market.

Following the logic of human capital theory as it relates to poverty, poor individuals either lack native ability, or have made economically "irrational" choices in their pursuit of education and/or training. Human capital theory fails to offer any explanation as to why individuals would make such seemingly poor judgments about their future earnings potential.

Human capital theory is largely mute on the mechanisms that give rise to group-wide disadvantages in education and labor force experience in the first place (Bowles and Gintis 1975). Models of status attainment that emerged during the 1960s and '70s began to fill this void by showing the important role that social background (e.g., parental education and occupational status) plays in the process of human capital achievement and subsequent status attainment (Blau and Duncan 1967; Sewell et al. 1970). This line of research documented significant direct and indirect effects of parental status on that of their offspring, suggesting that to some degree, the U.S. stratification system tends to reproduce social inequality over time. An important implication was that children who grew up poor were unfairly disadvantaged in the educational attainment process.

Additional failures of human capital theory lie in the assumptions that (1) all individuals receive the same returns to given human capital investments and thus, they all perceive the same benefits to such investments; (2) there are no differences across occupations and industries in the types of on-the-job training or employer-sponsored off-the-job training that augment skills; (3) upward mobility throughout a career does not affect returns to education and experience; and (4) local labor market conditions do not impact the returns individuals receive.

Problems with these assumptions behind human capital theory could potentially explain the differential educational attainment and lower returns to education and work experience for metro and nonmetro men and women found in prior empirical studies (e.g., Bibb and Form 1977; McLaughlin and Perman 1991a; Tickamyer and Bokemeier 1988). Such problems must be kept in mind as we explore the role of human capital in explaining the risk of poverty for household heads in metro and nonmetro areas.

Education and Work Experience

Higher levels of formal education can reduce the risk of poverty in at least two ways. First, schooling can impart general and, in some cases,

specialized skills that employers desire. Attaining certain levels of education also has been argued to serve a screening function for employers.
Individuals who have completed high school or college may be socialized
to function in large organizations or to have displayed the necessary drive
or ability employers desire, regardless of the type of education received
(Blaug 1976; Schiller 1980). In either case, those with higher levels of
education are preferred by employers and are given access to better jobs,
or to career paths that ultimately lead to better-paying jobs.

One problem observed in nonmetro America is that aggregate educational attainment has historically lagged behind that in metro areas (Mc-
Granahan 1991; Swanson and Butler 1988). As yet, researchers have failed
to explain this educational deficit. It may be that lower nonmetro earnings
lead nonmetro youth to decide that an investment in college education is
not economically rational. Many nonmetro youths may come from families
with incomes inadequate to finance college, or from families where education beyond high school is neither valued nor financially supported. The
outmigration of better-educated nonmetro youth to metro areas could
further explain the continued educational deficit in nonmetro areas (see
chapter 11 in this volume by Lichter, McLaughlin and Cornwell). The final
explanation for the educational deficit is the differences in age structures in
metro and nonmetro areas. Research by LeClere and McLaughlin (1988)
shows that even after adjusting for geographic differences in age, the
educational deficit in nonmetro areas remains.

Years of work experience "also features prominently in human capital
research." Theoretically, years of work experience bring opportunities to
learn new job skills that increase a worker's productivity. Formal on-the-
job training or formal training outside of work provide alternative sources
of skills and knowledge that increase the value of workers to employers,
improving the chances for lucrative and steady employment, and reducing
the prospect of poverty (Thurow 1969). What human capital theory fails to
acknowledge is that different types of jobs require different levels of skill
and knowledge and a different length of on-the-job training for workers to
become efficient in the position. In the same way, certain jobs offer more
opportunities for employer-sponsored formal training both on and off the
job. Research on industrial and occupational structure in metro and nonmetro areas suggests that jobs in nonmetro areas are more likely to be low
skill with little need or opportunity for additional training (Erickson 1981;
McLaughlin and Perman 1991; Teixeira and Mishel 1991). Work experience
may not carry the same value in jobs requiring little skill. It also has been
shown that opportunities for on-the-job training differ for men and women,
with women less likely to be offered training opportunities (Duncan and
Hoffman 1976).

While evidence of metro/nonmetro differences in work experience is lacking, studies have shown that the nonmetro poor have a stronger attachment to the labor force than their metro counterparts. Isaac Shapiro (1989) reports that in nonmetro and metro areas, respectively, 71 and 55 percent of able-bodied heads of poor households work. It seems reasonable that the greater attachment to the labor force among the nonmetro poor will be mirrored in geographic patterns of total work experience. If work experience is greater among nonmetro residents, then explanations for their greater poverty rates must lie elsewhere.

Human Capital and Anti-Poverty Policy

Human capital theory emerged at the same time that the War on Poverty was evolving, and much of the early empirical evidence strongly confirmed the theory. Not coincidentally, a number of anti-poverty policy initiatives of this era stressed human capital enhancement, either to help poor adults earn their way out of poverty, or to keep poor children from remaining poor in adulthood (Danziger and Weinberg 1986).

Rooted firmly in human capital theory, many of these programs, and a number of new ones, constitute an important part of the nation's anti-poverty policy. These programs are based on the fundamental premise that the quickest and most long-lasting route out of poverty is via gainful employment. They seek to improve the employability of the poor by facilitating or providing education and skills training. These include Head Start, means-tested assistance for college students such as Basic Education Opportunity Grants or work-study programs, and employment and training programs such as those provided under the Job Training Partnership Act (1982) and the Job Opportunities and Basic Skills Training provisions of the Family Support Act (1988).

The appeal of human capital enhancement as a strategy to ameliorate poverty is consistent with the strongly held value of individualism in U.S. society (Tussing 1975). Based on the assumption that the U.S. stratification system is reasonably permeable within and across generations, and that upward economic mobility is almost assured for those who try hard enough, this perspective places the blame for poverty squarely on the poor themselves. The assumption is that the able-bodied poor are in poverty largely as a result of personal deficiencies—notably in human capital.

The viability of human capital enhancement as an anti-poverty strategy has not gone without criticism. One problem is that even full-time work does not guarantee above poverty-level wages. Full-time work at the current minimum wage ($4.25 per hour) brings an income ($8,840) substantially below the 1990 poverty line for a married couple with two children ($13,254). Original computations from the 1990 CPS reveal that 6.9 percent of full-time, full-year workers do not have sufficient annual income to bring them above 150 percent of the poverty threshold, and that this "working poverty" is considerably worse in nonmetro areas (11.3 percent) than metro areas (5.8 percent).

A related problem concerns labor demand. As Schiller (1980:121) notes, "if there is only one job and four applicants, no amount of educational improvement or redistribution will succeed in leaving fewer than three persons unemployed." Increasing the education or training of some will only serve to shuffle people within the occupational queue (Tomaskovic-Devey 1987). The implication is that human capital enhancement will do little to ease the more systemic problems of low wages and insufficient labor demand for those at the bottom. From this perspective, structural changes that provide jobs at a living wage, are needed to resolve the problem of persistent poverty in the United States. This suggests another reason why anti-poverty strategies based on human capital enhancement are attractive. It seems easier, and it certainly is more politically feasible, to change individuals rather than engineer the economy itself (for an excellent review of these issues, see Lichter et al. 1993).

In the ensuing analysis, we address the following questions. First, are nonmetro Americans generally, and the nonmetro poor in particular, disadvantaged in terms of educational attainment and labor force experience? Second, what is the bivariate relationship between poverty rates and levels of human capital in nonmetro and metro areas? Third, to what degree can nonmetro/metro differences in poverty risks be accounted for by systematic differences in human capital endowments? And fourth, what are the effects of key background factors such as parental education, rural upbringing, and growing up poor on educational attainment and on the probability of being poor?

Data and Measures

Data

We analyze data from the 1988 wave of the *Panel Study of Income Dynamics* (PSID). First conducted in 1968 with a representative sample of over 5,000 U.S. families, this panel survey has been carried out annually ever since. Despite sample attrition among the original families, the sample size has grown because the PSID tracks new households that result when sample members leave the original household. The survey was initiated as part of the "war on poverty" and consequently, an overrepresentation of low-income groups was built into the sample design. It also contains a wide range of social background, economic, demographic and contextual variables not available in Census Bureau data such as the Current Population Survey, making it well suited for an analysis of the determinants of poverty in America (Survey Research Center 1984).

In past research, the longitudinal nature of the PSID has been fruitfully used to examine the dynamics of entries into and exits from poverty (Bane and Ellwood 1986). Our aim in this chapter is to describe the relationship between poverty and human capital in nonmetro America. Accordingly, we treat the 1988 wave of the PSID as a cross-sectional data set, and examine the likelihood that a given family was poor in 1987. In so doing, it is important to keep in mind that we are generalizing not to a 1988 sample of U.S. families, but to the situation in 1987 of a sample of 1968 families. We constrain our analysis to the human capital characteristics of family heads between the ages of 25 and 64. In all, we analyze a weighted sample of 5,212 heads and their families.[2] The average age of these heads was 41.6 years, 17 percent were non-white or Hispanic, 24 percent were female, 61 percent were married, 24 percent were nonmetro residents, and 31 percent resided in a Southern state.

Measures

For statistical purposes, the definition of a "rural" area often is the source of some confusion. While they are sometimes used synonymously, the U.S. Census Bureau definitions of "rural" and of "nonmetropolitan" are quite distinct (O'Hare 1988). Rural residents live outside of urban areas; the latter being communities with a population of at least 2,500 or other densely settled urbanized areas (Fuguitt et al. 1989). Nonmetro residents live outside of metro counties; the latter being counties with a large city (50,000 or more) and surrounding counties that have important ties to the central county. In this analysis, we draw on the metro/nonmetro distinction, however, the PSID allows us to subdivide each. Specifically, we use a four-category geographic identifier to differentiate between residents of central counties and other counties within metro areas; and within non-metro areas, counties that are adjacent and non-adjacent to metro areas. We pay particular attention to residents of nonmetro non-adjacent counties, since this is the most rural of the four county types and may be the most disadvantaged (Fuguitt et al. 1989).

We base our definition of poverty on the official thresholds set forth by the U.S. Census Bureau (1989).[3] According to this definition, a family is poor if their annual pre-tax cash income from all sources falls below a threshold considered necessary to provide a minimum standard of living. To account for differing need levels, we follow Census Bureau procedures by adjusting these thresholds by family size.[4] However, in this analysis we differ from the Census Bureau by defining as poor those families whose income is below 150 percent of the poverty line. This more liberal definition is consistent with mounting evidence that official thresholds are unrealistically low, i.e., that a poverty level income is insufficient to provide basic needs (Ruggles 1990). By this definition, 14.6 percent of the household heads in our study are poor. The pattern across county types highlights the severity of nonmetro poverty. The poverty rate for those in metro central, other metro, nonmetro adjacent, and nonmetro non-adjacent counties was 15.3, 10.9, 18.2 and 23.5 percent, respectively.

We employ two basic measures of the human capital of family heads. The first is completed years of formal education, and is measured as both a discrete and continuous variable. The second is work experience, and is based on two PSID variables: total years and total full-time years of labor force experience since age 18. We use the latter variables both in raw form and as a percentage of total years lived since age 18 (i.e., percent of adult years in the labor force). These measures of work experience are considerably superior to the more common proxy (i.e., age minus years of education minus five) which makes the questionable assumption (especially for women) that respondents finished school before entering the labor force and stayed in the labor force until the time of the survey.

Nonmetro-Metro Differences in
Human Capital Endowments

Whether human capital deficits are a particularly salient cause of poverty in nonmetro areas will depend in part on whether education and labor force experience among the nonmetro poor are especially low. Table 6.1 shows various indicators of human capital for poor and non-poor household heads residing in central metro, other metro, nonmetro adjacent and nonmetro non-adjacent counties. With respect to nonmetro-metro differences, a decidedly mixed picture emerges, depending on whether the focus is education or labor force experience.

On balance, the nonmetro poor, especially those living in non-adjacent counties (those most remote from metro areas), have lower levels of education. These differences are not particularly dramatic when education is measured as mean years of schooling completed. Poor heads in nonmetro non-adjacent counties received the least amount of formal education, an average of 10.5 years. However, this average was not much less than those for the other three residence categories. Mean completed education was 11.3, 11.7 and 11.1 years for those in central, other metro and nonmetro adjacent counties, respectively.

The deficit in education among the nonmetro non-adjacent poor is more apparent, however, with education measured as the percentage graduating from high school. Only 43.4 percent of poor family heads in non-adjacent

TABLE 6.1. Human Capital Attributes by Poverty Status and Residence, 1987.

	Total				Poor[a]				Non-Poor			
	Metro Counties		Nonmetro Counties		Metro Counties		Nonmetro Counties		Metro Counties		Nonmetro Counties	
	Central Counties	Other Counties	Adjacent	Non-Adjacent	Central Counties	Other Counties	Adjacent	Non-Adjacent	Central Counties	Other Counties	Adjacent	Non-Adjacent
Mean Education (years)	13.4	13.3	12.4	12.2	11.3	11.7	11.1	10.5	13.7	13.5	12.7	12.7
Percent High School Grad	81.8	82.1	70.2	69.4	50.9	56.2	57.6	43.4	87.4	85.3	73.0	77.4
Percent College Grad	29.8	27.4	17.3	16.8	5.0	6.8	2.6	1.2	34.3	29.9	20.5	21.6
Years worked since 18	17.3	19.1	18.2	19.4	10.6	14.1	12.4	15.6	18.5	19.7	19.5	20.5
Percent years worked since 18	73.8	77.2	76.7	76.4	51.1	61.1	60.5	62.6	77.7	79.1	80.3	80.5
Years worked full-time since 18	15.5	17.3	16.3	17.6	9.0	11.9	10.2	13.0	16.6	17.9	17.6	19.0
Percent years worked full-time since 18	64.0	68.0	67.2	68.6	43.8	50.0	49.3	52.2	67.4	70.1	71.1	73.3
Weighted N	1404	2529	580	700	214	276	105	164	1189	2253	474	535

Source: 1988 Wave of the Panel Study of Income Dynamics

[a]Heads are defined as poor if their total family income is less than 150% of the official poverty threshold. See text for definitions of other variables.

counties were high school graduates or better, the next lowest percent being among those in central counties (50.9 percent). While the percentages are substantially lower with human capital measured as percentage graduating from college, residents of nonmetro non-adjacent counties again are the most disadvantaged. The data for non-poor heads and all heads (total) are presented for comparison. They generally indicate lower levels of educational attainment in the two nonmetro county types.

These data indicate that part of the explanation for relatively high poverty rates in nonmetro areas may inhere in lower levels of formal education. However, data in the second panel of Table 6.1 suggest that, with human capital measured as labor force experience, quite the opposite is true. Regardless of which measure is considered, poor heads residing in non-adjacent counties have greater labor force experience and attachment than their counterparts in the other three residence types. By and large, poor heads in central counties have the least labor force experience and attachment. For example, poor heads in non-adjacent counties had on average 15.6 years of labor force experience since age 18 (13.0 full-time years), which compares to only 10.6 years among poor heads in central counties (9.0 full-time years). Those in the other two geographic categories fell between these extremes.

One plausible explanation for the apparent discrepancy in human capital attainment in nonmetro areas—lower levels of education combined with higher levels of work experience—may result because those individuals with lower levels of education spent fewer years after age 18 in school and were able to contribute more years to labor force activity. At an aggregate level, lower educational attainment and higher labor force experience among household heads in nonmetro non-adjacent counties could reflect the older age composition in nonmetro areas. Even though our sample is restricted to those aged 25 to 64, the outmigration of younger, better educated individuals from nonmetro areas leaves behind an older, less-educated population (see the Lichter, McLaughlin and Cornwell chapter in this volume). Older individuals may simply have more years of labor market experience because they have lived longer. The PSID allows us to separate the effects of age from years of labor force experience for individuals of the same age.

Total years of labor force experience is only one measure of human capital. Perhaps even more important for this study is attachment to the labor force. Continuous labor force attachment signals to employers a willingness to work and constitutes an uninterrupted period of on-the-job skill acquisition. Compared to the results for years of work experience, we find a similar pattern for percentage of years worked since age 18 and percentage of years worked full-time since age 18. In both instances poor heads in nonmetro non-adjacent counties are the most advantaged, while those in the central counties of metro areas are the most disadvantaged. Here however, the more obvious difference is between the residents of central counties and all other poor heads. Again, similar geographic patterns obtain for non-poor heads and all heads.

To summarize, Table 6.1 presents equivocal evidence regarding geographic differences in the human capital endowments of poor family heads. In terms of educational attainment, residents of nonmetro non-adjacent counties are the most disadvantaged. When human capital is measured as labor force experience or attachment, they are the least disadvantaged. Table 6.1 also provides evidence of the important link between poverty and human capital. Regardless of which indicator is used, human capital is substantially higher among non-poor than poor household heads. These bivariate relationships become even more evident in the next section as we document variation in poverty rates.

Explaining Poverty: The Relative Impact of Human Capital

The purpose of this section is to provide an empirical base from which to evaluate the potential usefulness of human capital enhancement as an anti-poverty strategy in nonmetro and metro areas. We begin with a descriptive presentation of poverty rates within categories of education and labor force experience of household heads. This establishes the degree of association between human capital and poverty, and variation in this association between nonmetro and metro areas. We then estimate logistic regression models of poverty to establish the effect of human capital relative to other determinants. In particular, we establish the degree to which nonmetro-metro differences in education and labor force experience and attachment account for higher poverty risks in nonmetro areas. Recognizing that the etiology of poverty is different for male and female household heads, we also present gender specific models of poverty.

Poverty Rates by Human Capital Characteristics

Table 6.2 shows family poverty rates by residence and head's educational attainment and labor force attachment. Higher levels of human capital sharply reduce the risk of poverty. The first panel indicates that poverty rates drop steadily with higher levels of education. Among all family heads, for example, the poverty rate for those with less than a high school education stood at 34.0 percent in 1987. This compares to only 15.8 percent for those with a high school diploma, 11.5 percent for heads of households with a diploma and some additional non-academic (vocational) degree, 11.1 percent for ones with some college, and only 2.9 percent for those with a college degree or better.

TABLE 6.2. Poverty Rates by Human Capital Attributes and Place of Residence, 1987[a].

		Metro Counties		Nonmetro Counties	
	Total	Central Counties	Other Counties	Adjacent	Non-Adjacent
Overall Poverty Rate	14.6	15.3	10.9	18.2	23.5
Weighted N	5212	1404	2529	580	700
Education					
Less than H.S.	34.0	42.9	27.3	26.5	43.2
High School	15.8	17.3	9.9	20.6	26.0
High School Plus	11.5	12.4	10.1	19.6[b]	6.9[b]
Some College	11.1	11.1	9.7	15.3[b]	14.8
College Degree	2.9	2.7	2.9	2.7	3.2
Percent of Years Worked Since Age 18[c]					
<75	26.2	27.6	20.2	33.6	39.9
75 - 87	10.1	9.2	8.3	14.5	15.3
>87	7.6	5.5	5.2	9.0	17.9
Percent Years Worked Full-time Since Age 18					
<63	24.2	24.7	18.4	32.3	37.7
63 - 83	9.4	6.7	8.5	13.6	16.3
>83	8.0	9.5	5.0	9.0	14.2

Source: 1988 Wave of the Panel Study of Income Dynamics

[a]Heads are defined as poor if their total family income is less than 150% of the official poverty threshold.
[b]Estimates are based on fewer than 100 cases.
[c]Includes part-time work.

Looking within geographic areas, with some aberrations, the same basic pattern obtains. The exceedingly high poverty rates among those with less than a high school diploma in nonmetro non-adjacent counties (43.2 percent) and central counties of metro areas (42.9 percent) are noteworthy. Stated differently, while a high school degree is important for keeping all family heads out of poverty, this is especially true for those in central metro and non-adjacent nonmetro counties. The only other noteworthy geographic difference pertains to the effect of having a non-academic degree in addition to a high school diploma. Heads with such vocational training have much lower poverty rates in non-adjacent counties (6.9 percent) when compared to those holding a high school degree alone (26.0 percent) or even some college training (14.8 percent). While caution is warranted since the 5.9 percent is based on 65 observations, it may be that returns to vocational training are particularly high in the most rural labor markets.

The bottom two panels of Table 6.2 describe the effect of labor force attachment on poverty rates. To simplify reporting of these comparisons, we trichotomize the labor force attachment variables to divide the sample roughly into thirds. We examine labor force attachment in this descriptive analysis because reports of years of labor force experience are confounded by age differences of respondents. For example, a category of ten or fewer years worked could include both a college-educated individual aged 32 with ten years of labor force experience, and a 62 year old with an eighth grade education and ten years of labor force experience. Using the labor force attachment measure, heads with more continuous attachment to the labor force (a higher percentage of years reported in the labor force since age 18) have significantly lower poverty rates than those with less attachment. The steady decline in poverty rates with higher levels of labor force attachment is generally consistent across residence categories.

Multivariate Models of Poverty

Taken together, these descriptive results indicate that greater labor force attachment and higher investments in education correspond with reduced poverty risks in both metro and nonmetro areas. However, with a few exceptions as noted above, the rates of poverty reported in nonmetro areas for each category of human capital and labor force attachment exceed those reported in metro areas. This suggests two possible explanations. First, household heads in metro and nonmetro areas differ from each other in other ways that explain the variations in poverty rates. Second, conditions in metro and nonmetro areas differ resulting in higher poverty rates among nonmetro household heads even when their individual characteristics are similar to those of their metro counterparts. Or, some combination of individual differences and variations in conditions in metro and nonmetro areas explain the higher nonmetro poverty rates.

To test these various explanations, we use logistic regression to estimate models of poverty among family heads, concentrating on the importance of the head's human capital in explaining the likelihood of a household being poor. Logistic regression is used because the dependent variable is dichotomous—either a household is or it is not poor. The operational definitions and distributions for the variables used in the multivariate analyses appear in Table 6.3.

Table 6.4 presents a series of five hierarchical logistic regression models. In addition to ordinary logit coefficients (B), we also present transformed coefficients (P), whose interpretation is the effect of a unit change in the

TABLE 6.3. Operational Definitions and Means for Variables in Multivariate Analysis

Variable	Definition	Mean[a]
Poverty	Total family income in 1987 less than 150% of U.S. Census Bureau poverty threshold.	.14
Residence in 1987		
Central Counties[b]	Central counties of metro areas of 1 million or more	.27
Other Metro	Other metro counties	.49
Nonmetro Adjacent	Nonmetro counties adjacent to metro areas	.11
Non Adjacent	Nonmetro counties not adjacent to metro areas	.13
Completed Education		
Less than High School[b]	Less than high school and no GED	.20
High School	High school or GED	.21
High School Plus	High school degree plus additional nonacademic (e.g. vocational) training	.10
Some College	Some college but not degree	.22
College Degree	College degree or more	.27
Labor Force Experience		
Total Full-time Years	Total years since age 18 worked full-time	16.78
Proportion Full-time Years	Proportion of years since age 18 worked full-time	.67
Head's Age	Age in years	41.6
Head's Race	Head is neither white nor Hispanic	.17
Head's Gender	Male = 1; Female = 2	1.24
Head's Parent's Education		
Father High School Grad	Head's father was high school grad or better	.50
Mother High School Grad	Head's mother was high school grad or better	.61
Presence of Children		
Ages 1 - 2	Children ages 1 - 2 present in family	.13
Ages 3 - 5	Children ages 3 - 5 present in family	.13
Ages 6 - 18	Children ages 6 - 18 present in family	.27
Head's Marital Status in 1987		
Never Married[b]	Head has never been married	.16
Married	Head was married	.61
No Longer Married	Head was divorced, widowed or separated	.23
Union Member	Head's 1987 job was covered by a union contract	.18
Work Disability	Head had a work disability in 1987	.15
Worked in 1987	Head worked in 1987	.85
Southern Residence	Southern residence in 1987	.31
County Unemployment Rate	County unemployment rate (percent)	5.4
Head's Origin Economic Status		
Well Off[b]	Grew up in a family that was pretty well off	.26
Average	Grew up in a family that was average - "it varied"	.43
Poor	Grew up in a family that was poor	.31
Head's Origin Residence		
City[b]	Grew up in a city	.39
Town-Suburb	Grew up in a town or suburb	.42
Farm-Rural	Grew up in farm, rural area, country	.19
Nonmetro	Grew up in a nonmetro county as defined in 1980	.43
Head's Total Siblings	Total number of natural brother's and sister's head ever had	3.62

[a]Means are for dummy variables code of 0, 1 except where indicated.
[b]Used as reference category in multivariate analysis.

TABLE 6.4. Logistic Regression Models of Poverty[a]

	Model I		Model II		Model III		Model IV		Model V	
	B	ΔP[b]	B	ΔP	B	ΔP	B	ΔP	B	ΔP
Residence										
Central Counties	—	—	—	—	—	—	—	—	—	—
Other Metro	-.368	-.039	-.384	-.040	-.275	-.030	-.261	-.029	-.096c	-.011
Nonmetro Adjacent	.276	.037	-.021c	-.003	.374	.051	.085c	.011	.362c	.049
Non Adjacent Nonmetro	.538	.078	.298	.040	.701	.107	.443	.062	.435	.061
Education										
Less than High School			—	—			—	—	—	—
High School			-1.140	-.091			-.937	-.080	-.734	-.068
High School Plus			-1.427	-.102			-1.152	-.091	-.924	-.079
Some College			-1.511	-.105			-1.370	-.100	-.942	-.081
College Degree			-2.931	-.131			-3.243	-.134	-2.406	-.126
Age			-.032	-.004	.015	.002	-.017	-.020	-.042	-.005
Labor Force Experience										
Total Full-time Years					-.024c	-.003	-.006c	-.001	.027c	.003
Proportion Full-time Years					-2.258	-.123	-3.213	-.133	-2.162	-.122
Non-white									.913	.149
Female									.257c	.034
Parent's Education										
Father High School Grad									-.294	-.032
Mother High School Grad									-.224c	-.025
Origin Residence										
City									—	—
Town-Suburb									.178c	.023
Farm-Rural									.514	.073

TABLE 6.4. Continued

	Model I		Model II		Model III		Model IV		Model V	
	B	ΔP[b]	B	ΔP	B	ΔP	B	ΔP	B	ΔP
Presence of Children										
Ages 1 - 2									.873	.139
Ages 3 - 5									.691	.104
Ages 6 - 18									.919	.148
Marital Status										
Never Married									—	—
Married									-1.087	-.087
No Longer Married									-.006	-.001
Union Member									-1.205	-.092
Work Disability									.668	.100
Worked in 1987									-1.731	-.110
Southern Residence									.442	.061
Constant	-1.794		-.761		-.779		1.877		2.220	
-2 Log Likelihood	4006.6		3544.6		3633.4		3175.3		2458.4	
DF	5074		5069		5071		5067		5052	

Source: 1988 Wave of the Panel Study of Income Dynamics.

[a] Heads are defined as poor if their total family income is less tha n 150% of the official poverty threshold.

[b] Logistic regression coefficients converted to reflect the effect of a unit change in the independent variables on the probability of poverty (see Peterson 1985).

[c] Coefficient *not* significant at .05 (two-tailed).

predictor variable on the probability that the household is poor (Peterson 1985). In Model I, poverty status is regressed on place of residence, with residents of central counties of metro areas serving as the reference group. This model confirms the descriptive results of Table 6.3. Compared to central county residents, those in other metro areas are significantly less likely to be poor, while those in nonmetro adjacent and especially nonmetro non-adjacent counties are significantly *more* likely to be in poverty. The transformed logit coefficient of .078 for nonmetro non-adjacent residents means that their estimated poverty rate is .078 (or 7.8 percentage points) more than that for residents of central counties. These differences roughly correspond to those seen in Table 6.3.

In Model II we enter variables indicating level of education attained. Because of the well known increase in educational attainment across birth cohorts, we also control for head's age. If the higher poverty rates in more rural counties are accounted for by lower levels of education, then the effects of residence should be less in Model II. There is some evidence for this. The coefficient for nonmetro non-adjacent residence declines in magnitude by nearly half, while that for nonmetro adjacent residents becomes insignificant. Also noteworthy are the effects of education on poverty risks. Compared to those with less than a high school education (the reference group), the poverty rate among those with college degrees is estimated to be 13.1 percentage points lower (P = -.131). In all cases, those with higher levels of educational attainment were less likely to be poor than those with less than a high school diploma.

Model III adds to Model I two variables indicating labor force experience. These are the total years of full-time labor force experience since heads were age 18, and the proportion of years heads worked full-time since they were 18. We enter both these variables under the assumption that they measure distinct and important features of labor force experience—total experience and degree of attachment, respectively. We also enter age in the model. The total number of years an individual potentially has available to contribute to the labor force is highly dependent on age. Accordingly, we felt it was important to attempt to distinguish the effects of age from those of total years of labor force experience. Previous studies of working age populations that have not had measures of actual experience available have found that earnings increased and the likelihood of being poor decreased with increasing age. In this study, we are able to more directly test whether increasing age, or more likely, increasing years of labor force experience explain the decreasing likelihood with age of being poor. We also include the labor force attachment measure to assess the relative importance of more continuous years of labor force experience. These three measures do not perfectly define each other since years of education after age 18 eliminate the definitional relationship between years of labor force experience and proportion of years in the labor force since age 18 and actual age.

Model III indicates that, of the two, proportion of adult years working full-time is the more important predictor of poverty status. The coefficient for total years of work is statistically insignificant. Compared to Model I, the positive effect of nonmetro residence increases when labor force experience is controlled in Model III. This suggests that if nonmetro residents were as disadvantaged in labor force experience as their counterparts in central metro counties, their already higher poverty rates would be that much greater. Unlike education, geographic differences in labor force experience serve to reduce the nonmetro disadvantage in poverty risks.

Compared to Model I, Model IV indicates that with both education and labor force experience controlled, the overall effect of nonmetro residence is reduced. However, geographic differences in human capital do not fully explain the greater poverty risks among the most rural residents—those in nonmetro non-adjacent counties. Model IV also indicates that both dimensions of human capital have significant, independent and negative effects on poverty. However, the effects of educational attainment are reduced, while those of labor force attachment increase when both education and labor force experience measures are included in the model. Finally, a comparison of fit statistics for Models II and III with those of Model I indicates that education and labor force experience, as measured here, improve the fit of the model to a roughly equal degree.

To gain a more complete picture of the net effect of human capital endowments on the probability of poverty, Model V includes several other individual, household and contextual predictors. These additional variables are defined in Table 6.3. The probability of poverty was higher if (1) the head was non-white, (2) there were children present in the household, (3) the head had a work disability in 1987, (4) the household was in a Southern state, or (5) the head grew up in a rural area (as compared to a city). Conversely, poverty risks were reduced when the head (1) had a better educated father (the effect for mother's education was marginally insignificant), (2) was married (as opposed to never married), (3) had a job that was covered by a union contract, or (4) worked in 1987. While the effects of education and labor force experience are attenuated somewhat in Model V, they remain negative and significant. After controlling for these various predictors of poverty, only non-adjacent nonmetro household heads continue to have a higher likelihood of poverty than their counterparts in central counties. In sum, these multivariate results confirm the importance of investments in human capital in predicting the likelihood that household heads and their families would be poor. However, controls for differences in human capital attainment were unable to completely eliminate the residential variation in the likelihood of being poor.

Gender-Specific Models of Poverty

The extremely high rates of poverty among households headed by women in both metro and nonmetro areas (McLaughlin and Sachs 1988) led us to examine the effects of human capital on the likelihood of poverty for female-headed and male-headed households separately. Prior research has clearly documented the disadvantaged position of women in the labor force, in particular the lower returns to human capital and work experience that employed women receive (McLaughlin and Perman 1991; O'Neill 1985; Tickamyer and Bokemeier 1988; Tienda et al. 1987). This is confounded by the less continuous labor force participation of women generally, and that many women who head households may have only recently re-entered the work force.

The models estimated separately by gender appear in Table 6.5. In this comparison of the two models, we first discuss those geographic and human capital coefficients that are significantly different statistically in the men's and women's models. We then point out those related to residence and human capital that differ in significance in predicting poverty status in the models. Among the human capital and residence coefficients, only one comparison was significantly different from a statistical standpoint for male-and female-headed households. Holding a college degree decreased the likelihood of poverty more in female- than male-headed households. This reflects both the relative advantage a college degree provides women heading households, but also shows the relative economic well-being of households headed by men. None of the coefficients for the effects of residence were statistically different in the men's and women's models. Equally important for our purposes are the differences in the significance of human capital and geographic residence in the two models. Both education and labor force attachment reduced poverty risks among male and female heads. However, among the latter, with age and proportion of adult years worked controlled, total years of labor force experience had a small, but positive, effect on the probability of poverty. Also, the results suggest that the economic detriment to living in nonmetro areas was stronger among female heads and remained after the full model had been estimated. All of the coefficients for residence were insignificant in the male-headed household model.

Explaining Educational Attainment

Many assume that, to a significant degree, poverty is transferred across generations and that background socioeconomic status is a critical determinant of poverty. In the development of the multivariate models of

TABLE 6.5. Logistic Regression Models of Poverty for Male and Female Household Heads.

	Male Heads		Female Heads	
	B	ΔP^b	B	ΔP
Residence				
Central Counties	-	-	-	-
Other Metro	.067[c]	.006	-.256[c]	-.050
Nonmetro Adjacent	.252[c]	.023	.761	.176
Non Adjacent Nonmetro	.383[c]	.037	.747	.173
Education				
Less than High School	-	-	-	-
High School	-.745	-.045	-.704	-.122
High School Plus	-.977	-.054	-.982	-.157
Some College	-1.062	-.057	-.725	-.125
College Degree	-2.139	-.078	-3.265[d]	-.275
Age	-.039	-.003	-.057	-.012
Labor Force Experience				
Total Full-time Years	.017[c]	.001	.065	.014
Proportion Full-time Years	-1.679	-.072	-3.238	-.274
Non-white	.764	.085	1.325[d]	.316
Parent's Education				
Father High School Grad	-.665	-.042	.376[c,d]	.083
Mother High School Grad	-.157[c]	-.012	-.312[c]	-.060
Origin Residence				
City	-	-	-	-
Town-Suburb	-.030[c]	-.002	.569[d]	.129
Farm-Rural	.495	.050	.495[c]	.111
Presence of Children				
Age 1 - 2	.953	.114	.653[c]	.150
Age 3 - 5	.715	.078	.629	.144
Age 6 - 18	.823	.094	1.106	.262
Marital Status				
Never Married	-	-	-	-
Married	-1.553	-.070	.009[c]	.002
No Longer Married	-.675	-.042	.366[c,d]	.081
Union Member	-1.144	-.059	-1.422	-.200
Work Disability	.581	.060	.995	.235
Worked in 1987	-1.622	-.071	-2.115	-.243
Southern Residence	.433	.042	.458	.102
Constant	2.764		2.773	
-2 Log Likelihood	1619.4		782.1	
DF	3810		1217	

Source: 1988 Wave of the Panel Study of Income Dynamics.

[a]Heads are defined as poor if their total family income is less than 150% of the official poverty threshold.

[b]Logistic regression converted to reflect the effect of a unit change in the independent variables on the probability of poverty (see Peterson 1985).

[c]Coefficient *not* significant at .05 (two-tailed).

[d]Difference between male and female coefficients significantly different at .05.

poverty presented above, in addition to parental education and rural origins, we tested other background variables. Simple correlations (not shown) revealed that poverty rates were higher among heads who grew up (1) in a poor family, (2) in a nonmetro county, and (3) with many siblings. While none of these variables achieved significance in the full poverty model, it is especially noteworthy that growing up poor had no direct effect. This suggests that while background status is important, its effects are largely indirect.

For our purposes, an important indirect effect is via educational attainment. Indeed, it is a fundamental assumption of programs, such as Head Start, that the cycle of poverty can be weakened by breaking down the barriers faced by disadvantaged youth in the attainment of an adequate education. While not discounting the important effect of labor force experience on poverty, we concentrate on education for two reasons. First, it is more amenable to policy intervention. Second, in view of nonmetro disadvantages in educational attainment, it may represent a way to narrow geographic differences in poverty risks.

Table 6.6 presents logistic regression models of high school completion. Because education increases across birth cohorts, all of the models control for age, which has the expected negative effects. Model I also shows a strong effect of socioeconomic origins. Compared to those who report having grown up in a family that was economically well-off, those who grew up poor have high school graduation rates that are twenty percentage points lower. Those of average economic origins do not differ from those well-off in this regard.

We also are interested in the effects of rural origins. Model II indicates that, after controlling for age, those who grew up in a rural area (farm, rural, open country) were significantly less likely to have completed high school than those from the city. Those of suburban origins did not differ significantly from their city-raised counterparts. This model also shows that, net of rural origins, those who grew up in a nonmetro county were less likely to have finished high school.

The latter result could simply reflect the fact that those of rural origins are more likely to have grown up poor, as suggested by the positive bivariate correlation between these two variables (not shown). However, Model III shows that both economic and geographic origins have significant and independent effects on high school completion, suggesting that something other than differences in economic well-being explain lower rates of high school completion in nonmetro areas. Another possible explanation for the lower educational achievement among those with rural origins is that formal education is simply less highly valued in rural areas and that this affects the educational aspirations of rural youth. However,

TABLE 6.6. Logistic Regression Models of High School Completion

	Model I		Model II		Model III		Model IV	
	B	ΔP[a]	B	ΔP	B	ΔP	B	ΔP
Age	-.029	-.005	-.037	-.006	-.027	-.004	-.023	-.004
Origin Status								
Well Off	—	—	—	—	—	—	—	—
Average	.136[b]	.021	—	—	.163[b]	.025	.258	.038
Below Average	-.999	-.204	—	—	-.927	-.187	-.401	-.072
Origin Residence								
City			—	—	—	—	—	—
Town - Suburb			-.100[b]	-.016	-.092[b]	.015	-.027[b]	-.004
Farm - Rural			-.440	-.080	-.332	.058	-.073[b]	-.012
Nonmetro			-.353	-.062	-.307	-.054	-.171	-.029
Other Background Variables								
Nonwhite							-.314	-.055
Father High School Grad							.728	.092
Mother High School Grad							.506	.069
Head's Total Siblings							-.125	-.021
Constant	2.953		3.247		3.091		2.552	
-2 Log Likelihood	4861.5		5013.5		4820.4		4473.2	
DF	5204		5203		5201		5197	

Source: 1988 Wave of the Panel Study of Income Dynamics.

[a]Logistic regression coefficients converted to reflect the effect of a unit change in the independent variables on the probability of high school graduation.

[b]Coefficient *not* significant at .05 (two-tailed).

existing evidence suggests that, if anything, rural people place a higher value on education than their urban counterparts (Lowe and Pinhey 1980).

Model IV includes other important background variables. They indicate that nonwhites and those with more siblings, were less likely to have completed high school, while those with parents who were high school graduates themselves, were more likely to have achieved at least this level of education. The inclusion of these variables greatly reduces the effects of rural, nonmetro, and poverty origins.

Summary and Discussion

Poverty in the United States has proven to be an intractable social problem. It also is one that, popular perception notwithstanding, is more prevalent in nonmetro than metro areas. We have addressed this issue by providing an analysis of the links between poverty and human capital. In this section, we briefly review our findings and discuss their implications for anti-poverty policy.

Ever since the War on Poverty began in the 1960s, an important ameliorative approach has been to increase worker employability and productivity via human capital enhancement (Sawhill 1988). Our analysis indicates that this approach is not without empirical foundation since the effects of human capital on poverty are substantial. We have shown that higher levels of education and more labor force experience significantly and independently reduce the likelihood of poverty, even after controlling for a wide range of other salient factors.

Our results also have implications for addressing the geographic imbalance in poverty risks. Compared to residents of metro counties, we document substantial disadvantages in educational attainment among nonmetro non-adjacent heads of households, disadvantages which partially account for their greater poverty rates. Of course, our cross-sectional results are not necessarily a prediction of what will happen in the future; and these findings would be less alarming if there were evidence of declining nonmetro-metro differences in educational attainment. Unfortunately, if anything, the opposite is true. Recent research is suggestive of persistently higher high school dropout rates in nonmetro than metro areas (Swaim and Teixeira 1991) and of an increasing metro/nonmetro disparity in average educational levels (McGranahan and Ghelfi 1991).

To increase educational attainment among nonmetro youth we suggest the following. Head Start, and other programs that seek to better prepare disadvantaged youth for school should be expanded, especially in areas of high nonmetro poverty concentration. Research shows that Head Start has positive effects on school performance, high school graduation rates, and ultimate employability (Levitan 1990). Such programs are especially important in view of the effects of social background on educational attainment which we documented here. They can help to break the intergenerational cycle of poverty. If Head Start were made an entitlement program, rural children would disproportionately benefit since there are fewer alternatives to Head Start in rural areas (Sherman 1992).

For those students already in school, states need to become more attentive to differences across nonmetro and metro school districts in their ability to fund quality education (Hobbs 1991). Institutional mechanisms need to be developed to channel state and federal funds toward disadvantaged districts in both nonmetro and metro areas. Funding formulae need to be attentive to differential costs across areas, for example, the higher costs of transportation in rural areas (Sherman 1992). Some of these monies could be set aside as a source of funding for innovative programs that seek to keep nonmetro children from dropping out of school. Other measures could be taken to improve the quality of rural teachers, for example, offering college loan forgiveness to promising young teachers who agree to settle in rural areas (Sherman 1992). In general, programs that seek to increase the educational attainment of economically disadvantaged students would be especially helpful in nonmetro America, since poverty rates are higher there.

We stress that there are reasons to suspect that such initiatives will only be modestly successful in reducing poverty in nonmetro America. This is because enhancing the skills of low-income workers does little to increase the availability of jobs which demand those skills and which pay a living wage. Indeed, there is ample evidence that the problem of working poverty is particularly endemic to nonmetro areas (Lichter 1989a; 1989b; Lichter and Costanzo 1987; Shapiro 1989). This is consistent with our own finding that the poor in nonmetro non-adjacent counties have greater labor force experience and attachment than their counterparts elsewhere—especially those in central counties (Table 6.1), and that the nonmetro advantage in this regard is keeping nonmetro residents from being even poorer (Table 6.4). The implication is that an anti-poverty strategy that emphasizes human capital enhancement may be particularly ill-suited in nonmetro areas. We concur with Janet Fitchen (1981:214), who calls for the dispelling of the myth that "education is *the* key to escaping poverty," and that schools are "societal panaceas, magic carpets out of poverty" (emphasis in original). In short, greater attention must be paid to increasing the demand for labor of disadvantaged adults.

Apropos of this, some call for increased educational attainment in nonmetro areas, not so much as a way to combat poverty among individuals, but to increase the aggregate human capital endowment of nonmetro places. The assumption is that this will better situate nonmetro areas in the competition for new industries. To the extent that resulting economic development provides good jobs for otherwise poor nonmetro adults, this strategy is sound. It makes particularly good sense if predictions of skyrocketing demand for skilled labor hold true (Johnston and Packer 1987). Unfortunately, Teixeira and Mishel (1991) offer evidence that no such jump in the demand for labor is in the offing. In fact, they predict stagnant demand for skilled workers in nonmetro areas during the 1990s. If this more pessimistic scenario obtains, then efforts to increase the education and training of nonmetro workers will only serve to reshuffle the queue of workers at the bottom of the occupational distribution (Tomaskovic-Devey 1987), resulting in little real progress in the battle against poverty. As always, nonmetro areas that educate their youth, but do not or cannot provide employment opportunities comparable to those in metro areas, run the risk of losing those they have educated through out-migration. As an individual-level strategy to escape poverty, education coupled with migration can be quite effective.

The fact is that societal investments in the human capital endowments of disadvantaged populations will do little good without commensurate concern for generating a demand for their labor through economic development. Perhaps this grim reality explains why, compared to means-tested income transfer programs (e.g., Aid to Families with Dependent Children), human capital enhancement programs have historically received far less funding (Burtless 1986).

On the bright side, however, Hobbs in chapter 12 of this volume notes that the school system, especially in nonmetro communities, may offer unrecognized opportunities for economic development. Innovative experiential learning programs—for example, school-business partnerships (Sherman 1992)—which get nonmetro high school students more intimately involved with their own community's development efforts—may generate new ideas, create stronger community bonds, and keep some of the best and brightest from leaving. This could help foment communication among community leaders and engender more coordinated and enlightened economic development strategies.

Notes

1. Respectively, the nonmetro and central city percent in poverty are 12.6 and 9.3 for non-Hispanic whites, 40.0 and 33.3 for African Americans, 34.5 and 29.4 for Hispanics, and 30.3 and 15.7 for Native Americans.

2. Throughout the analysis, we use the family weight, which we have divided by the mean family weight, to yield a weighted sample N approximately equal to the unweighted PSID sample size. This provides more conservative and realistic estimates of statistical significance.

3. We do not, therefore, define poverty using the special income to needs ratios provided in the PSID.

4. The adjustment for elderly heads (those 65 or more) is unnecessary since our analysis is restricted to those aged 25 to 64.

References

Auletta, Ken. 1982. *The Underclass*. New York, NY: Random House.

Bane, Mary Jo, and David T. Ellwood. 1986. "Slipping into and out of poverty: The dynamics of spells." *Journal of Human Resources* 21: 1-23.

Bibb, Robert, and William H. Form. 1977. "The effects of industrial, occupational, and sex stratification on wages in blue collar markets." *Social Forces* 55:974-99.

Blau, Peter, and Otis Dudley Duncan. 1967. *The American Occupational Structure*. New York: John Wiley and Sons.

Blaug, Mark. 1976. "The empirical status of human capital theory: A slightly jaundiced survey." *Journal of Economic Literature* 14 (Sept.): 827-55.

Bowles, Samuel, and Herbert Gintis. 1975. "The problem with human capital theory—A Marxian critique." *American Economic Review* 65 (2): 74-82.

Burtless, Gary. 1986. "Public spending for the poor: Trends, prospects, and economic limits." Pp. 18-49 in Sheldon H. Danziger and Daniel H. Weinberg, *Fighting Poverty: What Works and What Doesn't*. Cambridge, MA: Harvard University Press.

Danziger, Sheldon H., and Daniel H. Weinberg. 1986. *Fighting Poverty: What Works and What Doesn't*. Cambridge, MA: Harvard University Press.

Deavers, Kenneth L., and Robert A. Hoppe. 1992. "Overview of the rural poor in the 1980s." Pp. 3-20 in Cynthia M. Duncan (ed.), *Rural Poverty in America*. New York, NY: Auburn House.

Duncan, Greg J., and Saul D. Hoffman. 1979. "On-the-job training and earnings differences by race and sex." *Review of Economics and Statistics* 61 (4): 594-603.

Ehrenberg, Ronald G., and Robert S. Smith. 1982. *Modern Labor Economics: Theory and Public Policy*. Glenville, IL: Scott, Foresman and Company.

Erickson, Rodney A. 1981. "Corporations, branch plants, and employment stability in nonmetropolitan areas." Pp. 135-53 in John Rees, Geoffrey J.D. Hewings, and Howard A. Stafford (eds.), *Industrial Location and Regional Systems: Spatial Organization in the Economic Sector*. Brooklyn, NY: Bergin.

Fitchen, Janet M. 1981. *Poverty in Rural America: A Case Study*. Boulder, CO: Westview Press.

Fuguitt, Glenn V., David L. Brown, and Calvin L. Beale. 1989. *Rural and Small Town America*. New York, NY: Russell Sage Foundation.

Granovetter, Mark. 1981. "Toward a sociological theory of income differences." Pp. 11-47 in Ivar Berg (ed.), *Sociological Perspectives on Labor Markets*. New York, NY: Academic Press.

Hobbs, Daryl. 1991. "Rural education." Pp. 151-65 in Cornelia B. Flora and James A. Christenson (eds.), *Rural Policies for the 1990s*. Boulder, CO: Westview Press.

Jensen, Leif, and Marta Tienda. 1989. "Nonmetropolitan minority families in the

United States: Trends in racial and ethnic economic stratification, 1959-1986." *Rural Sociology* 54 (4): 509-32.

Johnston, W. B., and A. E. Packer. 1987. *Workforce 2000: Work and Workers for the 21st Century*. Indianapolis, IN: Hudson Institute.

Kalleberg, Arne L., and Aage B. Sorenson. 1979. "The sociology of labor markets." Pp. 351-79 in A. Inkeles et al. (eds.), *Annual Review of Sociology, 1979*. Palo Alto, CA: Annual Reviews.

LeClere, Felicia B., and Diane K. McLaughlin. 1988. "Educational attainment: Toward a better understanding of the rural-urban gap." Paper presented at the Rural Sociological Society Annual Meetings, Athens, GA (August).

Levitan, Sar A. 1990. *Programs in Aid of the Poor*, Sixth Edition. Baltimore, MD: Johns Hopkins University Press.

Lichter, Daniel T. 1989a. "Race, employment hardship, and inequality in the American nonmetropolitan south." *American Sociological Review* 54: 436-46.

Lichter, Daniel T. 1989b. "The underemployment of American rural women: Prevalence, trends, and spatial inequality." *The Journal of Rural Studies* 5: 199-208.

Lichter, Daniel T., Lionel J. Beaulieu, Jill L. Findeis, and Ruy Teixeira. 1993. "Human capital, labor supply, and poverty in rural America." Rural Sociological Society, Presidential Task Force on Persistent Rural Poverty, *Persistent Rural Poverty*. Boulder, CO: Westview Press.

Lichter, Daniel T., and Janice Costanzo. 1987. "Nonmetropolitan underemployment and labor force composition." *Rural Sociology* 52: 329-44.

Lowe, George D., and Thomas K. Pinhey. 1980. "Do rural people place a lower value on formal education?: New evidence from national surveys." *Rural Sociology* 45 (2): 325-31.

McGranahan, David A. 1991. "Introduction." Pp. 1-12 in *Education and Rural Economic Development*. Agriculture and Rural Economy Division, Economic Research Service, USDA. ERS Staff Report No. AGES 9153.

McGranahan, David A., and Linda Ghelfi. 1991. "The education crisis and rural stagnation in the 1980's." Pp. 40-92 in *Education and Rural Economic Development*. Agriculture and Rural Economy Division, Economic Research Service, USDA. ERS Staff Report No. AGES 9153.

McLaughlin, Diane K., and Lauri Perman. 1991a. "Returns vs. endowments in the earnings attainment process for metropolitan and nonmetropolitan men and women." *Rural Sociology* 56 (3): 339-65.

McLaughlin, Diane K., and Lauri Perman. 1991b. "The role of returns versus endowments in explaining the gender earnings gap in nonmetropolitan America." Paper presented at the Rural Sociological Society Annual Meetings, Columbus, OH (August).

McLaughlin, Diane K., and Carolyn Sachs. 1988. "Poverty in female-headed households: Residential differences." *Rural Sociology* 53 (3): 287-306.

O'Hare, William P. 1988. "The rise of poverty in rural America." *Population Trends and Public Policy* 15 (July): 1-16.

O'Neill, June. 1985. "The trend in the male-female wage gap in the United States." *Journal of Labor Economics* 3: S91-S116.

Peterson, Trond. 1985. "A comment on presenting results from logit and probit models," *American Sociological Review* 50 (1):130-31.

Ruggles, Patricia. 1990. *Drawing the Line: Alternative Poverty Measures and Their Implications for Public Policy.* Washington, DC: The Urban Institute Press.

Sawhill, Isabel V. 1988. "Poverty in the U.S.: Why is it so persistent?" *Journal of Economic Literature* 26: 1073-119.

Schiller, Bradley R. 1980. *The Economics of Poverty and Discrimination.* Third Edition. Englewood Cliffs, NJ: Prentice-Hall.

Sewell, William H., Archibald O. Haller, and George W. Ohlendorf. 1970. "The educational and early occupational status attainment process: Replication and revision." *American Sociological Review* 35 (December): 1014-27.

Shapiro, Isaac. 1989. *Laboring for Less: Working but Poor in Rural America.* Washington, DC: Center for Budget and Policy Priorities.

Sherman, Arloc. 1992. *Falling by the Wayside: Children in Rural America.* Washington, DC: Children's Defense Fund.

Survey Research Center. 1984. *User Guide: Panel Study of Income Dynamics.* University of Michigan: ICPSR.

Swaim, Paul L., and Ruy A. Teixeira. 1991. "Education and training policy: Skill upgrading options for the rural workforce." Pp. 122-62 in *Education and Rural Economic Development.* Agriculture and Rural Economy Division, Economic Research Service, USDA. ERS Staff Report No. AGES 9153.

Swanson, Linda L., and Margaret A. Butler. 1988. "Human resource based of rural economies." Pp. 159-80 in *Rural Economic Development in the 1980's: Prospects for the Future.* Agriculture and Rural Economy Economic Research Service, USDA Rural Development Research Report No. 69.

Teixeira, Ruy A., and Lawrence Mishel. 1991. "Upgrading workers' skills not sufficient to jump-start rural economy." *Rural Development Perspectives* 7 (3):19-24.

Thurow, Lester C. 1969. *Poverty and Discrimination.* Washington, DC: The Brookings Institution.

Tickamyer, Ann, and Janet Bokemeier. 1988. "Sex differences in labor market experiences." *Rural Sociology* 53: 166-89.

Tienda, Marta, Shelley A. Smith, and Vilma Ortiz. 1987. "Industrial restructuring, gender segregation, and sex differences in earnings." *American Sociological Review* 52: 195-210.

Tomaskovic-Devey, Donald. 1987. "Labor markets, industrial structure, and poverty: A theoretical discussion and empirical example." *Rural Sociology* 52 (1): 56-74.

Tussing, A. Dale. 1975. *Poverty in a Dual Economy.* New York, NY: St. Martin's Press.

U.S. Census Bureau. 1989. *Money Income and Poverty Status in the United States: 1988.* Current Population Reports, Series P-60, No. 166. Washington, DC: U.S. Government Printing Office.

Wilson, William J. 1987. *The Truly Disadvantaged.* Chicago: University of Chicago Press.

7

The Educational Attainments of American Indians[1]

C. Matthew Snipp

In 1990, the U.S. Bureau of the Census enumerated 1.96 million American Indians. As a group, American Indians amount to barely one-half of one percent of the total U.S. population. They are too few in number to swing national elections or affect national economic indicators. So one may wonder why American Indian education should merit much attention. There are, in fact, a number of compelling reasons why the education of American Indians is a significant social issue.

Throughout this century, while millions of Americans of European descent enjoyed the material benefits of an expanding urban industrial economy, American Indians remained in the peripheral backwaters of American society; often placed in remote, desolate areas following the cessation of conflicts with Euro-Americans. In 1930, when over half of American society were city dwellers, less than 10 percent of American Indians lived outside of rural areas (Snipp 1989). Today, they are still this nation's most rural minority.

The physical, social, and cultural isolation of American Indians from the rest of the nation is further reflected in their economic position. This was first documented in the historic Meriam Report (Institute for Government Research 1928) which described the unparalleled poverty and economic hardship among American Indians. Since this report's publication, studies have shown repeatedly that American Indians are the poorest of America's poor. They have been among the least educated, least employed, poorest, worst housed, most ill-fed, and least healthy groups in American society throughout most of this century (Levitan and Hetrick 1971; Levitan and Johnston 1975; Snipp 1989; Sorkin 1971).

That American Indians occupy the very lowest rung of the national socioeconomic hierarchy should be reason alone to make them the subject of serious sociological attention. Their experiences highlight unmet needs and urgent problems for policy makers and others concerned with economic well-being in American society. And for American Indians in particular, the harsh poverty and economic hardship characteristic of reservation life challenges American ideals about equality of opportunity and economic fairness.

Education, of course, has an unsurpassed role in shaping economic opportunities, so much so that the two are often perceived as synonymous. In the rhetoric of American ideals, education is the "great equalizer" that makes economic opportunities available to those of otherwise disadvantaged social origins. If education is among the most important vehicles of upward social mobility, then the economic position of American Indians is hardly surprising. Their education levels are among the lowest for any group in America (Snipp 1989).

Low levels of American Indian educational attainment have persisted in the face of a sizable bureaucracy. An entire branch of the Bureau of Indian Affairs is devoted to education (Taylor 1984) and the Department of Interior is currently considering whether to establish a separate "Bureau of Indian Education." There is also an Office of Indian Education in the Department of Education, and numerous programs in other federal agencies relevant to Indian education. In the Spring of 1991, the White House organized a major conference on Indian education. A recent estimate of the total annual federal outlays for programs directly and indirectly related to Indian education is not readily available but undoubtedly would be in the tens of millions of dollars.

The persistence of educational disadvantages in the face of this redoubtable institutional apparatus has many complicated explanations (AIPRC 1976), none of which can be fully described here. Certainly there is a history of institutional mismanagement (GAO 1978). However, another perhaps more important factor can be traced to the underlying purpose of education for American Indians.

Since the earliest days of contact with American Indians, Europeans have used pedagogy as a device for indoctrinating, "civilizing," and culturally subjugating American Indians in the guise of education (AIPRC 1976; Szasz 1977). Christian missionaries commonly established schools for the education and "civilization" of Indian children (Pearce 1965). As one of its missions, the original charter of Harvard University, one of America's oldest institutions of higher learning, provided for the education of American Indians. John Ross, the great nineteenth century chief of the Cherokees, attended a private academy in Tennessee. One of the first public school systems established west of the Mississippi river was not created to teach the children of white settlers. It was established by the Cherokee tribe in eastern Oklahoma after the tribe was relocated from their homes east of the Mississippi (Foreman 1934).

In the late nineteenth century, reformers advocated education as a way of hastening the cultural assimilation of American Indians into American society. These reformers hoped that by removing Indians from their home environments, they could be taught to give up their traditional culture and adopt the ways of white society (Hoxie 1984; Utley 1984). To carry out this policy, schools such as the Hampton Institute[2] in Virginia and Carlisle[3] in Pennsylvania were established. Indian students from areas across the United States were more or less forcibly recruited and brought to these schools by train (Utley 1984).

In the wake of the late nineteenth century reforms that established Hampton and Carlisle, the Bureau of Indian Affairs (BIA) also developed an extensive network of boarding schools for Indian youth. First allocated in 1877, appropriations for Indian schools initially supported 150 schools for Indian students, including 48 boarding facilities. By 1910, BIA was spending nearly $3.8 million to support 389 Indian schools, of which 106 were boarding schools with almost 20,000 students in residence—about 61 percent of all students in Indian schools (U.S. Bureau of Census 1915).

Cultural assimilation was the primary mission of these schools. In anticipation of them, the 1869 report of the Board of Indian Commissioners commented that:

> *By educating the children of these tribes in the English language these differences would have disappeared and civilization would have followed at once. Nothing then would have been left but the antipathy of race, and that, too is always softened in the beams of a higher civilization* (U.S. Bureau of the Census 1915:195).

The curricula of BIA schools were mostly confined to teaching basic literacy and vocational skills, and to cultural indoctrination. Some schools harshly punished students for speaking their native language and absolutely forbade other cultural practices such as participating in traditional ceremonies or using herbal remedies (Fuchs and Havighurst 1972; Szasz 1977).

For most of this century, for example, BIA boarding schools prohibited with punishments the practice of Indian culture, use of native language, and native dress. BIA curricula were entirely devoid of references to American Indian culture and lifestyles. Furthermore, the curricula offered little academic preparation and were heavily devoted to vocational training (Fuchs and Havighurst 1972: Szasz 1974).

In the 1950s and 1960s, the federal government absolved its obligations to American Indians in a series of policies known as Termination (Fixico

1986). One thrust of these policies involved the physical relocation of American Indians from rural reservations to pre-selected urban centers. Once settled there, Indians were given education and training to once again promote their assimilation into Euro-American urban society and the industrial labor force.

The termination and relocation programs (actually named "Employment Assistance") were attacked by many quarters (AIPRC 1976; Burt 1982; Fixico 1986; O'Brien 1989). Former supporters charged that it had failed to accomplish its aim of assimilating the Indians. Some critics pointed to the ineffectiveness of the program in improving standards of living for American Indians. Later studies corroborated these complaints by showing that there are few benefits from rural-urban migration for American Indians: poor, unemployed reservation Indians typically relocate to become poor, unemployed city dwellers (Gundlach and Roberts 1978; Snipp and Sandefur 1988). Other critics pointed to the "brain drain" caused by relocation programs. Very often, the best and the brightest were recruited for relocation to urban areas where they would have more opportunities for education and employment (Clinton et al. 1975).

The decade of the 1970s was an especially important period in the history of Indian education as Indian educators gradually gained more control over the curriculum, policies, and administration. During this time, developments such as the Indian Self-Determination and Educational Assistance Act of 1975 (Public Law 93-368), growing numbers of Indian school boards, tribally operated schools, institutions such as Navajo Community College and D-Q University, and a host of alternative schools in urban and reservation areas marked a first time large-scale involvement of Indian people in educational programs.

The 1970s also were important because during this decade, numerous public policies attempted to promote racial and ethnic minority education enhancements. Public schools and institutions of higher education made concerted efforts to increase minority graduates by sponsoring programs such as Upward Bound. In the context of public policy initiatives promoting Indian education, data from the 1980 Census are especially meaningful for judging the impact of these measures on the Indian population.[4]

Eventually, the programs of termination and relocation, and Euro-American dominated educational programs for American Indians, were formally repudiated with the passage of the American Indian Self-Determination and Educational Assistance Act of 1975. This act officially acknowledged the end of federal efforts to force cultural assimilation upon American Indians, and paved the way for greater participation by American Indians in their educational institutions. Despite the far-reaching implications of this legislation, the educational handicaps of American Indians are daunting.

American Indian educators working on reservations face particularly difficult obstacles. Reservation schools are often situated in remote and inaccessible places, thus, complicating recruiting and retaining teachers. This also discourages students' regular attendance, especially during the winter when weather makes travel hazardous, if not impossible. Furthermore, the limited resources of tribal governments and rural school districts are manifest in substandard school facilities, inadequate supplies, and outdated instructional material. These and numerous other factors play a role in limiting the educational opportunities for American Indians on reservations.

Compared with their reservation peers, urban Indian youth may have significantly better educational experiences. Yet, urban Indians are also confronted by the problems plaguing inner-city schools, in which there may be little awareness or sensitivity to American Indian student concerns. Thus, whether urban American Indians are more successful in school than their reservation counterparts is an empirical question.

The next section charts the educational status of American Indians. This means examining Indian educational attainments relative to other racial groups, and in relation to rural-urban differences.[5] This information is meant to show the extent to which the education of American Indians lags behind other groups, and the extent to which the education of rural, primarily reservation Indians lags behind their urban counterparts. Among the conclusions that can be drawn from these comparisons is that American Indians have fared poorly in obtaining post-secondary schooling. Consequently, this discussion also reviews the situation of American Indians in higher education. The chapter concludes with a brief discussion of the public policy implications of our findings.

Distribution of the American Indian Population

Because some of the information in this chapter is shown separately for American Indians living in metropolitan areas and on reservations, it will be useful to begin by showing the extent to which Indians are concentrated in these areas. Unlike most other Americans, Indians are often situated outside cities and their suburbs. As recently as 1980, less than half resided in metropolitan areas (Snipp 1989). In contrast, about 81 percent of blacks and 73 percent of whites were living in metropolitan localities.

The urban American Indian population is concentrated in a relatively small number of cities. About one-half of urban American Indians reside in 17 cities (shown in Table 7.1), each of which has 10,000 or more Indians. The largest urban Indian population is in southern California, numbering over 91,000 in 1980. Except for New York, large urban Indian populations are found only in cities of the western U.S., with Chicago and Detroit being the most eastern. One reason, among many, why these cities have large American Indian populations is that they are the former relocation centers. Between 1952 and 1972, eight of the 17 cities shown in Table 7.1 served as relocation centers for programs in which over 100,000 American Indians participated (Fixico 1986; Sorkin 1978).[6]

The majority of American Indians reside in "Indian Country"—on or near reservations, trust lands, and the former Indian territory of Oklahoma.[7] In 1980, approximately 340,000 American Indians were living on reservations and another 30,000 occupied special tribal trust lands. Figure 7.1 shows the distribution of the American Indian population by the different places of residence.

To complement these data, Map 1 shows the location of American Indian reservations across the nation. Although there are 278 federal and state reservations located throughout the U.S. (192 in the west), 16 reservations represent 57 percent of the reservation Indian population. The Navajo

TABLE 7.1. Standard Metropolitan Statistical Areas (SMSAs) with 10,000 or more American Indians, 1980.

SMSA	1980
Los Angeles, Long Beach CA	47,234
Tulsa, OK	38,463
Phoenix, AZ	27,788
Oklahoma City, OK	24,695
Albuquerque, MN	20,721
San Francisco, Oakland, CA	17,546
Riverside, San Bernadino, Ontario, CA	17,107
Minneapolis, St. Paul, MN	15,831
Seattle, Everett, WA	15,162
Tucson, AZ	14,880
San Diego, CA	14,355
New York, NY	13,440
Anaheim, Santa Ana, Garden Grove, CA	12,782
Detroit, MI	12,372
Dallas, Ft. Worth, TX	11,076
Sacramento, CA	10,944
Chicago, IL	10,415
Total in SMSAs	324,811

Percent of Total U.S. Indian Population   23.8

Source: U.S. Bureau of the Census, General Population Characteristics, U.S. Summary, 1980.

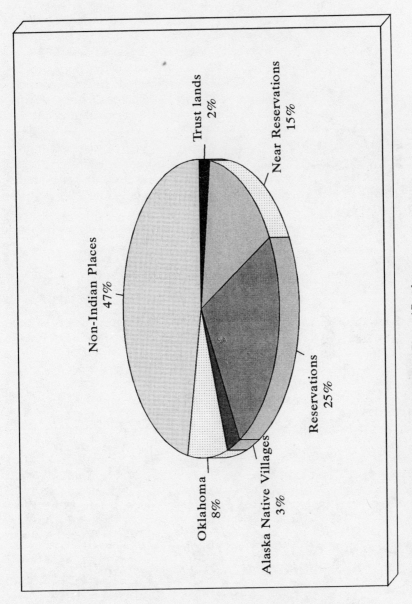

Trust lands
2%

Near Reservations
15%

Non-Indian Places
47%

Reservations
25%

Oklahoma
8%

Alaska Native Villages
3%

FIGURE 7.1 Distribution of American Indians by Place of Residence.

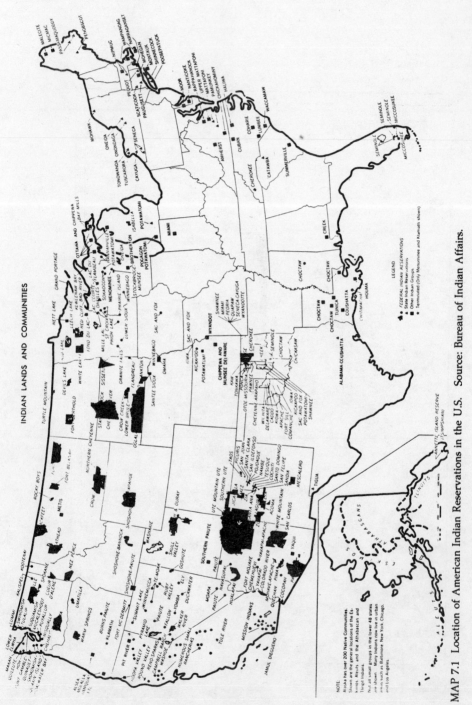

MAP 7.1 Location of American Indian Reservations in the U.S.   Source: Bureau of Indian Affairs.

reservation overlapping the Four Corners region of northeastern Arizona is clearly the largest in numbers and size. Over 100,000 Navajo occupy a territory approximately the size of West Virginia. Trailing far behind, but second in size, is the Pine Ridge reservation in South Dakota with a population of approximately 12,000 in 1980. All of these reservations, except the Navajo, involve relatively small numbers of people, especially compared to urban locations.

American Indians and Other Americans

To show the educational achievements of American Indians in relation to those of other Americans, Table 7.2 shows the school achievements of blacks, whites, and American Indians for the years of 1970 and 1980. By every measure, except median education in 1980, blacks and Indians have markedly lower levels of education than whites. In 1980, blacks, whites, and Indians had about the same levels of median education but this statistic, in relation to other indicators of educational success, is misleading because it suggests that there are few differences among these groups. In contrast, slightly over one-half of all blacks and Indians over age 25 have completed high school compared to over two-thirds of the white population who have graduated from high school. Similarly, 17 percent of the white population over age 25 have four or more years of college while the percent of blacks and Indians with a similar education is less than half of this figure.

Although Indians and blacks lag behind whites in their educational attainments, they made substantial gains in the 1970s. The largest educational gains are reflected in percentages of high school graduates for 1970 and 1980. At the beginning of the decade (i.e., 1970), American Indians were

TABLE 7.2 Educational Characteristics of American Indians, Blacks, and Whites, Persons Age 25 and Older 1970 and 1980.

	American Indian		Blacks		Whites	
	1970	1980	1970	1980	1970	1980
Percent with less than a sixth grade education	7.7	8.4	14.8	8.2	4.5	2.6
Percent with a twelfth grade education	22.0	55.5	31.4	51.2	54.5	66.6
Percent with four or more years of college	3.8	7.7	4.4	8.4	11.3	17.1
Median Education (years)	9.8	12.2	9.8	12.0	12.1	12.5

Source: Snipp (1989)

far behind blacks in terms of high school graduation. In the years following, they staged a remarkable increase in high school graduates, growing
from 22 percent in 1970 to 56 percent in 1980. This growth has meant that
the percent of high school graduates among American Indians is now
slightly higher than that of blacks. As a milestone, the 1970s was a decade
in which a majority of Indians and blacks attained a high school diploma,
and this is further evidenced in almost identical increases in median education.

The remarkable improvements in American Indian educational levels
between 1970 and 1980 should be viewed in light of two qualifications. One
is that shifting patterns of ethnic identification between 1970 and 1980 may
have altered to some unknown extent the composition of the Indian
population (Snipp 1989). A large number of individuals who identified
themselves as American Indian in 1980 did not identify themselves as such
in 1970. If this resulted in an influx of well-educated persons newly
identifying themselves as American Indian, it would artificially raise
educational levels. Whether this is actually the case is impossible to ascertain because the characteristics of persons who have changed their ethnic
identity cannot be determined.

Another qualification is that the 1980 census instructed persons with a
GED certificate to report their education as twelve years of completed
schooling. Programs to help students obtain GEDs became widespread in
the 1970s. Assuming that American Indians participated heavily in these
programs, the increase in Indian education may reflect a larger number of
GEDs more than it does a real increase in the number of school years
completed.

Despite increases in secondary schooling, growing numbers of high
school graduates have not produced significant increases in college
graduates for Indians or blacks. The percent of Indians and blacks with four
or more years of post-secondary education doubled between 1970 and 1980
but the gap between these groups and the white population increased
slightly. For example, the percentage difference between whites and
American Indians completing four years or more of college was 9.4 points
in 1980 compared to a gap of 7.5 points in 1970. In other words, the percent
of the American Indian population with advanced education grew during
the 1970s but it expanded less than the percent of the white population
pursuing college educations. In view of the numerous programs designed
to promote college attendance by minority students, these data may be
disappointing. However, without such programs, it is conceivable that the
gap between whites and American Indians (and blacks) might be much
larger.

Another way of looking at this problem is simply to compute the crude
multiplier by which increases in secondary school completion are con-

verted into post-secondary education.[8] Among whites, a 14.3 percent increase in high school graduates produced a 5.8 percent rise in four year college attendance, yielding a multiplier of .406. For whites, this means that each one percent increase in high school graduates results in an increase of .406 percent in persons with four or more years of college. Alternatively, for every 100 additional whites graduating from high school, an additional 41 will achieve four or more years of college. For American Indians, this multiplier is only .116 signifying that for each additional 100 Indians who finish high school, only an additional 12 will complete four or more years of college. If Indians in 1980 attended college at the same multiples as whites, 13.8 percent should have completed at least four years of post-secondary schooling. This means that six percentage points, or two-thirds of the 9.4 point deficit between whites and Indians, can be accounted for by lower rates of college attendance by American Indians.

There are many possible explanations for why American Indians have not converted their secondary schooling gains into similar gains in higher levels of education. One reason is that in spite of public policy initiatives, discrimination and other factors limit opportunities for higher education, or otherwise prevent Indian students from completing college. Admitting Indian students to college does not guarantee their retention. Another possible problem is that Indian education has traditionally emphasized short-term vocational training instead of academic studies. In the past, BIA boarding schools and other educational assistance programs heavily favored vocational training for Indian students (Fuchs and Havighurst 1972). By the same token, a baccalaureate degree in literature, political science, or other academic pursuits may have little apparent value to Indian youths making their homes on a reservation or in an inner city.

A third, and perhaps most disturbing possibility is that the universality of high school diplomas has forced Indian students to acquire this degree as a minimum requirement for entering the job market, but not for the purpose of continuing their education. The widespread availability of programs to assist Indian high school drop-outs with GED examinations also might increase the numbers of persons reporting a high school education, or its equivalent, without improving college attendance or abating the Indian high school drop-out rate.

Recall that the 1980 Census questionnaire instructed respondents with GEDs to report their schooling as 12 years. Assuming that persons with GED certificates are less likely to attend college than persons completing four years of high school, this would explain at once the striking increase in high school completion and the dismally low rates of college attendance by American Indians. Unfortunately, this matter cannot be explored further because it is impossible to distinguish in Census data persons with GEDs from those with high school diplomas.

Although national studies are not available, an educational survey of the Northern Cheyenne reservation in Montana lends support to these ideas (Ward and Wilson 1989). This study found that Northern Cheyenne are much more likely than neighboring non-Indians to have a GED. Predictably, among Northern Cheyenne, those possessing a GED were significantly less likely to attend college than those having a high school diploma.

However, the Northern Cheyenne attended college at about the same rates as local non-Indians, suggesting, perhaps, that Northern Cheyenne high school graduates attend college in numbers sufficient to compensate for those with GEDs who were less likely to attend college. Nonetheless, few Northern Cheyenne ever complete college as 81 percent of Northern Cheyenne who had ever attended college did not hold a degree. Ward and Wilson (1989) do not offer any further insights about why college completion rates are so low among American Indians. However, from personal observation and anecdotal accounts, the Northern Cheyenne are not unique—college retention for American Indian students is a serious problem across the nation and one that desperately needs careful study.

School Enrollment and Progress

Enrollment

There are indications that a relatively large number of Indian youths are curtailing their education before finishing high school. Preliminary evidence of this behavior can be seen in the age-specific rates of school enrollment among American Indian youth in Table 7.3. Not surprising, this table shows that very few children under age five are enrolled in school,

TABLE 7.3. Percent of American Indian and Alaska Native Youths, 19 Years Old and Under, Enrolled in School.

Age	Metropolitan	Reservation
Under 5	15.5	15.4
5 - 6	85.2	87.4
7 - 8	98.3	97.5
9 - 10	98.8	98.6
11 - 12	98.5	97.8
13 - 14	97.9	96.3
15 - 16	88.3	87.8
17 - 18	60.6	60.0
19	28.3	20.4

Source: 1980 Census of Population: Public Use Microdata Sample, 5 percent A File: Reservation Supplementary Questionnaire Public Use Microdata Sample.

and most likely those enrolled are in pre-school programs or in programs such as Head Start, which are often tribally sponsored. Tribal involvement in pre-school programs may explain why there is virtually no difference in under-age-five school enrollments for reservation and nonreservation areas. Indian children living on a reservation may have about the same access to pre-school programs as students living outside reservation boundaries.

The data for school enrollment indicate that most Indian and Alaska Native children, as other children, generally begin school around the ages of five or six. The figures in Table 7.3 also show that primary school attendance is almost universal for these students. Regardless of residence, the percent of Indian students ages seven to 14 enrolled in school is no less than 94 percent. The balance of students not enrolled may be a function of reporting errors, the extreme isolation of students in areas such as Alaska and the southwest U.S., and a small number of families who withhold their children from school for religious, health, or other reasons.

While primary school attendance is almost universal among Indian children, this is by no means the case for secondary school enrollment. At ages 13 and 14, most Indian students have entered or are about to enter their first year of high school. From the data in Table 7.3, it is very clear that student retention is most problematic in these years. In some areas, age 16 is the earliest that students may legally withdraw from school. The upshot of this rule is that school enrollments for 15 and 16 year olds is significantly lower than for students age 13 and 14. Another sharp drop appears among students age 17 and 18. Only about six out of 10 Indian youths in this age group are enrolled in school. This estimate of non-attendance is as pronounced in urban areas as it is on reservations. A further indication of the low levels of post-secondary school attendance is that over two-thirds of 19 year old Indian youths are not enrolled in school.

Needless to say, many students graduate and, hence, are not enrolled at ages 17 or 18. However, these data are consistent with other reports indicating extremely high dropout rates for American Indians (AIPRC 1976; Szasz 1977; Ward and Wilson 1989). For reservation youth in 1980, the Census Bureau reported that 27 percent between the ages of 16 and 19 had not completed school and were not enrolled (U.S. Bureau of the Census 1985). In this same report, reservation drop-out rates fluctuated from 15 to 50 percent for larger reservations , and to as high as 100 percent for very small reservations with only a handful of youth.

Explanations for why American Indian youth dropout of school at exceedingly high rates focus on economic opportunities (or the lack thereof), and the cultural alienation of American Indian students in public schools. For reservation youth, the link between education and a high-paying job simply does not exist. Reservations have extraordinarily high rates of unemployment, sometimes exceeding 50 percent (Snipp 1989), and the few jobs that are available are low-skill, low-wage work that requires little education. Furthermore, some tribal cultures place a very low value on material possessions, rewarding instead those who adhere to tribal lifestyles, including ceremonial and spiritual traditions. In this scheme, Anglo education has minimal relevance.

Another perspective suggests that as American Indian students grow older, they become increasingly aware of the differences that separate them from the cultural values touted in Anglo curriculums. The cultural differences separating American Indian students from their non-Indian teachers and classmates create a sense of alienation and makes schooling seem an inappropriate, if not uncomfortable experience. The response of American Indian students to this situation is to emotionally and physically withdraw from school. Margaret Szasz (1977:187) sums up this perspective in her commentary on Indian education in the twentieth century:

> ...one of the most persistent problems [of American Indian students] was that of poor attendance and high dropout rates. Lack of motivation, general defeatism, and a seminomadic pattern of existence—all of these combined to make the Indian child feel there was no reason for attending or continuing school....Social integration became more difficult for the child as he went beyond the primary years. Although young children might have close friends among other ethnic groups, this often decreased to the point where they clung to their own ethnic group by the time they were in junior high school.

Other studies have reached similar conclusions (see Fuchs and Havighurst 1972 for a discussion).

Progress

It is not correct to assume that all students age 17 and 18 who are not in school are dropouts, or that all enrolled 19 year olds are in college. Some of the former may have graduated from high school at age 17 or the latter may still be finishing high school. Another way of viewing the magnitude of the high school dropout problem among Indians is from the vantage point of school progress. The success of Indian students in their school careers is especially important. Students who fall behind in their schooling are more likely to drop out and less likely to complete post-secondary schooling than students who are unimpeded in their school achievement.

The Census Bureau does not collect information about school progress, but it can be estimated by making certain assumptions about school attendance patterns and then comparing ages with educational levels. The percentages in Table 7.4 are based on the assumption that by age five or six,

TABLE 7. 4. School Progress by American Indians and Alaska Natives 5 to 18 Years Old.

Age	Percent Metropolitan		Reservation	
	Behind	Ahead or On Time	Behind	Ahead or On Time
5 - 6	0.0	100.0	0.0	100.0
7 - 8	4.3	95.7	6.1	93.9
9 - 10	8.9	91.1	10.7	89.3
11 - 12	9.3	90.7	13.8	86.2
13 - 14	11.5	88.5	17.6	82.4
15 - 16	17.7	82.3	24.2	75.8
17 - 18	33.0	67.0	40.2	59.8

Source: 1980 Census of Population: Public Use Microdata Sample, 5 percent A File; Reservation Supplementary Questionnaire Public Use Microdata Sample.

most Indian children enrolled in school will be in the first grade and thereafter, will be promoted one grade each year. By ages 17 and 18, these students should be enrolled in, or have completed, the twelfth grade.

According to these assumptions, no child age five or six years old starts behind in school; they are enrolled in the first or higher grades, i.e., ahead or on time. However, at each older age group, the percent of students who are behind in grade grows quickly. For example, in reservation areas, the percent of seven and eight year old children behind in school is around six percent. Among children four years older (age 11 or 12) in the same areas, about 14 percent appear to be behind.

As in the preceding table, the impact of dropout behavior becomes most obvious at about age 16. Students in reservation areas have the most dismal record of progress with over 24 percent of youths age 15 and 16 behind in school, and 40 percent of 17 and 18 year olds behind, showing the impact of dropouts. At best, in metropolitan locations, a third of Indian students who should be juniors or seniors in high school appear to be below this level or out of school altogether.

Comparing Table 7.4 with Table 7.3 shows how well enrollment figures reflect school achievement. This is most easily seen for the 17 and 18 year old age group. In Table 7.3, 61 percent of metropolitan youth 17-18 years old are shown enrolled in school. In Table 7.4, 67 percent of these youth are ahead or on time in their school progress. Reconciling these figures means that seven percent of metropolitan youth not enrolled in school are probably early high school graduates. The remaining 33 percent are most likely behind because they are dropouts. Notably, the slippage between school enrollment and normal progress is much lower in reservation locations, suggesting that early graduation is less common in these areas.

High School and Beyond

High School Graduates

The data in Table 7.5 show the distribution of high school graduates among cohorts of American Indians over the age of 25.[9] Gender differences are not large in this table but there are consistent differences with regard to residence. Regardless of age or sex, reservation Indians have lower levels of education than urban Indians.

Predictably, educational attainment is closely related to age. Younger American Indians, like other segments of the U.S. population, are better educated than their elders. Except in metropolitan areas, over three-fourths of the Indian population age 25 to 30 report 12 years or more of completed schooling. In contrast, the percent of the Indian population age 70 and over reporting 12 or more years of school ranges from 29 percent among metropolitan women to a low of 13 percent for reservation males. Another way of looking at this distribution is to note that the majority of urban American Indians age 55 and younger have at least a high school education or its equivalent. However, in reservation locations, the high school educated majority is younger, ages 36 to 40 and under.

Another interesting pattern in Table 7.5 is that residential differences

TABLE 7.5. Percent of American Indians and Alaska Natives 25 Years Old and Over With 12 or More Years of Education Completed.

Age	Metropolitan		Reservation	
	Males	Females	Males	Females
25 - 30	78.5	78.8	73.0	72.3
31 - 35	77.9	78.3	68.5	66.7
36 - 40	74.9	68.1	58.7	57.2
41 - 45	64.8	62.7	49.4	47.2
46 - 50	63.2	56.8	40.5	40.5
51 - 55	50.2	50.5	33.1	35.5
56 - 60	48.4	50.1	34.2	31.7
61 - 65	44.2	45.6	28.6	28.3
66 - 70	34.2	29.7	22.1	23.3
Over 70	22.5	28.5	12.6	16.0

Source: 1980 Census of Population: Public Use Microdata Sample, 5 percent A File; Reservation Supplementary Questionnaire Public Use Microdata Sample.

between the old and the young become larger around the ages of 40 and over. This is interesting because it raises many questions about the impact of education. For example, among the youngest American Indians, the narrow gap between reservation and metropolitan residents may represent similar educational opportunities in these areas. Or, it may indicate that better-educated individuals do not migrate from reservation areas until they are older. In other words, the large differences among persons over 40 may represent persons who acquired higher (or lower) levels of education by virtue of their residence, or better-educated persons who left the reservation for economic opportunities elsewhere.

College Experience

The earlier observation that gains in secondary schooling are not translated into gains at the post-secondary level is reinforced by Table 7.6. These numbers are the probabilities of obtaining four years or more of post-secondary schooling among persons who have acquired at least 12 years of school.[10] They correspond to the probabilities that high school graduates will pursue their education at least to the baccalaureate level.

Table 7.6 shows the probabilities of post-secondary education across age groups. The results vary predictably with respect to differences by place and gender. Men are generally more likely to attain four years or more of post-secondary schooling, and the probabilities of this achievement are higher in metropolitan areas than reservations. However, across age groups, the data reveal a somewhat surprising set of results.

Gender and residential differences notwithstanding, the likelihood of completing four years of college is remarkably small for younger persons, especially individuals 30 years of age and under. This reinforces several points already made about American Indian college attendance, but it is surprising in other respects. It is most unexpected because conventional wisdom ordinarily presumes that younger people, especially the post-Sputnik "baby boom" generation have had many more opportunities for attending college than their elders.[11] This finding is also surprising in the context of numerous social programs aimed at encouraging higher educational achievements among minority populations in general, and American Indians in particular. Have these programs failed and did educational opportunities actually decline in the 1970s? The answer to this question is probably no.

In absolute numbers, the number of Indians with four years or more of college in 1980 exceeded 53,000, more than in any previous census. However, the rise in secondary schooling among younger persons is not, as mentioned, being converted to yet higher levels of post-secondary education. This is producing a proportionally smaller segment of college-educated persons relative to the number of persons finishing high school. In this respect, the prospects for post-secondary education among younger American Indian high school graduates are virtually the lowest in the adult Indian population. This also means that pursuing a college degree as a reward for high school graduation is not readily available to the vast majority of young American Indian high school graduates.

For older American Indians, particularly males, the results in Table 7.6 reveal another important and somewhat unexpected insight. It appears that the most significant public policies promoting higher education among American Indians were not the initiatives of the 1960s and 1970s but, instead, were the opportunities made available through the post-World War II GI bill. During World War II, about 25,000 American Indians served in all branches of the armed forces (Hagan 1979). This number is more impressive from the standpoint that it suggests about one-third of all Indian men between the ages of 15 to 44 in 1940 were in the war.

The post-war GI legislation made available financial assistance for higher education on an unprecedented scale to tens of thousands of returning veterans. Among these veterans, it appears that American Indian GIs also benefitted. The best evidence for this claim appears in the probabilities of advanced schooling for Indian males in metropolitan locations. Indian veterans who were age 20 to 30 in 1945 were age 55 to 65 in 1980. This age group overlaps the 56 to 60 year olds who have the second highest probability of college attendance for high school graduates. The high school graduates with the highest probability of having an advanced

TABLE 7.6. Age-specific Conditional Probabilities of Completing Four or More Years of Post-Secondary Education Given the Completion of Secondary Schooling, 1980.

Age	Metropolitan		Reservation	
	Males	Females	Males	Females
25 - 30	.156	.136	.099	.093
31 - 35	.214	.148	.153	.114
36 - 40	.192	.130	.151	.116
41 - 45	.209	.132	.118	.102
46 - 50	.220	.110	.123	.079
51 - 55	.245	.121	.099	.079
56 - 60	.230	.105	.106	.096
61 - 65	.204	.148	.148	.170
66 - 70	.186	.124	.087	.142
Over 70	.154	.176	.162	.152

Source: 1980 Census of Population: Public Use Microdata Sample, 5 percent A File; Reservation Supplementary Questionnaire Public Use Microdata Sample.

education are men now residing in metropolitan areas and those who reached their eighteenth birthday between the years 1942 and 1947, i.e., men who were age 51 to 55 in 1980.

The likely impact of the GI bill on American Indian men is visible, though less pronounced, in other areas. Urban Indians with GI bill assistance had more opportunities to pursue their education. And by the same token, reservation or nonmetropolitan Indians were faced with the situation of having fewer educational opportunities or migrating to urban areas. There is evidence that after World War II, Indians migrated to and remained in cities for the purpose of getting an education and taking advantage of job opportunities (Fixico 1986; Price 1968). Indian women, most of whom were not veterans, do not have the same age-specific variations as Indian men, lending further evidence of the GI bill's impact on Indian education.

Finally, the over 70 age group also has relatively high rates of completing four years of college. However, this age group also has a very low rate of high school graduation. The figures in Table 7.6 most likely reflect the attainments of a small group of extraordinary individuals who, once over-coming the barriers to finishing high school, were able also to acquire additional years of schooling. Ironically, the conditional probability of attending four years or more of college by high school graduates is consid-erably higher for this age group than for Indians 30 and under.

American Indians in Higher Education

Enrollment Patterns

Beyond what is available from the Census, there are few other sources of data for American Indians in higher education. However, some informa-tion is available from the Center for Education Statistics in the Department of Education. This final series of tables draws on this source.

The information presented in Table 7.7 yields some insight into the preceding data showing that relatively few American Indians acquire four or more years of college. These percentages show distributions of American Indian students over time in public and private, two- and four-year institutions. These numbers are remarkably stable and suggest several conclusions about American Indians in higher education.

One observation that is not very surprising, but nonetheless extremely apparent in these data, is that relatively few American Indians attend private institutions. The percentage of American Indian students in private colleges and universities ranges from a low of 10 percent in 1982 to a high of 13 percent in 1984. Among private institutions, American Indian stu-

TABLE 7.7. American Indian Enrollment 1976-1984 in Public and Private Two-Year and Four-Year Institutions.

	1976	1978	1980	1982	1984
Public					
Four Year	37.2	34.9	34.6	35.9	35.8
Two Year	51.5	53.0	53.8	53.7	50.9
Private					
Four Year	8.9	10.0	9.4	8.3	9.6
Two Year	2.4	2.1	2.2	2.1	3.8
Total[1]	100.0	100.0	100.0	100.0	100.0

Source: Center for Education Statistics (1987), Table 7.2.

[1]Numbers may not add up to 100 percent due to rounding error.

dents are most likely to be enrolled in four-year programs by a margin of about four or five to one.

Compared with private schools, the differences in enrollments are reversed for public institutions. Around 90 percent of American Indian students are enrolled in public institutions, and nearly one-third more of these students are enrolled in two-year than in four-year institutions. Most likely, these two-year programs are local community colleges in which students are working toward an associate's degree or vocational certificate. Although tranfers of college credits from two- to four-year programs are certainly common, the concentration of American Indian students in two-year programs may partially explain why relatively few American Indians acquire four or more years of post-secondary education.

Finding a large concentration of American Indian students in two-year public programs is especially interesting because there are now 22 tribal colleges operating as public institutions on reservations across the U.S. Most of these are two-year institutions and this may play some role in the concentration of Indian students in two-year programs. However, there is little information about total enrollments, curricula, and educational plans and outcomes for students in these schools (Carnegie Foundation 1989).

While local community colleges may attract Indian students by virtue of their proximity, especially those on reservations, they may also limit their educational attainments. Indian students may be reluctant to transfer because it would mean leaving their home and community. And transfers may experience difficulty adjusting to their new environment stemming from their experiences in smaller programs, possibly in less demanding academic environments, and the stresses of changing academic homes midstream in their undergraduate career. Fewer American Indians with baccalaureate degrees are the result of this situation.

Academic Degrees

The distribution of baccalaureate degrees received by American Indians between 1975 and 1981 are shown in Table 7.8. From the mid-1970s to the early 1980s, the years shown in this table, the number of degree recipients in each year was virtually constant—about 3500. This number is only slightly more than five percent of the total number of American Indians enrolled in undergraduate programs in 1980 (U.S. Office of Education 1987:14). Despite the constancy in the number of baccalaureate degrees awarded, it is noteworthy that the number of two-year associate's degrees increased from 2,522 in 1975-76 to 3,574 in 1980-81, a 42 percent increase (U.S. Office of Education 1987:18). Perhaps because of the proximity of two-year community colleges, American Indians are clearly increasing their presence in these institutions, but for less obvious reasons, they are not choosing to continue their education beyond this level.

Nevertheless, the degrees obtained by American Indians in 1975-76 were not very different from those obtained in 1980-81. For example, the social sciences were the most popular subject areas between 1975 and 1981: about 27 to 29 percent of all undergraduate degrees received by American Indians were in these fields. In fact, the most significant shifts in subject areas mirrored trends in American undergraduate preferences as a whole. Baccalaureate business degrees received by American Indians increased by about 45 percent, rising from 12 percent in 1975-76 to nearly 18 percent in

TABLE 7.8. Percent distribution of baccalaureate degrees received by American Indians awarded for major fields of study, 1975-76 to 1980-81.

Major	1975-76	1978-79	1980-81
Physical Sciences, including Mathematics and Engineering	8.8	8.9	8.9
Biological Sciences, including Agriculture and Health Professions	12.7	12.9	12.3
Humanities	17.5	15.8	18.1
Social Science	27.6	28.6	27.1
Education	21.2	18.9	15.9
Business	12.2	14.9	17.7
Total	100.0	100.0	100.0
N	3498	3404	3584

Source: Center for Education Statistics (1987), Table 7.6.

1980-81. In the same years, baccalaureate degrees in education declined from 21 to 16 percent, a 25 percent decrease. Very clearly, American Indian students have not been immune to the rising popularity of business as an undergraduate major, nor to the decreasing attractiveness of education.

To close this discussion, Table 7.9 shows the distribution of doctoral degrees received by American Indians. The number of American Indians who receive an advanced degree is extremely small. Though unlike baccalaureate degrees, this number has been growing, from 93 in 1975-76 to 130 in 1980-81, a 40 percent rise.

The distribution of doctoral degrees across subject areas fluctuates across the years shown but in large measure, this reflects the instability associated with the very small numbers of degrees in each category—small differences in absolute numbers cause large percentage changes. This makes it difficult to assess trends over time. However, it is very apparent that doctorates in education account for the largest share of the advanced degrees received by American Indians. Doctorates in the social sciences and in "Other Fields"[12] compete as distantly trailing second-place candidates.

Concluding Remarks

For understanding the educational status of American Indians, this chapter has tried to make several points. One is that exposure to educational institutions is not a new development among American Indians. However, mass education for American Indians is relatively new. Between

TABLE 7.9. Percent Distribution of Doctoral Degrees Received by American Indians Awarded for Major Fields of Study, 1975-76 to 1980-81.

Major	1975-76	1978-79	1980-81
Biological Science	4.3	5.8	6.2
Business	6.5	2.9	3.8
Education	37.6	41.3	43.8
Letters	5.4	2.9	5.4
Physical Sciences, including Engineering	11.8	9.6	6.9
Social Sciences	12.9	26.0	16.9
Other Fields	21.5	11.5	17.0
Total	100.0	100.0	100.0
N	93	104	130

Source: Center for Education Statistics (1987), Table 7.8.

Note: "Other Fields" includes those fields for which less than five degrees were awarded in any given year.

1900 and 1930, school attendance by American Indians age five to 20 years increased from 40.4 to 60.2 percent. By 1980, this figure exceeded 90 percent. Furthermore, Indian control over Indian schools is a very recent development which spread most rapidly during the 1970s. An added point is that American Indians have made significant strides in secondary schooling. Comparing 1980 with 1970, statistics show a remarkable increase in the number of Indians reporting a high-school level of education. On the other hand, younger American Indians are highly prone to dropping out of high school and are not inclined to attend college, even if they complete high school. The rise in secondary school completion may be due to growing numbers of American Indians acquiring GED degrees.

A final observation is that in relative terms, opportunities for attaining four years of college are lowest for American Indians 30 years of age or less. Some of these individuals will undoubtedly complete additional years of higher education. But in the absence of substantial numbers of over 30 year old college students, the proportion of high school graduates attaining four or more years of college is at an alarming low post-World War II level among younger Indians. In an economy demanding ever higher levels of knowledge from workers, this development is an ominous sign for the future. It means, in particular, that the economic disadvantages facing American Indians due to their limited educational attainments are likely to persist.[13]

In terms of public policies to promote the education of American Indians, it hardly needs to be stated that two problems must be addressed. One, stemming the problem of high school dropouts must be a key priority. Clearly this is much easier said than done. Yet, it is equally obvious that this problem poses one of the most significant barriers to further progress in educating American Indians. Furthermore, programs to promote GEDs should not be viewed as an acceptable remedy. A GED is at best a post-hoc, band-aid measure for a much more serious problem. In the absence of documentary evidence, it is still fair to assert that students with GEDs, as opposed to successfully completing their secondary education, face more disadvantages, are less employable, and are less likely to pursue any type of higher education.

A second problem needing attention is that efforts must be made to encourage American Indians to pursue higher educations. In a society that is becoming better educated and increasingly information intensive, higher education is absolutely essential for American Indians to compete successfully for jobs and economic resources. Opportunities for higher education need to be expanded in post-World War II veterans benefits. Furthermore, retention of American Indian college students should be a matter of serious concern.

In a recent study, Scott (1986) noted that retention of Indian college students could be improved by taking steps to facilitate their integration into the academic community. Specifically, he suggested that academic institutions become more sensitive to, and supportive of, Indian students committed to Indian cultural values and lifestyles. In the absence of such support, academic success among American Indians is likely to remain limited.

This discussion was not intended to end on a pessimistic note. Yet, the prognosis for Indian education in the foreseeable future is not good. Data from the 1980 census show that, despite some improvements, there are lingering, long term barriers to educational achievement among American Indians. Statistics from the 1990 census are not yet available but past experience suggests that the recent circumstances of American Indians are not a great deal different than in 1980. High drop-out rates and limited success in college were problems plaguing Indian education 30 years ago (Berry 1969; Miller 1971). They were problems that went unsolved in the 1970s, and lacking a strong commitment to deal with these issues in the 1990s and beyond, they are likely to remain problematic well into the future.

Notes

1. Support for this research was provided by the Russell Sage Foundation and the Ford Foundation. The author assumes responsibility for all opinions and inadvertent errors herein.

2. The Hampton Institute was also assigned the duty of teaching newly freed slaves. Today, it is a predominantly black university.

3. Jim Thorpe, the great Indian athlete, attended Carlisle.

4. For this discussion, the term "American Indians" is shorthand for "American Indians, Eskimos, and Aleuts". This is done only for the sake of editorial convenience. Unfortunately, most data from the Census Bureau are not reported separately for these groups.

5. The data for this paper are taken from the 1980 decennial census of population. Data about American Indian educational progress are extremely scarce, and ideally, more up-to-date information would be desirable. However, the large scale surveys that provide educational statistics for the nation as a whole, such as the Department of Education's National Assessment of Educational Progress or the Census Bureau's Current Population Surveys, despite their size, are not large enough to generate reliable information about American Indians. As a result, the 1980 census is one of the few sources of data for the American Indian population.

The data for American Indians residing in metropolitan areas are taken from published sources (U.S. Bureau of the Census, 1973, 1983). Metropolitan areas are those defined by the Census Bureau as Standard Metropolitan Statistical Areas (SMSAs). The definition of an SMSA is very complex and based on a number of alternative criteria. Details about this definition are available in various Census publication.

Data for urban American Indians are also extracted from the 1980 Public-Use Microdata Sample (PUMS-A File) distributed by the Census Bureau. This file is based on the 1980 Census of Housing and Population and it is widely used in social science research. It is a five percent sample of the total U.S. population and it contains information about 11.3 million individuals residing in 4.7 million households. American Indians number about 77,000 in this file, representing the total American Indian population of 1,423,043, or about one-half of one percent of the U.S. total.

In 1980, along with the regular census, American Indians in reservation households were the objects of a special survey. This survey covered approximately 75 percent of households with at least one American Indian occupant on reservations and portions of Oklahoma known as "Historic Areas." "Historic Areas" of Oklahoma are areas with boundaries corresponding to the old Indian Nation boundaries that existed prior to statehood in 1907. Besides the usual information collected by the census, this survey also gathered information unique for reservation Indians. For example, information was collected about whether the children in the household (if any) were enrolled in a Bureau of Indian Affairs (BIA), tribal, or other type of school.

This survey is known as the 1980 American Indian Supplementary Questionnaire, and it is available from the Census Bureau in machine readable and published form. This file can be purchased from the Census Bureau. Readers should also be aware that 1980 was *not* the first census in which a supplementary questionnaire was distributed to American Indians. A special enumeration of American Indians was first conducted on 1890, and again in the 1910, 1930, and 1950 censuses.

In this chapter, the data for reservation Indians are tabulated from the Supplementary Questionnaire Public-Use Microdata Sample (SQ-PUMS). The SQ-PUMS file contains information about 50,000 individuals residing in 13,000 households on reservations and historic areas of Oklahoma. The 10 percent sample of the SQ-PUMS is representative of the national population of American Indians living in "Indian Country."

6. Relocation programs were initiated in 1952 and were not officially terminated until 1981. However, the emphasis on relocation was sharply curtailed in 1972. The cities which served as official relocation centers were Chicago, Cleveland, Dallas, Denver, Los Angeles, Oakland, San Francisco, and San Jose, California. In 1968, centers were opened in Tulsa and Oklahoma City. For more details, see Sorkin (1978) or Fixico (1986).

7. Urban and reservation populations are not always mutually exclusive. There are a few reservations located within or adjacent to metropolitan areas. For example, the Osage reservation is part of the Tulsa, Oklahoma SMSA, the Puyallup reservation is within the Tacoma, Washington SMSA, and a number of very small reservations known as rancherias are located in SMSAs in southern California.

8. This is simply the ratio of the percentage change in college graduates relative to the percentage change in high school graduates.

9. Age 25 is a conventional standard. It is assumed to be the age by which most persons have completed high school.

10. These estimates are calculated as the age-, gender-, and residence-specific

proportion of American Indians with four or more years of post-secondary schooling relative to the total American Indian population with twelve years or more
schooling within age-, gender- and residence-specific groups.

11. In the context of this discussion, there is a fine distinction between educational
opportunities and the probability of completing four or more years of schooling.
Educational opportunity may refer to *access* to education, regardless of whether a
degree is received. Or, it may refer to the opportunity to complete an educational
program and acquire a degree by having access to the resources to overcome barriers
such as financial needs, educational deficiencies, racial discrimination, and personal
hardships. Probabilities of college completion are very closely related to the latter
view of opportunity.

12. The category of "Other Fields" includes degrees in subjects outside of traditional disciplinary distinctions. This would include most doctorates in interdiscipli-
nary programs and some area studies.

13. The relationship between education and economic well-being is well known.
See Mincer (1974) and Sewell and Hauser (1975).

References

American Indian Policy Review Commission (AIPRC), "Task force five: Indian
    education. 1976." *Report on Indian Education*. Final report to the American Indian
    Policy Review Commission. Washington, DC: U.S. Government Printing Office.
Berry, Brewton. 1969. *The Education of American Indians: A Survey of the Literature*.
    Washington, DC.: U.S. Government Printing Office.
Brophy, William A., and Sophie D. Aberle. 1966. *The Indian: America's Unfinished
    Business*. Norman, OK: University of Oklahoma Press.
Burt, Larry W. 1982. *Tribalism in Crisis: Federal Indian Policy 1953-1961*. Albuquer-
    que, NM: University of New Mexico Press.
Carnegie Foundation for the Advancement of Teaching. 1989. *Tribal Colleges:
    Shaping the Future of Native America*. Princeton, NJ: Princeton University Press.
Clinton, Lawrence, Bruce A. Chadwick, and Howard M. Bahr. 1975. "Urban
    relocation reconsidered: Antecedents of employment among Indian males."
    Rural Sociology 40: 117-133.
Fixico, Donald L. 1986. *Termination and Relocation: Federal Indian Policy, 1945-1960*.
    Albuquerque, NM: University of New Mexico Press.
Foreman, Grant. 1934. *The Five Civilized Tribes*. Norman, OK: University of Ok-
    lahoma Press..
Fuchs, Estelle, and Robert J. Havighurst. 1972. *To Live on this Earth: American Indian
    Education*. Garden City, NY: Doubleday.
Gundlach, James H., and Alden E. Roberts. 1978. "Native American Indian migra-
    tion and relocation: Success or failure." *Pacific Sociological Review* 12: 117-128.
Hagan, William T. 1979. *American Indians*, revised edition. Chicago, IL: University
    of Chicago Press.
Hoxie, Frederick E. 1984. *A Final Promise: The Campaign to Assimilate the Indians,
    1880-1920*. Lincoln, NE.: University of Nebraska Press.
Institute for Government Research. 1928. *The Problem of Indian Administration* [The
    Meriam Report]. Baltimore, MD: Johns Hopkins University Press.

Levitan, Sar A., and Barbara Hetrick. 1971. *Big Brother's Indian Programs with Reservations*. New Yor k, NY: McGraw-Hill Book Company.

Miller, Frank C. 1971. "Involvement in an urban university." Pp. 313-340 in Jack O. Waddell, and O. Michael Watson (eds.), *The American Indian in Urban Society*. Boston, MA: Little, Brown and Company.

Mincer, Jacob. 1974. *Schooling, Experience and Earnings*. New York, NY: National Bureau of Economic Research.

O'Brien, Sharon. 1989. *American Indian Tribal Governments*. Norman, OK: University of Oklahoma Press.

Pearce, Roy Harvey. 1965. *The Savages of America: A Study of the Indian and the Idea of Civilization*. Baltimore, MD: The Johns Hopkins Press.

Price, John A. "The migration and adaption of American Indians to Los Angeles." *Human Organization* 27: 168-175.

Scott, Wilbur J. 1986. "Attachment to Indian culture and the 'difficult situation': A study of American Indian college students." *Youth and Society* 17: 381-395.

Sewell, William H., and Robert M. Hauser. 1975. *Education, Occupation, and Earnings*. New York, NY: Academic Press.

Snipp, C. Matthew. 1989. *American Indians: The First of This Land*. New York, NY: Russell Sage.

Snipp, C. Matthew, and Gary D. Sandefur. 1988. "Earnings of American Indians and Alaskan Natives: The effects of residence and migration." *Social Forces* 66: 994-1008.

Sorkin, Alan L. 1971. *American Indians and Federal Aid*. Washington, DC: The Brookings Institution.

Sorkin, Alan L. 1978. *The Urban American Indian*. Lexington, MA: DC Heath and Company.

Szasz, Margaret Connell. 1977. *Education and the American Indian: The Road to Self-Determination Since 1928*, second edition. Albuquerque, NM: University of New Mexico Press.

U.S. Bureau of the Census. 1983. *General Social and Economic Characteristics, United States Summary, 1980 Census of Population*. Washington, DC: U.S. Department of Commerce.

U. S. Bureau of the Census. 1973. *American Indians. Subject Report*. Washington, DC: U.S. Government Printing Office.

U. S. Bureau of the Census. 1915. *The Indian Population in the United States and Alaska, 1910*. Washington, DC: U.S. Government Printing Office.

U.S. Department of Education, Center for Education Statistics. 1987. *The American Indian in Higher Education 1975-76 to 1984-85*. Washington, DC: U.S. Government Printing Office

U.S. Government Accounting Agency (GAO). 1978. "Bureau of Indian Affairs not operating boarding schools efficiently." *Report of the Comptroller of the United States*, CED-78-56. Washington, DC: U.S. Government Accounting Office.

Utley, Robert M. 1984. *The Indian Frontier of the American West 1846-1890*. Albuquerque, NM: University of New Mexico Press.

Ward, Carol, and David R. Wilson. 1989. *1989 Educational Census of the Northern Cheyenne Reservation*. Lame Deer, MT: Northern Cheyenne Tribe, mimeo.

8

Down and Out in Rural America:
The Status of Blacks
and Hispanics in the 1980s[1]

Thomas A. Lyson

The 1980s was a decade of social and economic contradictions in the United States. After a sharp recession in 1981 and 1982, the economy rebounded into what became the longest sustained period of growth in the nation's history. However, during a period of economic recovery that has lasted into the 1990s, poverty rates remained high, the income gap between the rich and the poor widened, and many regions of the country, including large, rural sections of the South and Midwest, stagnated (Littman 1989; Lyson 1989; Lyson and Falk 1993).

Apart from the macro trends and conditions that typified economic life in the U.S. during the 1980s, the social and economic problems of America's minority populations remained high on the nation's agenda throughout the decade. Several scholarly studies documented the intractability of poverty and poor living standards among blacks and Hispanics (see for example, Jaynes and Williams 1989; Jensen 1990; Sandefur and Tienda 1988; Wilson 1987). It is worth noting that virtually all of the attention directed toward assessing the social and economic conditions of minorities in this country has had either a national or an urban focus. This is not surprising, perhaps, since almost three-fourths of the nation's population reside in urban areas and over 40 percent live in metropolitan areas with one million or more residents. Places like New York City, Chicago and Los Angeles are sufficiently large that problems of race, poverty and the underclass attract attention collectively as well as individually. On the other hand, although almost 60 million Americans live outside metropolitan areas, including almost five million blacks and nearly two million Hispanics, the social and economic welfare problems, human capital needs, and opportunity structures facing rural Americans rarely receive collective recognition or individual attention.

In recent years, there has been a growing awareness that blacks and Hispanics living in rural America face distinctive sets of opportunities and life chances that are qualitatively different from those facing their counterparts in urban areas (Jensen 1991). Not only do rural minorities confront a more restrictive set of occupational opportunities, but these jobs often pay less than comparable positions in urban areas and have fewer job benefits attached to them. Likewise, the social amenities, welfare benefits, and infrastructure that sustain a decent standard of living are deficient in many rural areas, especially areas with large minority populations (Tickamyer and Duncan 1990).[2]

While one could argue that rural areas, in general, compare unfavorably to urban areas on a range of quality of life measures, it is also true that the stock of human capital in rural places is not up to urban standards. The average level of schooling is lower in rural areas, illiteracy is higher and the dropout rate surpasses that found in urban areas (Lyson 1989). Hence, many social scientists have argued that for rural areas to close the gap with urban places, the human capital of rural places must be enhanced.

Beyond issues of equity between rural and urban America, there is a question of inequality within rural America itself. We know, for example, that minorities living in cities tend to fare worse than urban whites. While we expect to find a similar pattern in rural areas, it is unclear exactly how blacks and Hispanics living in rural America compare to their white counterparts. In this chapter, an assessment is made of the changing social and economic status of rural blacks and Hispanics in the U.S. during the 1980s. This inquiry is woven around two interrelated questions. First, did these groups ride the crest of the economic boom that swept the country during the decade or did they become further mired in the economic backwaters of the country? And second, what factors and conditions are associated with the changes in the economic experiences of rural blacks and Hispanics? After these two questions are examined, an analysis of some innovative programs and policies that have the potential to improve socioeconomic conditions for minorities in lagging rural regions is explored.

The Geography of Rural Minorities

While both the rural and urban white populations are dispersed across all regions of the country (Table 8.1), the same pattern does not hold true for rural blacks and Hispanics. Nearly 95 percent of all rural blacks reside in the South and over half of these people are found in the South Atlantic

TABLE 8.1.   Residence Patterns of Whites, Blacks and Hispanics.

Region	White		Black		Hispanic	
	Rural	Urban	Rural	Urban	Rural	Urban
		- - - - - - Percent - - - - - -				
New England	5.0	6.8	.7	2.3	1.1	1.9
Middle Atlantic	7.1	18.8	1.0	18.1	2.6	15.5
East No. Central	20.8	18.0	.8	19.1	3.4	5.6
West No. Central	15.2	6.2	1.8	3.1	3.6	.6
South Atlantic	16.8	16.4	52.0	28.1	3.0	10.7
East So. Central	12.9	4.3	22.2	7.6	2.8	.2
West So. Central	9.9	8.9	20.5	11.4	34.3	21.6
Mountain	5.8	5.3	.4	1.5	43.2	7.1
West	6.5	15.3	.6	8.8	6.0	36.8

Source: Current Population Survey, 1988

states. There are 276 counties in the South in which blacks account for 30 percent or more of the total population. Over 2.5 million of the five million rural blacks live in these 276 counties. This residence pattern contrasts sharply with that of urban blacks. Less than half of the nation's urban blacks live in the South. The Northeast and North Central regions together contain over 40 percent of the urban black population, while over one in 10 urban blacks lives in the West and Mountain regions.

Rural Hispanics display a similar pattern of geographic specificity. Nearly half of all rural Hispanics live in the West and Mountain regions. The bulk of these are found in the Mountain states of Arizona, New Mexico and Colorado. Another 40 percent of the rural Hispanic population reside in the South, mainly Texas. There are 81 nonmetropolitan counties in which Hispanics make-up 30 percent or more of the population. Nearly 650,000 Hispanics live in these 81 counties. Urban Hispanics, like their black counterparts, are more geographically dispersed with about one in six living in the Northeast. As Sandefur and Tienda (1988) note, most rural Hispanics are Mexican-American, while the urban Hispanic population is a polyglot of Mexican-Americans, Puerto Ricans, Cubans and other people of Spanish descent.

The geographic concentrations of rural blacks and Hispanics have important implications for understanding the problems they face today and their prospects for the future. The geographic concentration of rural blacks in the South and rural Hispanics in the Southwest is no accident, but rather the result of historical patterns of economic development. Rural blacks in the South today represent the legacy of the old plantation system of agriculture and the tenant and sharecropping system that followed the Civil War. For generations, rural blacks in the South worked in the region's cotton fields as tenant farmers, sharecroppers or as agricultural laborers. When cotton production was mechanized in the 1950s and 1960s, the source of economic livelihood for millions of blacks disappeared. Many of the more highly motivated rural blacks migrated to cities in the North in search of employment. Those blacks who opted to remain in the rural South now frequently live in places devoid of significant economic opportunities (Falk and Lyson 1988).

Unlike rural blacks, the geographic concentration of rural Hispanics does not have its roots in slavery and plantation agriculture. Rather, rural Hispanics in the Southwest have come in waves from Mexico, especially after the Mexican Civil War in 1910. Because many of these immigrants were poorly educated and did not speak English, they were relegated to lowest rungs on the job ladder. Often the only employment open to them was as agricultural workers. Like rural blacks, many rural Hispanics were able to eventually leave agricultural work and move to urban centers in the North. However, a residual of low-skilled, poorly educated Hispanics has remained in the rural Southwest.

TABLE 8.2. Income Levels of White, Black and Hispanic Workers: 1979 and 1987.

	White		Black		Hispanic	
	1979	1987	1979	1987	1979	1987
Male			- - - - - - 1987 Dollars - - - - - -			
Rural	22,897	22,224	12,477	11,233	16,745	15,065
Urban	28,243	28,585	17,454	16,538	20,270	17,883
Female						
Rural	8,053	9,325	6,247	7,534	5,637	5,938
Urban	10,167	13,016	9,801	10,884	7,673	8,553
	Ratio of Rural Income to Urban Income					
	- - - - - - Percent - - - - - -					
Male	81.1	77.7	71.5	67.9	82.6	84.2
Female	79.2	71.6	63.7	69.2	73.5	69.4

Source: Current Population Survey, 1980 and 1988. Data are for workers 25 years old or older.

Deteriorating Economic Conditions:
1979-1987

Between 1979 and 1987, rural workers in general, and black and Hispanic workers in particular, saw their economic positions deteriorate relative to their urban neighbors. Only black women and Hispanic men were able to improve their situations. At the same time, within rural areas, the income gap between white workers and workers in the two minority groups also widened (Table 8.2).

The ratio of rural income to urban income for white men fell from 81.1 percent in 1979 to 77.7 percent in 1987. The drop in the ratio of rural to urban income for black men during this same period was from 71.5 percent to 67.9 percent, while Hispanic income increased from 82.6 percent to 84.2 percent. For women, the largest drop was experienced by white women. Rural white women had incomes that were 79.2 percent of urban white women in 1979. By 1987, rural white women's income had fallen to 71.6 percent of their urban peers. Hispanic women saw their income fall from 73.5 percent to 69.4 percent during this period. Rural black women, on the other hand, improved their economic situation vis-a-vis urban women.

Within rural areas, black and Hispanic men lost ground to whites. Black men had incomes that were 54.5 percent of white men in 1979. By 1987, the average income of rural black men had fallen to just 50.5 percent of white men. Similarly, rural, Hispanic men saw their incomes fall from 73.1 percent of white men in 1979 to 67.8 percent in 1987.

Interestingly, rural black women fared better than black men vis-a-vis whites. Between 1979 and 1987, black women saw their incomes increase from 77.6 percent of rural white women to 80.8 percent. Rural Hispanic women, on the other hand, lost ground to whites. Their incomes fell from 70 percent of the white average in 1979 to 63.7 percent in 1987.

Another way to assess the changing economic status of rural blacks and Hispanics is presented in Table 8.3. Here, rural white, black, and Hispanic households are grouped into categories based on their total household income. Thus, for example, 22.9 percent of all rural white households in 1979 had incomes that placed them in the top 20 percent income group nationally. On the other hand, only 7.8 percent of rural black households had incomes high enough to place them in the top 20 percent.

Two points stand out in Table 8.3. First, rural black and Hispanic households were disproportionately concentrated in the lowest income categories in both 1979 and 1987, while the income distribution for white households is more evenly dispersed across the income quintiles. Second, the economic situation for all rural households, and especially for black and Hispanic households, deteriorated substantially during the 1980s. By 1987,

TABLE 8.3. Income Quintiles for Rural White, Black and Hispanic Families: 1979 and 1987.

	White		Black		Hispanic	
	1979	1987	1979	1987	1979	1987
Quintile						
1) Top 20%	22.9	15.0	7.8	3.3	11.7	6.6
2) Next 20%	25.6	21.2	14.3	11.8	17.1	15.3
3) Next 20%	23.9	24.0	21.1	17.7	23.1	20.9
4) Next 20%	17.3	22.7	25.5	27.9	27.8	31.2
5) Bottom 20%	10.3	17.1	30.3	39.2	19.3	26.0
Percent of Families with Income in 1987:						
Less than $7,500	9.9	10.4	24.3	27.3	14.5	15.4
More than $40,000	23.6	23.7	8.4	7.1	14.6	12.3

Source: Current Population Survey, 1980 and 1988.

nearly four in 10 rural black households were in the bottom income quintile, while only three out of every 100 rural black households had incomes that placed them in the top 20 percent. The situation for rural Hispanics was only slightly better. About one in four Hispanic households fell into the bottom income category in 1987, while 6.6 percent had household incomes large enough to be in the top 20 percent.

Two other pieces of data in Table 8.3 document racial and ethnic-based inequalities in rural America. First, over one in four rural black households had incomes less than $7,500/year in 1987 compared to one in seven Hispanic households and one in 10 white households. Phrased differently, black households are nearly three times as likely as white households to have very low incomes. Second, and conversely, white households are three times as likely as black households to have high incomes (i.e., over $40,000/year). It should also be noted that between 1979 and 1987 the percentage of black and Hispanic households with low incomes increased, while the percentage with high incomes decreased.

Not only do rural blacks and Hispanics have relatively low incomes compared to whites, but counties in which blacks and Hispanics are concentrated rank low on the income scale. The average income rank of nonmetropolitan counties without large concentrations of blacks or Hispanics is 1733 (out of 3049). The average income rank of the 81 counties in which Hispanics account for 30 percent or more of the population is 2339. Among the 276 counties with 30 percent or more black population, the average ranking is only 2419. To briefly summarize, the data presented above illustrate several important facts about the economic situation of minorities in rural America in the 1980s. First, black and Hispanic workers in rural areas earn less than their urban counterparts. Second, the income gap between rural workers and urban workers widened during the decade. Third, within rural areas, blacks and Hispanics are at the bottom of the economic ladder. Fourth, areas with large concentrations of blacks and Hispanics rank well below other nonmetropolitan counties on the income ladder. Finally, during the 1980s, the income situation for rural minorities deteriorated considerably.

In the next section of this chapter, an assessment is made of the nature of the opportunity structure in rural America and how employment opportunities have been allocated across racial, ethnic and gender lines. The working hypothesis is that the racially and ethnically-linked economic inequalities in rural areas are due in part to the inability of blacks and Hispanics to secure well-paying jobs in the local economy.

Employment Opportunities
for Rural Minorities

The data in Table 8.4 indicate that the nature and range of employment opportunities available in rural areas varies considerably by race, ethnicity and gender. Looking first at the industrial makeup of the rural work force, it is apparent that black men, and to a lesser extent Hispanic men, confront more restricted sets of occupational alternatives than whites. Over 40 percent of rural black men hold manufacturing jobs. This compares with 25 percent of white men and 21 percent of Hispanic men who work in manufacturing. Hispanic men, on the other hand, are disproportionately found in agriculture. One in five Hispanic workers holds an agriculturally-related job. Overall, rural white men are more evenly allocated across the industrial spectrum.

Although the patterns of industrial employment for rural women also reveal variation across racial and ethnic lines, there are remarkable similarities as well. Most notable, for example, is the fact that over half of all rural women are employed in service-related industries. Beyond this, over 35 percent of rural black women hold manufacturing jobs. Together, manufacturing and service industries account for over 85 percent of all jobs held by black women. This incredibly restricted range of industrial employment alternatives is no doubt tied to the low levels of income reported by black females in Table 8.2.

Hispanic women, like Hispanic men, are overrepresented in agriculture. Over one in eight Hispanic women work in agriculture. This is four times

TABLE 8.4. Industrial and Occupational Employment of Rural White, Black and Hispanic Workers: 1988.

	White		Black		Hispanic	
	Male	Female	Male	Female	Male	Female
Industry			------Percent------			
Agriculture	9.2	3.3	6.7	0.0	19.4	13.3
Construction	15.2	1.6	14.9	.4	17.9	0
Manufacturing	25.1	17.2	42.9	35.5	21.4	13.6
Utilities	9.3	3.1	5.5	1.0	4.6	1.8
Trade	15.9	20.3	10.6	9.8	14.2	15.0
Services	20.4	50.1	16.1	50.4	15.9	51.1
Government	4.9	4.4	3.3	2.9	6.6	5.2
Occupation						
Professional/						
Technical/Managerial	22.6	25.7	6.6	11.9	12.2	17.3
Sales/Clerical	12.8	36.8	5.2	15.0	8.3	22.5
Craft Worker	24.2	2.9	16.2	4.9	29.6	1.3
Operative	24.9	13.5	52.1	32.4	23.9	17.3
Service Worker	6.1	18.5	11.6	35.8	6.0	30.3
Farmer	6.0	1.3	.5	0.0	2.0	1.4
Farm Worker	3.4	1.3	7.8	0.0	18.0	9.9

Index of Dissimilarity	*Men*	*Women*
White vs. Black	37.1	38.2
White vs. Hispanic	20.0	24.3
Hispanic vs. Black	33.8	24.2

Source: Current Population Survey, 1988. Data are for workers 25 years old and older.

the percent of white women in agriculture and five times the percent of black women.

The data on occupational placement (Table 8.4) complement the industrial data and provide a good indication of the types of jobs rural workers hold. As might be expected, rural white men occupy the more favorable positions in the occupational structure. Nearly half hold professional, managerial, technical or skilled blue-collar jobs. Only about 23 percent of rural black men and 42 percent of rural Hispanic men are found in these types of jobs.

Conversely, over half of the rural black male workforce holds semi-skilled and unskilled blue-collar positions. This is more than double the percentages of white men and Hispanic men in these positions. Finally, in line with the disproportionate percentage of Hispanic men in the agricultural sector, 18 percent of rural Hispanic men are classified as farmworkers.

Like black men, rural black women are confined to a narrow range of occupational positions. Over 68 percent are found in relatively low level blue-collar and service jobs. Comparable figures for Hispanic and white women in these types of occupations are 48 percent and 32 percent respectively. On the other hand, over 60 percent of rural white women hold white-collar positions compared to 27 percent of rural black women and 50 percent of rural Hispanic women.

To better understand the differences in occupational opportunity structures that confront white men, black men and Hispanic men, three indexes of dissimilarity were computed. The index of dissimilarity (D) is a widely used measure of segregation (Rosenfeld and Sorenson 1979). When applied to occupational distributions, it is based on the absolute differences between the proportion of one group in a particular occupational category and the proportion of a second group holding jobs in that category. These differences are summed across occupational categories and divided by two. Scores for the D coefficient can range from 0, indicating no differences in the occupational distributions between the two groups, to 100, indicating that the groups share no common occupations.

For men, the greatest occupational discrepency among the three groups is between whites and blacks. Over 37 percent of whites and blacks would have to change occupational positions for there to be parity in the distributions. For blacks and Hispanics to have identical occupational distributions, 33.8 percent of the groups would need to change positions. And for whites and Hispanics, the D coefficient is 20 percent.

Similar patterns of dissimilarity are evident for women. Nearly 40 percent of black and white women would have to change positions for occupational parity to be achieved. Likewise, nearly 25 percent of Hispanic women would have to change place with either white women or black women before distributions became identical.

It is evident from the results in Table 8.4 that race, ethnicity, and gender are powerful determinants of job placement in rural areas. Part of the reason why blacks and Hispanics fare worse than whites in terms of industrial and occupational placement is probably tied to the geographic concentrations of blacks in the South and Hispanics in the Southwest. As we have noted elsewhere (Falk and Lyson 1988:135), areas of the rural South with high concentrations of blacks "....remain saddled with an economic base dominated almost entirely by slow-growing, stagnating, and declining industries....consequently, most occupational opportunities in the Black Belt are at the low-wage, low-skill end of the job ladder." In a similar vein with respect to Hispanics, Tienda (1981:536) notes: "Agricultural activities continue to provide employment for nonmetro Chicanos.... This means that many are subjected to low standards of living with their attendant implications for limited mobility and social acceptance."

Lagging Educational Attainment

Any agenda to improve or enhance the life chances of rural residents in the U.S. must focus on the nexus between education and schools, on the one hand, and the nature and range of employment opportunities in an area, on the other hand. It has become an accepted social fact that the disadvantaged positions of rural minorities in the U.S. are due in part to deficiencies in levels of human capital (Beaulieu 1989; Wilson 1987; Snipp et al. 1993). According to Jensen (1991:186), "Employment opportunities for nonmetro minorities will increase in direct proportion to improvements in the human capital they bring to the labor market." This may be true insofar as there already exists a set of "good" jobs in an area. However, to date there is little empirical evidence to indicate that simply improving the stock of human capital in an area will enhance employment opportunities. It is likely that most of the better paying and stable jobs in the economy will continue to be disproportionately found in urban areas rather than in rural areas. Rural areas with high concentrations of blacks and Hispanics are likely to find favor only with employers who are seeking a low wage and relatively unskilled pool of labor.

TABLE 8.5. Educational Attainment of Rural White, Black and Hispanic Adults: 1980 and 1988.

	White		Black		Hispanic	
	1980	1988	1980	1988	1980	1988
Men		------ Percent ------				
Less than 8 Years						
of Schooling	13.4	8.5	34.7	19.3	40.7	34.7
High School Graduate	72.7	78.8	45.8	61.4	45.5	50.6
Some College	34.9	35.1	17.9	17.4	18.1	18.4
College Graduate	19.0	17.8	6.2	6.2	8.7	8.3
Women						
Less than 8 Years						
of Schooling	10.4	6.9	27.1	16.5	40.1	33.9
High School Graduate	74.3	81.3	46.6	60.8	42.5	52.7
Some College	27.9	32.6	15.3	17.1	13.3	16.5
College Graduate	12.9	13.5	8.2	6.8	4.5	4.8

Source: Current Population Survey, 1980 and 1988. Data are for persons 25 years old and older.

Data on educational attainment are presented in Table 8.5. These data show that the percentage of blacks and Hispanics with less than an eighth grade education decreased substantially during the 1980s. However, in 1988, one in five rural black men and one in three rural Hispanic men still had less than an elementary school education. To employers seeking qualified workers, these individuals would be judged to be functionally illiterate and suitable for only low-skill, marginal employment. Similar patterns hold for rural black and Hispanic women as well.

While there has been some success in raising the educational floor of rural minorities, similar improvements are not evident at the top range of the educational ladder. The percentage of rural blacks and Hispanics who graduated from college generally stayed the same or in some instances decreased during the 1980s. The percentage of rural Hispanic men who had graduated from college, for example, declined from 8.7 percent in 1980 to 8.3 percent in 1988. The percentage of rural black women who graduated from college went from 8.2 percent in 1980 to 6.8 percent in 1988.

It is also worth noting that rural whites hold a decided educational advantage over rural blacks and Hispanics. Not only are there proportionately fewer rural whites with less than eight years of schooling, but there are also substantially more whites with college degrees. Falk and Lyson (1988:128) note one of the consequences of unequal educational attainment for blacks and whites in the rural South: "White men disproportionately occupy good jobs, black women (and to a lesser degree, black men) occupy bad jobs. Given this, the gap between blacks and whites seems intractable. Historical inequalities seem bound to continue, and the class system in the South will reproduce itself yet again."

Part of the reason why rural blacks and Hispanics manifest lower educational attainments vis-a-vis rural whites may be linked to the geography of rural minorities noted earlier. Both rural blacks and rural Hispanics are concentrated in relatively poor regions of the country. One consequence of living in an economically depressed area is that local funds for schooling are more limited. In the 276 nonmetropolitan counties in which 30 percent or more of the population is black, local expenditures for schooling are 17.8 percent less than they are in other nonmetropolitan counties. Likewise, in the 81 nonmetropolitan counties with large concentrations of Hispanics, expenditures are 12.2 percent less than the nonmetropolitan average.

More importantly, however, the socioeconomic context that characterizes these lagging regions no doubt has a detrimental effect on educational performance. As James Coleman (1966) noted 25 years ago, student achievement is tied directly and strongly to the socioeconomic climate of the neighborhood school. This, of course, presents a conundrum to researchers and policy makers who see increased educational achievement as a stimulus to local economic development. Low income rural areas are unlikely to produce the level of human capital necessary to attract good jobs to the area. Conversely, the lack of desirable employment alternatives in poor rural areas forces the better educated blacks and Hispanics in these places to migrate to urban areas where their skills and abilities can be better compensated. A scenario of this sort illustrates why education-based programs for local economic development have traditionally had little impact on improving socioeconomic conditions in low income rural areas and are unlikely to have significant impact in the future.

What Will Happen in the 1990s?

By most social and economic yardsticks, the 1980s were not good to many rural blacks and Hispanics. After several decades of slow but steady economic progress, the 1980s are best viewed as a period of either marginal improvements, stagnation or even decline. The data presented in Tables 8.2-8.5 illustrate the growing divergence between rural whites and rural blacks and Hispanics on a range of social and economic indicators. Ironically, the eroding social and economic situation for rural minorities has occurred during what was widely touted by recent Republican administrations as the longest sustained period of economic growth since World War II.

In the best of all worlds, the disadvantaged positions of rural blacks and Hispanics would become an issue of national concern in the 1990s and a federally directed and supported initiative would be launched to alleviate the inequalities that currently exist. However, times have changed since President Johnson declared his War on Poverty in the 1960s and the political mood has turned away from large-scale, federally sponsored programs to a belief that poverty and economic development are issues that are most appropriately addressed at the local level. At best, the federal government in the 1990s can be counted on to provide bits and pieces of a social safety net to keep at least some groups and some places from falling further behind the economic mainstream. Some examples of the types of programs that are targeted at specific economically disadvantaged and vulnerable groups include Headstart, the Women and Infant Care (WIC) program, and the Job Training Partnership Act (JTPA).

During the 1980s, the federal government's role in rural development changed dramatically. Instead of offering leadership and guidance in helping to address problems in rural America, the federal government abrogated this responsibility to state and local officials. This position was articulated during the Reagan Administration by John Block, former Secretary of Agriculture: "The fundamental premise of this strategy is that local and state governments have the right—and should have the authority—to decide how public resources should be spent in rural America. The federal role becomes one of support rather than direction, and the agenda for action is set primarily by rural citizens themselves" (USDA 1984:1).

In the 1990s the problems of poverty, low educational attainment and limited employment opportunities that face rural minorities are most likely to be addressed in the marketplace. That is, the key to improving the plight of rural blacks and Hispanics must be framed in terms of the "market." The social and economic conditions of all rural Americans will improve when people are able to find good jobs. The challenge facing policy makers and program planners, then, is to find new and innovative ways of nurturing sustainable economic development in rural America.

The problem of creating and sustaining a broad range of employment opportunities is compounded by the fact that rural areas in the U.S. are becoming part of an increasingly globalized economy. In a free market and global economy, capital and jobs will naturally flow to areas where the greatest profit can be extracted. This means that rural areas in the U.S., especially those with limited human capital such as the rural South and Southwest, will be relegated to the economic backwaters and forced to compete with Third World countries for foot-loose multinational plants. Over the long term, it is questionable whether or not rural areas will be able to sustain themselves economically by following this strategy.

The benign neglect the federal government has displayed toward the problems of rural areas generally, and rural minorities in particular, coupled with the inability of traditional industrial development strategies to alleviate these problems, suggests that new and innovative efforts are needed. One potentially useful conceptual framework that can be used to frame a "market oriented" policy and program response to rural economic development in the 1990s was put forth recently by Michael Piore and Charles Sabel (1984) in their book, *The Second Industrial Divide*. These authors argue that economic development is most viable and sustainable in a political environment in which local municipalities take an active hand in nurturing and supporting small-scale, industrially diverse, flexibly specialized enterprises. This contrast sharply with traditional rural development strategies that are aimed at attracting branch plants of large corporations. Rather than pursuing a strategy of smokestack chasing, Piore and Sabel believe that many areas, both rural and urban, have an untapped potential for indigenous local development. The key to this strategy's success is the ability of local and state governments to provide the technical assistance, financial backing and infrastructure to stimulate and nurture local economic development.

Along this line, an agenda to enhance human capital in rural communities shifts its focus from training workers primarily for highly skilled, and presumably highly paid, jobs in large organizations to inculcating the traits and characteristics compatible with work in small scale, diverse and flexibly specialized enterprises. It should be noted here that not all of these small and diverse enterprises will require technically sophisticated workers. There are a myriad of very productive and profitable businesses that require little more than basic literacy and an innovative approach to problem solving (Thornburgh 1988). This is not to deny, however, that knowledge-based industries will be one component of a prosperous rural America. It is important to remember, however, that the needs of rural people, in general, and rural minorities, in particular, may be best served by presenting them with a broad range of employment opportunities.

According to the Piore and Sabel framework, the economic landscape of rural America should strive to become a multidimensional mosaic of large-scale, mass-production enterprises and small-scale, flexibly specialized, craft-oriented units. The small-scale, flexibly specialized firms would articulate in several ways with the larger economy. First, these businesses would provide products for local consumption that are not readily available in the mass market. Some examples of these types of enterprises would be specialty foods, custom clothing, and handcrafted furniture. Second, small-scale, technically sophisticated enterprises would be able to fill niche markets in the national economy that are too small for mass producers. Professional business services, computer software design, and specialty apparel manufacturers are examples of some of these types of businesses. Third, small, craft-based, flexibly specialized enterprises can alter production quickly to exploit changing market conditions.

This is not to say that a strategy of small business development is not vulnerable (O'Farrell and Hitchens 1988). There is at least some evidence that the apparent growth of small businesses is an artifact of a recent trend towards subcontracting-out of various manufacturing and/or service functions by large corporations. For example, rather than maintain a janitorial and custodial staff, a large corporation may find it advantageous to purchase these services in the local market. This means that the ability of small firms to grow and diversify may be limited by contractual obligations to larger corporations. Furthermore, by limiting its freedom to operate, the small business is subjected to the same market vagaries as the large corporation. Beyond this, there is some evidence that many small businesses pay lower wages and offer fewer fringe benefits than large establishments (Fisher 1989; Gordon 1979).

Despite these caveats, however, there may be considerable payoff to the establishment and nurturing of small business. David Birch (1987) has noted that between 1980 and 1986, the Fortune 500 companies reduced their work forces by 2.8 million people. During this period, one million new jobs were added to the economy. Many small businesses represent the leading edge of technological development in the product cycle. Rural areas that are able to provide the infrastructure, venture capital and trainable labor for these small businesses are likely to outperform the economy as a whole (Johnson 1989). While an agenda to develop and nurture small business development may not be a direct panacea to the plight of rural minorities, it offers a rarely tried alternative to traditional rural development strategies. If the federal government will not launch a major initiative to alleviate the economic problems facing rural minorities in the 1990s, then it is incumbent upon policy makers and program planners at state and local levels to formulate strategies that foster and sustain economic growth. The best tonic for the problems facing rural minorities and lagging rural regions is a process to fully utilize the human capital that exists there now. If the development of small-scale, local enterprises shows promise, the 1990s will be a period of transition for rural America. Whites, blacks and Hispanics all stand to benefit from these efforts.

Notes

1. Support for this research was provided in part by funds from the Cornell University Agricultural Experiment Station in conjunction with USDA/CSRS regional research project S-229.

2. In this chapter, the terms rural and nonmetropolitan are used synonomously. In both cases, the terms refer to "nonmetropolitan" or "non-MSA" counties as defined by the U.S. Census.

References

Beaulieu, Lionel J. 1989. *Building Partnerships for People: Addressing the Rural South's Human Capital Needs.* Mississippi State, MS: Southern Rural Development Center.

Birch, David L. 1987. *Job Creation in America: How Our Smallest Companies Put the Most People to Work.* New York, NY: MacMillan.

Coleman, James S. 1966. *Equality of Educational Opportunity.* Washington, DC: U.S. Government Printing Office.

Falk, William W., and Thomas A. Lyson. 1988. *High Tech, Low Tech, No Tech: Recent Industrial and Occupational Changes in the South.* Albany, NY: SUNY-Albany Press.

Fisher, Peter S. 1989. "Risk capital and rural development." Pp. 130-48 in *Towards a Rural Development Policy for the 1990's: Enhancing Income and Employment Opportunities.* The Congressional Research Service, Joint Economic Committee, Congress of the United States.

Gordon, David M. 1979. *The Working Poor: Towards a State Agenda.* Washington, DC: Council of State Planning Agencies.

Jaynes, Gerald D., and Robin M. Williams (eds.). 1989. *A Common Destiny: Blacks and American Society*. Washington, DC: National Academy Press.

Jensen, Leif. 1991. "The doubly jeopardized: Policy perspectives on nonmetropolitan blacks and Mexicans." Pp. 181-93 in Cornelia B. Flora and James A. Christenson (eds.), *Rural Policies for the 1990's*. Boulder, CO: Westview Press.

Johnson, Thomas A. 1989. "The role of entrepreneurship in rural economic development." Pp. 156-62 in *Towards Rural Development Policy for the 1990's: Enhancing Income and Employment Opportunities*. The Congressional Research Service, Joint Economic Committee, Congress of the United States.

Littman, Mark S. 1989. "Poverty in the 1980's: Are the poor getting poorer?" *Monthly Labor Review* 112 (6): 13-18.

Lyson, Thomas A. 1989. *Two Sides to the Sunbelt: The Growing Divergence Between the Rural and Urban South*. New York, NY: Praeger Publishers.

Lyson, Thomas A., and William W. Falk. 1993. *Forgotten Places: Uneven Development in Rural America*. Lawrence, KS: University Press of Kansas.

O'Farrell, P.N., and D. Hitchens. 1988. "Alternative theories of small firm growth." *Environment and Planning* A 20 (9):1365-83.

Piore, Michael J., and Charles F. Sabel. 1984. *The Second Industrial Divide*. New York, NY: Basic Books.

Rosenfeld, Rachel A., and Aage B. Sorenson. 1979. "Sex differences in patterns of career mobility." *Demography* 16 (February): 25-31.

Sandefur Gary D., and Marta Tienda (eds.). 1988. *Divided Opportunities: Minorities, Poverty and Social Policy*. New York, NY: Plenum Press.

Snipp, Matthew, Hayward D. Horton, Leif Jensen, Joane Nagel, and Refugio Rochin. 1993. "Persistent rural poverty and racial and ethnic minorities." Pp. 171-99 in *Persistent Poverty in Rural America*. Boulder, CO: Westview Press.

Thornburgh, Dick. 1988. "The state's role in an era of economic transition: The Pennsylvania experience." *Economic Development Quarterly* 2 (3): 203-10.

Tickamyer, Ann R., and Cynthia M. Duncan. 1990. "Poverty and opportunity structure in rural America." *Annual Review of Sociology* 16: 67-86.

Tienda, Marta. 1981. "The Mexican-American population." Pp. 502-50 in Amos H. Hawley and Sara Mills Mazie (eds.), *Nonmetropolitan America in Transition*. Chapel Hill, NC: University of North Carolina Press.

United States Department of Agriculture. 1984. *Rural Development and the American Farm*. Office of Rural Development Policy, Washington, DC: U.S. Government Printing Office.

Wilson, William J. 1987. *The Truly Disadvantaged*. Chicago, IL: University of Chicago Press.

9

Gender Differences in Human Capital in Rural America

Jill L. Findeis

The dramatic increase in the number of women engaged in market work in the U.S. nonmetropolitan labor force emphasizes the need to assess the human capital that rural or nonmetropolitan women possess.[1] Whether women prefer market work or enter the labor force in response to economic need, their productivity in the labor market and their earnings in part reflect their human capital. Additional human capital investment may improve labor market outcomes and experiences of rural women and thus serve to benefit rural families.

Further, human capital investment among rural women can have benefits beyond those realized in the workplace. Parents are important mentors for children, and can provide education beyond the elementary and secondary education provided by often weak rural schools. Women in nonmetropolitan communities can also provide important leadership and community services, and it can be argued that human capital investment for women provides benefits not limited to the labor market (Schultz 1989).

Policymakers seeking to adopt policies and design programs to improve the human capital of rural America should consider if differences exist in the patterns of human capital investment and utilization by rural men as compared to rural women, and assess if these populations have special needs not met by current policies and programs. The reliance of the U.S. economy on a well-trained workforce that is increasingly comprised and dependent on women makes this an important task (Johnston and Packer 1987). Differences may exist in the extent to which rural men and women participate in alternative forms of human capital development—elementary and secondary education, post-secondary and adult education programs, on-the-job training and public job-training programs, and work experience. Differences may also exist in the extent to which rural men and women benefit from investment in their own human capital.

It will ultimately be necessary to determine which patterns of human capital investment are relevant to rural women. Further, investment in the human capital of women will pay off for society only if this human capital can be productively used to increase the earnings of women and the well-being of the families they support. Thus, from a policy perspective, answers to two questions are critical: (a) What are the most meaningful ways to supplement the human capital of rural women? and (b) Can women utilize this additional human capital in the rural environment in which they work? Any examination of the influences of gender must examine these dual issues.

This chapter examines the basic question: Are women rewarded in rural labor markets for human capital investment? The chapter examines (a) the relationship between schooling and employment adequacy in rural areas, and (b) the differential returns to acquired human capital in rural labor markets. This assessment is followed by an examination of rural labor market conditions that inhibit positive incentives for human capital investment, particularly among rural women unwilling or unable to migrate. To the extent that gender-related differences in patterns of human capital investment and utilization are observed, reasons for differences are assessed. Finally, avenues for change are recommended.

Labor Market Experiences of Rural Women

Studies of the labor market experiences of rural or nonmetropolitan women (e.g., Bokemeier and Tickamyer 1985; Findeis 1993; Lichter 1989; McLaughlin 1990) have shown that women are economically disadvantaged in rural labor markets. Substantial numbers of rural women are not adequately employed and experience high rates of *economic underemployment*—they are unemployed, are "discouraged workers," earn low wages, or are unable to find enough work. In each case, the labor market forces of supply and demand have resulted in outcomes that may be economically efficient but result in hardship for individuals and families. Women, and particularly rural women, are at risk of being among the economically underemployed.

The Labor Utilization Framework (LUF) used by Clogg and Sullivan (1983), Mutchler (1985), Lichter (1987, 1989), Tigges and Tootle (1990), Findeis (1993) and Bird (1990), among others, can be used to measure rates of different forms of underemployment.[2,3] Although alternative measures of labor market experiences can be posited, the extent to which an individual is underemployed in the LUF (i.e., is not adequately employed) reflects both inadequacies in wages and insufficiencies in the hours of work available. The specific forms of *economic underemployment* differentiated in the Labor Utilization Framework include (a) unemployment, (b) sub-un-employment, (c) underemployment by low hours, and (d) underemployment by low earnings.[4,5] The sub-unemployed are principally "discouraged workers," those individuals who have dropped out of the labor force because they are unable to find work. The underemployed by low hours are part-time workers who prefer to work more hours; whereas those underemployed by low earnings are those who receive low wages. All forms of economic underemployment reflect inadequacies in employment—i.e., situations where individuals and families experience hardship related to their participation (or externally-imposed inability to participate) in the labor market.

Studies of rural labor utilization in the U.S. have typically used data from the March Current Population Survey (CPS Annual Demographic File) conducted annually by the Bureau of the Census for the Bureau of Labor Statistics. The economic underemployment rates presented in this chapter were estimated from the March Current Population Survey (CPS) for the years 1980-88, for working-age individuals between 18 and 64 years of age, inclusive. The four major components of economic underemployment in the LUF are measured as follows using CPS individual-level data (Lichter 1987):

1. *Unemployed:* (a) individuals without work who have been searching for employment during the previous four-week period, and (b) employed persons in the process of job transition or lay-off.
2. *Sub-unemployed:* (a proxy for "discouraged workers"): (a) individuals currently not working because they are unable to find work, and (b) part-year workers who are currently out of the labor force but looking for full-time work.
3. *Underemployed by low hours:* employed persons working less than 35 hours per week due to an inability to find full-time employment (i.e., involuntary part-time workers).
4. *Underemployed by low earnings:* individuals whose labor market-related earnings are less than 1.25 times the individual poverty thresholds of the Social Security Administration.

Comparisons of aggregate economic underemployment rates by gender and by metro/nonmetro location are made in Figure 9.1.[6] Underemployment rates are observed to be higher among women residing in non-metropolitan areas than among women residing in metropolitan areas. Furthermore, unemployment rates of women are higher than for men across both locations. Since 1980, rates of economic underemployment

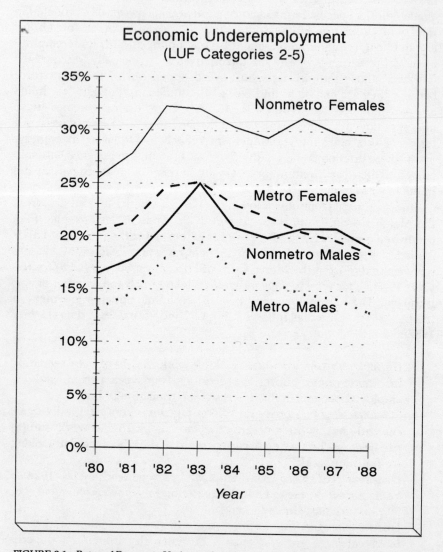

FIGURE 9.1. Rates of Economic Underemployment Among U.S. Metro and Nonmetro Men and Women, 1980-88.

among nonmetropolitan women have exceeded rates for nonmetropolitan men by roughly ten percentage points, on average. These high rates may result from insufficient human capital or from the underutilization of human capital stocks, or from both deficiencies.

Economic underemployment rates for U.S. metro and nonmetro men

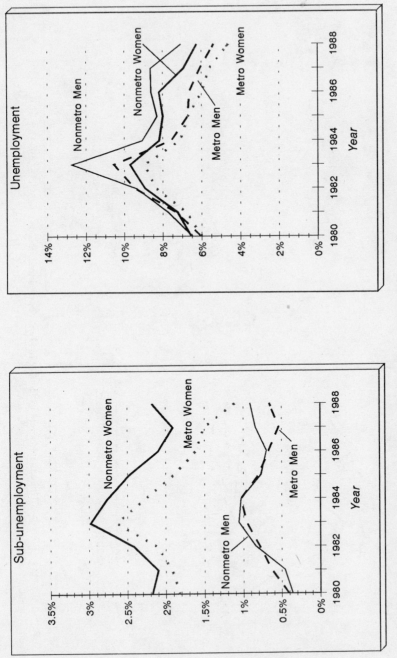

FIGURE 9.2. Rates of Underemployment by Gender in Metro/Nonmetro Locations in the U.S., 1980-88.
Source: Estimated from March Current Population Survey.

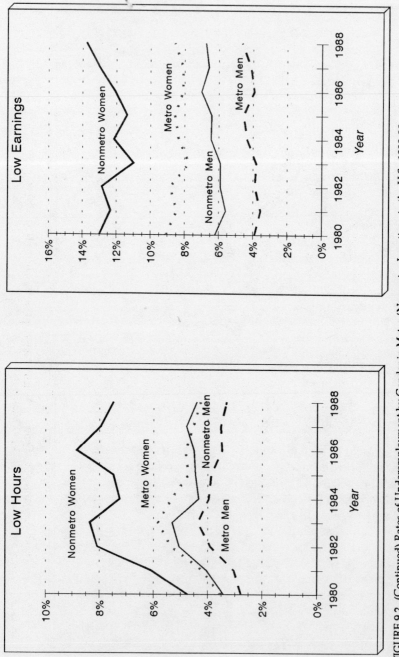

FIGURE 9.2. (Continued) Rates of Underemployment by Gender in Metro/Nonmetro Locations in the U.S., 1980-88.

Source: Estimated from March Current Population Survey.

and women, further disaggregated by type of underemployment, are shown for the years 1980-88 in Figure 9.2. The disaggregated underemployment rates indicate that the substantial gender differences in Figure 9.1 are largely attributable to significantly higher rates of underemployment by low hours and low earnings for nonmetropolitan women.[7] Significant numbers of employed nonmetro women receive low wages and frequently only "poverty wages," as indicated by the high rates of underemployment by low earnings observed among nonmetropolitan women. Estimates based on the CPS generally indicate that nonmetro women are twice as likely as nonmetro men to be underemployed by low earnings. In addition, many rural women would prefer to work more hours than their jobs afford. Based on the estimates presented in Figures 9.1 and 9.2, the widely-held perception that women working part-time prefer to work part-time is *potentially* erroneous, since the LUF estimates indicate that many nonmetro women working part-time are doing so *involuntarily* and would prefer to work more hours.[8]

The underemployment rate estimates support the observation that significant numbers of nonmetropolitan women lack adequate employment in the U.S. Rural women are less likely to be sufficiently employed than rural men, or than their urban counterparts. What can be done to reduce the high underemployment rates found among rural women is clearly an important policy question. Specifically, can human capital development by rural women improve their labor market experiences and thus reduce the underemployment and the economic hardship that they often experience?

Human Capital and Employment Adequacy

Investment in human capital occurs through elementary and secondary education, post-secondary and adult education programs, on-the-job training, public job-training programs, and work experience. Rural women have somewhat higher rates of participation in adult education programs compared to men, but are less likely to receive financial support from employers for schooling (McCannon 1985). Federal Job Training Partnership Act (JTPA) Title II-A programs have comparable participation rates across gender (Redman 1990), but may not serve women most in need because the 15 percent limit on trainee support may reduce access to training by low-income households (Swaim and Teixeira 1991)—many being female-headed households. Further, given gender-related differences in occupational structure, it is reasonable to posit that women are less likely than men to have access to employer job-training programs, but Swaim and Teixeira (1991) argue that little employer-provided training is

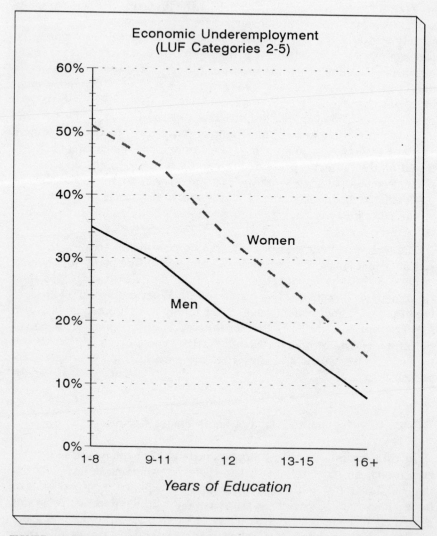

FIGURE 9.3. Rates of Economic Underemployment Among U.S. Nonmetro Men and Women, by Education.

available in the U.S., anyway. Although formalized employer job-training programs are not a major contributor to human capital development in the U.S. and are less prevalent in rural areas, apprenticeships may perform this function in rural economies on a smaller scale. However, participation rates in informal arrangements that serve a skill-building function in the

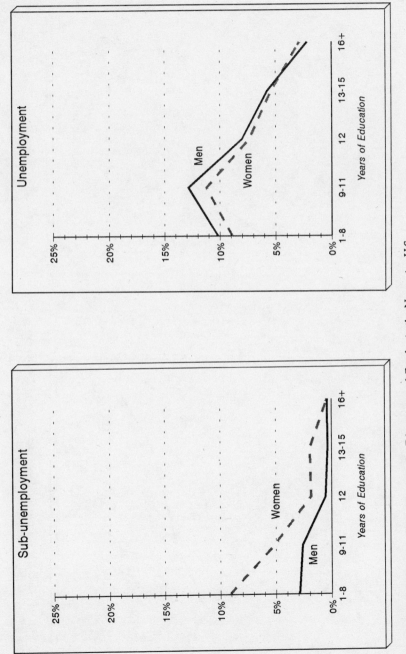

FIGURE 9.4. Rates of Underemployment by Education and Gender in the Nonmetro U.S.
Source: Estimated from 1988 March Current Population Survey.

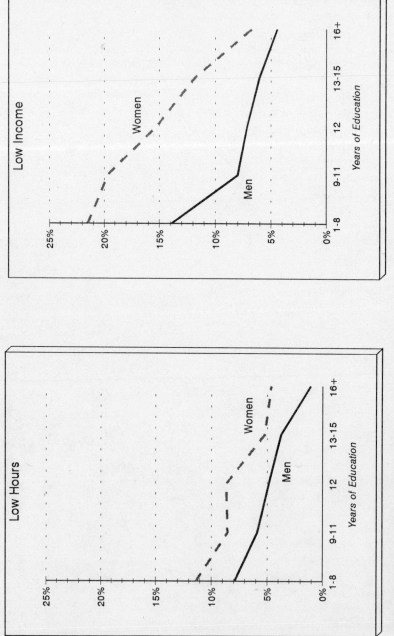

FIGURE 9.4. (Continued) Rates of Underemployment by Education and Gender in the Nonmetro U.S.
Source: Estimated from 1988 March Current Population Survey.

workplace are, at best, hard to measure and the influence of gender is even more difficult to establish.

The Current Population Survey can, however, be used to examine the influence of educational attainment on employment adequacy and to determine if both men and women employed in rural labor markets benefit economically from additional education.[9] For both women and men, additional years of formal education are associated with better labor market outcomes (Figures 9.3 and 9.4). Regardless of gender, individuals not completing high school are significantly disadvantaged in the labor market. However, nearly half of all rural women in the labor force with 1-8 years of formal education are economically underemployed, compared to one of every three rural men. With additional education beyond eighth grade, underemployment rates decline, especially for women. Over half of nonmetro working women with at most an eighth grade education are underemployed. This rate declines to 45 percent for working women with 9-11 years of education, and to 33 percent for those with a high school education. Nonmetro men with 1-8 years of education experience a 35 percent economic underemployment rate, that declines to approximately 21 percent for high school graduates with no additional education.

Education beyond high school further reduces rates of economic underemployment. For nonmetro males, 21 percent of those with a high school education are economically underemployed. This compares to 16 percent for males with 1-3 years of post-secondary education, and 8 percent for those with four or more years of college education. For women remaining in nonmetropolitan areas, the same pattern emerges; 33 percent of female high school graduates in the rural labor force are not adequately employed, 24 percent of female workers with 13-15 years of education are economically underemployed, whereas only 15 percent of women in the labor force with 16 or more years of education are not adequately employed.

The observed positive effects of education on employment adequacy are applicable across all major industrial sectors—services, manufacturing, and the resource-based industries.[10] The proportions of workers adequately employed (not with low earnings or low hours, and currently working) in services, manufacturing, and the resource-based industries increase significantly with education (see Figure 9.5). Further, with few exceptions, the gap between the disparate rates of adequate employment between rural men and women narrows, *and narrows significantly*, with more education.

This effect is most evident among the service industries, possibly reflecting the low-skill/high-skill extremes of the jobs that characterize the service sector (see Teixeira and Swaim 1991). Similar effects are observed in the resource-based industries, although lower proportions of both rural men and women with more education are adequately employed than is the case in services. In the manufacturing sector, education also improves rates of

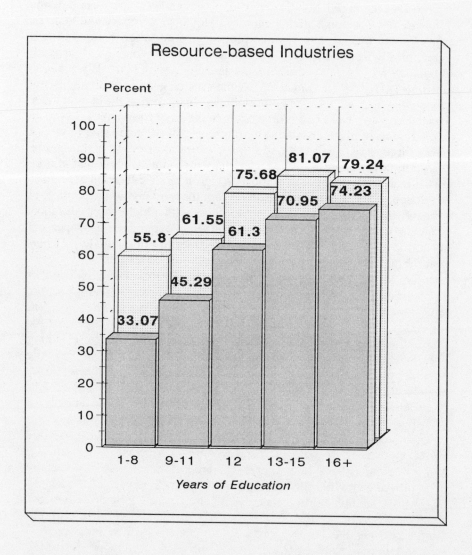

FIGURE 9.5. Rates of Adequate Employment by Education in Major Industries in Non-metro U.S.
Source: Estimated from 1988 March Current Population Survey. The shaded bar represents the rate of employment adequacy for women. The unshaded bar represents the rate for men.

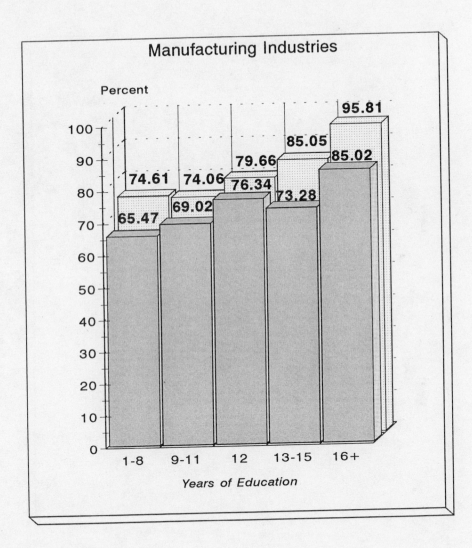

Manufacturing Industries

Percent

65.47	69.02	76.34	73.28	85.02
74.61	74.06	79.66	85.05	95.81

Years of Education: 1-8, 9-11, 12, 13-15, 16+

FIGURE 9.5. (Continued) Rates of Adequate Employment by Education in Major Industries in Nonmetro U.S.
Source: Estimated from 1988 March Current Population Survey. The shaded bar represents the rate of employment adequacy for women. The unshaded bar represents the rate for men.

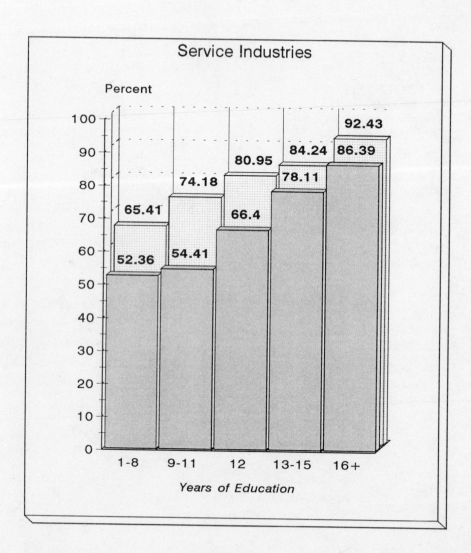

FIGURE 9.5. (Continued) Rates of Adequate Employment by Education in Major Industries in Nonmetro U.S.
Source: Estimated from 1988 March Current Population Survey. The shaded bar represents the rate of employment adequacy for women. The unshaded bar represents the rate for men.

employment adequacy, but because more rural men and women in manufacturing are adequately employed (generally at all education levels) than in either services or the resource-based industries, the rates of increase are less pronounced. Except at very low levels of education (1-8 years) or at higher levels of educational attainment (13+ years), the gap based on gender is comparatively small. Manufacturing is the only major industrial sector where the gap between employment adequacy for men and women actually widens as levels of education extend beyond the high school level.

Figures 9.3 through 9.5 demonstrate that for both rural men and women, underemployment rates decrease and employment adequacy increase with additional schooling in all sectors. The higher rates of employment adequacy should induce investment in more education by both men and women. However, as Table 9.1 indicates, while more women complete high school and have higher academic achievements during their high school tenure, fewer rural women than men attend college or technical school (see Donaldson 1984; Schwarzweller 1976). For instance, nearly 43 percent of male high school graduates who maintained residence in rural areas pursued some form of education beyond high school. This figure was ap-

TABLE 9.1. Distribution of Educational Attainment Levels for U.S. Rural Men and Women by Region, 1980.[a]

Years of Education Completed	South		West		Northeast		North Central	
	Men	Women	Men	Women	Men	Women	Men	Women
	—%—		—%—		—%—		—%—	
Elementary								
0 - 4 years	8.83	5.61	3.92	3.05	1.60	1.38	1.98	1.33
5 - 7 years	13.80	12.33	4.78	3.59	5.72	4.22	5.54	3.86
8 years	9.75	9.88	8.01	6.46	10.45	9.38	14.60	12.62
	—	—	—	—	—	—	—	—
Total: 0 - 8 years	32.38	27.82	16.71	13.10	17.77	14.98	22.12	17.81
High School								
9 - 11 years	17.71	21.65	13.03	14.63	14.61	14.97	13.86	15.02
12 years	28.75	32.97	33.82	40.59	36.12	43.06	40.48	45.68
College or Technical School								
13 - 15 years	11.03	10.06	19.34	19.65	12.94	14.26	12.04	12.98
16 + years	10.12	7.49	17.10	12.04	18.55	12.74	11.53	8.51
Percent Graduated from High School	49.90	50.52	70.26	72.28	67.61	70.06	64.05	67.17

[a]Individuals 25 years old and older.
Source: U.S. Bureau of the Census. *United States Summary.* Pp. 1-187/88.

proximately 36 percent among rural women. Regardless of the region of the country being considered, men who work in rural labor markets are more likely than rural women to have received technical school or college-level training to enhance their labor productivity. This raises a critical question: "Why do women who remain in rural areas often fail to invest in their own human capital beyond high school?"

Constraints to Human Capital Development
by Rural Women

The lack of post-secondary education that is observed among the majority of rural men and women (and particularly among women) reflects the strong trend toward out-migration of more highly educated men and women from rural areas and the interplay of economic and social incentives and expectations affecting women that remain in rural locations. The out-migration of more highly educated women, as well as men, is well-documented (e.g., Fuguitt et al. 1989; Wilson 1987) and remains a serious problem for rural economies. However, this trend is principally the result of better opportunities elsewhere that attract the most highly educated labor resources from rural labor markets. From the individual's perspective, out-migration remains an important avenue for enhancing the returns to investment in human capital through improvement in the opportunities for better labor market outcomes.

At the same time, rural women who have the *ability* to pursue post-secondary education often do not pursue this option. Several explanations for the observed lower rates of human capital investment among rural adult women can be posited. First, the educational experiences of females are often not comparable to those of males who attend the same schools in the same communities (American Association of University Women 1991). In public schools, gender differences exist in terms of access to education mentors and effective role models in the education system (Dunne 1979), placement in educational tracks, and career guidance (Clarenbach 1977). Rural public schools often do not facilitate the further development and utilization of human capital (Caldwell and Trainer 1989), particularly for females (Dunne 1979).

Much of the literature examining gender differences in rural education has supported the view that the curriculum, counseling and career guidance efforts in rural school districts have tended to be sex-stereotyped, channeling rural women into traditional female occupations (Clarenbach 1977). Educators may view this approach as being "realistic" and consistent with the preferences of high school students, their families, and the jobs available to women in rural communities. However, this approach ignores the fact that traditional female occupations pay considerably less and offer fewer benefits than nontraditional occupations, many of which are suitable for women who have acquired the necessary skills. Mentors should help students establish lifestyle patterns that are realistic but do not result in poverty. Role models and mentors in schools can have significant positive impacts, if these individuals seek to broaden the life choices of rural women.

Second, the traditional culture of rural areas has historically placed a greater emphasis on family formation, rather than human capital formation, for young rural women. The failure of many rural public schools to provide forward-looking and innovative career guidance to female students simply reflects the attitudes held by many rural communities. Women in rural communities are affected by the prevailing sex-role expectations of their families, peers, and communities and by the influence of traditional role models that emphasize family, often to the exclusion of market work. Early marriages, early child bearing, and the bearing of more children, have historically been the typical experiences of rural women (Dunne 1979, Kleinsasser 1986). Marriage and parenthood can delay education (Teachman and Polonko 1988) and entrance into the labor market where on-the-job experiences contribute to human capital. Furthermore, those women who work usually work in traditional female occupations. Donaldson (1984) argues that young women that remain in rural communities or later return as adults are compelled to "narrow their choices." Studying the life choices of female high school students in rural "Sawyer, Maine," Donaldson (1984) found that the majority of females exhibited a strong desire to remain in Sawyer as young adults, but as a result experienced a reduction in the choices and priorities that were available to them.[11] Living in Sawyer meant strong expectations of family roles for women, and the availability of fewer and poorer job opportunities (Donaldson 1984).

Rural communities have generally continued to maintain a strong commitment to family support roles for women. However, the on-going focus on a family-supportive role for women to the virtual exclusion of their roles in the economy is problematic. The family-oriented expectations for women, in addition to their low rates of human capital investment beyond high school, may leave many rural women unprepared to enter or re-enter the formal economy. Their job-specific human capital is often minimal and this limitation is further confounded by the constraints of child care, transportation, and families that may not be supportive of women working outside the home (despite economic necessity). These constraints also serve to inhibit the participation of rural women in adult education programs (McCannon 1985).

Finally, women who do not migrate to better employment opportunities in urban economies are faced with limited employment choices. While the employment opportunities available in rural areas for both genders are more limited than in urban economies, rural women usually fare worse than men, regardless of major industry of employment. Figures 9.6 through 9.8 demonstrate the uneven distribution of earnings for wage and salary workers (excluding self-employed labor) on the basis of gender in manufacturing, service, and resource-based industries.[12] As shown in Figure 9.6, 79 percent of all women employed in rural service industries in the 1988 March Current Population Survey earned wages equalling $7.00 per hour or less, or $14,000 or less annually for full-time work. This compares to 55 percent of rural men (see Figure 9.6). Similarly, rural manufacturing employment for women is principally low-wage; 76 percent of the women in manufacturing earned $7.00 per hour or less, compared to 42 percent of rural men.

What is disturbing is the small proportion of women employed in "good jobs"—jobs that provide incentives for substantial financial investments in post-secondary education. For example, only 7 percent of nonmetro women employed in the service industries earned wages exceeding $10.00 per hour, or $20,000 annually for full-time employment, and only 5 percent of rural women employed in the manufacturing sector earned this wage. On the other hand, 24 percent of all nonmetro men employed in the service industries and 28 percent of males in manufacturing had wages that exceeded the $10.00 per hour mark (Figures 9.6 and 9.7). A similar distribution of wages is observed in the resource-based industries (Figure 9.8).

Dunne (1980:398) has argued that rural youth, both male and female, "perceive only a narrow range of low-level jobs as realistic for themselves." The lack of a range of job opportunities has long characterized rural labor markets in the U.S. Rural women are predominantly concentrated in occupations characterized by low returns to labor (Bloomquist 1990; Lichter 1989), with few nontraditional jobs held by women (Pennsylvania Economic Development Partnership Board 1989). Strong sex-based occupational segregation is observed, with women employed in low-wage, low-status occupations and industries (Bloomquist 1990; Bokemeier and Tickamyer 1985; McLaughlin 1990). Women are often unable to fully utilize the human capital acquired through education or work experience (Donaldson 1984). Research on male-female differentials in labor market experiences (e.g., Bielby and Baron 1986; McLaughlin 1990; Tickamyer and Bokemeier 1988) has confirmed that women generally earn less, receive fewer benefits, have less time flexibility, have fewer supervisory duties on the job, have fewer opportunities for advancement, and experience more job turnover. Discrimination against rural women in rural labor markets may also be exacerbated by traditional values that fail to recognize or support the economic role of women (Maret and Chenoweth 1979).

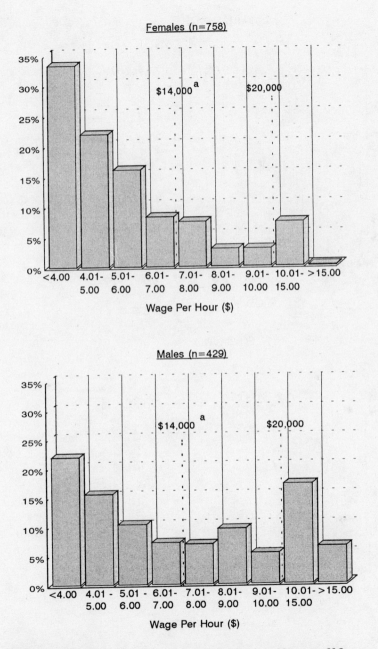

FIGURE 9.6. Distribution of Wages in Service Industries in Nonmetro U.S.
Source: 1988 March Current Population Survey.
[a]$14,000 and $20,000 represent annual earnings for full-time work at associated hourly wages.

202

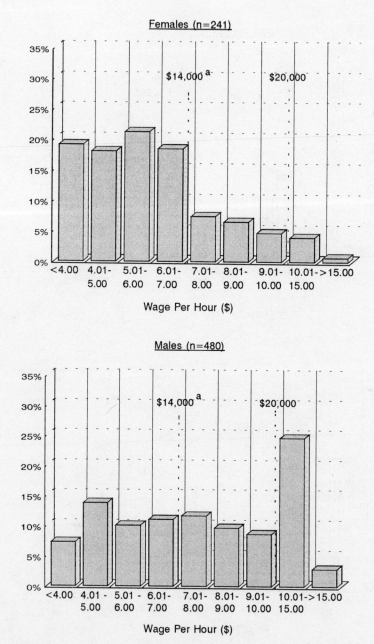

FIGURE 9.7. Distribution of Wages in Manufacturing Industries in Nonmetro U.S.
Source: 1988 March Current Population Survey.
[a]$14,000 and $20,000 represent annual earnings for full-time work at associated hourly wages.

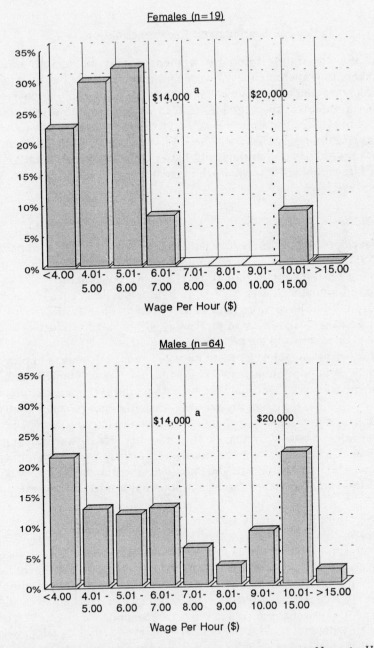

Females (n=19)

$14,000 a $20,000

Wage Per Hour ($)

Males (n=64)

$14,000 a $20,000

Wage Per Hour ($)

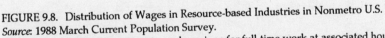

FIGURE 9.8. Distribution of Wages in Resource-based Industries in Nonmetro U.S.
Source: 1988 March Current Population Survey.
ᵃ$14,000 and $20,000 represent annual earnings for full-time work at associated hourly wages.

Policy Implications and Recommendations

Given the constraints faced by women, it may be tempting for policymakers to perpetuate the *status quo* for rural women. But the high rates of economic underemployment and the costs of the resulting poverty make this alternative unacceptable. Given current concerns with the capacity of the U.S. public education system to provide a productive future workforce (Murnane 1988; Swaim and Teixeira 1991), it is timely for policymakers to consider strategies to better train and more effectively integrate large numbers of women who currently are, or are soon to be, in the labor force.

Policy Choices

The development policies that are pursued will have differential impacts on rural individuals and rural communities. By pursuing a policy of encouraging greater human capital development, policymakers will expand the individual's choices; that is, individuals with higher levels of human capital will have more (and better) options open to them. As a result, those *choosing* to remain in rural areas will be more productive and will have greater access to the better jobs that exist.

Alternatively, those who choose to migrate from rural areas to improve their employment opportunities will also have that choice. Human capital development can serve to facilitate out-migration (and contribute to further community decline) if human capital development is not pursued jointly with national policies for employment generation and improvement. Fearing higher rates of out-migration, rural community leaders may not support human capital development policies. Further, rural community leaders may choose to perpetuate the *status quo,* or maintain the low-wage image of the rural U.S. labor force as a potential attractant to some industries.

Out-migration is less likely for rural women compared to men (see chapter 11 in this volume by Lichter, McLaughlin, and Cornwell). The challenge to rural communities is how to use the human capital of women productively, so as to increase the returns to human capital investment by women. Appropriate policies and programs focusing on human capital investment will be most effective for women if they combine human capital improvement with enhancements in the basic economic conditions of jobs available to women. As Hobbs (1986:34) observes, "rural development would not be well-served if education limited rural residents' options." Alternatively, funds for rural economic development will not be efficiently allocated if improvements in human capital are financed but cannot be effectively utilized.

The need for rural communities to work simultaneously to improve human capital and employment opportunities is not new. McLaughlin (1990), Tickamyer and Bokemeier (1988), Hobbs (1986), Chu (1980), Swaim and Teixeira (1991) and other rural development researchers and practitioners have argued for the coordination and simultaneous implementation of both efforts. Hobbs (1986) has noted that rural communities can maximize their benefits from development by coordinating employment development efforts with education, secondary education for youth and post-secondary education for adults. For nonmetro women, coordination appears to be even more critical. McLaughlin's (1990) research indicates that human capital development in the absence of efforts to change employment opportunities for women will have *no impact* on job characteristics, and therefore on underemployment. That is, existing employment opportunities are unable to effectively utilize improvements in women's human capital. In fact, it is likely that underemployment will actually *increase* among rural women if rural employment opportunities are not simultaneously improved.

Given these concerns, the following recommendations for policy should be considered:

1. At the national and state levels, there should be a strong commitment to human capital development for females as well as for males. It should be recognized that investment in human capital allows individuals options to choose life patterns consistent with individual preferences. Federal and state educational programs should be gender-balanced, reflecting a fair commitment to girls and women.

2. Rural public schools should be cognizant of the preferences of their constituencies, but should not deny young women access to role models and mentors, as well as educational tracks and career guidance that will qualify them for better (often nontraditional) employment opportunities. Further, rural schools, as well as schools nationwide, need to improve the basic and vocational educations of students who do not pursue post-secondary education (Murnane 1988; Weiss 1990)—i.e., those students most likely to become rural adults.

3. Post-secondary institutions that serve rural residents (e.g., two-year colleges and technical schools) should seriously consider the needs of the growing population of returning adult students in the U.S. Adult education is an important avenue for women re-entering the workforce, and for displaced men and women adjusting to changes in labor markets. While there is a realization by many that this population is increasing in size, the provision of support services

needed for this population has not kept pace with the expanded numbers of older students.

4. There should be a strong commitment to rural job creation and retention efforts. Industrial diversification efforts should include specific consideration of *occupational diversification* for women, thus allowing women the option to move into better jobs and/or nontraditional occupations. Rural women and men should not be satisfied with education and job training programs that qualify them for the poorest employment opportunities.

5. Rural communities and policymakers concerned with rural development should also attempt to *simultaneously* improve human capital and rural employment opportunities. The benefits of human capital development increase when employment experiences improve, but investment in human capital will not occur as long as the costs of human capital investment exceed the benefits. This "vicious cycle" affects both rural men and women, but is a particularly pernicious problem for rural women because of their limited employment opportunities.

Notes

1. The terms "rural" and "nonmetropolitan" will be used interchangeably in this chapter, as will the terms "urban" and "metropolitan". However, the estimates from the Current Population Survey are based on metro/nonmetro designations.

2. The Labor Utilization Framework (LUF), applied to the U.S. population by Clogg and Sullivan (1983); Clogg (1985); Mutchler (1985); and Clogg, Sullivan, and Mutchler (1986); among others, has been recently applied to nonmetro areas in the U.S. by Lichter (1987, 1989); Bird (1990); Findeis (1993); and Tigges and Tootle (1990). Alternative frameworks have been suggested by Tipps and Gordon (1985) and Nord, Phelps, and Sheets (1988).

3. It is important that the hierarchical nature of the LUF be understood. LUF requires that individuals simultaneously experiencing different forms of underemployment (e.g., underemployment by low hours and underemployment by low earnings) are sorted into only one underemployment category, based on a priority scheme. The hierarchy prevents double-counting.

4. The Labor Utilization Framework also includes an underemployment category termed "occupational mismatch." The "occupational mismatch" category is not included as a form of *economic underemployment*.

5. One category of underemployment in the LUF is "underemployment by low income," but an anonymous reviewer suggests that "underemployment by low *earnings*" is a more appropriate term. The author agrees and will use "earnings."

6. It should be noted that in 1984 the metro/nonmetro classifications in the CPS were updated, and therefore the metro/nonmetro estimates of underemployment are not directly comparable between the pre-1984 period and later years. In 1984,

some nonmetro areas were redefined as metro. As a result, shifts should be observed in both the metro and nonmetro trends that reflect the change in metro/nonmetro designations. However, it is likely that similar trends in underemployment rates by gender and by metro/nonmetro location hold, despite this change.

7. The Current Population Survey allows respondents to classify their activities as "looking for work" or "doing housework." Unemployed women may answer that they are "doing housework" when involved in multiple activities including both housework and looking for market work. If this occurs, the estimates of sub-unemployment and unemployment rates for women are biased downward.

8. The issue of *voluntary* versus *involuntary* part-time employment among rural women presents an interesting, researchable question. Some women may prefer to work full-time because of improved access to employee benefits. Also, there may be significant numbers of women that work part-time and would prefer *more* part-time work but not full-time work as used in the LUF.

9. Educational attainment reflects years of education as well as attainment of specific thresholds or credentials (e.g., high school degree). Findeis et al (1991) found that "lack of degrees that employers want" (not only education) was cited by women participating in the 1991 Rural Livelihood Strategies Survey as an important reason why they were unable to work.

10. The industry composition of each of the major industrial sectors is given in Appendix A.

11. Donaldson (1984) used a fictitious name for the actual town in the study of "Sawyer."

12. The March Current Population Survey Annual Demographic File includes hourly earnings data for wage and salary earners, excluding individuals self-employed in incorporated businesses. Separate weights are used for this variable.

References

Bielby, W. and J. Baron. 1986. "Men and women at work: Sex segregation and statistical discrimination." *American Journal of Sociology* 4: 759-99.

Bird, A. 1990. *Status of the Nonmetro Labor Force, 1987*. Rural Development Research Report No. 79. Washington, DC: Agriculture and Rural Economy Division, Economic Research Service, U.S. Department of Agriculture.

Bloomquist, L. 1990. "Local labor market characterics and the occupational concentration of women and men." *Rural Sociology* 55 (2): 199-213.

Bokemeier, J., and A. Tickamyer. 1985. "Labor force experiences of nonmetropolitan women." *Rural Sociology* 50 (1): 51-73.

Caldwell, C., and J. Trainer. 1989. "An ethnographic study of low participation rates in higher education in southcentral Pennsylvania." Paper prepared for the American Education Research Association, San Francisco, CA (March).

Chu, L. 1980. *Education for Rural Women: A Global Perspective*. Austin, TX: National Educational Laboratory Publishers, Inc. [ERIC available]

Clarenbach, H. 1977. *Educational Needs of Rural Women and Girls*. Report of the National Advisory Council on Women's Educational Programs. Washington, DC: National Advisory Council on Women's Educational Programs.

Clogg, C., T. Sullivan, and J. Mutchler. 1986. "Measuring underemployment and inequality in the work force." *Social Indicators Research* 18 (4): 375-93.

Clogg, C. 1985. "The effect of changing demographic composition on recent trends in underemployment." *Demography* 22 (Aug.): 395-414.

Clogg, C., and T. Sullivan. 1983. "Demographic composition and underemployment trends, 1969-1980." *Social Indicators Research* 12: 117-52.

Donaldson, G. 1984. "Growing up means moving away: Developmental dilemma for the rural adolescent." Revision of a paper presented at the National/Second International Institute on Social Work in Rural Areas. Orono, ME (July 28-31) [ERIC available].

Dunne, F. 1980. "Occupational sex-stereotyping among rural young women and men." *Rural Sociology* 45 (3): 396-415.

Dunne, F. 1979. "Traditional values/contemporary pressures: The conflicting needs of America's rural women." Paper presented at the Rural Education Seminar. College Park, MD (May) [ERIC available].

Findeis, J. 1993. "Utilization of rural labor resources." Pp. 49-68 in D. Barkley (ed.), *Economic Adaptation: Alternatives for Nonmetropolitan Areas.* Boulder, CO: Westview Press—Rural Studies Series.

Findeis, J., et al. 1991. "Rural labor market experiences and rural poverty." Paper presented at the 1991 Annual Meetings of the American Agricultural Economics Association. Manhattan, KS (August 4-7).

Findeis, J., and S. Saxena. 1987. "Labor force transitions and nonmetropolitan unemployment." Paper presented at the Annual Meetings of the Southern Regional Science Association. Atlanta, GA (March).

Fratoe, F. A. 1979. "Rural women and education." Paper presented at the Annual Meetings of the Rural Sociological Society, University of Vermont (August) [ERIC available].

Fuguitt, G., D. Brown, and C. Beale. 1989. *Rural and Small Town America.* New York, NY: Russall Sage Foundation.

Ghazalah, I. 1987. *Long Term Follow-Up of Vocational Education Graduates: A Study Based on Federal Income Tax Data.* Athens, OH: Ohio University, Department of Economics.

Hanson, S. 1982. "The effects of rural residence on the socio-economic attainment process of married females." *Rural Sociology* 47 (1): 91-113.

Hobbs, D. 1986. "Knowledge based rural development: Adult education and the future rural economy." Mimeo, Columbia, MO: University of Missouri.

Johnston, W., and A. Packer. 1987. *Workforce 2000: Work and Workers for the 21st Century.* Indianapolis, IN: Hudson Institute.

Jones, J., and R. Rosenfeld. 1989. "Women's occupations and local labor markets: 1950 to 1980." *Social Forces* 67 (3): 666-692.

Kleinsasser, A. M. 1986. "Exploration of an ambiguous culture: Conflicts facing gifted females in rural environments." Paper presented at the Annual Conference of the National Rural and Small Schools Consortium. Bellingham, WA (October) [ERIC available].

Lichter, D. 1987. "Measuring underemployment in rural areas." *Rural Development Perspectives* 3 (Feb.): 11-14.

Lichter, D. 1989. "The underemployment of American rural women: Prevalence, trends and spatial inequality." *Journal of Rural Studies* 5 (2):199-208.

Maret, E., and L. Chenoweth. 1979. "The labor force patterns of mature rural women." *Rural Sociology* 44 (4):736-53.

McCannon, R. 1985. *Serving the Rural Adult: A Demographic Portrait of Rural Adult Learners*. Manhattan, KS: Action Agenda Project.

McGranahan, D., and L. Ghelfi. 1991. "The education crisis and rural stagnation in the 1980's." Pp. 40-92 in *Education and Rural Economic Development: Strategies for the 1990's*. Staff Report No. AGES 915: Washington, DC: Agriculture and Rural Economy Division, Economic Research Service, U.S. Department of Agriculture.

McLaughlin, D. 1990. *Influence of Labor Market Structure on Differences in Outcomes and Operation in Local Labor Markets*. Ph.D. dissertation, University Park, PA: The Pennsylvania State University.

Murnane, R. 1988. "Education and the productivity of the work force: Looking ahead." In R. Litan, R. Lawrence and C. Schultze (eds.), *American Living Standards: Threats and Challenges*. Washington, DC: The Brookings Institution.

Mutchler, J. 1985. *Underemployment and Gender: Demographic and Structural Indicators*. Ph.D. dissertation, Austin, TX: University of Texas.

Nord, S., J. Phelps, and R. Sheets. 1988. "An analysis of the economic impact of the service sector on underemployment in major metropolitan areas in the United States." *Urban Studies* 25: 418-32.

Ollenburger, J., S. Grana, and H. Moore. 1989. "Labor force participation of rural farm, rural nonfarm, and urban women: A panel update." *Rural Sociology* 54 (4): 533-50.

Parcel, T., and C. Mueller. 1983. *Ascription and Labor Markets: Race and Sex Differences in Earnings*. New York, NY: Academic Press.

Pennsylvania Economic Development Partnership Board, Working Committee on Economic Equality for Women. 1989. *Human Capital + Opportunity = Economic Vitality: Women's Significance in Pennsylvania's Economic Growth*. Harrisburg, PA.

Peterson, R. 1989. "Firm size, occupational segregation, and the effects of family status on women's wages." *Social Forces* 68 (2): 397-414.

Redman, J. 1990. *Metro/Nonmetro Program Performance Under Title II-A, Job Training Partnership Act*. 1990. Staff Report No. AGES 9072. Washington, DC: Agriculture and Rural Economy Division, Economic Research Service, U.S. Department of Agriculture.

Schultz, P. 1989. "Women and development: Objectives, frameworks, and policy interventions." Working Paper, Population and Human Resources Division, World Bank (April).

Schwarzweller, H. 1976. "Scholastic performance, sex differentials and the structuring of educational ambition among rural youth in three societies." *Rural Sociology* 41 (2): 194-216.

Stafford, M., and M. Fossett. 1989. "Occupational sex inequality in the nonmetropolitan south: 1960-1980." *Rural Sociology* 54 (2): 169-94.

Swaim, P., and R. Teixeira. 1991. "Education and training policy: Skill upgrading options for the rural workforce." Pp. 122-62 in *Education and Rural Economic Development: Strategies for the 1990's*. Staff Report No. AGES 915; Washington,

DC: Agriculture and Rural Economy Division, Economic Research Service, U.S. Department of Agriculture.

Teachman, J., and K. Polonko. 1988. "Marriage, parenthood, and the college enrollment of men and women." *Social Forces* 67 (2): 512-23.

Teixeira, R., and P. Swaim. 1991. "Skill demand and supply in the new economy: Issues for rural areas." Pp. 13-39 in *Education and Rural Economic Development: Strategies for the 1990's.* Staff Report No. AGES 915; Washington, DC: Agriculture and Rural Economy Division, Economic Research Service, U.S. Department of Agriculture.

Tickamyer, A., and J. Bokemeier. 1988. "Sex differences in labor market experiences." *Rural Sociology* 53 (2): 166-89.

Tienda, M. 1986. "Industrial restructuring in metropolitan and nonmetropolitan labor markets: Implications for equity and efficiency." In M. S. Killian, L. Bloomquist, S. Pendleton and D. A. McGranahan (eds.), *Symposium on Rural Labor Market Research Issues.* Economic Research Service Staff Report No. AGES860721. Washington, DC: Agriculture and Rural Economic Division, Economic Research Service, U.S. Department of Agriculture.

Tigges, L., and D. Tootle. 1990. "Labor supply, labor demand, and men's underemployment in rural and urban labor markets." *Rural Sociology* 55 (3): 328-56.

Tipps, H. C., and H. A. Gordon. 1985. "Inequality at work: Race, sex, and underemployment." *Social Indicators Research* 16 (Jan.): 35-49.

Weiss, L. 1990. *Working Class Without Work: High School Students in a Deindustrializing Economy.* New York, NY: Routledge Press.

Wilson, F. 1987. "Metropolitan and nonmetropolitan migration streams: 1935-1980." *Demography* 24: 211-28.

Wilcox, K. 1982. "Differential socialization in the classroom: Implications for equal opportunity." In G. D. Spindler (ed.), *Doing the Ethnography of Schooling: Educational Anthropology in Action.* New York, NY: Holt, Rinehart, and Winston, Inc.

APPENDIX A. Industry Composition of Major Industrial Sectors.

Major Sector	Industries
Resource-based	Agriculture
	Mining
	Forestry and Fisheries
Service	Transportation
	Communications
	Utilities and Sanitary Services
	Wholesale Trade
	Retail Trade
	Banking, Finance, and Insurance
	Private Household Services
	Business Services
	Repair Services
	Entertainment and Recreation
	Hospital and Health
	Educational Services
	Social and Other Professional Services
	Public Administration
Manufacturing	Construction
	Lumber and Wood
	Furniture and Fixtures
	Stone, Clay, Glass, and Concrete
	Primary Metals
	Fabricated Metals
	Machinery
	Transportation Equipment
	Food and Kindred Products
	Tobacco Manufacturers
	Textiles and Apparel
	Paper
	Printing and Publishing
	Chemicals
	Rubber and Plastic Products
	Leather and Leather Products

10

Adapting to Economic Change: The Case of Displaced Workers

Paul Swaim

Increased global competition, new automation technologies, and numerous plant closings suggest that many workers have found themselves suddenly without jobs in recent years. Furthermore, workers displaced from declining industrial sectors may often have little prospect of finding similar jobs. Helping workers adapt to changing employment opportunities is thus an important goal for rural human capital policies.

Human capital deficiencies may mean that many rural displaced workers have poor prospects for finding good jobs in expanding industries and occupations. Strong literacy and math skills are especially valued by employers in technologically dynamic sectors of the economy. Workers with good cognitive skills, thus, command greater labor market flexibility following displacement than workers lacking these skills. The rural work force, however, has fewer years of schooling than the urban work force and is particularly deficient in math and science. In contrast, the largely manual skills possessed by rural workers displaced from production jobs may count for very little in today's job market.[1]

Rural labor market conditions may also create adjustment difficulties for displaced workers. For example, the rural unemployment rate rose more than the urban rate in the recession at the beginning of the 1980s and has remained higher ever since. Workers displaced in rural areas, thus, face intense competition from other job searchers. As a result, many may require longer to become reemployed; many may have to settle for new jobs that do not make adequate use of their skills.

Even in better economic times, the sparseness of rural labor markets may represent a disadvantage for the rural displaced worker. A job seeker with a specific combination of skills (i.e., human capital) and needs has a greater probability of finding a good job match with many potential employers. Since the pool of potential employers is larger and more diversified in an urban area as compared to a small or dispersed rural market, laid-off job seekers should generally fare better in the urban market.[2]

Moreover, the benefit of a large urban labor market may be even greater in a mass-layoff situation. A mass layoff in a small labor market will put large numbers of similarly qualified displaced workers in competition with one another for existing vacancies. This congestion effect will be less, perhaps even negligible, in an urban market where labor turnover is large.

Finally, the industrial and occupational mix of rural employment may mean that rural workers are displaced more frequently than their urban counterparts. Manufacturing and resource-based industries, such as farming and mining, are disproportionately rural. And many firms in these industries have been among the most affected by changing international trade patterns, new technologies, cyclical downturns, and other economic trends believed to cause displacement.

If substantiated, these arguments suggest that rural human capital policies should place a high priority on helping displaced workers to adapt to changing employment opportunities. It simply has not been known, however, whether rural workers are at relatively high risk of being displaced from their jobs. Nor has it been known how the personal losses resulting from displacement differ for rural and urban workers. Empirical study is, thus, needed to verify the severity of the rural displacement problem and to identify promising policy responses. This chapter uses information on job displacement from the Current Population Survey (CPS) to analyze these issues.

The chapter is organized as follows. The unique data set assembled for this analysis is described in the following section. Next, a descriptive overview of the worker displacement problem in rural labor markets is provided. The major conclusion of this section is that rural workers have been somewhat more likely than urban workers to be displaced and have experienced larger economic losses following displacement. Further, regression analysis is used to estimate the contributions of human capital deficiencies and labor market conditions to the larger rural losses. The importance of both sets of factors is confirmed. The final section summarizes the chapter's findings and discusses implications for rural human capital policy.

Data

The basic data sources for this study are the 1986 and 1988 Displaced Worker Surveys (DWS). These surveys were special supplements to the January CPS in those years and were designed to identify a large, nationally representative sample of workers displaced from jobs due to plant shut-downs or other permanent layoffs.[3]

In 1986 and 1988, all respondents from the roughly 60,000 households in the January CPS were asked whether they or any adult member of their household had "lost or left a job" in the five years before the survey "because of a plant closing, an employer going out of business, a layoff from which [the worker] was not recalled or other similar reasons." An affirmative response triggered a series of questions concerning the nature of the job lost and subsequent labor market experience. These supplemental questions, which comprise DWS, augment the extensive demographic and labor force data in the basic monthly CPS.

This study focuses on workers who lost full-time wage and salary jobs or became unemployed through the failure of a full-time, self-managed business in the years 1981-1986. The sample is also restricted to workers between the ages of 20 and 64, because workers 65 or older will generally be eligible for Social Security retirement payments (and possibly private pensions as well). Thus, these older individuals face a different set of choices regarding the labor market than do younger workers. Finally, only workers who have been displaced from their previous job for a year or more are included in the sample.[4]

In the following analysis, an "urban" worker is defined as one who resided in a Metropolitan Statistical Area (MSA), as designated by the Bureau of the Census. MSAs range in size from 50,000 up to several million, and may include two or more cities and surrounding suburbs and com-munities. A "rural" worker is, thus, one who does not reside in an MSA.[5]

The basic DWS is not well suited for studying differences in the incidence and effects of displacement across geographic areas. The problem is that the information for job displacement and place of residence refer to dif-ferent times. Because only a very small number of workers are displaced in any given week, respondents were asked to describe job displacement experience in the five years *before* the survey interview. Unfortunately, the information on residence is limited to residence *when* surveyed.

If a worker moved in the one-to-five years that had elapsed since losing his or her job, survey week residence differs from residence at the time of displacement. In fact, 21.7 percent of the workers indicated making an employment-related move since being displaced. The total number moving since losing their jobs may be even higher, because some workers may have moved for other reasons.

The residence of these workers, at the time they were displaced, can be more accurately distinguished for many of the more than 8,000 displaced workers identified in the 1986 and 1988 DWS. The CPS staggered sampling procedure means that half of the January respondents in any given year are re-interviewed in March. The March survey contains five-year retrospective information on residence, which corresponds almost exactly with the period covered by the January survey. The migration history from the March survey can, thus, help to identify residence when displaced.[6]

A three-step procedure was used to identify rural displaced workers. First, individual questionnaire responses from the January and March CPS were combined for displaced workers re-interviewed in March. Second, the January information on the year of displacement and whether the worker subsequently made an employment-related move was used together with that of March on place of residence (when interviewed, one year before the interview, and five years before the interview) to make a best guess of each worker's residence when displaced. Finally, residence when displaced was used to distinguish urban from rural workers.

Although this procedure for identifying rural displaced workers involves some imprecision, it is more reliable than relying on residence when interviewed. One indicator of the importance of post-displacement migration is that 11 percent of the displaced workers identified by the three-step procedure as rural had moved to urban locations by the time they were interviewed. The post-displacement experience of individuals moving between urban and rural areas also appears to be atypical. Thus, misclassifying these individuals could bias estimates of the individual costs resulting from rural displacements.[7]

The outcome of these restrictions is a nationally representative sample of 3,927 workers displaced from full-time jobs in the years 1981-1986. Twenty-nine percent of this sample were rural workers. The remainder of this chapter examines who these workers were and what happened to them following displacement. The role of human capital characteristics in facilitating or impeding labor market adjustment is particularly emphasized.

Overview of the Job Displacement

Incidence of Displacement

DWS data indicate that 1.7 million workers were displaced annually between 1981 and 1986 (Table 10.1).[8] Despite the severe 1981-1982 recession, total displacements for 1981-1984 were only slightly higher than for 1983-1986. The latter period contains only recovery years in which employment grew and unemployment rates fell. Apparently, most of the job displacement in recent years reflects structural changes in the economy rather than cyclical downturns.

Of the 10.1 million workers displaced between 1981 and 1986, 2.5 million (25 percent) resided in rural areas. By comparison, average monthly employment in 1985 was 100.7 million, with just 21 percent in rural labor

TABLE 10.1. Displacement by Industrial Sector, Region, Cause, and Receipt of Advance Notice[a]

| Item | Unit | Displaced workers | | | All employed |
		1986 DW survey: 1981-84	1988 DW survey: 1983-86	Annual Average: 1981-86	1985
Total	1,000	6,875	6,556	1,679	100,718
Goods producing	percent	61.0	55.8	58.5	35.5
Plant shutdowns	percent	47.5	54.1	50.7	NA
Advance notice	percent	51.1	53.1	52.2	NA
Urban	1,000	5,116	4,923	1,255	79,471
Goods producing	percent	58.6	52.6	55.7	33.5
Plant shutdowns	percent	47.2	55.2	51.1	NA
Advance notice	percent	51.7	52.7	52.2	NA
Rural	1,000	1,759	1,633	424	21,248
Goods producing	percent	68.0	65.4	66.8	44.2
Plant shutdowns	percent	48.1	50.6	49.3	NA
Advance notice	percent	50.3	54.3	52.2	NA
Rural share	percent	25.6	24.9	25.3	21.1
Regional distribution					
Urban:					
Northeast	percent	19.1	16.7	18.0	24.2
Midwest	percent	26.1	25.0	25.5	23.0
South	percent	31.3	35.6	33.4	31.0
West	percent	23.5	22.7	23.1	21.8
Rural:					
Northeast	percent	9.7	9.2	9.5	10.4
Midwest	percent	29.5	29.1	29.3	32.0
South	percent	46.4	43.2	44.8	43.5
West	percent	14.4	18.5	16.4	14.1

[a]"Displaced workers" denotes adult workers displaced from full-time jobs in 1981-1986; "All employed" denotes annual average employment of adults in 1985; and "NA" denotes "not applicable."

markets. Because rural workers were a larger share of those displaced than of all workers, it follows that the rate of displacement was (moderately) higher in rural than in urban labor markets.

Just over half of all displaced workers were displaced because of total plant shutdowns or relocations. This rate was somewhat lower in rural areas, where "slack work" and "failure of own business" were more frequently cited than in urban areas. Although the DWS identified relatively few displaced farmers, they tended to have been self-employed, hence contributing to the relative importance of "own business failure" in the rural displacement data.

During this period, employers generally were not required to provide advance notice to workers affected by permanent layoffs. Nearly half of the workers said they were neither notified nor otherwise expected to lose their jobs. Since February 1989, Federal law has required 60 days notice for many large layoffs. Thus, an increased share of workers are likely to receive advance notice of impending displacements now than in 1981-1986.

Rural displaced workers were more likely to live in the South and Midwest than were urban displaced workers, consistent with regional differences in the level of urbanization. For example, in 1981-1986, 45 percent of all rural displacements occurred in the South compared with 33 percent of urban displacements. Those figures reflected the South's employment pool: 44 percent of all rural workers and 31 percent of urban workers. The two regions with the highest rural rates of displacement relative to employment were the West and South. The pronounced increase in the rate of displacement in the rural West between the 1981-1984 and 1983-1986 periods reflects the mid-1980s downturn in the energy sector.

Overall, 59 percent of the displaced workers had been employed in the goods-producing industries (agriculture, mining, construction, and manufacturing). Since just 36 percent of employment was in this sector, displacement rates were substantially higher in the goods-producing than in the service sector. It is interesting to note, however, that the service sector share of displacements appears to be increasing and was nearing 50 percent in urban areas by the mid-1980s. Consistent with differences in the mix of employment, rural displaced workers were substantially more likely to have worked in goods-producing industries than were urban workers.

An examination of the occupation of these workers confirms the relative vulnerability of production workers to displacement (Table 10.2). Although just 43 percent of rural employment was in blue-collar occupations, 61 percent of the rural displaced workers lost such jobs. To better gauge occupational differences in displacement rates, relative risk rates—defined as the ratio of an occupation's share of total displacements to its share of total employment—are reported (see columns 3 and 6 in Table 10.2). Thus, a risk value above 1.0 indicates an above-average rate of displacement. In

TABLE 10.2. Occupational Distribution of Displacement[a]

	Urban			Rural		
Occupation	Displaced	All employed	Relative risk	Displaced	All employed	Relative risk
	Percent		*Index*	*Percent*		*Index*
Total	100.0	100.0	1.0	100.0	100.0	1.0
Blue collar	47.7	28.2	1.7	60.6	43.1	1.4
Farming, forestry, and fisheries	1.5	1.8	.8	3.5	8.4	.4
Craft	18.0	12.1	1.5	23.3	13.8	1.7
Operatives	17.5	6.6	2.7	19.8	10.1	2.0
Laborers and tranport operatives	10.7	7.7	1.4	14.0	10.8	1.3
White collar and service	52.3	71.8	.7	39.4	56.9	.7
Managerial	11.4	12.3	.9	8.4	7.9	1.1
Professional and technical	10.9	16.8	.6	7.3	12.1	.6
Clerical	13.2	17.2	.8	8.9	12.2	.7
Sales and service	16.8	25.4	.7	14.8	24.7	.6

[a] "Displaced" denotes adult workers displaced from full-time jobs in 1981-1986; and "All employed" denotes annual average employment of adults in 1985.

rural areas, blue-collar occupations had a relative risk level of 1.4, double the 0.7 rate for white-collar occupations. There is also considerable variation between blue-collar occupations with the highest displacement rates experienced by craft workers and machine operatives. Among white-collar occupations, managers were most at risk.

A higher proportion of rural than urban employment was in blue-collar jobs (43 versus 28 percent), and this difference was a major source of the higher rural displacement rate. Indeed, occupational differences in displacement risks were very similar in urban and rural areas. One exception is that the relative risk was very low for rural workers in farming, forestry, and fisheries occupations.[9]

The demographic composition of displaced workers indicates potential human capital deficits that could impede adjustment (Table 10.3). Perhaps of greatest concern to policy makers, rural displaced workers were less educated than both urban displaced workers and rural workers generally. More than one in five rural displaced workers had not finished high school.

TABLE 10.3. Demographic Characteristics of Displaced Workers[a]

	Urban			Rural		
Occupation	Displaced	All employed	Relative risk	Displaced	All employed	Relative risk
	Mean years		*Index*	*Mean years*		*Index*
Age	37.8	38.1	NA	37.0	38.7	NA
	Percent		*Index*	*Percent*		*Index*
Total	100.0	100.0	1.0	100.0	100.0	1.0
Male	65.5	57.0	1.1	66.8	58.4	1.1
Black	11.3	11.3	1.0	8.8	7.4	1.2
Hispanic	8.9	6.2	1.4	2.6	1.6	1.6
Years of schooling completed						
Total	100.0	100.0	1.0	100.0	100.0	1.0
Less than high school	17.7	12.8	1.4	21.0	17.8	1.2
High school	43.0	36.8	1.2	52.5	46.5	1.1
More than high school	39.4	50.4	0.8	26.6	35.7	0.7

[a] "Displaced" denotes adult workers displaced from full-time jobs in 1981-1986; "All employed" denotes adults working full-time one or more weeks in 1985; and "NA" denotes" not applicable."

Although many of these workers may have developed valuable production skills on their old jobs, there may be little demand for these largely manual skills in growing service and high-tech industries.

Rural displaced workers were slightly younger and considerably more likely to be male than other workers. Blacks and Hispanics generally had above average displacement rates. Ethnic minorities were, however, a larger share of urban than rural displaced workers. The uneven incidence of displacement reflects the concentration of men and minorities in production jobs. However, displacement is widespread with no groups enjoying immunity.

Economic Losses from Displacement

Both short and long-term economic losses may result from displacement. The major source of short-term losses is the unemployment that often follows permanent layoffs. Once reemployed, however, losses will con-

TABLE 10.4. Personal Economic Losses from Displacement[a]

Loss measure	Urban	Rural
Time jobless:[b]		
More than 6 months (in percent)	39.8	43.5
Median weeks	20	24
Unemployment rates (in percent)		
Displaced workers (when interviewed)	9.7	14.0
Total labor force (1986-1988 average)	5.9	7.2
Wage loss:[c]		
More than 25 percent loss	30.4	36.1
Median percent loss	6.6	10.4
Health insurance loss rate:[d]		
Workers not covered by any group plan		
(when interviewed)	25.5	33.9

[a] Adult workers displaced from full-time jobs in 1981-1986.
[b] Sample limited to workers in the 1986 DWS.
[c] Sample limited to workers reemployed in the survey week.
[d] Sample limited to workers covered by a group health insurance plan on their former job.

tinue if the new job pays a lower wage or offers fewer benefits than the former.

In DWS, interviewers were to ascertain the number of weeks workers were without work following displacement. While many rural displaced workers found jobs relatively quickly, a large group experienced a very long spell of joblessness following displacement.[10] For example, 40 percent of the rural workers were without work for 14 or fewer weeks. At the other extreme, a similar 44 percent were still not working after six months, and many of these experienced more than a year of joblessness (Table 10.4). Although the pattern is similar for urban workers, they spent less time jobless. Median time without work in rural areas was about a month longer than in urban areas (24 versus 20 weeks) and the probability of six months or more of joblessness was higher.

It may be that the long jobless periods reported in DWS are misleading. Workers were asked about events that occurred up to five years prior to the survey interview and they may not have remembered accurately the time required to find a new job. It is also possible that reported jobless times included periods during which the workers were not actively searching for a new job. If so, some workers reporting six months or more of joblessness may not have suffered large adverse effects.

Data on the labor force status of these workers at the time of the survey interviews suggest that long jobless spells frequently do indicate serious adjustment difficulties. In DWS, all displaced workers were asked the standard questions used each month to calculate official unemployment rates. In both urban and rural areas, this information was used to calculate unemployment rates for the displaced workers. These rates far exceeded the corresponding rates for the total labor force. This difference confirms that between 1 and 5 years after being displaced, a significant share of displaced workers were still having difficulty adjusting.[11]

How do the earnings on the new job compare with those on the old job when displaced workers are reemployed? As with weeks jobless, earnings losses ranged from negligible or even nonexistent to very large. At one extreme, 38 percent of the rural displaced had current weekly earnings that at least equaled their former earnings. This group seems to have experienced no lasting reduction in earnings.[12] At the other extreme, 36 percent earned less than three-quarters (and 17 percent less than half) of their former rate of pay. Many in this group likely experienced large reductions in their standard of living. As with long spells of unemployment, earnings losses—particularly severe losses—were more frequent in rural areas (Table 10.4).

Displaced workers also face a high risk of losing health insurance. For many Americans, health insurance is a fringe benefit of their job or the job of another family member. When the job is terminated, however, this benefit may terminate as well. Health insurance loss rates were calculated as the percent of displaced workers formerly covered by a group health insurance plan on their old job who were not covered by *any* group plan when interviewed. The loss rate for rural workers was 34 percent, which exceeds the 26 percent urban rate.[13]

Overall, rural workers face a higher risk of job displacement than do urban workers, and they suffer larger economic losses. These findings indicate that job displacement has been a greater source of economic insecurity for rural than for urban workers in recent years. The descriptive analysis in Tables 10.1-10.4 does not indicate, however, the relative importance of human capital deficits versus labor market conditions in generating larger rural displacement costs. As a result, appropriate policy responses are difficult to identify. The final two sections of this chapter address these issues.

Regression Analysis

Individual Determinants of Economic Losses

In order to assess the causes of higher rural losses, a series of multivariate regression models were estimated. In each case, the dependent variable is a measure of post-displacement economic status, such as weeks jobless or earnings on the new job. These dependent variables are regressed on 15 human capital variables and 5 labor market conditions variables. The estimated coefficients then indicate the effects of these individual characteristics and labor market conditions on post-displacement labor market status. Both sets of factors turn out to be important determinants of individual adjustment success.

Table 10.5 reports least squares coefficients for the combined sample of rural and urban displaced workers. Seven measures of post-displacement labor market status are used. The first three dependent variables measure the time required to become reemployed, while the fourth and fifth measure the quality of the new job. Finally, the sixth and seventh dependent variables indicate whether the worker changed occupation or moved in response to displacement. Although neither need be undesirable, high rates of occupational and geographic mobility probably reflect a scarcity of suitable job openings in the local economy.[14]

Among the human capital variables, the benefits of a good education stand out. More educated workers became reemployed more rapidly and found new jobs with better wages and benefits. The facts that displacement losses were higher for less educated workers and that the rural work force had less schooling, are consistent with the hypothesis that human capital deficiencies contributed to higher rural losses.

The work histories of these workers also left some better positioned to find good new jobs. Workers formerly employed in skilled occupations or who earned higher wages, hence likely possessed above average human capital, and as a result generally fared better. For example, craft, managerial, and professional-technical workers became reemployed at higher wages and with better health insurance coverage than less skilled workers. By contrast, workers with many years of tenure on their old job experienced large earnings losses. Some of high-tenure workers' earnings on their prior job probably reflected on-the-job learning with little application to other employers (i.e., "specific" rather than "general" human capital). However, high tenure workers had a below average health insurance loss rate and only an average amount of unemployment.

Several of the other individual characteristics also suggest that human capital investments can enhance labor market adaptability.[15] Displacement costs were higher for Blacks and older workers. By contrast, married men

TABLE 10.5. Regression Analysis of Post-Displacement Labor Market Status: Coefficient Values (Standard Errors in Parenthesis)[a]

Independent variable	(1) Probability jobless 6 months or longer	(2) Logarithm of weeks jobless	(3) Probability reemployed	(4) Logarithm of usual weekly earnings on new job	(5) Probability lost group health insurance	(6) Probability changed occupation	(7) Probability job-related move
Human capital variables:							
Age	0.006***	0.020***	0.002***	-0.002*	0.001	-0.002**	-0.004***
	(.001)	(.006)	(.001)	(.001)	(.001)	(.001)	(.001)
Education (years)	-0.016***	-0.083***	0.020***	0.026***	-0.020***	-0.003	0.010***
	(.006)	(.023)	(.003)	(.005)	(.004)	(.004)	(.003)
Race (Black = 1)	0.233***	0.640***	-0.104***	-0.090***	0.102***	0.065**	-0.055***
	(.043)	(.172)	(.023)	(.036)	(.030)	(.030)	(.020)
Job tenure (years)	0.001	-0.003	0.001	-0.009***	-0.007***	0.002	-0.004***
	(.002)	(.009)	(.001)	(.002)	(.001)	(.002)	(.001)
Sex (male = 1)	-0.078*	-0.151	-0.024	0.117***	0.031	-0.012	0.031
	(.047)	(.088)	(.025)	(.037)	(.034)	(.031)	(.023)
Married	0.061	0.357**	-0.090***	-0.060*	-0.101***	-0.010	-0.055***
	(.042)	(.068)	(.023)	(.035)	(.031)	(.029)	(.021)
Married * Male (interaction)	-0.074	-0.460**	0.164***	0.210***	-0.044	-0.030	0.019
	(.056)	(.222)	(.030)	(.045)	(.040)	(.037)	(.027)
Log of weekly wage (prior job)	0.030	-0.093	0.060***	0.479***	-0.039*	-0.081***	0.071***
	(.029)	(.120)	(.015)	(.023)	(.021)	(.018)	(.013)
Occupation (prior job):[b]							
Craft	-0.035	-0.426*	-0.005	0.181***	-0.001	-0.106***	0.038
	(.051)	(.201)	(.029)	(.044)	(.040)	(.036)	(.026)
Machine operative	0.001	-0.193	0.005	0.109**	-0.012	-0.044	-0.044*
	(.050)	(.197)	(.028)	(.043)	(.039)	(.036)	(.025)
Manager	-0.102	-0.598**	0.030	0.236***	-0.073	-0.037	-0.003
	(.063)	(.252)	(.035)	(.051)	(.047)	(.042)	(.031)
Professional and technical	-0.074	-0.317	0.099***	0.318***	-0.115**	-0.162***	-0.013
	(.061)	(.244)	(.035)	(.051)	(.047)	(.042)	(.031)
Sales	-0.050	-0.476*	0.065*	0.081	-0.056	-0.013	-0.029
	(.062)	(.245)	(.034)	(.051)	(.048)	(.041)	(.031)

TABLE 10.5. Continued

Independent variable	(1) Probability jobless 6 months or longer	(2) Logarithm of weeks jobless	(3) Probability reemployed	(4) Logarithm of usual weekly earnings on new job	(5) Probability lost group health insurance	(6) Probability changed occupation	(7) Probability job-related move
Human capital variables:							
Occupation (prior job):[b]							
Clerical	-0.075	-0.418*	0.037	0.144***	-0.072	-0.022	-0.069**
	(.060)	(.237)	(.034)	(.050)	(.045)	(.041)	(.030)
Service	-0.189***	-0.652**	0.014	0.130**	-0.015	-0.150***	-0.038
	(.070)	(.283)	(.038)	(.057)	(.058)	(.047)	(.034)
Labor market variables:							
Union coverage (prior industry)	0.341***	0.910***	-0.102**	-0.160***	-0.003	0.074	0.022
	(.069)	(.276)	(.040)	(.059)	(.049)	(.049)	(.040)
Area unemployment rate	0.030**	0.141***	-0.012***	0.001	0.008**	-0.003	-0.005*
	(.005)	(.022)	(.003)	(.005)	(.004)	(.004)	(.003)
Total plant shutdown	-0.076***	-0.488***	0.032**	0.008	-0.008	-0.069***	0.003
	(.025)	(.101)	(.014)	(.021)	(.018)	(.017)	(.012)
Advance notice of Layoff	-0.001	-0.047	0.043***	0.052**	-0.044**	0.045***	-0.009
	(.025)	(.099)	(.014)	(.020)	(.017)	(.016)	(.012)
Rural worker	0.024	0.023	-0.035**	-0.134***	0.068***	0.053***	0.042***
	(.028)	(.112)	(.015)	(.023)	(.020)	(.019)	(.014)
Number of observations	1421	1030	3927	2590	2635	2824	3923
Adjusted R²	.135	.152	.121	.379	.081	.059	.078

***, **, * Coefficient significantly different from zero at 1%, 5%, and 10%.

[a]Ordinary least squares regressions for workers aged 20 - 61, displaced from full-time jobs in 1981 - 1986, with the following exclusions: estimation sample in columns 1 and 2 limited to workers in the 1986 DWS; estimation sample in columns 4 and 6 limited to workers employed when interviewed; estimation sample in column 5 limited to workers covered by a group health plan on their prior job. All models also included an intercept term and a control variable for the number of years elapsed between the time of the layoff and the survey week. The models in columns 3 - 7 also included a dummy variable identifying observations from the 1986 survey, whose coefficient was always very small and statistically insignificant.

[b]The excluded occupational group is laborer.

experienced less unemployment than other groups, and men found higher paying jobs than women. Married women were least likely to be left without group health insurance, perhaps because they are frequently covered by their husband's employer-provided plan.

Labor market conditions also matter. In particular, lower area unemployment rates sped reemployment. The higher average unemployment rates in rural areas in the 1981-1986 period, thus, contributed to the longer unemployment spells of rural displaced workers. By contrast, high unemployment rates did not depress wages or benefits once reemployed.

Two labor market conditions that facilitate adjustment are advance notice of the impending layoff and layoffs from total plant shutdowns, rather than partial reductions in force. The potential benefits of advance notice seem clear, but the fact that total shutdowns result in less unemployment is perhaps surprising. A possible explanation is that laid-off workers postpone aggressive job searches if they believe that they may be recalled to their former job. Such a belief may be more easily sustained when the employer continues to operate.

The coefficient of the rural (zero-one) variable provides an estimate of the independent effect of residing in a rural area, once the other individual characteristics and labor market conditions included in the model have been controlled. Rural residence does not appear to have been an important cause of the longer periods of joblessness experienced by rural workers. Thus, higher rural joblessness following displacement appears to be a result of rural-urban differences in the human capital and (other) labor market conditions variables.

Rural residence is associated with significant reductions in weekly earnings once reemployed. The rural coefficient indicates an incremental earnings loss of approximately 13 percent. Rural residence also significantly increased the probability of losing health insurance coverage. These results suggest, but do not prove, that rural residence has an independent effect on losses. An alternative explanation would be that the rural coefficients are picking-up omitted determinants of labor market status. For example, if rural schools are lower quality than urban schools, then the rural coefficient may reflect this difference, rather than a pure rural effect. The evidence on occupational change and migration in columns 6 and 7 of Table 10.5, however, supports the interpretation that a true rural effect is present.

How might rural residence exercise an independent effect on economic losses? As was noted in the introduction, the sparseness of rural labor markets may reduce the probability that any given job-seeker can locate a job within commuting distance that provides a good match for that worker's particular skills and needs. If a shortage of good job-worker matches characterizes rural labor markets, workers displaced in rural areas should more frequently end up accepting jobs in different occupations or moving to areas offering better employment opportunities.

Rural workers frequently report both occupational changes and job-related moves to a new city or county. Seventy-nine percent of the rural workers found new jobs in a different occupation from their old job, while 25 percent report job-related moves. Urban displaced workers were less likely to switch occupation or move (73 and 21 percent, respectively). The regression results in Table 10.5 confirm the independent importance of rural residence for occupational change and migration. Rural residence increased the probability of changing occupation by approximately 5 percentage points and the probability of out-migration by approximately 4 percentage points. Workers displaced in urban areas, thus, appear to have better prospects of finding a similar job locally than do rural workers.

It is striking that rural residence had no independent effect on time unemployed, yet was associated with larger earnings and fringe benefit losses. Job search theory suggests a possible characterization of this difference: Reemployment opportunities are less favorable in rural areas, but workers reduce their job aspiration levels sufficiently so as not to experience longer joblessness. As was just discussed, one way in which aspirations can be lowered is through accepting jobs in different, low wage occupations. In fact, rural workers switching to a new occupation had especially large earnings losses, with two-fifths of this group reporting a reduction in weekly earnings of 25 percent or more.

Decomposition of Rural-Urban Differences

The regression framework can also be used to assess the relative importance of human capital deficiencies versus unfavorable labor market conditions in generating larger rural losses. The regressions in Table 10.5 can be represented by the following equation:

$$Y_i = X_i^{HC}\beta^{HC} + X_i^{LM}\beta^{LM} + \varepsilon_i \qquad (1)$$

where Y denotes a measure of post-displacement labor market status, X^{HC} denotes the vector of personal characteristics related to human capital levels, X^{LM} denotes the vector of labor market conditions, β^{HC} and β^{LM} are the vectors of regression coefficients, ε is the mean zero error term, and subscript i denotes the i-th individual. If model 1 is fit separately for rural and urban workers, then the estimated coefficients can be used to decompose the urban-rural difference in the mean value of Y (i.e., the outcome) into the share attributable to differences in human capital (i.e., due to differences in the mean of X^{HC}) and the share attributable to differences in labor market conditions (i.e., due to differences in the mean of X^{LM} and in the β^{HC} and β^{LM} coefficients).[16]

The basis for this decomposition is that the fitted value for Y calculated at the means of the independent variables is the mean of Y.[17] Denoting means for rural and urban workers by the subscripts r and u, respectively:

$$Y_r = X_r^{HC}\beta_r^{HC} + X_r^{LM}\beta_r^{LM} \tag{2a}$$
and
$$Y_u = X_u^{HC}\beta_u^{HC} + X_u^{LM}\beta_u^{LM} \tag{2b}$$

The share of the difference between Y_r and Y_u that is due to the relative human capital deficits of rural workers can be estimated by calculating the predicted value of an average urban worker if (s)he had instead been in a rural labor market:

$$Y_{u,r} = X_u^{HC}\beta_r^{HC} + X_r^{LM}\beta_r^{LM} \tag{3}$$

The relative importance of human capital differences is then indicated by the ratio:

$$S_1^{HC} = (Y_r - Y_{u,r})/(Y_r - Y_u) \tag{4a}$$

A second estimate of the human capital share can be calculated from the predicted Y value for an average rural worker if (s)he had instead been in an urban labor market:

$$S_2^{HC} = 1 - ((Y_r - Y_{r,u})/(Y_r - Y_u)) \tag{4b}$$

Table 10. 6 presents the fitted values used in decompositions 4a and 4b, as well as the two estimated shares, S_1HC and S_2HC. [18] These results confirm that human capital deficiencies play a significant role in worsening the labor market status of rural displaced workers. However, rural-urban differences in labor market conditions generally play a larger role in causing higher average adjustment costs for rural displaced workers.

The results of the decomposition are fairly clear for models 3-5, which predict labor market status in the survey week (i.e., the probability of being employed and wages and benefits on the new job). Human capital differences accounted for 13-36 percent of the higher rural displacement losses. Thus, human capital deficiencies were an important barrier to finding good new jobs, but rural labor market conditions were even more of a barrier.

The results are less clear for weeks jobless (models 1-2). Human capital deficiencies appear to have accounted for a large share of the higher average total weeks jobless, but only a small share of the higher probability of 6 months or more of joblessness. These somewhat contradictory estimates

TABLE 10.6. Decomposition of Rural-Urban Differences in Post-Displacement Labor Market Status.

| Dependent variable | Predicted values[a] | | | | Human capital share of rural-urban gap[b] | |
	Urban Mean Y_r	Rural HC in urban LM $Y_{r,u}$	Urban HC in rural LM $Y_{u,r}$	Rural Mean Y_r	Estimate 1: $S_1^{HC}*100$	Estimate 2: $S_2^{HC}*100$
1. More than 26 weeks jobless (percent)	42.6	43.3	46.2	46.8	14.3	16.7
2. Weeks jobless[c]	13.9	14.3	13.7	14.9	120.0	40.0
3. Reemployed (percent)	73.5	71.8	69.9	68.0	34.5	30.9
4. Weekly earnings[c] on new job (dollars)	315	295	270	259	19.6	35.7
5. Lost health insurance (percent)	27.6	29.1	34.7	35.8	13.4	18.3
6. New occupation (percent)	71.5	72.4	77.7	78.1	6.1	13.6
7. Job-related move (percent)	18.0	17.0	22.7	21.1	-51.6	-32.3

[a] "HC" denotes the human capital variables and "LM" denotes the labor market conditions variables used in the Table 5 regressions. Fitted values were calculated for four combinations of the rural and urban coefficient vectors and mean values for the HC and LM variables. (See text for details.)

[b] Two different estimates of the relative importance of the human capital variables for explaining the rural-urban differences in mean outcomes can be calculated from the four fitted values: $S_1^{HC} = (Y_r - Y_{u,r}) / (Y_r - Y_u)$ and $S_2^{HC} = 1 - ((Y_r - Y_{r,u}) / (Y_r - Y_u))$. (See the text for a full discussion.)

[c] Fitted values for models 2 and 4 are antilogarithms of the mean fitted values for log (weeks jobless) and log (weekly earnings), respectively.

suggest that the contribution of human capital deficits to greater rural unemployment is not precisely estimated.

Models 6 and 7 test whether human capital differences explain higher rural rates of occupational change and out-migration following displacement. Human capital differences accounted for approximately 10 percent of the greater propensity for rural workers to change occupations, but none of the greater propensity to move. The small (or negative) contribution of human capital factors is consistent with the hypothesis that good job matches are more difficult to find in rural labor markets. That is, sparse rural labor markets impede adjustment.

Conclusion

The essence of human capital theory is that individuals can acquire skills that enhance their future earnings capacity. The labor market returns to any particular skill, however, depend on employers' job requirements. It follows that shifts in the structure of skill demands will change the employment opportunities of individual workers. The need to adapt to shifting labor market conditions is particularly evident for displaced workers. Workers possessing—or able to learn—skills in increased demand will fare better. Workers lacking such skills will be vulnerable to prolonged unemployment or confinement to low wage jobs.

The analysis in this chapter shows that worker displacement was an important source of economic insecurity in the 1981-1986 period. Furthermore, the displacement problem was more severe in rural than in urban areas. Rural workers were more likely to be displaced and experienced higher economic costs following displacement. Finally, the human capital deficits of many rural displaced workers and the labor market conditions in many rural areas represented important barriers to adjustment success.

Displacement may be an unavoidable cost of economic change. The data for 1981-1986 suggest that the high rate of displacement reflected ongoing economic restructuring more than intermittent cyclical downturns. The challenge to rural human capital policy is, thus, less to avoid displacement than to render it less disruptive. To do so will require both the creation of new jobs to replace those lost to economic change and assistance to workers to move from declining to growing sectors of the economy.

The first of these challenges can be characterized as the need to diversify the economic base in many rural communities. This is one of the traditional focuses of rural development policy and the potential contribution of human capital investments to rural diversification is widely recognized. The severe dislocation pains experienced by many rural displaced workers, however, indicates a second need: worker flexibility to adapt to changing employment opportunities.

In the long run, more and improved schooling for the rural labor force can provide cognitive skills, including the ability to learn, that can increase adaptability. Even if successfully implemented, educational reforms will be of limited value for the majority of the existing work force which has already left school. A second tool for easing the adjustment following displacement is job counselling and retraining programs like those funded by Title III of the Job Training Partnership Act. Evaluation studies have shown that these programs can be cost effective (Leigh 1989). Yet, funding levels fall far short of what is needed to serve the 1.5 million workers displaced annually.

Since States have considerable discretion in allocating Title III funds (and limited reporting requirements), we do not know if the share of services provided to rural workers adequately reflects the greater severity of the rural displacement problem. It is also unclear whether the mix of services provided meets rural workers' particular needs, because most evaluation studies of Title III programs have focused on urban workers. However, it is known that job search assistance programs, which seek rapid placement of workers in new jobs, have been emphasized (U. S. Department of Agriculture 1991: chapter 5). These programs assume that most displaced workers are qualified to accept good, locally available jobs. Job search assistance is probably less appropriate for rural than for urban displaced workers. Rural displaced workers may frequently require more intensive (and expensive) forms of assistance, such as occupational retraining and relocation assistance.

Notes

1. See U. S. Department of Agriculture (1991) for a detailed discussion of these issues and extensive citations.

2. The number of job vacancies relative to the number of job searchers is not necessarily lower in rural labor markets. The small number and limited diversity of local employers means, however, that good matches between the specific job skills and needs of an individual searcher and the job requirements and conditions associated with local vacancies are scarcer in "thin" rural labor markets than in "thick" urban labor markets. See Mortensen (1988) for an overview of matching models and Howitt and McAfee (1987) for a discussion of the efficiency gains due to "thick" labor markets.

3. See Flaim and Sehgal (1985) for a more extensive description of the DWS. Several earlier studies used these data to study national patterns in job displacement (Podgursky and Swaim 1987a,b; 1989; Swaim 1989). Those studies concluded that approximately 1.5 million workers are displaced annually from full-time jobs and

that a significant minority experience high losses. Economic losses are higher for certain groups (blacks, women, older workers) and for workers with less schooling or in less skilled blue-collar occupations.

4. Earlier research with DWS data has shown that many workers laid off in the year immediately prior to the survey interview are eventually rehired by their former employer, hence, are not permanently displaced. Limiting the analysis to workers who have had at least a year to adapt to the loss of their former job should also better capture the long run effects of displacement. One additional sample restriction is that workers with missing information for key variables were excluded from the sample.

5. In Census Bureau terminology, these are "metropolitan" and "non-metropolitan," rather than "urban" and "rural" workers. The more colloquial terms "urban" and "rural" are used throughout the chapter.

6. Two caveats concerning the data should be noted. First, both the displacement and the migration information come from survey questions that rely on the memory of survey respondents concerning events up to five years in the past. As a result, this information is probably less accurate than the widely-analyzed data on current employment and residence in the basic CPS. Second, workers are classified as urban or rural on the basis of residence and not where they worked. It is likely that some workers classified as rural commuted to urban labor markets to work (and *vice versa*). The CPS provides no information on work location.

7. For example, workers living in rural areas when interviewed had somewhat higher personal economic costs from displacement than did the group actually displaced from rural jobs. They were also older and less educated. These differences reflect the tendency of younger and better educated workers to gravitate toward urban labor markets following displacement.

8. Census population weights provided with the CPS data were used to inflate sample counts into the national and regional totals reported in Table 10.1.

9. The DWS records relatively few displacements of wage and salary workers from agricultural jobs. The seasonal nature of much hired agricultural employment may mean that these jobs rarely achieve the degree of permanence required for displacement to be meaningful. Seasonal and migrant work is probably best viewed as a distinct source of employment insecurity, which generally is not reflected in the DWS data.

10. The wording of these questions was changed between the 1986 and 1988 DWS, so that responses from the two surveys cannot be pooled. The following discussion uses data from the 1986 survey, because the question in that year better measures total joblessness caused by displacement. The results for the jobless data from the 1988 DWS are qualitatively similar to those presented here.

11. The unemployment rates in Table 10.4 probably understate reemployment difficulties. Fourteen percent of the rural and 12 percent of the urban displaced workers were classified as "out of the labor force" when interviewed. Because all of these workers held full-time jobs before being laid-off, some of those dropping-out of the labor force probably should be viewed as "discouraged" job seekers rather than voluntary nonparticipants.

12. Before making this comparison, the worker's former earnings were adjusted

to approximate what the worker would have been earning when interviewed had he or she remained at their former job. Thus, past earnings were inflated by an index based on the worker's former occupation, sector of employment (government versus private), and year of displacement using the wage and salary component of the Employment Cost Index published by the Bureau of Labor Statistics.

13. One reason for the higher loss rate for rural workers is that they were less likely to be employed on the survey date. Although some of these workers were covered by their spouse's employer-provided plan or a public plan such as Medicare, many were not. Another reason for the lower rate of health insurance coverage in rural areas is that rural workers often accepted new jobs that did not provide this important benefit.

14. In every case, theoretical arguments can be advanced for using more complex statistical models, appropriate for limited dependent variables (Maddala 1983). The author has estimated such models and found that the results presented here are robust. For expositional ease, only the simpler, ordinary least squares specifications are reported.

15. Many of these individual characteristics may reflect—at least in part—determinants of labor market status other than human capital (i.e., job skill) differences. For example, the generally poorer outcomes for Blacks may reflect labor market discrimination.

16. Rural-urban differences in the estimated values of the β coefficients indicate differences in the labor market returns to the independent variables (e.g., years of education), hence are a component of labor market conditions.

17. See Oaxaca (1973) for an early application of this decomposition technique to the analysis of male-female earnings differences.

18. Several of the mean values in Table 10.6 differ from values reported in Table 10.4. These differences have two sources. First, Table 10.4 reports sample means; whereas Table 10.6 reports fitted values for mean individuals, which do not equal sample means for the log-linear models used for weeks jobless and weekly earnings (models 2 and 4). Second the Table 10.4 values were weighted by the population weights supplied with the CPS, but these weights were not used in the regression analysis in Tables 10.5 and 10.6.

References

Flaim, Paul, and Ellen Sehgal. 1985. "Displaced workers of 1979-83: How well have they fared?" *Monthly Labor Review* 108 (June): 3-16.

Howitt, Peter, and R. Preston McAfee. 1987. "Costly search and recruiting." *International Economic Review* 28 (February): 89-107.

Leigh, Duane. 1989. *Assisting Displaced Workers: Do the States Have A Better Idea?* Kalamazoo, MI: W.E. Upjohn Institute Press.

Maddala, G.S. 1983. *Limited Dependent and Qualitative Variables in Econometrics.* Cambridge, MA and New York, NY: Cambridge University Press.

Mortensen, Dale T. 1988. "Matching: finding a partner for life or otherwise." *American Journal of Sociology* 94 (Supplement): S215-40.

Oaxaca, Ronald L. 1973. "Male-female wage differentials in urban labor markets." *International Economic Review* 14 (October): 693-709.

Podgursky, Michael, and Paul Swaim. 1987a. "Duration of joblessness following displacement." *Industrial Relations* 26 (Fall): 213-226.

Podgursky, Michael, and Paul Swaim. 1987b. "Job displacement and earnings loss: Evidence from the displaced worker survey." *Industrial and Labor Relations Review* 41 (October 1987): 17-29.

Podgursky, Michael, and Paul Swaim. 1989. "Do more-educated workers fare better following job loss." *Monthly Labor Review* 112 (August): 43-46.

Swaim, Paul. 1989. "Worker displacement in the 1980's: An overview of recent trends." Pp. 133-39 in T. J. Kozik and D. G. Jansson (eds.),*The Worker in Transition: Technological Change.* New York, NY: The American Society of Mechanical Engineers Press.

U.S. Department of Agriculture. 1991. "Education and rural development: Strategies for the 1990's." Economic Research Service Staff Report AGES 9153, Washington, DC: G.P.O.

11

Migration and the Loss of Human Resources in Rural America[1]

Daniel T. Lichter
Diane K. McLaughlin
Gretchen T. Cornwell

The stock of human resources in rural areas is inextricably linked to past and current migration trends. During the 1970s, the net in-migration experienced by nonmetropolitan areas generated new hope for rural America (Fuguitt 1985; Morrison and Wheeler 1979). The exodus of people from nonmetropolitan areas not only slowed substantially during this period, but in-migration from metropolitan areas also accelerated (Tucker 1976). This unprecedented turnaround of historic patterns of non-metropolitan out-migration fueled new optimism about the potential for rural economic revitalization and signalled a possible end to the longstanding erosion of the human resource base in nonmetropolitan America. Indeed, the loss of the "best and brightest" from nonmetropolitan areas slowed noticeably in the 1970s (Zuiches and Brown 1978). Unlike the past, the people left behind in rural areas no longer seemed limited to the aged, the undereducated, and the unskilled.

Unfortunately, the optimism of the 1970s was short-lived. The 1980s marked the return to nonmetropolitan net out-migration, as metropolitan areas once again were growing at the expense of nonmetropolitan areas (Beale and Fuguitt 1986; Johnson 1989). During the 1980-87 period, non-metropolitan areas experienced a net out-migration rate of -1.3 percent after recording a net in-migration rate of 9.0 percent during the 1970s (Johnson 1989). Nonmetropolitan areas, dependent on a stagnating natural resource base (e.g., timber and mining) and faced with increasing international competition for product markets in the nonagricultural sector, were especially vulnerable to the national economic downturn of the early 1980s.

They have also been much slower than metropolitan areas to recover (Henry et al. 1987). It is not surprising then that the end of the population "turnaround" has rekindled longstanding concerns about the drain of human resources from rural areas.

The main objective of this chapter is to document changes in the flow of human resources between metropolitan and nonmetropolitan areas during the 1974-75 and 1987-88 periods. We focus on both the *quantitative* (e.g., volume of people) and *qualitative* (e.g., human capital of migrants) dimensions of migration to and from rural areas. Specifically, has the 1980s re-reversal in nonmetropolitan migration patterns contributed to a deepening erosion of the rural human resource base? Are nonmetropolitan areas once again providing a refuge primarily for the oldest, the least educated, and those with job skills ill-suited to the labor demands of a changing economy?

The Demographic Context of
Rural Human Resource Development

Changing rural migration patterns often provide the demographic context for either success or failure of rural human resource development programs (e.g., job training or vocational education). Indeed, out-migration affects the stock of human resources through its impact on the size and composition of rural populations (Lichter and De Jong 1990). Historically, rural out-migration has been highly selective of the youngest and the most highly educated, as the lack of rural jobs caused many to leave in search of better economic opportunities in larger urban centers (Fuguitt et al. 1989; Wilson 1987). As a result, the promise of public investments in human resource development programs (e.g., job training or vocational education) has often gone unfulfilled. Migration is a demographic mechanism that frequently perpetuates—or even reinforces—existing deficits in the stock of human resources in rural areas. Rural schools have educated their young people, only to see many of the most talented leave for better jobs in the city.

Rural development policy designed to enhance the human resource base of rural America can achieve full success only if the exodus from rural areas is slowed. At a minimum, this requires some attention to the match between labor supply and demand—between the human capital characteristics of rural people and the jobs available to them (Tigges and Tootle 1990). The 1970s was a period of optimism precisely because nonmetropolitan areas enjoyed employment growth and some measure of success both in retaining its highly-skilled people and in attracting better-educated persons from urban centers (Zuiches and Brown 1978). Indeed, an expanding rural human resource base was regarded as clear evidence of continuing rural economic development and the growing interdependence of the rural and urban sectors of the national economy (Greider and Krannich 1984; Wardwell 1978). Migration was viewed as an equilibrating mechanism that redressed spatial inequalities in human capital and contributed to a leveling of rural-urban differences in standards of living.

The present study examines the link between nonmetropolitan migration and human capital losses in the late 1980s, and thus builds on previous studies of the 1970s turnaround period (Brown and Zuiches 1978; Lichter et al. 1979; Wilson 1987). The fact that nonmetropolitan areas today are losing people on balance to metropolitan areas raises several critical questions about the changing size and character of the rural human resource base. For example, was the return to nonmetropolitan net out-migration caused primarily by an accelerated exodus from nonmetropolitan areas or by a reduction in the number of metropolitan people migrating to rural areas? Any increases in the volume of out-migration from nonmetropolitan areas could easily offset the population gains of the "turnaround" period. Such evidence would also raise serious concerns about the long-term ability of rural labor markets to retain its people, including those with skills that directly or indirectly affect the productive capacity of rural areas and the potential for economic development (see Morrison and Wheeler 1978).

The comparative human capital endowments of migrants and non-migrants are thus critically important in evaluating human capital flows between metropolitan and nonmetropolitan areas during the 1980s. Evidence from the 1950s through the early 1980s revealed that younger, more highly educated individuals employed in white-collar occupations were overrepresented in both the nonmetro-to-metro and metro-to-nonmetro migration streams (Fuguitt et al. 1989; Lichter et al. 1979). Even during the early 1970s, nonmetropolitan counties had significantly higher out-migration rates among young and highly-educated persons, while retirement age cohorts experienced higher in-migration than out-migration rates (Zuiches and Brown 1978). Nonmetropolitan areas suffered a net loss of 642,000 individuals aged 20-29 during the 1975-80 period alone (Fuguitt et al. 1989). Fortunately, this period also brought a modest reduction in the selectivity of out-migration from nonmetropolitan areas of individuals with high levels of human capital. Nonmetropolitan out-migration, compared to the previous decades, was less selective of the young and those with higher educational and occupational attainment (Lichter et al. 1979). An important question today is whether migration selectivity has continued to decline during the current period of net out-migration from rural areas.

How nonmetropolitan out-migrants compare socially and economically with nonmetropolitan in-migrants—those people originating from metropolitan areas—is an equally critical issue. Clearly, the relative sizes and comparative socioeconomic composition of the two migration streams— the migration exchange—lie at the heart of the human capital issue. If the streams to and from nonmetropolitan areas are similar in size *and* composition, then the base of human capital in nonmetropolitan areas is unaffected by migration. The rural net in-migration of the 1970s added 2.9 million to the nonmetropolitan population base (Fuguitt et al. 1989). But despite the decreasing selectivity of nonmetropolitan out-migration, those moving away from nonmetropolitan areas were nevertheless younger, more highly educated, and more occupationally-skilled than those moving to nonmetropolitan areas. Even during the period of the population "turnaround," nonmetropolitan areas continued to lose their youngest and best-educated individuals to metropolitan areas. Moreover, recent evidence in upstate New York indicates that some rural areas may now be importing metropolitan poor people in increasing numbers (Fitchen 1991), which further exacerbates spatial inequalities in the distribution of human resources. No doubt, an important issue today is whether the metro-nonmetro *exchange* of highly-educated and occupationally-skilled people has exacerbated the loss of human capital in rural areas.

Migration clearly affects the size and composition of the human resource base of nonmetropolitan America. In this chapter, we have three specific objectives. First, we document the changing volume and rates of metro-to-nonmetro and nonmetro-to-metro migration during the rural growth period of the mid-1970s, as well as during the late 1980s when rural areas experienced net out-migration. Second, we examine changes in selective out-migration from metropolitan and nonmetropolitan areas on several sociodemographic traits (e.g., education and employment) that directly or indirectly reflect human capital endowments. We evaluate whether migration has become more or less selective of young and highly-skilled persons, especially after the turnaround period of the 1970s. Third, we compare the socioeconomic characteristics and human capital endowments of individuals comprising the migration flows between metropolitan and nonmetropolitan areas. As we describe below, our analysis provides rather striking evidence that recent U.S. migration patterns have further eroded the human capital base of rural America.

Data

We use data from the 1976 and 1988 March annual demographic supplements of the *Current Population Survey (CPS)*. The *CPS* provides a nationally-representative sample of roughly 60,000 American households.[2] In addition to providing general socioeconomic and demographic information for respondents, the *CPS* files include data on current residence and retrospective information on place of residence in 1975 and 1987, respectively. As a result, we can distinguish four migrant groups: (1) metro-to-nonmetro movers, (2) nonmetro-to-metro movers, (3) metro stayers, and (4) nonmetro stayers during the 1975-76 and 1987-88 periods. Movers from abroad have been eliminated from our analysis. In addition, we do not attempt to examine metro-to-metro or nonmetro-to-nonmetro migration in this study; these migrant streams have been classified as metro stayers and nonmetro stayers, respectively.[3] This classification is appropriate given our concern with overall losses/gains of human capital in nonmetropolitan areas, as opposed to intra-area variation *within* nonmetropolitan areas.

These data for the mid-1970s and the late 1980s allow comparisons of the changing flows of human resources between metropolitan and non-metropolitan areas during a period of substantial change in migration patterns. In the current analysis, rural human resources are defined broadly. Like previous research for the 1970s (Lichter et al. 1979; Zuiches and Brown 1978), we examine the flow of population groups distinguished by the demographic variables of *sex, race,* and *age*. The age selectivity of migration is a particularly important dimension affecting the rural human resource base. High out-migration rates among young adults in their reproductive prime seriously diminishes the potential for continuing natural increase and future population growth in rural areas (Johnson 1989). In addition to these demographic characteristics, we also consider *education* and several job-related or socioeconomic characteristics commonly associated with deficiencies in human capital.[4] The latter include *occupation* (e.g., white-collar, blue-collar, and service workers/farm), *labor force status* (i.e., in or out of the labor force), *employment hardship* (i.e., jobless, part-time or working poor, or adequate), and *poverty status*. Employment hardship is measured using the Labor Utilization Framework (for technical details, see Lichter [1989] or Tigges and Tootle [1990]). Poverty is defined using official income thresholds established by the U.S. Bureau of the Census (Ruggles 1990).

The Return to Nonmetro Net Out-migration in the 1980s

Table 11. 1 shows the size of the migration streams for 1975-76 and for the post-1980 re-reversal of migration flows between metropolitan and nonmetropolitan areas. During 1987-88, nonmetropolitan areas experienced a net out-migration of 178,000 persons aged 18 and older. This compares with a net in-migration of 251,000 persons during 1975-76. The return to net out-migration in the 1980s is nearly as striking—at least

TABLE 11.1. Net Migration Between Metropolitan and Nonmetropolitan Areas, Ages 18 and Older, 1975-76, and 1987-88.

	1975-76	1987-88
Volume (in 1000;s):		
Metro-to-Nonmetro	1,733	1,157
Nonmetro-to-Metro	1,482	1,335
Nonmetro Net Migration	251	-178
Rates:[a]		
Metro-to-Nonmetro	17.5	10.1
Nonmetro-to-Metro	32.3	34.8
Nonmetro Net Migration	5.5	-4.6
Metro Net Migration	-2.5	1.5

[a] Calculated as: [Movers/(Stayers + Movers); x 1000. Movers from abroad are excluded.

numerically—as the largely unexpected nonmetropolitan net in-migration of the 1970s. Indeed, after a net in-migration rate of 5.5 persons per 1000 during 1975-76, nonmetropolitan areas lost on balance nearly 4.6 persons per 1000 during the 1987-88 period.

Previous research has shown that the 1970s nonmetropolitan turn-around was a consequence of both increases in metro-to-nonmetro migration and decreases in the rate of gross out-migration from nonmetropolitan areas (Tucker 1976). This pattern was reversed in the 1980s. Although there was a slight upturn in rural out-migration in the post-1980 period, the rural re-reversal was due primarily to the slowing of in-migration from metropolitan areas (Table 11.1, bottom panel). The gross rate of metropolitan out-migration to nonmetropolitan areas dipped from 17.5 per 1000 in 1975-76 to about 10 per 1000 in 1987-88. The magnitude of this shift over a relatively short period raises questions about future prospects for rural population growth from metropolitan in-migration (see Johnson 1989). The corresponding high rate of nonmetropolitan out-migration likewise raises the specter of incipient declines in the human resource base of rural America, especially if out-migration is selective of those with the highest levels of human capital.

Migration Selectivity—How Migrants Compare with Nonmigrants

If the human capital endowments of nonmetropolitan out-migrants are identical to those of stayers, the population composition of non-metropolitan areas will be unaffected by out-migration, regardless of its magnitude. The higher migration propensities among certain groups of individuals—those who are younger, better-educated, and hold white-collar occupations—means that migration affects the human resource base at both origin and destination locations. Decreases in the selectivity of non-metropolitan out-migration reported in previous studies (Lichter et al. 1979) suggest that migrants and nonmigrants have become increasingly similar over time. This dilutes the potentially deleterious effects on the quality of human capital accumulated in rural areas, even though the size of the human resource base is diminished by out-migration. Data in Table 11.2 provide a basis for determining whether the declining selectivity of migration continued into the 1980s.

These data clearly reveal that out-migrants from both metropolitan and nonmetropolitan areas tended to have more human capital (as defined here) than stayers, both in the 1970s and 1980s. For the 1987-88 period, 41.2 percent of the metro-origin migration stream were aged 18-29, compared with 28.4 percent of the stayers. In the nonmetro-origin stream, 51.7 percent of the migrants were aged 18-29 compared with 23.2 percent of the stayers. In both streams, the proportion of individuals aged 18-29 in the migrant stream declined between 1975-76 and 1987-88, which suggests some reduction in selectivity of young adults. For each migration period, however, the nonmetro-origin movers included a higher proportion of young individuals than the metro-origin mover group.

Migration streams were also highly selective on education, a key human capital indicator. For 1975-76, persons with 13 or more years of education represented a much higher percentage of the migration streams than of the metropolitan and nonmetropolitan stayer populations. This pattern continued for the 1987-88 period, but only for the nonmetro-origin stream. Among nonmetropolitan out-migrants, 45 percent had 13 or more years of education as compared with about 26 percent of the stayers. This pattern of educational selectivity contrasts sharply with the metro-origin stream. Only 38 percent of movers had 13 or more years of education, compared with 41 percent of the metro stayers. Unlike the mid-1970s, metropolitan areas are now exporting a disproportionate share of their least educated. The silver lining is that these in-migrants nevertheless compare favorably with the nonmetropolitan stayers they are joining.

Migration selectivity is also apparent on the occupational status of workers, on employment hardship, and on poverty status. In both the mid-1970s and late-1980s, nonmetro-origin migrants were comprised disproportionately of white-collar workers. On the other hand, white-collar occupations were *underrepresented* among those migrating from metro-to-nonmetro areas. Moreover, the metro-to-nonmetro stream was disproportionately comprised of the jobless, as well as the poor and the near poor (i.e., with incomes less than twice the poverty threshold). Indeed, the

TABLE 11.2. Percent Distributions of Sociodemographic Characteristics, by Migration Status, 1975-76, and 1987-88.

	Metropolitan				Nonmetropolitan			
	1975-76		1987-88		1975-76		1987-88	
	Stayer	Mover	Stayer	Mover	Stayer	Mover	Stayer	Mover
Sex:								
Female	52.8	50.1	52.4	49.8	52.5	52.5	52.4	51.0
Male	47.2	49.9	47.6	50.2	47.5	47.5	47.6	49.0
Race:								
Black	11.2	5.2	12.6	6.5	7.9	7.6	8.8	9.1
Non-black	88.3	94.8	87.4	93.5	92.1	92.4	91.2	90.9
Age:								
18-29	30.1	53.9	28.4	41.2	28.1	63.9	23.2	51.7
30-59	49.7	36.4	51.2	47.0	47.3	30.6	50.7	41.5
60+	20.2	9.6	20.4	11.8	24.6	5.5	26.1	6.8
Education:[a]								
0-11	32.4	27.1	21.6	23.2	44.3	23.5	31.1	17.6
12	36.7	38.5	37.2	39.1	35.4	33.1	42.7	37.4
13 or more	30.8	34.4	41.2	37.7	20.3	43.4	26.2	45.0
Labor Force Status:								
Non-participant	35.6	34.6	36.0	39.9	39.7	28.1	43.2	29.0
Participant	64.4	65.4	64.0	60.1	60.3	71.9	56.8	71.0
Employment Hardship:[b]								
Jobless	9.1	16.4	6.5	11.4	8.3	13.6	6.5	5.5
Marginal[c]	8.9	11.4	10.3	18.6	13.9	14.7	17.3	20.7
Adequate	82.0	72.1	83.1	69.9	77.8	71.7	76.2	73.9
Occupation:								
White-collar	54.0	52.6	59.7	51.8	39.2	54.1	42.4	50.5
Blue-collar	31.2	31.1	25.4	29.3	38.6	28.9	35.1	27.5
Service/Farm	14.8	16.2	14.9	18.9	22.2	16.9	22.5	22.1
Poverty Status:								
Poor	8.7	12.4	10.1	18.7	13.8	16.2	14.3	17.6
1-2 times poor	8.7	12.8	7.4	13.9	12.9	13.2	11.5	13.4
2+ times poor	82.5	74.7	82.5	67.4	73.3	70.5	74.2	69.1

[a]Restricted to ages 25 and older.
[b]Refers to participation in the modified labor force.
[c]Includes involuntary part-time and low-wage workers.

TABLE 11.3. Changes in Migration Selectivity: Index of Dissimilarity.[a]

	Metro-to-Nonmetro Stream			Nonmetro-to-Metro Stream		
	1975-76	1987-88	Change	1975-76	1987-88	Change
Sex	2.7	2.6	-.1	.0	1.4	1.4
Race	6.0	6.1	.1	.3	.3	.0
Age	23.9	12.8	-11.1	35.8	28.5	-7.3
Education	5.4	3.5	-1.9	23.1	18.8	-4.3
Labor Force Status	1.0	3.9	2.9	11.6	14.2	2.6
Employment Hardship	9.9	13.2	3.3	6.1	3.4	-2.7
Occupation	1.6	7.9	6.3	15.0	8.1	-6.9
Poverty Status	7.9	15.1	7.2	2.9	5.1	2.2

[a]Compares characteristics of migrants to origin residents.

percentage poor comprised a larger proportion of both streams during the 1980s than in the earlier period.

The results in Table 11.2 give a rather complex picture of changing patterns of migration selectivity between 1975-76 and 1987-88. Consequently, we calculated an index of dissimilarity (D), which summarizes mover-stayer differences in the percentage distributions of each of the sociodemographic characteristics considered in Table 11.2. The values of D, which are presented in Table 11.3, indicate the percentage of migrants that would have to shift categories before the percentage distribution of the migrant stream was equal to that of stayers.[5] Thus, the degree of migration selectivity is indicated by the size of the D value.

The results in Table 11.3 support two general conclusions. First, the declines in migration selectivity from nonmetropolitan areas observed for the 1975- 76 period (Lichter et al. 1979) generally persisted through the 1987-88 period. For 1975-76, 35.8 percent of nonmetro-to-metro migrants would have had to change age categories before migrants and stayers had similar age distributions. Indeed, the age selectivity of nonmetropolitan out-migration is greater than for any other characteristic. But the value of D for age declined to 28.5 by 1987-88. The results in Table 11.3 likewise indicate declines over time in the selectivity of migration by education level (i.e., 23.1 to 18.8) and occupation (i.e., 15.0 to 8.1). The extent of sex, race, and employment status selectivity of nonmetropolitan out-migration was small regardless of period, with little change in selectivity observed for the other indicators of socioeconomic status considered here.

A second general conclusion is that patterns of out-migration from metropolitan areas suggest a much less optimistic demographic future for rural America. Although the metro-to-nonmetro stream, like its counterstream, revealed declines in age selectivity (i.e., 23.9 to 12.8 over

1975-76 to 1987-88 period), the Ds indicate that metro-origin out-migrants became *more* selective over time on employment status, occupation, and poverty status. Specifically, the metro-to-nonmetro stream became increasingly overrepresentative of the jobless, the marginally employed, blue-collar and service/farm workers, and the poor (see full detail in Table 11.2). Thus, compared to the turnaround period of the 1970s, metropolitan areas in the late 1980s were more likely to export their least skilled and their poor to nonmetropolitan areas. Thus, the declines in selectivity of the youngest and most educated from nonmetropolitan areas must be balanced against the evidence of increases in *negative* selectivity of metropolitan-origin migrants on several socioeconomic characteristics.

Out-migration Rates—Nonmetro Areas
Experience Widespread Upswing in 1980s

The overall return to nonmetropolitan net out-migration in the 1980s was due to declining in-migration and increasing out-migration (see Table 11.1). But does this pattern exist for various population subgroups? For example, evidence of increasing nonmetropolitan out-migration of the highly educated and skilled, but decreases among the less skilled, will magnify the potential deleterious effects of migration on the stock of human resources in rural areas. An alternative scenario—with much different implications for rural human capital—is one in which the overall increase in nonmetropolitan out-migration is comprised primarily of the less skilled. The different mix of in-migration and out-migration rates across population subgroups will have quite different implications for rural human capital.

Table 11.4 contains out-migration rates (per 1000) for the metro-to-nonmetro and nonmetro-to-metro migration streams for both the 1975-76 and 1987-88 periods. These data for nonmetropolitan areas provide a single overarching conclusion: The 1980s upturn in nonmetropolitan out-migration was generally widespread across population subgroups. The only nonmetropolitan group that experienced a decline in gross out-migration was the jobless. Thus, most nonmetropolitan population subgroups—young or old, highly educated or less educated, occupationally-skilled or less-skilled—shared in the upward shift in out-migration in the 1980s. Nonmetropolitan areas are increasingly exporting their "best and brightest," as well as their least skilled and least educated.

The results showing subgroup participation in the post-1980 downturn in metropolitan out-migration rates provide more equivocal and less optimistic conclusions for rural America (Table 11.4). While most segments of the metropolitan population shared in the decline in rates of out-migra-

TABLE 11.4. Outmigration Rates (per 1000) for Selected Sociodemographic Subpopulations, 1975-88 and 1987-88.

	Metro-to-Nonmetro Stream		Nonmetro-to-Metro Stream	
	1975-76	1987-88	1975-76	1987-88
Sex:				
Female	16.6	9.9	32.2	33.9
Male	18.5	10.6	32.3	35.9
Race:				
Black	8.2	5.3	31.1	36.1
Non-black	18.7	10.7	32.2	34.7
Age:				
18-29	30.9	14.5	70.4	74.3
30-59	12.9	9.2	21.1	28.7
60+	8.4	5.9	7.5	9.3
Education:				
0-11	12.2	9.8	11.5	15.4
12	15.3	9.6	20.1	23.5
13 or more	16.2	8.4	44.9	45.0
Labor Force Status:				
Non-participant	17.0	11.1	23.4	23.6
Participant	17.8	9.5	38.2	43.2
Employment Hardship:				
Jobless	31.6	16.5	61.1	36.9
Marginal	22.7	17.0	40.4	51.2
Adequate	15.7	8.0	35.3	41.9
Occupation:				
White-collar	17.7	9.1	50.4	49.8
Blue-collar	18.1	12.1	28.1	33.3
Service/Farm	15.7	8.0	28.4	41.4
Poverty Status:				
Poor	24.7	18.5	37.9	42.3
1-2 times poor	25.4	18.7	33.0	40.1
2+ times poor	15.9	8.2	31.1	32.5

tion, it is nevertheless clear that declines were most apparent among the young, highly educated, and occupationally skilled. Such a pattern reinforces the results in Table 11.2 on metropolitan migration selectivity. For example, the rate of metropolitan out-migration among young adults was cut in half between 1975-76 and 1987-88 (i.e., from 30.9 to 14.5 per 1000).

Indeed, most of the decrease in metropolitan out-migration was due to greater metropolitan retention of young adults. Likewise, the pattern of out-migration by educational level reversed between the 1970s and 1980s. The most educated group had the highest rate of metropolitan out-migration for 1975-76. By 1987-88, the highly educated in metro areas had the *lowest* rate of out-migration. A similarly disquieting pattern also occurred for the poverty variable: out-migration of the wealthiest declined the most, while it declined the least (on a percentage basis) among the poor.

In summary, subgroup differentials in patterns of nonmetropolitan out-migration provide the basis for a rather neutral assessment of the effects on rural human capital accumulation. The results of changing metropolitan out-migration (or alternatively, nonmetropolitan in-migration) tell a much different story. The 1980s have not only brought significant reductions in the level of in-migration from metropolitan areas, but these reductions have been primarily among the youngest, most educated, and the skilled. The flow of human capital to nonmetropolitan areas—both from a quantitative and qualitative standpoint—shifted noticeably between the mid-1970s and late-1980s.

Migration Exchange—The Changing Impact of Net Migration on Human Capital Resources in Nonmetro Areas

To this point, we have described the changing migration selectivity patterns—how migrants compare to nonmigrants—and recent shifts in differential out-migration from metropolitan and nonmetropolitan areas. Yet unanswered is the central question of whether the migration re-reversal has adversely affected the rural stock of human capital. Simply, what is the impact of the new migration patterns on the sociodemographic composition of nonmetropolitan areas? In this section, we consider several different approaches to this question.

An initial approach asks how the socioeconomic composition of the metro-to-nonmetro stream compares with that of the nonmetro-to-metro stream. Are migration streams becoming more similar to each other over time? Table 11.5 provides indexes of dissimilarity that summarize the differences in percentage distributions between metro-to-nonmetro and nonmetro-to-metro migrants for the various socioeconomic traits. The results support two general conclusions. First, the D values indicate rather remarkable similarity in the socioeconomic composition of each stream. Indeed, for both migration periods, the two migrant streams were generally more similar to each other than to their origin nonmigrants (cf., Table 11.3), a finding consistent with earlier studies (Lichter et al. 1979). The composi-

TABLE 11.5. Nonmetropolitan Net Migration Rates (per 1000), Metro-Mover to Nonmetro-Mover Interchange Ratios, and Indices of Dissimilarity (Ds)[a].

	1975-76			1987-99		
	Net Migration	Interchange		Net Migration	Interchange	
	Rate	Ratio	D	Rate	Ratio	D
Sex:			2.4			1.2
Female	3.7	1.12		-5.2	.85	
Male	7.3	1.23		-4.1	.89	
Race:			2.4			2.6
Black	-6.3	.80		-13.6	.62	
Non-black	6.5	1.20		-3.8	.89	
Age:			10.0			5.0
18-29	-.8	.99		-23.0	.69	
30-59	8.2	1.39		-.6	.98	
60+	7.7	2.04		4.7	1.51	
Education:			9.0			7.3
0-11	7.9	1.67		4.9	1.32	
12	14.0	1.70		1.4	1.06	
13 or more	7.1	1.16		-6.9	.85	
Labor Force Status:			6.5			10.9
Non-participant	10.3	1.44		4.5	1.19	
Participant	2.4	1.06		-11.5	.73	
Employment Hardship:			3.3			5.9
Jobless	17.3	1.28		19.9	1.53	
Marginal	-7.0	.83		-17.2	.66	
Adequate	2.5	1.07		-12.8	.69	
Occupation:			2.2			3.2
White-collar	3.0	1.06		-9.4	.81	
Blue-collar	4.8	1.17		5.1	.85	
Service/Farm	1.2	1.04		-13.3	.68	
Poverty Status:			4.2			1.7
Poor	-3.9	.89		-3.3	.92	
1-2 times poor	4.4	1.13		-3.8	.90	
2+ times poor	7.4	1.24		-5.0	.85	

[a]D compares sociodemographic characteristics of Metro-to-Nonmetro Movers with Nonmetro-to-Metro Movers.

tional similarity of streams undoubtedly dilutes any potentially adverse effects of migration on either origin or destination populations. Second, the results in Table 11.5 provide only partial indication that the two streams have become increasingly similar over the period considered here. For four of the eight characteristics, the D values declined in size. Such a result is inconsistent with Wardwell's (1978) prediction that the continuing spatial homogenization of America society—both socially and economically— would contribute to declining socioeconomic differences between migrants moving to and from nonmetropolitan areas.

The problem with comparisons of percentage distributions (which provide the basis for calculating Ds) is that the impact of volume of migration streams is ignored. As a second approach, the nonmetropolitan net migration rate provides an alternative measure of the impact of net migration— the balance of the exchange between metropolitan and nonmetropolitan areas—on the nonmetropolitan population.[6] These rates clearly reveal that the 1980s re-turnaround to nonmetropolitan out-migration has had rather pervasive effects across the sociodemographic groups considered here. But perhaps even more significant is that the highest net out-migration rates were observed among the youngest, best educated, and labor force participants. For example, between 1975-76 and 1987-88, the nonmetropolitan net out-migration rate of young adults increased from -.8 to -23.0, a change greater than for any other characteristic. Similarly, net out-migration of the most educated reversed from 7.1 to -6.9 over this period. Migration flows upgraded the educational capital of rural America during the 1970s, but diminished the human capital base in the 1980s. Indeed, during the late-1980s, the least educated groups continued to experience net in-migration in nonmetropolitan areas.

The results for occupational characteristics give a similarly pessimistic story. Net out-migration rates in the 1980s were highest among those most attached to the labor force, i.e., labor force participants (-11.5), white-collar (-9.4), and service workers (-13.3). Moreover, while nonmetropolitan areas experienced a net gain (i.e., 7.4 per 1000) of higher income groups during the 1970s, this pattern was reversed in the late 1980s by net out-migration (i.e., -5.0 per 1000) among those with incomes two or more times the official poverty threshold. Conversely, nonmetropolitan areas in the 1980s experienced high net in-migration rates only among the jobless (i.e., 19.9 per 1000). Clearly, patterns of net migration in the late 1980's have had a serious impact on the human resource base of nonmetropolitan areas.

Our final approach is to compare the relative and absolute sizes of subgroup streams to and from nonmetropolitan areas. The *relative* size of the metro-to-nonmetro and nonmetro-to-metro streams is given by the interchange ratio, calculated as the ratio of nonmetropolitan in- to out-migration (Table 11.5, Columns 2 and 5). This ratio has a straightforward interpretation. For example, the number of males moving from metro-to-nonmetro was 23 percent higher than the number migrating from non-metro-to-metro areas over the 1975-76 period (i.e., the interchange ratio was 1.23). Overall, the interchange ratios reinforce a familiar theme: the post-1980s nonmetropolitan re-reversal, while being experienced broadly across population groups, was nevertheless particularly pronounced among the youngest (.69), most educated (.85), and those with job skills (e.g., as reflected in the interchange ratio [.69] for the adequately employed).

More important, these interchange ratios translate into sizable shifts between 1975-76 and 1987-88 in the *absolute* population gained or lost in the migration exchange between metropolitan and nonmetropolitan areas. The rather striking magnitude of these changes are illustrated in Figures 11.1 -11.7. They reveal quite vividly the changes in aggregate levels of net migration over the past decade or so. In each instance, the data paint a pessimistic picture of recent migration change for nonmetropolitan America. For example, the interchange ratio (Table 11.5) among young adults (aged 18-29) indicates that the nonmetropolitan in-migration stream

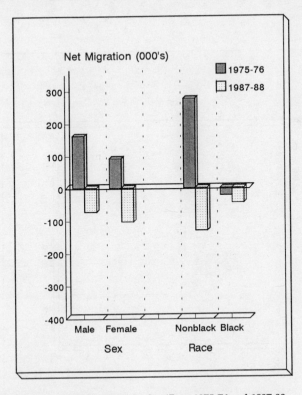

FIGURE 11.1. Nonmetro Net Migration, by Sex/Race, 1975-76 and 1987-88.

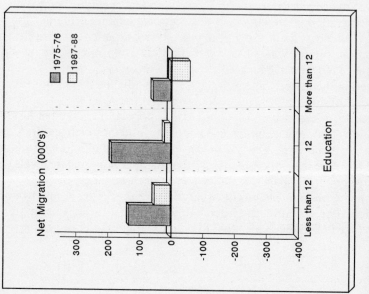

FIGURE 11.3 Nonmetro Net Migration, by Education, 1975-76 and 1987-88.

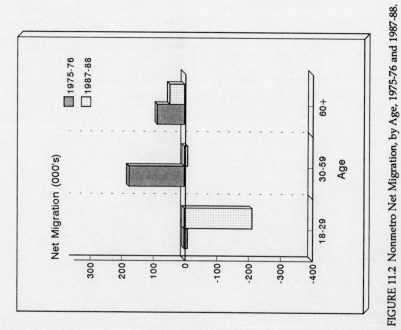

FIGURE 11.2 Nonmetro Net Migration, by Age, 1975-76 and 1987-88.

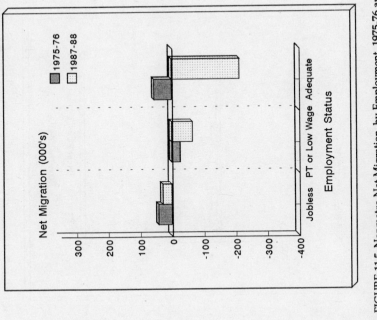

FIGURE 11.4 Nonmetro Net Migration, by Labor, 1975-76 and 1987-88.

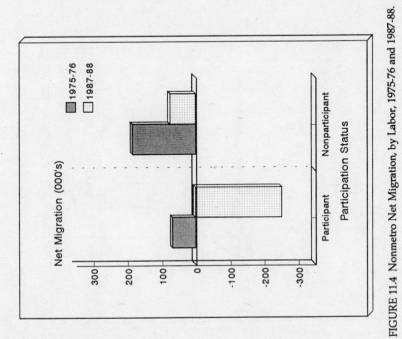

FIGURE 11.5 Nonmetro Net Migration, by Employment, 1975-76 and 1987-88.

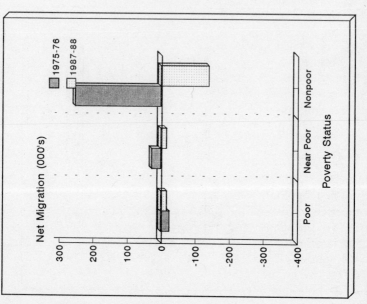

FIGURE 11.6 Nonmetro Net Migration, by Occupation, 1975-76 and 1987-88.

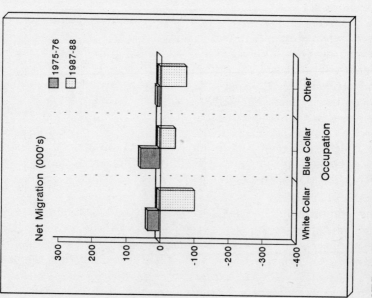

FIGURE 11.7 Nonmetro Net Migration, by Poverty Status, 1975-76 and 1987-88.

was only 66 percent of the out-migration stream in the late 1980s. But this represents a substantial aggregate loss of over 200,000 young adults over a one-year period (Figure 11.2). These data for nonmetropolitan areas similarly highlight the large aggregate losses of the highly educated (Figure 11.3), labor force participants (Figure 11.4), the adequately employed (Figure 11.5), white-collar workers (Figure 11.6), and the nonpoor (Figure 11.7) during the late 1980s. Despite the optimism implied by growing similarity in the characteristics of nonmetropolitan in- and out-migrants, the nonmetropolitan migration re-reversal was a significant source of aggregate losses of human capital in rural areas.

Conclusion

The nonmetropolitan turnaround of the 1970s, heralded by some as a renaissance period for rural America (Morrison and Wheeler 1978), was not sustained into the 1980s. As a result, recent trends have again raised the specter of nonmetropolitan America being depleted of one of its most valuable resources—its people. Indeed, our analysis suggests that the 1980s represented an unwelcome departure from the 1970s when migration contributed—both quantitatively and qualitatively—to the stock of human resources in rural areas. The message for the 1980s is much different.

1. Nonmetropolian net out-migration during 1987-88 nearly equalled the volume of net in-migration in nonmetropolitan areas for 1975-76. This reversal reflected both increases in nonmetropolitan out-migration and decreases in in-migration from metropolitan areas.

2. Despite declines in selective nonmetropolitan out-migration of the highly educated and occupationally skilled between the mid-1970s and late-1980s, metropolitan areas *increasingly* exported those with the lowest levels of education and job skills.

3. Increases in nonmetropolitan out-migration over 1975-76 and 1987-88 were broadly experienced across population subgroups. Conversely, declines in metropolitan out-migration were differentially observed among the young, the highly educated, adequately employed, and the nonpoor. Metropolitan areas thus, are increasingly retaining their "best and brightest."

4. The optimism implied by an apparent convergence in the socio-economic characteristics of migrants to and from nonmetropolitan areas must be tempered by the aggregate exchange of migrants that on balance strongly favored metropolitan areas in 1987-88. More significant, the exchange of population between metropolitan and non-

metropolitan areas resulted in large absolute losses of the young, educated, and highly skilled in nonmetropolitan areas.

In conclusion, the 1980s has caused many observers to retreat from their often unabashed optimism of the nonmetropolitan population turnaround period. The upswing in nonmetropolitan out-migration has instead renewed our appreciation of the historic role of migration in perpetuating or even reinforcing longstanding spatial inequalities in human resources and in the quality of life in America. Indeed, given the evidence presented here, the post-1980s period has marked a return to an earlier historic trend, one where migration diminished rather than added to the base of human resources in rural America.

Notes

1. The authors acknowledge the helpful comments and/or assistance of Bo Beaulieu, John Cromartie, Glenn Fuguitt, Terry Glantz, Ken Johnson, David Mulkey, and Lou Ploch.

2. For these analyses we use the recently-released 1988 CPS file that has been corrected for previous inaccuracies in the coding of migration between metropolitan and nonmetropolitan areas over the 1987-88 period.

3. One problem with using the *CPS* files is that nonmetropolitan or metropolitan areas have been redefined over the 1975-76 and 1987-88 periods. That is, some nonmetropolitan areas have been reclassified as metropolitan between 1975-76 and 1987-88. Fortunately, the volume of migration between metropolitan and non-metropolitan areas for either 1975-76 or 1987-88 is not affected by reclassification.

4. One limitation of these job-related characteristics is that they are measured at the end of the migration period (i.e., in 1976 and 1988). Consequently, the problem is that end-of-period characteristics may be a function of either (1) the individual human capital or skills of the migrants; and/or (2) the limited (or expanded) employment opportunities in the place of destination. On the other hand, whether new in-migrants *were* jobless or *became* jobless when they moved to rural areas is largely immaterial to the questions posed in this paper. The essential point is whether the new in-migrants have become economically assimilated in the place of destination and are contributing (or not) to the productive potential of rural America.

5. The index of dissimilarity is calculated as:

$$D = 1/2 \quad | \ m_i - s_i |$$

where m_i is the percentage of movers in category i and s_i is the percentage of stayers in category i. Obviously, if migrants and stayers where distributed in the same proportions over categories, D would be 0. A D of 100 would indicate that there is no overlap between movers and stayers in the distribution, a result that would indicate substantial selectivity in migration.

6. Nonmetropolitan net migration rates are calculated as:

$$\frac{\text{Metro Movers} - \text{Nonmetro Movers}}{\text{Nonmetro Stayers} + \text{Nonmetro Movers}} \times 1000$$

The denominator is the population at time 2 in the absence of either in- or out-migration. Consequently, this rate reveals the "impact" of migration by expressing population change (resulting from in-and-out migration) as a proportion of population size.

References

Beale, Calvin L., and Glenn V. Fuguitt. 1978. "The new pattern of nonmetropolitan population change." Pp. 157-77 in K.E. Taeuber, L.L. Bumpass, and J.A. Sweet (eds.), *Social Demography*. New York, NY: Academic Press.

Fitchen, Janet M. 1991. *Endangered Spaces, Enduring Places*. Boulder, CO: Westview Press.

Fuguitt, Glenn V. 1985. "The nonmetropolitan population turnaround." *Annual Review of Sociology* 11: 259-80.

Fuguitt, Glenn V., David L. Brown, and Calvin L. Beale. 1989. *Rural and Small Town America*. New York, NY: Russell Sage.

Greider, Thomas, and Richard S. Krannich. 1984. "Diffusion and development in the Rocky Mountain Region, 1940-80." *Growth and Change* 15: 41-49.

Henry, Mark, Mark Drabenstott, and Lynn Gibson. 1987. "Rural growth slows down." *Rural Development Perspectives* 3 (June): 25-30.

Horan, Patrick M., and Charles M. Tolbert II. 1984. *The Organization of Work in Rural and Urban Labor Markets*. Boulder, CO: Westview Press.

Johnson, Kenneth M. 1989. "Recent population redistribution trends in non-metropolitan America." *Rural Sociology* 54: 301-26.

Lichter, Daniel T. 1989. "Race, employment hardship, and inequality in American nonmetropolitan south." *American Sociological Review* 54: 436-46.

Lichter, Daniel T., and Gordon F. De Jong. 1990. "The United States." Pp. 391-417 in C.B. Nam, W.J. Serow, and D.F. Sly (eds.), *International Handbook on Internal Migration*. New York, NY: Greenwood.

Lichter, Daniel T., Tim B. Heaton, and Glenn V. Fuguitt. 1979. "Trends in the selectivity of migration between metropolitan and nonmetropolitan areas: 1955-1975." *Rural Sociology* 44: 645-66.

Morrison, Peter A., and Judith P. Wheeler. 1976. *Rural Renaissance in America? The Revival of Population Growth in Remote Areas*. Population Bulletin 31. Washington, D.C.: Population Reference Bureau.

Parcel, Toby L., and Charles W. Mueller. 1983. *Ascription and Labor Markets: Race and Sex Differences in Earnings*. New York, NY: Academic Press.

Ruggles, Patricia. 1990. *Drawing the Line: Alternative Poverty Measures and Their Implications for Public Policy*. Washington, DC: Urban Institute.

Tigges, Leanne, and Debra Tootle. 1990. "Labor supply, labor demand, and men's underemployment in rural and urban labor markets." *Rural Sociology* 55: 328-56.

Tucker, C. Jack. 1976. "Changing patterns of migration between metropolitan and nonmetropolitan areas in the United States: Recent evidence." *Demography* 13: 435-43.

Wardwell, John M. 1977. "Equilibrium and change in nonmetropolitan growth." *Rural Sociology* 42: 156-79.

Wilson, Franklin D. 1987. "Metropolitan and nonmetropolitan migration streams: 1935-1980." *Demography* 24: 211-28.

Zuiches, James J., and David L. Brown. 1978. "The changing character of the nonmetropolitan population, 1950-75." Pp. 55-72 in T.R. Ford (ed.), *Rural U.S.A.: Persistence and Change.* Ames, IA: Iowa State University Press.

PART FOUR

Strategies for Strengthening the Human Capital Resources of Rural America

12

Capacity Building:
Reexamining the Role of
the Rural School

Daryl Hobbs

The schools of rural America have generally served their students and the nation well. A near constant throughout the 20th century has been an uninterrupted flow of workers from rural to urban America. Thanks to the ubiquity and effectiveness of rural schools, this migration has represented a massive transfer of human capital—most of the migrants have been educationally well prepared to fill the greater job opportunities in urban areas. Thus, the nation has benefitted from this contribution to economic growth. But a further consequence continues to be a widening gap in economic growth and income between rural and urban America. As we complete the final years of the 20th century, these trends continue and the consequences accumulate. A slow erosion of the relative economic well-being of rural America continues. Accordingly, there is a need to re-think economic development strategies for rural areas and the role that education (investments in human capital) could play in an alternative prescription for rural development.

This chapter focuses on the need for rural (economic) development and examines the limitations of some of the traditional approaches to economic development and school improvement. It begins by raising some questions about the economic development role of human capital and proceeds through some further modifications of that concept necessitated by rural conditions. It then considers rural schools and their relationship to rural development. A conclusion is that there is a need for re-thinking the relationship between education in rural areas and its linkage to development.

Human Capital and Economic Growth

The idea of human capital has become an integral component of American orthodoxy surrounding both education and economic growth. The logic is deceptively simple and direct. The orthodoxy specifies that economic growth in an increasingly technical, complex and interrelated global economy is vitally dependent on a nation's stock of human capital. The greater the amount of human capital, the greater the likelihood of national economic growth and the greater the economic well-being of those in possession of human capital. The most widely used measure of human capital has been educational attainment of workers. The more education, presumably the more human capital. Thus, the syllogism is completed; economic growth is significantly dependent on human capital, human capital is produced by education, therefore economic growth is quite dependent on education.

In elaborating the idea of human capital, Schultz (1961, 1967) reasoned that in the U.S. during the 20th century, residual growth—the difference between the amount of economic growth and growth in the traditional factors of production (land, labor and physical capital)—could most validly be explained by improvements in the skills, knowledge and habits of the work force. In an effort to verify this conceptual relationship, the most convenient longitudinal measure of those characteristics of labor was the amount of schooling workers had received. Thus, typical human capital analyses took the form of determining the correlation between schooling attainment and earnings of workers, based on the further assumption that earnings are a reflection of the greater skill and ability of workers.

Correspondingly, education came to be regarded as an investment, since it comes at a cost, is associated with a prospect of future returns, and is subject to obsolescence—characteristics shared with physical capital. The fact that early analyses found those correlations to be positive and strong helped root the idea in the public (and private) mind regarding a direct linkage between economic growth, human capital, and the amount and quality of workers' education. That idea has been gaining in prominence and influence in the face of growing concern about U.S. economic competitiveness and the growing cost, and presumed declining effectiveness, of public education. The book *Nation At Risk* (1983) strongly reinforced that linkage and has catalyzed a spate of educational reforms. Indeed educators have increasingly emphasized the presumed relationship between education and economic growth in order to sustain public support for education in the face of broad-based challenges.

Human Capital in the Rural Context

To reiterate, the education/economic growth relationship is deceptively simple. Recent research supports the existence of a *correlation* between education and earnings but raises many questions about *cause and effect*. Assuming validity of the human capital concept, researchers have raised important empirical questions concerning how human capital is acquired, where it is acquired, what human capital materializes in economic growth and individual well-being, and who benefits from human capital investments. Those questions take on particular significance for rural areas as recent trends have documented an *increase* in rural education attainment and expenditures, concurrent with a *relative decrease* in rural income and higher paying employment (Porterfield 1990). Rural areas are providing further evidence that human capital without employment that uses it does not contribute much to economic growth.

As of 1990, nonmetropolitan income averaged only 73 percent of metropolitan income. Further, given the extant mix of nonmetropolitan economic activity, the National Governor's Association (1988) projects that nonmetropolitan income will grow at only 75 percent of the national rate during the 1990s. Rural poverty rates have crept up to a level nearly 50 percent higher than metropolitan rates (Reid and Frederick 1990). Despite these indicators of a growing gap between rural and urban economic well-being, nonmetropolitan counties have outspent metropolitan counties for education in all but seven states (Jansen 1991). Furthermore, nonmetro patterns of employment growth were not found to be related to average schooling levels of the population for either the 1969-1979 or 1979-1986 periods (Killian and Parker 1991). These findings do not suggest that education is not valuable or worth the investment, but it does cast doubt on the simplistic connection between education and employment growth. The relationship is more complex, especially for rural areas.

In this chapter we will review recent rural economic development and education research that has added complexity to the human capital-economic development equation and suggest ways that human capital might become a component of a more effective development strategy for rural localities. In the process, we will review the circumstances of rural schools and consider how rural educational investments might be more effectively linked with economic development strategies to produce greater benefit to rural localities.

Needed Modifications for Rural Localities

If the idea of investments in human capital (education) is to become an effective part of local rural development strategies, it is necessary to consider modifications in the human capital-economic growth nexus. Following are some of the constraints on that relationship as they affect rural areas.

Migration

The 20th century has produced a massive migration of educated (and some uneducated) workers from rural to urban areas. Obviously, those workers took with them whatever human capital (education, skills, work habits) they possessed, based on the generally valid assumption that they would obtain a greater return in the form of higher wages in the urban area. Indeed Schultz (1961) contended that migration itself is a form of individual investment in human capital—it involves a cost and can yield a return.

The conceptualization of human capital identifies returns on investments to individuals and to the nation, but not necessarily to the locality that produces the human capital. The theory does not attempt to identify returns to localities because mobility of the work force is assumed. Human capital (if it is equated with schooling) can be produced anywhere, but in order to achieve its productive potential it must be linked with the other factors of production. If the other factors of production are not present in the environment in which the human capital is acquired, those who acquire human capital have shown a great propensity to move to where they can achieve a return on their investment (Lichter and Costanzo 1987). Educated (trained, skilled) people tend to move to where there are jobs that utilize their education and/or training and pay them accordingly.

The problem for the rural locality is that migrants take with them the locality's investment in their education, along with their own. And the amount of the locality's investment continues to be substantial. While there are variations between regions and states, nearly half (44 percent) the cost of U.S. public elementary and secondary education comes from local sources, although that is down from 83 percent in 1920 (Jansen 1991). Consequently, as Deaton and McNamara (1984) emphasize, it has been very difficult for many rural localities to capture the benefit of their human capital investments. Indeed it could be argued that rural localities have, for most of this century, subsidized urban economic growth. While rural localities continue to lose from this out-migration, they have little alternative but to continue to invest in education of their youth. The locality would achieve little economic benefit if those trained/educated persons were to remain, but without opportunities for employment of their skills. Without jobs that utilize acquired human capital, there is little return on either the individual's or the locality's investment. Thus, human capital represents but one side of a rural development equation—an important and necessary, but not sufficient, condition.

Lack of Rural Demand for Higher Level Skills

Migration has been attributable to a long term and persistent urban-rural differential in the distribution of industries and occupations within the American economy (Reid 1990). As McGranahan (1988) and others (e.g., Falk and Lyson 1988; Killian and Parker 1991; Rosenfeld et al. 1985) have shown, within all industries there has been a pronounced tendency for the more highly skilled managerial and technical occupations to be located in urban areas. The less skilled, less well-paid, and more routine production jobs tend to be concentrated in rural areas.

That difference was exacerbated, especially during the 1960s and 1970s, when a significant relocation of routine manufacturing firms occurred as those firms, in search of lower labor costs, moved plants in great numbers from urban areas to rural areas (Falk and Lyson 1988; Rosenfeld et al. 1985). That pattern of re-location greatly expanded low wage, low skill rural employment opportunities and temporarily contributed to a reversal of the rural to urban migration pattern in some rural regions during the 1970s. However this re-located job growth had little association with human capital; local rural economies are more likely to specialize in resource-based and routine manufacturing industries, neither of which demand much education (Killian and Parker 1991). Indeed, much of the re-location of routine manufacturing was directed toward the rural South, a region characterized as having the nation's lowest average levels of adult education attainment (Falk and Lyson 1989). It was that kind of rural job growth that contributed to Killian and Parker's (1991) inability to find a significant relationship between rural educational attainment and job growth during the 1970s and '80s. It is the existence of such seeming incongruities that have led some analysts such as Smith (1989) and Stallmann et al. (in Chapter 15 of this book) to argue that economic growth leads to human capital investment instead of the other way around.

It is important for rural localities to take into account the consequences of a development strategy aimed solely at attracting outside investment—especially that dependent on low skill, low wage industries. As observed by Reid: "reliance on outside investors has helped little to develop the capacity of rural people to improve their economic alternatives. Low wage jobs seldom taught useful skills to rural workers, who were valued for their low cost rather than their talents and were readily replaced when machines and foreign workers offered further economies" (1990:8). Indeed the emergence of an international market for low wage industries has caused many rural localities to lose the manufacturing plant they had only recently acquired (Hansen 1979; Rosenfeld et al. 1985).

Similarly, McGranahan and Ghelfi (1990) and Lichter and Costanzo

(1987) conclude from such evidence that, in the end, the principal current constraint on rural economic development is not a shortage of workers to fill existing jobs, but rather a lack of demand for skilled workers in rural locations. As a consequence, they argue for caution in assuming that rural economic development is likely to result from a simple expansion in resources devoted to instructing rural pupils. More succinctly, Bluestone (1972) contends that training workers for nonexistent careers is a cruel hoax played upon those who can least afford it.

The Emergence of a Two Tier Economy

Much has been reported about the growth in lower skill service sector employment in both rural and urban areas. This has been occurring simultaneously with growing employment in higher paying, higher skill managerial and technical fields (Johnston and Packer 1987). A result has been the emergence of a dual economy, a consequence of what some analysts refer to as labor market segmentation (Falk and Lyson 1988). An especially significant effect in rural areas has been employment growth without corresponding increases in income. Porterfield (1990) found, for example, that the five categories of jobs generating the largest employment increases in nonmetropolitan areas during the 1980s were all service jobs. Conversely, of the 5 job categories producing the greatest decline in employment, 4 were in goods production. It is of greater rural development significance however, that the 5 job categories producing the greatest gains in employment paid an annual average wage of $12,000, while the 5 with the greatest decrease paid an average of $24,000 per year.

Clear evidence of these two tiers is demonstrated in analysis carried out by Killian and Parker (1991). For the 1979 to 1986 period, they found that average educational attainment of a metropolitan area's population was not significantly related to its employment growth. But, employment growth was significantly and positively related to the proportion of college graduates in the population and to *the high school dropout rate*. The greater the employment growth of a metropolitan areas, the higher the school dropout rate. This finding appears more logical when it is considered that in rapid growth areas, there has been an especially great increase in demand for workers in consumer services, e.g. retail, food and travel services, etc. In such areas, students who become disillusioned with high school have little difficulty finding a job, although it is frequently of the kind many refer to as "dead-end" (Falk and Lyson 1989).

Unless there is economic development in rural areas, rural-urban differences will be compounded as correspondingly rapid growth occurs in occupations demanding higher levels of skill and reasoning power (Johnston and Packer 1987). Present trends show rural employment gains to be largely in the lower skill, lower pay occupations; urban areas are also gaining such employment but they are gaining in the higher skill, higher paying occupations as well, while rural areas are not. That differential sustains the prospect of continued out-migration of more highly educated from rural to urban areas.

Human Capital and Education

Another issue concerning the role of human capital investment in rural development concerns how human capital is acquired and whether number of years of schooling completed is a valid measure. An obvious issue is whether schooling produces human capital directly (skills, abilities that are rewarded in the work place) or whether schooling provides a credential that serves as a basis for acquiring human capital elsewhere—on-the-job experience. DeYoung (1989) reports that most human capital theorists agree that on-the-job training is a primary location for acquisition of occupational skills. Thurow (1983) states even more directly that on-the-job training is *the* dominant mode of acquiring human capital. The human capital argument with regard to on-the-job training is that it represents a cost to the individual in the form of lower wages while undergoing training and therefore, along with education, qualifies as human capital. The credentials provided by schooling can, however, be a major factor in determining which individuals gain entrance into which forms of on-the-job training—the screening function of schooling (Bowles and Gintis 1974). A college degree, for example, is almost certainly a requirement for entering advanced managerial/technical training with any large enterprise.

Changes in the market for various skills, technology and the supply of education all effect the value of education as well. The human capital value of education varies over time with the type of education received. While it is clear that some forms of education (such as an M.D. degree) have almost always translated directly into higher paying employment, those tend to be exceptions rather than the rule. In general, the rate of return on investment for a college graduate will vary greatly over time with what the graduate majored in and even which college they graduated from. To some extent, these reflect changes in demand for various kinds of skills. Also, like other economic factors of production, the relative supply of education/human capital affects its price. It is clear that during the past several decades there has been a substantial increase in the educational attainment of the population. There has been a long term inflation in education credentials, thus serving to reduce the market value of any given level of educational attainment (DeYoung 1989). As DeYoung observes: "With an overall inflation in educational attainment, obtaining a high school diploma (for example) may help one only to retain, not improve, current economic standards of living (standards once requiring no high school education)" (1989:128).

A more troubling aspect of the human capital implications of education is the fact that non-educational worker characteristics such as age, sex, and race are highly related to worker earnings, regardless of their level of educational attainment (DeYoung 1989). Although American society continues to endorse education as a key to social and economic mobility, evidence over the past 30 years makes it clear that education does not produce the same rate of return for all persons (Bowles and Gintis 1974; Falk and Lysen 1988). With the same level of education, whites earn more than African-Americans, men earn more than women and so on. The market value of human capital credentials is clearly influenced by who possesses them. Those factors are also known to effect student school performance—an issue discussed in greater detail below.

How to Define Rural Development

We have suggested that the weakness of the relationship between educational attainment and job growth is, in part, due to inadequacies of education as a measure of human capital in the contemporary economic environment and, in part, due to structural changes having occurred in the economy and patterns of employment over the past several decades. Yet, another possible explanation lies in how economic (rural) development is defined and conceptualized. For example, the re-location of routine manufacturing jobs and expansion of the low skill service sector has contributed to increased rural employment, but is not proving to be productive in realizing long term economic development.

Thus, some recent analyses have been devoted to distinguishing between economic growth and economic development. Reid (1990:1), for one, distinguishes between them as follows:

Economic growth refers to an expansion in the amount of economic activity in an area, without reference to concomitant changes in the technology employed in generating that economic activity, the number and quality of local institutions, or the manner in which the benefits of growth are distributed. Growth is typically measured by an expansion in the population of an area, or in the number of persons employed in its industries.

Development, on the other hand, implies that some change has occurred in the structure and function of local institutions, the application of technological innovations, or in economic structure.... development implies an improvement in human welfare and individual opportunity. Development is measured by expansion in the value of product from local industries, usually expressed in terms of rising per capita incomes.

Of the two, Reid contends that development is the more essential because it is development that "leads to progress in improving the human condition through a rising standard of living" (1990:1). Development implies a higher value use of resources—human, institutional and physical. But the analyses considered above have generally used growth measures rather than development measures as the dependent variable. Indeed, it can be fairly stated that most rural development efforts over the past several decades have been oriented principally toward growth. The re-location of factories to rural areas was largely based on that perspective.

Throughout the remainder of the chapter we will use development, rather than growth per se, as the preferred goal for rural development activities. As Reid distinguishes between the two, it is reasonable to expect that education (depending on how it is specified) could play a more important role in producing development than in producing growth. But for that to occur, changes are needed in both how education is defined and produced and in how rural localities approach economic development. That is the focus of the remainder of the chapter.

Rural Education, Human Capital and Rural Development

Despite an abundance of research showing little relationship between education and job growth in rural areas, we take the position that human capital (skills, abilities, knowledge) has an indispensable role to play in rural community development. One feature of that perspective is that rural localities need to improve their capacity to identify economic opportunities and to translate those opportunities into higher value employment— employment that utilizes and rewards higher levels of skill, training, and knowledge. For that to occur, however, a re-assessment is needed of how rural localities define and approach economic development and how human capital is produced. A part of that re-assessment includes how rural schools are structured and how they operate.

Rural Schools

Apart from their generally smaller size, rural schools have come to differ little from urban schools in structure, organization, curriculum, or appearance. That is because making rural schools more like urban schools has been the dominant and successful strategy for rural school "improvement" throughout most of this century. The most prominent part of that strategy was the consolidation of rural schools and districts. As a result of publicly induced consolidation, the number of school districts in the U.S. declined from 128,000 in 1930 to 15,500 in 1989; most of that consolidation occurred between 1930 and 1975. The number of school districts declined by only 1,200 between 1975 and 1989.

Despite past consolidation, rural schools and districts remain generally smaller in enrollment than their urban counterparts. According to the Common Core Data files on schools, there were 79,307 regular public schools in the 50 states and District of Columbia during the 1989-90 school year, enrolling just under 40 million students. About 62 percent of public schools are metro and 38 percent nonmetro. But using the Census definition of rural (population living in open country and in towns of less than 2,500), about 6.6 million students attend 22,412 rural schools, accounting for 16.6 percent of all public school students and 28.3 percent of all regular public schools.

About three-fourths of rural secondary schools enroll fewer than 400 students, while fewer than 20 percent of urban secondary schools are that small. Nearly 20 percent of rural schools have fewer than 100 students, while only 4 percent have enrollments of over 800. Districts with fewer than 300 students account for over 43 percent of rural districts, compared with just over 10 percent of the urban districts. Rural schools and districts are usually smaller because they serve low density populations.

The small size of rural schools, until recently, has been widely thought to reflect academic deficiency and therefore, lower educational quality. Accordingly, the rural education "problem" has persistently been framed in terms of rural schools (districts) being too small to economically offer the full range of academic specialties and accoutrements thought to be associated with quality education (Mulkey 1989). A variety of recent reviews seeking to examine years of accumulated research on school size have helped set aside somewhat the issue of school size as a determinant of school effectiveness or even of economic efficiency. One such review, reported by Monk (1986:1), observes:

The study (of curricular offerings) is motivated by theories of production which hold that economies are available in large compared to small schools. To say that such scale or size economies exist is to say that it is possible for larger schools to operate more efficiently than smaller schools. It is quite another matter to say that larger schools in fact take advantage of whatever scale economies are available to them.

With regard to academic performance, there is little evidence that rural students (schools) contribute to lowering the national average, as is sometimes charged (Sher 1986a). The 1990 version of the Nation's Report Card shows rural students scoring at, or above, the national average in history and civics at all grade levels (Jansen 1991). Numerous research studies (e.g. Giesbrecht 1978; Sher 1986a; Walberg and Fowler 1987) generally show school size, if it is related to school performance at all, tends to favor smaller rather than larger schools. Goodlad (1984), in a prominent comprehensive study of public schools, reports that most of the schools clustering in the top group of their sample were small, compared with schools clustering at the bottom. Of the various factors influencing the academic performance of rural students (and their school completion rate), research supports a conclusion that school size is not a very important consideration. This is not to say that school size is educationally or economically irrelevant. Sher (1986a) is among those who conclude that there could be some educational and economic benefit from further, selective school consolidation, but that such initiatives should be evaluated on a case by case basis rather than imposed by broad public directives. Rural circumstances are too diverse to effectively and uniformly accommodate and implement broad mandates.

Although academic performance of students, whether rural or urban, is not greatly affected by expenditures per pupil (Mulkey 1989; Walberg and Fowler 1987), financial support is nevertheless essential to retaining quality schools. Compared with urban schools, there is greater variation in level of funding of rural schools. There are far more "poor" rural districts and generally rural localities find it necessary to commit a higher proportion of local government revenues to education in order to keep school doors open. Jansen (1991), for example, reports that in 1982 (the latest year for which standardized county data are available), nonmetro counties outspent metro counties for education in all but seven states. At the local district level, even with some equalization of funding through state and federal supplements, low income rural counties spend less per pupil than wealthier counties, contributing to significant variation even within the same state.

Considering the slow growth of the rural economy during the 1980s and immediate prospects for more of the same, there is growing concern about the ability of many rural localities to sustain even their existing level of support for education. As Jansen concludes: "Without rural economic development, increased educational spending will likely come from intergovernmental aid. If patterns of the 1980s continue, this responsibility will increasingly fall on the states" (1991:14).

Many rural localities also confront conditions which limit their ability to adopt some currently advocated educational reform measures. The idea of school choice, i.e. offering parents/students an option of which school they attend, continues to be prominent among educational reform strategies. However, even if choice (open enrollment) proves to be an effective school improvement strategy, it would have limited application for many rural districts because of low population density. Many rural districts are what Nachtigal (1980) refers to as "necessarily existent"—the schools are so far apart that consolidation is not feasible. In such cases, generally encountered in the West, choice would be a no more practical alternative than consolidation.

Although school size and expenditures are not reliably related to the academic performance of rural students, the socioeconomic status of students (regardless of whether rural or urban) is a powerful and reliable predictor of student performance. From his analysis of nearly 200 research studies, White (1982) reports that almost all studies show a strong link between parent's socioeconomic status and student achievement, especially when data are aggregated to the level of a school, district, region or state. Such studies and conclusions are numerous. Even when research finds rural-urban differences in student academic achievement, or differences related to school size, those differences tend to disappear when the effect of student's socioeconomic status is controlled (Edington and Martellaro 1985). These studies clearly show that student academic performance is as much or more attributable to social and economic factors outside the school than to differences in the presumed quality of instruction within the school.

The effect of family income on student performance is especially pertinent to evaluating rural schools since the family income of rural students is generally well below that of urban students; the nonmetropolitan poverty rate in the U.S. is nearly 50 percent higher than the metropolitan rate, and rural income averages only 73 percent of urban income (Reid and Frederick 1990). Although average rural income falls well below urban income, there are, in addition, rural regions of long-term and extreme poverty. Bender and associates (1985) identify more than 200 rural counties (about 10 percent of all rural counties) as persistent poverty counties. Many of these counties include substantial minority populations.

Because of the great effect of socioeconomic status on student performance, and because of the greater incidence of low income in rural areas, no comparison of the academic performance of rural and urban students can be considered valid that does not control for differences in the economic condition of the respective student populations. Accumulated research makes it difficult to escape a conclusion that in order for rural school improvement to occur, proportional attention must be devoted to the well-being of families and communities along with the quality of instruction and facilities within the school.

Social Capital in the Production of Human Capital

It was a recognition of the importance of strong family and community reinforcement on student performance that led Coleman (1987) to label this effect as social capital—borrowing and extending the idea of human capital. Coleman emphasizes that reforms aimed at making schools more effective should concentrate on family, community and school relationships that build social capital. His contention is that greater success in improving the effectiveness of schools is more likely to be achieved by developing more supportive family and community connections for children, rather than by fine-tuning the school curriculum to presumed human capital needs. Illustrative of the importance of social capital is the research of Beaulieu and associates (1990) who extended Coleman's operational measures of social capital and found that a combination of low community and low family social capital was highly predictive of student dropout rates.

The idea of enhancing and improving social capital is a particularly applicable approach for rural areas because smaller schools and smaller communities can make the task of building closer relationships between school, community and families potentially easier.   Furthermore, important to the broader idea of rural development and the role of education in it, there is growing evidence that social capital can be developed and changes can occur within schools that do affect educational outcomes. Chubb (1988), for example, reports that the *way schools are organized* directly affects gains in student performance. Using a large data base of 500 high schools and 12,000 students, Chubb found no correlation between education gain and such conventional measures as expenditures per pupil, class size, and graduation requirements. What the research did find was that the most successful schools had educational leaders who consciously sought academic achievement for their students and were allowed flexibility in accomplishing that end.   Similarly, McCormick et al (1991), in a longitudinal study of South Carolina schools, found that counties with multiple school districts and districts with elected, rather than appointed, trustees were more responsive to local concerns, more flexible and correspondingly were operating higher quality schools. They conclude that how schools are organized and managed is one of the best indicators of school effectiveness.

These results present a parallel with our earlier distinction between economic growth and economic development.   Growth was defined as simply expansion, while development was described in terms of changes in structure and function of local institutions, including the relationship between institutions. That includes schools. Changes in the structure and function of rural schools can contribute to a broader notion of rural community (economic) development. Indeed, some authors (e.g. Higbee 1990; Nachtigal and Hobbs 1988) suggest that greater participation of students in studying their community and developing ideas for its improvement is itself an effective means of improving the relevance and effectiveness of education, as well as building social capital. The research findings that such school organizational characteristics as leadership, flexibility and localized decision-making, and the extent of social capital in the school environment, can significantly affect educational outcomes, underscores the importance of school-community restructuring.

The above was intended to lay a foundation for looking at the school in rural localities not only in terms of academic basics, but also as a potentially integral part of a process of rural community development. To be sure, rural schools must continue to provide students with the requisite academic skills to prepare them for post-secondary education and training and to enable them to take advantage of economic opportunity beyond the locality, but that need not occur at the expense of closer interaction with community and considering prospects for development within the locality.

What Human Capital for Rural Economic Development?

There has been a general tendency to limit thinking of human capital to specific job related skills. While that has proven to be an important component of economic growth, we have suggested that the institutional changes associated with the idea of community economic development, in order to occur, must be supported by the addition of abilities to identify community problems and mobilize organization and effort to solve those problems, whether economic or institutional. Much recent thinking about rural development has shifted from simply attracting outside investment (growth) to strategies in which local communities take major responsibility for their own development, with the goal being to create rural economies that are competitive in the more innovative and lucrative sectors (Reid 1990:8). In order to be effective, such self-development strategies depend on the community's ability to identify their comparative economic advantages as well as underutilized resources. As suggested by Shaffer (1990:75):

Building economically viable communities requires two major ingredients in varying proportions. The first... is an understanding of how small, open economies work and change through time. The second is referenced in various ways but common labels include leadership, community cohesion, and decision-making capacity."

Economic development self-help strategies are predicated on the idea that even though the resources of communities vary, as well as their possibilities for economic development, the viable community will identify and take advantage of available opportunities. It is the community's ability to identify those possibilities and engage in collective analysis and decision-making that is fundamental to the institutional side of development. But since communities vary with regard to resource base, location, and economic structure, a premium is placed on creativity and insight, characteristics that Shaffer suggests are easier to manipulate than more traditional assets. Correspondingly, Shaffer reports four non-economic characteristics usually found in economically viable communities: (a) a slight level of dissatisfaction; (b) a positive attitude toward experimentation; (c) a high level of intracommunity discussion; and, (d) a history of implementation (1990:76)

Community economic development self-help efforts have become sufficiently commonplace to enable research on their characteristics and effectiveness. One such effort has been reported by Green et al. (1990). For purposes of their research they defined community self-development as:

the implementation of a project or the creation or expansion of a firm that increases income to the community and/or generates a net increase in jobs. In addition, a self-development project must include the following three characteristics: (1) involvement by a local organization (in most cases a local government); (2) investment of substantial local resources; and (3) local control of the enterprise or activity (1990:56).

Their research procedure yielded 249 communities nationally that had engaged in activities that met their definition of community self-development. Of those 249, 105 case communities were verified and research information obtained. They found that the most frequent self-development activities were directed toward tourism and cultural activities, followed by retention and expansion of existing business. Forty seven percent of the self-development projects were community-based, 21 percent were county-wide and 25 percent were multi-county. Private business, city government, and local development organizations were reported as most frequently involved in the projects. Significantly, none of the projects made reference to involvement of the public school, although 9 percent did involve a local university or community college. Green and associates conclude that the projects worked best when there was a general local conviction that the community shared a major economic problem.

Rural community self-development requires a capacity for local analysis, organization and mobilization of both internal and external resources. A capacity to do those things involves human capital; a form of human capital somewhat different from how it is ordinarily conceptualized; and, a form of human capital that many rural localities lack as presently structured and organized. But just as importantly, rural community self-development depends on social capital—building a sense of cohesion and a comprehensive commitment to achieving community goals. Social capital can be both a goal and a means for self-development.

Roles for Schools in Rural Community Development

Schools in rural communities are usually a centerpiece of community life. In many rural localities, the school district forms the social borders of the community; the school is frequently the largest employer and the largest claim on the public treasury; school events are typically community events. Schools have a vested interest in the well-being of the community and vice versa. Where this reciprocity is acknowledged and becomes mutually reinforcing, it forms a part of the social capital important to student success while simultaneously increasing a community's capacity for economic development. Where it is missing, the school may be *in*, but not *of*, the community. In those cases, the school misses an opportunity for more effective student learning in the "laboratory" of the community, and the community misses an opportunity for an active partnership in its quest for improved economic and social viability.

Ironically, despite the social and physical proximity of school and community in the rural environment, there has been a long-term tendency toward separation and isolation of the school from the locality. This has occurred as schooling has become more national in focus and more standardized in organization and procedure. Once the school bell rings, even in small rural communities, students direct their efforts to a standardized curriculum, taught largely through standardized textbooks, with progress evaluated by standardized tests. All this occurs in remarkably similar classrooms. While school is in session, the community is "out there"—outside the curriculum, texts, and tests. It is more through extra-curricular than curricular activities that the school links with the community outside. In this regard, there has come to be little difference between rural and urban schools (Schmuck and Schmuck 1992).

But this conventional model of the school is being challenged in light of national concern about student academic performance and continuing high dropout rates. That concern has been expressed in a plethora of school reforms (small scale changes within the conventional model of the school). However, reform measures have so far been disappointing and growing emphasis is being placed on restructuring, e.g. changes of the conventional model (Elder and Hobbs 1990). Restructuring is taking the form, both nationally and in many states, of encouraging innovative schools. The National Governor's Association in their report *New Alliances for Rural America* (1988) specifically recommended educational policies that provided flexibility for schools to "adapt to local circumstances." And, as was reported above, the research of Chubb (1988) and McCormick et al. (1990) both found flexibility to be a key feature of effective schools. Indeed effective schools, defined by their organizational characteristics, is rapidly becoming a new standard for evaluating schools. Thus, the door is opening for rural schools to break from the conventional model of schooling and to try some new approaches. One such approach is to forge a closer link between school and community.

For schools already burdened with financial difficulties and attempting to improve their performance, it may seem that an emphasis on schools becoming a partner in rural community development is impractical. But interestingly, the growing emphasis on "effective schools" stresses many of the same attributes Reid (1990) and Shaffer (1990) described as characteristic of community self-development and economically viable communities. Kane (1989), for example, describes the attributes of effective schools as including: (a) a clear specification of goals and core values; (b) leadership; (c) good people and a good environment; (d) ability to solve problems and improve schools; (e) ability to work with the community; and, (f) control and discretion. The specifics of each of these attributes are expected to take a different form in each school as the effective school adapts to its particular community and environmental circumstances. Thus, the notion of "effective schools," just like the idea of community self-development, is based on a capacity of the organization to analyze its environment and devise strategies to improve its effectiveness. Effective schools and community self-development have much in common. Innovation and creativity are an expected result of each.

Without forsaking their principal role of providing basic education, Reid (1990:8) suggests that there are at least three ways rural schools could help strengthen rural communities: (a) by improving the basic skills of the rural labor force; (b) by helping rural communities understand and adapt to the changing world; and (c) by directly participating in rural community development. Indeed, it has been contended that these foci could improve the educational effectiveness of the school by providing students with opportunities to connect what they learn in the classroom with the world outside (Brendtro et al. 1990; Wigginton 1985).

Improving Basic Skills of the Rural Labor Force

As we have emphasized, there are many skills pertinent to rural community development; some are specific to jobs, some are pertinent to community organization and change. Below are several types of skills schools make an important contribution in producing.

1. Quality of Workforce. Although we previously presented mixed results concerning the relationship between educational attainment and economic growth, there is some evidence that education has a positive impact on a community's ability to attract and maintain a manufacturing sector (McNamara 1991). McNamara reviewed 11 recent studies of the relationship between community education investments and their success in attracting outside manufacturing investments and found that, although those results too were mixed, on balance communities making greater investments in education did improve their prospects. McNamara contends that a weakness of the research is that measures of both education and economic growth used were too general—this chapter concurs with that assessment.

2. Community Analysis Skills. As we have emphasized, community self-development depends not only on job skills but also on analytical, organizational, and leadership skills. Potentially, students can acquire both sets of skills if the school turns more frequently to the community as a learning laboratory. Tucker (1986) stresses that in terms of the human capital needs of the emerging economy (including the local one), students need to acquire an ability to learn how to learn. He argues that the widely adopted practice of separating students into vocational and academic tracks is counterproductive and that all students, whether vocationally or academically oriented, need "an education designed to provide a constant interplay between theory and application, between head and hand, between ideas and the world of action" (1986:37). Such an experientially based approach to education can fit logically and easily into the environment of the rural school-community, as numerous rural schools are now demonstrating.

To cite an example, a South Dakota high school has instituted a research and development course in their school (Higbee 1990). The students are researching their community—its economy, history, government, geology, etc— and "developing" ideas for its improvement. They receive a grade by writing papers; papers graded not only for content but for spelling, punctuation, grammar, and syntax as well. The goal of the high school is to improve the quality of their instruction by linking learning with application in the real world outside the school. By being active participants, students acquire an ability to learn how to learn—a skill that can be applied within the community or can be as transferable as any acquired in the conventional classroom. But the benefit does not end there. The papers become an actual or potential community resource. The students in the class make periodic reports to the Chamber of Commerce and other community organizations. Making such reports is a part of the educational experience. As Wigginton (1985) has observed, from his years of experience with Foxfire, most successful educational experiences involve the student producing a product for an audience beyond the teacher. In addition, students acquire a new awareness of their community—an understanding not included in the conventional school curriculum. Equally as important, the community can gain a new appreciation of school and students. Such an approach to learning appears to involve the co-production of marketable and community development human capital.

3. Entrepreneurial and Practical Business Skills. Entrepreneurial skills can be especially critical to rural community development because of a need for job creation and because self-employed and business owners constitute a growing share of the rural work force. Sher (1986b) observes the prominence and necessity of entrepreneurship in rural community economies and finds it odd that entrepreneurship is seldom, if ever, a part of the rural school curriculum. Sher contends that it is logical that schools could serve as a form of new business incubator and in the process, teach students skills in the analysis of economic opportunity, development of a business plan, actual operation of a business, etc. Indeed, Sher and associates have been involved in helping a number of rural schools establish school based development enterprises. Numerous examples of rural schools initiating such programs can be found, and include such enterprises as a community day care center, delicatessen, community television program, school stores and food services, community newspaper, community magazine, etc. Key features in each of those examples is that the business enterprises are real, they are operated by students and they are undertaken for two equally important purposes—a more pertinent education of the students involved and the addition of needed businesses or services to the locality.

4. Linkage with Private Sector Training Opportunities. As emphasized at the outset, much, if not most, human capital is acquired on the job, although education reinforces the existing distribution of economic opportunity by determining who gains access to what training. Rural schools are typically too small to offer comprehensive vocational training—training which, according to Tucker (1986), may be of questionable value, especially from a locality frame of reference. In addition, rural labor markets are generally too small to gainfully absorb all the trainees of a class sufficiently large to be economically feasible for the school to offer. But those conditions should not preclude the school developing training relationships with skilled personnel in the community. Even in smaller rural localities, a substantial number of occupational specialties can be found. The school, therefore, can play a role by negotiating training relationships with such community "trainers" to take responsibility for customized training for a few or even one student. Developing such relationships depends on a different kind of counseling than is usually encountered in public schools. Elliott (1988) suggests a need for both personal and career counseling in rural schools that would include working relationships with a range of business and industrial concerns representative of the occupational options available beyond high school. The principal student population for such counseling would be those who have no immediate aspirations for post-secondary education. The benefit of such school-community collaboration is an expansion of career training opportunities beyond those the school is able to offer under its own auspices.

Such targeted training has the additional benefit of "fitting" local needs. As suggested by Killian and Parker (1991:7): "For many employers,.. the kinds of specific job skills and relevant work experiences of the local labor force may be more important than simply the average number of years of school completed."

Helping Rural Communities Understand and Adapt to Changing Economic Circumstances

Although most schools in rural localities occupy a prominent place in the life of the community, their facilities tend to be underutilized (Sher 1986b). The following provide two key ways that schools can become more integrally involved in the activities of the local community.

1. The School as a Community Learning Resource Center. With the pace of economic and technological change, most people's need for education will not be exhausted with completion of high school or even college. School facilities with their library, classrooms, computers, distant learning technology, etc. are the logical location for on-going community educational and learning activities. Such utilization can provide the community with needed educational services, and reinforce the school as the location where important community activities occur. Economically viable communities, as Shaffer (1990) describes them, are localities that take the initiative to gain access to outside resources. Important among those resources are outreach programs of universities, extension services of land grant universities, regional and community colleges, state economic development agencies, etc. By employing the school as the location for such educational services, an opportunity is also created for such sources of technical assistance to be utilized to supplement regular classroom instruction.

Although outside sources of expertise can make useful contributions to rural community development, locally led consideration of problems, priorities, and issues can be more critical to community success. Using the school as the location for such meetings could lead to students being invited to participate, thereby contributing to their feeling of having a greater stake in the locality and its future and thus reducing what Brendtro (1990) refers to as a "crisis of unimportance" felt by many of today's youth.

Not to be overlooked in re-thinking the school as a community learning resource center is the role of technology (Mulkey 1991). Mulkey emphasizes that rural schools should focus on preparing rural residents to accept and use modern technology. Increasingly rural schools are employing distance learning technology to supplement their curriculum, provide for teacher in-service training, etc. Such technology is now being used for a much wider range of programming, including educational programs from extension services of land-grant universities. For many rural localities, it could be of substantial community benefit to utilize the community's investment in the technology beyond one or a few classes offered in the high school.

2. *The School as a Facilitator of Community Analysis and Planning.* Most larger urban communities employ professional personnel to conduct community analyses, needs assessments, develop plans, write grants, etc. In rural localities, such public business is carried out mostly by lay volunteers including elected officials. As volunteers, they usually lack the time and do not have access to the pertinent and relevant information needed for effective analysis and planning.

There are several potential supporting roles that could be played by the school, both as a community service and as a mechanism for improving education. One of those roles was described earlier in our discussion of the South Dakota high school that offered a research and development course. Through that course, students have produced studies and analyses of benefit to the community, as well as themselves. Another high school in South Dakota has, through their high school economics course, conducted surveys to determine community needs for different services. Another supporting role the school can play is to become a repository and point of access for current demographic and economic data necessary for community analysis and planning. Being located in the school, such data could be utilized for in-school education and be made available for public use.

Direct Participation in Community Development Activities

There are many ways in which schools in rural localities participate in community development, although they may not be thought of as such. It is likely that in most rural localities the school now has become the principal vehicle of community identity—many rural residents think of their community as their school district. In most rural areas, school events bring together a greater cross-section of the community more often than any other organization or institution. As Nachtigal (1980) observes, in most rural communities school business is community business. But there are additional and more explicit ways that the school can become involved in community development. We mention two specific examples.

1. *The School as a Vehicle for Attracting Outside Resources.* One asset of the school in most rural localities is that it includes the highest concentration of professional personnel in the community and typically includes administrative support personnel and services. With the benefit of these assets the school could, with the collaboration of other units of local

government, serve as the organizational agency to apply for grants, contracts, and other sources of supplementary community/school funding. It is likely that the promise of such collaboration would prove to be attractive to foundations, government agencies, and other sources of grant funds. It would not be reasonable to expect the school to take this on as an added responsibility, but it does seem reasonable that the school could serve as the organizational vehicle for such activities.

2. *The School as a Locus for Provision of Social Services.* We have emphasized the extent to which children in many localities, because of their low income status, are eligible for, and in need of social services. Yet, for many rural communities, such services tend to be located some distance from the community and often at several different locations. Nachtigal and Hobbs (1988) suggest this problem of small community access to needed social services could be addressed by bringing together under one roof the array of specialized services (health, education, manpower training, etc.) into an integrated service model, a "general store" of social services delivery. They observe that the school, or school grounds, would be a logical location for such an integrated service because children are among the clients in greatest need; because many of the needed services are education-related such as training and counseling; and because the school is open, accessible and prominent. As well, the presence of such services at, or near the school, could create education and community service opportunities for secondary students.

Conclusion

Creating a more viable economy for more rural communities depends importantly on human capital, social capital and a corresponding production and utilization of locality relevant knowledge. But in order for those assets to produce benefit for the locality, modifications are needed in the conventional human capital approach. As we have reported, students from rural schools generally hold their own academically in relation to national averages, especially considering the higher proportion of low income students in rural areas. Additionally, rural localities spend, on average, more per student than do urban schools. But rural schools have been doing that for a long time while concurrently the rural share of national income has declined. The limiting condition for rural communities, as several researchers have reported, is not so much a lack of human capital (rural communities export human capital in abundance) but rather an absence of employment opportunities that provide a return on human capital investments. A part of the challenge for rural localities then is to more effectively link the skills and abilities of their workforce with attracting and creating higher paying employment. That requires economic development and the institutional change that defines it. With regard to schools/education, simply more additions to the conventional curriculum and higher test scores for the upper half of the students is not likely to contribute much to rural economic development. New approaches to education that are more participatory for students and that utilize the student's environment as a learning laboratory can better provide students an ability to learn how to learn, while also adding to their locality's development resource base.

A purpose of community development is to identify under-utilized resources and bring them to bear in accomplishing community goals. The school, its program, personnel, and facilities can be one of the most important assets at a community's disposal in trying to achieve or sustain social and economic viability; but it is also an asset that is often not recognized as such and, therefore, is seldom explicitly incorporated into community development. But most rural schools, as they are presently structured and organized, find themselves fully occupied and perhaps overloaded as they attempt to accomplish all that is being imposed on them. It could be expected that many rural school administrators and teachers would raise objections if asked to take on additional community responsibilities without additional resources and personnel. What we have tried to emphasize, however, are possibilities for a more reciprocal relationship between school and community—a relationship which can potentially lead to greater school and community effectiveness. We have not, for example, suggested that schools add on to their curriculum a focus on application in the community outside the school, but rather that schools explore such possibilities as a way of making instruction more meaningful and effective, while simultaneously adding to community resources and contributing to achieving community goals. It is the integration of these activities, rather than their separation, which we emphasize as a part of the capacity needed for effective community development. It is conceivable as well, that some of the activities (especially non-educational) currently maintained as a school responsibility could be taken over by individuals and organizations within the community, thus freeing educational resources while mobilizing greater community involvement—building social capital.

This chapter has taken the individual rural community as a frame of reference for examining the relationship between education and community development. That should not be interpreted as suggesting that state and federal policies do not have a role to play. But, at a minimum such policies, as recommended by the National Governor's Association (1988), need to be sufficiently flexible to provide for adaptation to very different local circumstances in rural localities. But such flexibility would be of little value if rural communities lack the capacity and vision to devise their own strategies and to effectively utilize all resources available to them, including their own.

References

Beaulieu, Lionel J., Glenn D. Israel, and Mark H. Smith. 1990. "Community as social capital: The case of public high school dropouts." Paper presented at the Annual Meeting of the Rural Sociological Society, Norfolk, VA (August).

Bender, Lloyd, Bernal L. Green, Thomas F. Hady, John A. Kuehn, Marlys K. Nelson, Leon B. Perkinson, and Peggy J. Ross. 1985. *The Diverse Social and Economic Structure of Nonmetropolitan America*. Rural Development Research Report No. 49. Washington, D.C.: U.S. Department of Agriculture, Economic Research Service.

Bluestone, Barry. 1972. "Economic theory and the fate of the poor." *Social Policy* 2 (January/February): 30-48.

Bowles, Samuel, and Herbert Gintis. 1974. *Schooling in Capitalist America: Educational Reforms and the Contradictions of Economic Life*. New York, NY: Harper.

Brendtro, Larry K., Martin Brokenlegn, and Steve VanBockern. 1990. *Reclaiming Youth At Risk*. Bloomington, IN: National Educational Service.

Chubb, John. 1988. "Comments." Included in Nathan Glazer, John Chubb, and Seymour Fliegel, Manhattan Paper No. 5, Manhattan Institute. New York, NY.

Coleman, James. 1987. "Families and schools." *Educational Researcher* 16 (6): 32-38.

Coleman, James. 1988. "Social capital in the creation of human capital." *American Journal of Sociology* 94 (Supplement): S95-S120.

Deaton, Brady, and Kevin McNamara. 1984. *Education in a Changing Environment*. Mississippi State, MS: The Southern Rural Development Center (February).

DeYoung, Alan J. 1989. *Economics and American Education*. White Plains, NY: Longman, Inc.

Edington, Everett, and Helena Martello. 1985. *Does School Size Have Any Relationship to Academic Achievement?* Department of Educational Management and Development. Las Cruces, NM: New Mexico State University.

Elder, William L., and Daryl Hobbs. 1990. "From reform to restructuring: New opportunities for rural schools." *The Rural Sociologist* 10 (Summer): 10-13.

Elliott, Judi. 1988. *Rural Students At Risk*. Chicago: North Central Regional Educational Laboratory.

Falk, William W., and Thomas A. Lyson. 1988. *High Tech, Low Tech, No Tech: Recent Industrial and Occupational Change in the South*. Albany, NY: State University of New York Press.

Giesbrecht, Edwin C. 1978. *The Attainment of Selected Mathematical Competencies by High School Students in Saskatchewan*. Research Centre Report (November).

Goodlad, John I. 1984. *A Place Called School: Prospects for the Future*. New York, NY: McGraw-Hill.

Green, Gary P., Jan L. Flora, Cornelia Flora, and Frederick E. Schmidt. 1990. "Local self-development strategies: National survey results." *Journal of the Community Development Society* 21 (2): 55-73.

Greenstein, Robert. 1988. Barriers to rural development. Paper presented at the

Annual National Rural Electric Cooperative Manager's Conference. Baltimore, MD (August).

Hansen, Niles. 1979. "The new international division of labor and manufacturing decentralization in the United States." *The Review of Regional Studies* 9 (1): 1-11.

Higbee, Paul. 1990. *Rural Experiment*. Sturgis, SD: Black Hills Special Services Cooperative.

Jansen, Annica. 1991. "Rural counties lead urban in education spending, but is that enough?" *Rural Development Perspectives* 7: 8-14 (October-January).

Johnston, William B., and Arnold E. Packer. 1987. *Workforce 2000: Work and Workers for the 21st Century*. Indianapolis, IN: Hudson Institute.

Kane, Cheryl Chase. 1989. "Implementation of promising practices in rural settings: Necessary conditions." Pp. 55-60 in *Rural Education: A Changing Landscape*. Washington, D.C.: Office of Educational Research and Improvement. U.S. Department of Education (May).

Kiker, B.F. 1966. "The historical roots of the concept of human capital." *Journal of Political Economy* 74: 481-99.

Killian, Molly S., and Timothy S. Parker. 1991. "Higher education no panacea for weak rural economies." *Rural Development Perspectives* 7: 2-7 (October-January).

Lichter, Daniel T., and Janice A. Costanzo. 1987. "Nonmetropolitan underemployment and labor force composition." *Rural Sociology* 52 (Fall): 329-44.

McCormick, Robert, Cora Moore, and Bruce Yandle. 1991. *Private and Public Choices in Public Education: An Investigation of Trustee Effects*. Working Paper WP050191. Department of Economics, Clemson University.

McGranahan, David A. 1988. "Rural workers in the national economy." Pp. 29-47 in David L. Brown, J. Norman Reid, Herman Bluestone, David A. McGranahan and Sara Mazie (eds), *Rural Economic Development in the 1980s: Prospects for the Future*. RDRR-69. Washington D.C.: U.S. Department of Agriculture, Economic Research Service (September).

McGranahan, David A., and Linda Ghelfi. 1990. "The education crisis and rural stagnation in the 1980s." Unpublished manuscript (February).

McIntire, W., R. Cobb, and P. Pratt. 1986. "Vocational and educational aspirations of high school students: A problem of rural America." Paper presented at the meeting of the American Educational Research Association. San Francisco, CA.

McNamara, Kevin. 1991. "Education as an investment in local community development." *Proceedings of Conference on The Role of Education in Rural Community Development*. Mississippi State, MS: Southern Rural Development Center.

Monk, David. 1986. *Secondary School Enrollment and Curricular Comprehensiveness*. Ithaca, NY: State University of New York, College of Agriculture and Life Sciences, Cornell University. ERIC ED 287 628 (August).

Mulkey, David. 1989. "Research needs in rural education." Paper presented at the National Rural Education Research Forum. Reno, NV (October).

Mulkey, David. A. 1991. "Changing rural America: The context for school/community development." *Proceedings of Conference on The Role of Education in Rural Community Development*. Mississippi State, MS: Southern Rural Development Center.

Nachtigal, Paul. 1980. *Improving Rural Schools.* Washington, D.C.: U.S. Department of Education. National Institute of Education (September).

Nachtigal, Paul, and Daryl Hobbs. 1988. *Rural Development: The Role of the Public Schools.* Background paper; National Governor's Association. Washington, D.C.

National Commission on Excellence in Education. 1983. *Nation At Risk.* Washington, D.C.

National Governor's Association. 1988. *New Alliances for Rural America: Report of Task Force on Rural Development.* Washington, D.C.

Porterfield, Shirley. 1990. "Service sector offers more jobs, lower pay." *Rural Development Perspectives* 6 (June-September): 2-7.

Reid, J. Norman. 1990. "Education and rural development: A review of recent experience." Paper presented at the American Educational Research Association Annual Conference. Boston, MA. (April).

Reid, J. Norman, and Martha Frederick. 1990. *Rural America Economic Performance, 1989.* Agriculture Information Bulletin 609. Washington, D.C. U.S. Department of Agriculture. Economic Research Service (August).

Rosenfeld, Stuart A. 1985. Edward Bergman, and Sarah Rubin. *After the Factories: Changing Employment Patterns in the Rural South.* Research Triangle Park, NC: Southern Growth Policies Board.

Schmuck, Richard A., and Patricia A. Schmuck. 1992. *Small Districts Big Problems: Making School Everybody's House.* Newbury Park, CA: Corwin Press, Inc.

Schultz, Theodore W. 1961. "Investment in human capital." *American Economic Review* 51 (1): 1-17.

Schultz, Theodore W. 1967. "The rate of return in allocating investment resources to education." *The Journal of Human Resources* 11 (3): 293-309.

Shaffer, Ron. 1990. Building economically viable communities: A role for community developers. *Journal of the Community Development Society* 21 (2): 74-87.

Sher, Jonathan. 1986a. *Heavy Meddle: A Critique of the North Carolina Department of Public Instruction's Plan to Mandate School District Mergers Throughout the State.* Raleigh, NC: North Carolina School Boards Association (April).

Sher, Jonathan. 1986b. "Rural development worthy of the name." Pp. 515-22 in *New Dimensions in Rural Policy: Building Upon Our Heritage.* Joint Economic Committee of Congress. Washington, D.C.: U.S. Government Printing Office.

Smith, Eldon D. 1989. "Reflections on human resources in the strategy of rural economic development." *Review of Regional Studies* 19 (Winter): 13-32.

Tucker, Marc. 1986. "Facing an international economy: The need for structural change in education." In Stuart A. Rosenfeld (ed.), *Technology, the Economy and Vocational Education.* Research Triangle, NC: Southern Growth Policies Board.

Thurow, Lester. 1983. *Dangerous Currents.* New York, NY: Random House.

Walberg, Herbert J., and William J. Fowler. 1987. "Expenditure and size efficiencies of public school districts." *Educational Researcher* 16 (October): 5-13

White, K. R. 1982. The relation between socio-economic status and academic achievement. *Psychological Bulletin* 91 (3): 461-81.

Wigginton, Eliot. 1985. *Sometimes a Shining Moment: The Foxfire Experience.* Garden City, NY: Anchor Press/Doubleday.

13

The Influence
of Health and Health Care on
Rural Economic Development[1]

W. Bruce Vogel
Raymond T. Coward

The influence that a health care system exerts on a local economy can be represented by two paths (see Figure 13.1). First, the health care sector contributes indirectly to the local economy by enhancing the health of its residents (left vertical arrow in Figure 13.1). The health of residents, in turn, improves their potential participation and productivity in the work force, which, ultimately, contributes positively to the local economy. Second, there are more direct effects of the health care sector on a local economy (right vertical arrow in Figure 13.1). By that we mean, the health care sector of a community (including hospitals, private physician offices, health care clinics, home health agencies, and all other health-related services and facilities) makes direct contributions to the local economy through the salaries and wages paid to employees, and through the goods and services that are purchased in the community (McDermott et al. 1991).

Unfortunately, for many of the residents of rural America, there are significant differences, compared to urban and suburban Americans, in the health care systems to which they have access. As a consequence, rural economies are affected by a much different health care sector than are more urban and suburban communities. Rural communities tend to have access to a smaller number and a narrower range of health care services. Yet, at the same time, certain types of people (e.g., the poor and the medically uninsured) are disproportionately represented among rural populations and have health status profiles that place them among the most needy in our country (Clarke and Miller 1990; Rosenblatt and Moscovice 1982). As a consequence, comprehensive community development strategies that are

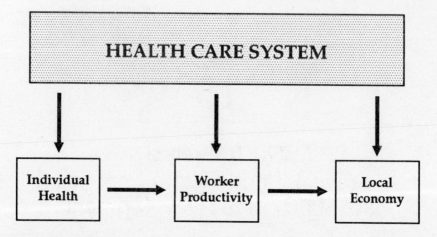

FIGURE 13.1. Illustration of the influence that a health care system exerts on the local economy of a community.

intended to bolster rural America through investments in human capital may well need to include specific actions to improve both the existing rural health care system and the health status of rural populations (Cordes 1990).

Following the reasoning underlying Figure 13.1, we begin this chapter with an examination of rural-urban differences in the availability of health care resources—to illustrate the significant variation between rural and urban communities with respect to the health care systems that contribute to their economies. Then, residential differences are examined in the prevalence of selected at-risk populations and in the rates of mortality—illustrating the differences in the health-related human capital stock that exists in rural versus urban contexts. Next, the connection between health and labor force participation is discussed and illustrated. Finally, the chapter concludes with a description and discussion of the impact of health care expenditures on the level of local and regional economic activity.

Residential Comparisons of Health Care Systems

Substantial evidence indicates that the range of health care services available to residents of small towns and rural communities is more narrow, that fewer alternatives are available within any one type of service, and that fewer health care providers exist to offer particular services (Christianson and Grogan 1990; Hicks 1990; Kindig and Ricketts 1991a; Mick and Morlock 1990; Wagenfeld 1990). In the sections that follow, the maldistribution of both providers and facilities is illustrated and described in order to reinforce our argument that the health care system that contributes to local *rural* economies (as illustrated in Figure 13.1) is distinctly different from that which advances urban and suburban economies.

Residential Maldistributions in Health Care Providers

Although there was a steady improvement during the 1980s in the number of physicians that practiced in small towns and rural communities, those gains did not offset the continued significant discrepancy that exists between different sized communities (Kindig and Movassaghi 1989;

TABLE 13.1 Trends in Physician (MD and DO) by Place of Residence: 1980-1986.[a]

	1980	1983	1986
United States			
Total Population	226,542,000	233,980,000	241,392,000
Total Physicians	462,322	518,565	569,787
Total MDs	433,502	496,947	544,308
Total DOs	18,820	21,618	25,479
Physicians/100,000 Pop.	204	222	236
MDs/100,000 Pop.	196	212	225
DOs/100,000 Pop.	8	8	11
Metropolitan Areas			
Total Population	172,455,000	177,927,000	185,261,000
Total Physicians	391,764	438,553	487,006
Total MDs	385,365	431,203	478,343
Total DOs	6,399	7,350	8,663
Physicians/100,000 Pop.	227	246	263
MDs/100,000	223	242	258
DOs/100,000	4	4	5
Nonmetropolitan Areas			
Total Population	54,087,000	56,053,000	56,131,000
Total Physicians	70,558	80,012	82,781
Total MDs	58,137	65,744	65,965
Total DOs	12,421	14,268	16,816
Physicians/100,000 Pop.	130	143	147
MDs/100,000 Pop.	107	117	118
DO/100,000 Pop.	23	25	30

Sources: Bureau of Census, *Statistical Abstract of the United States*, 1989; American Medical Association, *Physician Characteristics*, 1987; American Osteopathic Association, *Yearbook & Directory, 1988.*

[a]Adapted from Lanis L. Hicks (1990). Availability and accessibility of rural health care. *The Journal of Rural Health* 6(4): 485-505.

Langwell et al. 1985; Wright and Jablonowski 1987). For example, Hicks (1990) has reported that the number of physicians (MDs and DOs combined) in nonmetropolitan areas grew from 70,558 in 1980 to 82,781 in 1986 (a 17.3 percent increase). Yet, that increase left the 1986 nonmetropolitan ratio of physicians to population equal to only 55.9 percent of the metropolitan ratio (see Table 13.1).[2] Moreover, a number of studies during that period demonstrated that "while many of the larger nonmetropolitan areas were gaining in physicians as the overall supply of physicians expanded, the smallest communities and those more remote from metropolitan areas were losing physicians" (Hicks 1990: 486). Indeed, "during the 1980s, the gap in the availability of physicians in metropolitan versus nonmetropolitan areas widened" (Hicks 1990: 485). As a consequence, those rural communities that were often most in need of additional medical services (i.e., very small or very remote towns) were the least likely to have experienced growth in the number of health care providers practicing in their region during the 1980s.

Beyond this simple relative disadvantage, small towns and rural communities are also often judged to have an "undersupply" or an "inadequate" supply of primary care physicians (see the supplemental issue of *The Journal of Rural Health* edited by Kindig and Ricketts [1991a], for a fuller discussion of these issues). Although determining what constitutes an adequate supply of physicians for a given population is a complex task (Office of Technology Assessment 1990), traditional approaches have either used a physician-to-population ratio (i.e., experts determining how many persons a single physician can adequately serve), a needs-based approach (i.e., estimating the population-specific, disease-dictated needs of an area by examining population characteristics), a demand-based method (i.e., examining past patient utilization patterns to estimate a population's future requirements), or some mixture, or combination, of these approaches (Pathman 1991). Using any one of these techniques, many small towns and rural communities would be judged as falling below what is considered to be an adequate supply of physician providers (Kindig and Ricketts 1991b).

This historical trend for physicians to locate their practices in larger communities that offer greater professional and personal amenities is mirrored in the other health professions as well. For example, although rural parts of the United States contain approximately 25 percent of the nation's population, only about 19 percent of practicing nurses are employed in rural settings (American Nurses' Association 1987). Similarly, in 1982, 78 percent of the federally designated dental shortage areas (752 of 964) and 87 percent of the federally designated pharmacist shortage areas (115 of 132) were located in nonmetropolitan areas (U.S. Department of Health and Human Services 1984).

A study of health care professionals in Georgia illustrates another interesting aspect of the maldistribution problem (Wright and Jablonowski 1987). For some rural communities it is not just a matter of having fewer providers available, they may have nobody providing certain types of health care within their region! For example, Wright and Jablonowski (1987) reported that a majority of nonmetropolitan counties in Georgia had *no* practicing physical therapists (55 percent), opticians (67 percent), podiatrists (91 percent), speech pathologists/audiologists (93 percent), psychologists (79 percent), or occupational therapists (82 percent). Clearly, this does not mean that residents have *no* access to proper health care services just because they do not exist within their county borders—many rural people travel miles to obtain appropriate services. But, the farther an individual has to travel to receive services, the less frequently they use such services and the more apt they are to delay usage until they are more seriously ill (Clarke and Miller 1990).

Thus, although there are some notable exceptions (Cordes 1989), in general, smaller towns and rural areas with widely dispersed populations tend to have fewer health care providers practicing in their locales. And, as a consequence, health care systems in rural areas have a different impact on the local economy, both directly and indirectly, compared to the urban and suburban health care sector. This residential disadvantage extends, as well, to a range of health care facilities.

Residential Differences in Health Care Facilities

The health care facilities that are available to rural Americans are quite different in both quantity and nature from those located in more urban settings. Consider, for example, hospitals. The hospital is frequently the core or anchor of a rural health care system. Almost half of all community hospitals in the United States are located in small towns and rural communities (about 2,500 such hospitals), although they contain only about 23 percent of all the hospital beds in the country (American Hospital Association 1988). Indeed, many rural hospitals are very small institutions—approximately 1,000 have less than 50 beds (Hart et al. 1990).

But bed size is not the only difference between rural hospitals and their larger urban counterparts. Rural hospitals have lower occupancy rates; shorter lengths of stay; and, as the inpatient diagnostic and procedural mix of these institutions suggests, they provide care for medical and surgical conditions that are of a lower complexity than their urban counterparts (Hart et al. 1990). In addition, rural hospitals are more dependent on Medicare reimbursement as a revenue stream; they have lower, and in some cases negative, operating margins; and, a larger number of them are experiencing financial distress (Cleverly 1989a, 1989b; Mick and Morlock 1990).

In addition, the cost containment efforts instituted by a number of third-party payers during the 1980s have caused many hospital facilities—both rural and urban—to alter their operations, seek new organizational affiliations, or close (Smith and Piland 1990). For example, of the 397 hospital closures experienced between 1981 and 1989, just under half (47.9 percent or 190) were rural hospitals (Merlis 1989). Clearly, the decade of the 1980s was a time of enormous change within the health care industry, and rural and urban communities both experienced alterations in their infrastructures. But it is unclear, at this point in time, just how these transformations will continue to evolve. And, indeed, there are *some* disturbing indicators for rural communities. Examining 1989 closings, Friedman (1990) reported that, for the first time, twice as many rural hospitals closed as urban institutions (44 versus 21).

Changes in the nature and composition of hospital care, however, is not the only health care system characteristic that differentiates rural from urban. The decade of the 1980s, for example, witnessed a number of other alterations in the structure, organization, and delivery of American health care—e.g., the expansion of managed care systems and an increase in the number of organized group practices. But, the implementation of each of the alternatives that have emerged in recent years (substitutes for the solo, fee-for-service physician model), have developed more rapidly in urban, as opposed to rural, locations. Indeed, the distinctive aspects and difficulties of making these alternative models work in sparsely populated areas are still poorly understood (Christianson and Grogan 1990).

The Use of Health Care

Given the lesser availability of health care providers and facilities in rural areas, it should be no surprise that the use of formal health care services by rural residents is less than that of their urban neighbors. In 1985, nonmetropolitan residents had a smaller number of physician contacts than did metropolitan residents (4.9 vs. 5.4) and a smaller percentage of them had seen a physician in the last year (73.3 percent of nonmetropolitan residents and 76.0 percent of metropolitan residents)(Norton and McManus 1989).[3] Indeed, Hicks (1990) has argued that there is evidence to suggest that the gap between the medical care utilization patterns of nonmetropolitan residents and that of metropolitan residents may be widening (she compared metropolitan and nonmetropolitan differences in physician visits for 1980 and 1986).

These lower utilization rates of health care services by rural residents cannot be attributed to a uniformly higher health status. The use of fewer medical services by rural folks is *not* because there is less need. Indeed, rural communities contain a disproportionate share of certain types of individuals who have profiles of greater illness. In the next section, examples of these high-risk rural populations are offered.

High-Risk Rural Populations

There are a number of examples of particular segments of the rural population who would appear to be at greater risk of needing health care and medical services. For example, we will illustrate the residential maldistribution of the poor and the medically uninsured.

We know that the health status of poor people is not as good as those with more adequate incomes. In addition, we know that poverty is not evenly distributed across the residential continuum. Higher proportions of rural populations than urban or suburban populations have incomes below the poverty level (Cordes 1989; Rural Sociological SocietyTask Force on Persistent Rural Poverty 1993). Indeed, in 1987, a person living in a nonmetropolitan area was almost as likely to be poor as someone living in the central city of a metropolitan area—16.9 percent of the nonmetropolitan population versus 18.6 percent of the central city population (Porter 1989). Thus, to be poor *and* rural may be a kind of "double jeopardy" in terms of health—poverty increases the probability of illness, while rurality decreases the probability of having access to health care.

In addition, a significant segment of rural poverty is associated with persistently poor, depressed areas and, therefore, can affect the health and health care of individuals across a lifetime (Bender et al. 1985). Hoppe (1985) has reported that higher percentages of the populations of these rural persistently low-income counties were black, disabled, or lived in families headed by women than were observed in nonmetropolitan counties.

Another example of a factor that places individuals at risk of having health problems is the absence of medical insurance coverage. The growing number of persons in the U.S. who lack such coverage represents a serious and disturbing social problem. Without coverage, many individuals do without medical care and experience unnecessary pain, suffering, disability, and even death (Freeman et al. 1987, 1990). Again, there appear to be residential differences in the degree to which people have medical insurance coverage. Analyzing data from the 1987 National Medical Expenditure Study (Patton et al. 1990) have reported that 17.4 percent of the nonmetropolitan population were without health insurance coverage while 14.8 percent of the metropolitan population lacked such coverage. Moreover, rural residents are more apt to be underinsured than their urban counterparts and are more likely to be without insurance for the entire year (Farley et al. 1985; Walden et al. 1985; Wilensky and Berk 1982).

Both of these population characteristics, poverty and lack of health insurance, place persons at greater risk of acquiring health-related problems. In addition, both conditions are more apt to be present in small towns and rural communities. As a consequence, the poor health of some rural workers may reduce their labor force participation and productivity which, in turn, may affect negatively the local economy (see Figure 13.1).

We could offer more examples (e.g., the concentration in rural areas of high-injury occupations like farming and mining; or, the presence of certain other special population groups with profiles of greater illness like migrant and seasonal workers or Native Americans), but we hope that the point is clear. The demographic composition of rural areas suggests that there are segments of the rural population who would seem to have higher health risk profiles. Certainly, there is reason to doubt the commonly held belief that it is universally "healthier" to live in the country (Hicks 1990). This may be true for certain elements of the rural population, but it certainly is not characteristic of all rural people. Moreover, these high-risk rural populations exist in a health care environment that is less well-staffed than more urban settings and offers a narrower range of health care options. As a consequence of compositional differences in population, combined with a distinctly different health care system, higher death rates have been observed among rural populations (Norton and McManus 1989). In the next section, the association between residence, risk factors, and death is examined.

Our purpose in examining mortality statistics is to illustrate, once again, the interaction of the factors represented in Figure 13.1. Earlier, we described the less comprehensive health care system that exists in most rural, as compared to urban, communities and speculated about the attenuation of both direct and indirect effects that the smaller size might have on a local economy. Then we suggested that the health stock of rural communities might likewise be less than in urban areas—affecting still further the vigor of a local economy by possibly reducing worker productivity. By examining mortality statistics, we hope to illustrate the manner in which poor health can diminish the human capital stock of a rural community by causing higher crude rates of mortality.

Residential Differences in Mortality

Miller et al. (1987), when examining 1980 *crude death rates* for all causes in the United States,[4] reported that the most rural counties experienced rates that were 17.7 percent higher than their metropolitan counterparts, and 13.4

TABLE 13.2. Death Rates Per 1,000 Population From All Causes, Cardiovascular Disease and Cancer for the Continental U.S., 1980.[a]

Cause of Death	U.S. Rate	Rural-Urban Difference[b] (Percentage)	Rural-U.S. Difference[c] (Percentage)
All Causes			
Crude Rate	8.59	17.7	13.4
Adjusted Rate[d]	7.74	-0.7	-0.8
Cardiovascular Disease			
Crude Rate	4.30	21.2	15.0
Adjusted Rate	3.81	-2.1	-2.7
Cancer			
Crude Rate	1.81	5.1	3.5
Adjusted Rate	1.67	-10.9	-9.2

[a]Data extracted From Tables 1,2, and 3 of Michael K. Miller, C. Shannon Stokes, and William B. Clifford (1987). "A comparison of the rural-urban mortality differential for deaths from all causes, cardiovascular disease, and cancer." *Journal of Rural Health* 3 (2): 23-34. Rates are two-year averages for 1979 and 1980. The original tables included data aggregated along a nine-point residence continuum in addition to the comparisons presented here. The pattern of differences observed in the more detailed categorization is similar in direction to the differences observed when the "tails" of the continuum are compared.

[b]The rural-urban percentage differences were calculated by dividing the average difference between the three most rural county groups and the most urban county groups, by the average of the three most urban county groups.

[c]The rural-U.S. percentage differences were calculated by subtracting the average rate for the three most rural county groups from the U.S. rate and dividing the difference by the U.S. rate.

[d]These rates are adjusted for age, gender, and race.

percent higher than the national average (see Table 13.2). Moreover, their analyses demonstrated that the smallest, most isolated rural counties had the highest rate of any group. This pattern of rural disadvantage was also found by Miller et al. (1987) when they compared crude death rates from two of the leading causes of death in the United States: cardiovascular disease and cancer (see Table 13.2). In 1980, rural residents exhibited a crude death rate from cardiovascular disease that was 21.2 percent higher than in urban areas, and a crude death rate from cancer that was 5.1 percent higher.

In epidemiology, crude death rates are an important indicator of the differential distribution of illness in a population. Thus, within the context of Figure 13.1, crude death rates are an important indicator of the health stock of a population. Yet, given the significant residential population differences described earlier, *adjusted death rates* are also an important indicator to consider when attempting to clarify the association between place of residence and mortality. When crude rates were adjusted for the effects of existing compositional differences in the populations, Miller et al. (1987) observed quite different patterns.

For example, we know that cardiovascular disease rates are heavily influenced by age (Kyle 1983). For example, older segments of the population have higher rates of death from cardiovascular disease. And we also know that a higher proportion of the populations of small towns and rural communities are elderly (Clifford et al. 1985). Therefore, without introducing appropriate adjustments, crude death rate comparisons are unable to differentiate that difference which is due to the existence of certain high-risk populations (like the elderly) and that which is associated with life in a particular type of locale.

Thus, when Miller et al. (1987) examined residential differences in *adjusted death rates*, they observed a distinctly different pattern (again, see Table 13.2). They computed mortality rates that were simultaneously adjusted for the three major demographic determinants of differential mortality in the United States: age, gender, and race. Under those conditions, rural residents were found to have a *lower* crude death rate (-0.7 percent), a *lower* death rate from cardiovascular disease (-2.1 percent), and a *lower* death rate from cancer (-10.9 percent) than their urban counterparts. In other words, as the authors concluded, "the difference between rural and urban counties is due not to residence *per se*, but to differences in demographic structure, particularly age composition" (Miller et al. 1987:31).

For the purposes of making public policy, stimulating community development, and investing in human capital, this mathematical adjustment does not eliminate the need to take special actions to address residential differences in health. Rather, it suggests that the reason small towns and rural communities have higher crude death rates is because of the composition of the people who live in such places. But, the differences in crude death rates still suggest that the poorer health status of rural communities may affect worker productivity and, in turn, diminish contributions to the local economy.

Health Care Resources, Labor Force Participation, Labor Supply, and Labor Productivity

Economists originally believed that individuals viewed medical care services as pure consumption goods. In other words, medical care was a source of consumer satisfaction, much like other goods and services. Since the 1960s, however, economists have come to recognize that medical care services, in combination with other inputs, are used by the consumer to invest in health-related human capital (Grossman 1972; Mushkin 1962). In this sense, health is not simply a state or condition, but rather a stock or store of well-being that can be augmented or depleted based upon consumer behavior. For example, by exercising and obtaining regular medical check-ups, a consumer can invest in his or her health-related human capital stock. This stock of health then yields a flow of benefits over time that both contributes to consumer satisfaction directly (a consumption benefit) and increases the individual's ability to engage in work and leisure (an investment benefit).[5] In this way, medical care services have both consumption and investment dimensions.

Following Grossman (1972), Figure 13.2 shows how various inputs (including medical care, the consumer's own time allocation to health, and his genetic predisposition to illness) are combined to produce gross investment in the health stock—a specific form of human capital. This health-related human capital stock, which is subject to depreciation, then provides a flow of services that benefits the consumer.

Figure 13.2 also includes both direct and indirect impacts of the health-related human capital stock on labor force participation and labor productivity. This health stock may have a direct impact on labor force participation since many acute and chronic illnesses may reduce the health stock to the point where the individual, regardless of his/her preferences for work, may be judged unfit for many or all types of work (arrow A). The health stock may have a direct impact on labor force productivity when acute or chronic illnesses reduce the individual's health stock to the point where participation is still possible, but productivity is reduced (arrow B). Finally, the health stock may have an indirect effect on labor force participa-

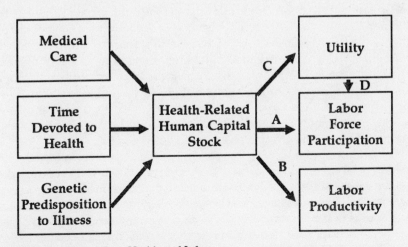

FIGURE 13.2. Medical Care, Health, and Labor

tion by altering the individual's preferences for labor versus leisure (arrows C and D).

The Literature on Health and Labor

A number of empirical studies have examined the influence of health-related human capital on labor force participation, labor supply, and wages. This literature clearly shows that: (1) health status has substantial effects on labor force participation, labor supply, and labor productivity; and (2) these effects exist specifically in rural populations. This section reviews selected studies in this area, with a special emphasis on the impact of health-related human capital on the labor market behavior of rural populations.

Chirikos and Nestel (1985) used data from the 1976-1977 National Longitudinal Surveys to estimate the short- and long-term effects of health problems on labor force participation and wage rates. This study is particularly noteworthy for its use of longitudinal data. They found that poor health reduces current economic welfare, and that this reduction is not overcome by either the other resources available to the household or the willingness of individuals with a history of poor health to devote greater effort to labor. They also found that blacks were less able than whites to maintain labor force activity and earnings when faced with a health problem.

Using data for middle-aged and older men from the 1967 Survey of Economic Opportunity, Scheffler and Iden (1974) examined the impacts of primary and secondary disabilities,[6] along with rural poverty on labor force participation and labor supply. Using a standard framework where the decision to enter the labor force is estimated separately from labor supply once in the labor force, Scheffler and Iden (1974) found that the presence of disabilities reduced the likelihood that individuals were in the labor force. In addition, given that individuals were in the labor force, the presence of disabilities reduced both the number of weeks the individual was in the labor force and the number of weeks worked over the past year. These results were found in separate models stratified by race (whites versus blacks) and age (middle-aged versus older individuals).

Scheffler and Iden (1974) also found that rural poverty affected labor market behavior. This is of interest since rural poverty is likely related to health status.[7] Table 13.3 shows the signs of the relationships between rural poverty and three measures of labor market behavior (labor force participation, weeks in the labor force over the past year, and weeks worked during the past year) for four demographic groups (black males age 55-64, white males age 55-64, black males age 25-64, and white males age 25-64). In

Table 13.3, a plus sign (+) indicates a statistically significant positive relationship between rural poverty and the specific measure of labor market behavior. A negative sign (-) indicates a statistically significant negative relationship, while a zero indicates no statistically significant relationship. The results in Table 13.3 reveal that rural poverty reduced labor market activity in four of the six cases where it was statistically significant. Unfortunately, for purposes of this review, the authors did not test for interactions between their measures of health-related human capital and the rural poverty variable.

In a particularly relevant paper, Scott et al. (1977) used 1973 household survey data from four rural southern counties to estimate models of labor force participation for seven age-gender subgroups of primary and secondary workers. Their independent variables included marital status, non-labor income, health status, expected wage,[8] school attendance, child care responsibilities, and child care availability. In six of their seven subgroups, poor health (measured as the presence of a work-inhibiting health problem) had a statistically significant negative effect on the probability of labor force participation.[9] This result is especially relevant to the topic of this chapter since their survey data focus on rural counties exclusively.

Finally, it is unfortunate that none of the studies reviewed above have examined both urban and rural data and at the same time, examined the possibility of interactive effects of residence, health-related human capital, and poverty on labor market behavior. Such an investigation could answer important questions about the economic impact of poor health on the rural disadvantaged. Also, it is unfortunate that studies published in the 1970s and 1980s using data from the 1960s and 1970s have not been replicated and extended using more recent data. Given the economic difficulties of

TABLE 13.3. Directions of Effects of Rural Poverty on Labor Market Behavior.

	Labor Force Participation	Weeks in the Labor Force over the Past Year	Weeks Worked During the Past Year
Black Males Age 55 - 64	+	0	+
White Males Age 55 - 64	-	0	-
Black Males Age 25 - 64	0	-	-
White Males Age 25 - 64	0	0	0

Source: Scheffler and Iden (1974: 128-130)

rural America in the 1980s, such replication and extension could add much to our understanding of the evolution of the relationship between health and labor market behavior, both generally and in rural settings specifically.

Health Services, Health Status, and the Time Price Elasticity

The literature clearly shows the following: (1) that poor health has adverse effects on labor force participation, labor supply, and labor productivity; and (2) that these effects are present in rural, as well as urban, populations. While these effects may vary in magnitude by age and sex, and by primary versus secondary labor status, they nevertheless emphasize the critical role of health-related human capital in influencing the size and productivity of the rural labor force.

Given a clear connection between health-related human capital and labor, the next logical question centers on the connection between formal health services and health status. Beyond some moderate amount, does the consumption of additional medical care services lead to a measurable improvement in health status? The answer to this question is important in any assessment of the contribution of the rural health care sector to economic development. If additional medical care services yield sizable additional health benefits (measured as improvements in health status),

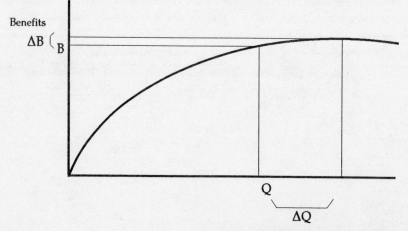

FIGURE 13.3. Benefits of Medical Care Versus Quantity of Medical Services Consumed.

hen changes in the amount of rural health care services may have significant health consequences. If, on the other hand, additional medical care services yield negligible additional health benefits, then changes in the amount of rural health care services may not have significant health consequences.

While medical care services undoubtedly contribute to improvements in health status in total, some work has suggested that the health benefit of additional medical care services beyond some moderate amount is, overall, much smaller (Auster et al. 1969; Manning et al. 1987). Such a situation is depicted in Figure 13.3, where total health benefits are graphed against the quantity of medical services consumed. While the total health benefits, B, are quite large at a high level of health care consumption, Q, the additional health benefits, ΔB, of consuming additional medical services, ΔQ, are quite small. At Q, we are operating on the flat portion of the total health benefits curve, where small changes in the consumption of medical services produce very small changes in total health benefits.

There are, however, reasons to believe that the benefit of additional health service consumption in rural areas is greater than in urban areas. First, the lower consumption of health care in rural localities suggests that marginal health benefits would be greater in rural areas, all other factors being held constant. Second, evidence from the RAND Health Insurance Experiment (Manning et al. 1987) suggests that additional health services are of measurable health benefit to the poor with respect to common medical problems. Given the high incidence of poverty in rural areas (Cordes 1989), additional medical care services may further benefit the health of residents of these localities. Third, hospital closure in rural areas, and concomitant reductions in the size of the health care sector, may be of sufficient magnitude to influence the level of health benefits markedly. In other words, rural hospital closure may lead to significant reductions in the size of the rural health care sector, and such reductions may, in turn, reduce access to health care by a sufficient amount to increase significantly the additional health benefit of increased formal health services (again, see Figure 13.3).

It is important to note that the additional health benefits discussed above refer to improvements in health status. In order for such improvements to translate into improved economic well-being, appropriate employment opportunities must be available. Given the depressed nature of many rural economies in the U.S., such opportunities cannot be taken for granted. That is, adequate health status should be viewed as necessary but not sufficient for adequate economic well-being. In this sense, health care resources sufficient to maintain and/or improve the health status of rural residents can be viewed as part of the essential infrastructure for economic development.

From an economic perspective, the time price elasticity of the demand for medical care may play a key role in determining how changes in the size of the rural health care sector will affect the quantity of medical care demanded. The time price elasticity of the demand for medical care measures the responsiveness of the quantity of medical care demanded to changes in the implicit price of an individual's time spent traveling, waiting, and receiving medical care. For employees without sick leave, this implicit time price clearly includes foregone wages, while for homemakers, the time price may include foregone household productivity or child care expenses. To the extent that the quantity of medical care demanded is quite responsive to changes in time price (i.e., it exhibits a high time price elasticity), an increase or decrease in time price will lead to a sizable decrease or increase, respectively, in the quantity of medical care demanded. Shifts in the size of the rural health care sector will likely change the time price of medical care by altering travel requirements. Given a sizable time price elasticity, such changes in the time price will modify the quantity of medical care demanded as well.

Initial attempts to measure the time price elasticity of the demand for medical care suggested that it may be of roughly the same magnitude as the money price elasticity (Acton 1975). More recent work applied to rural populations, however, suggests that office waiting time (for black households) and travel time to the provider (for both black and white households) have a greater impact on demand than out-of-pocket price (Miners et al. 1978). Such estimates suggest that reductions in the size of the rural health care sector may lead to significant reductions in the quantity of medical care demanded through increases in time prices. By the same token, expansion in the size of the rural health care sector may lead to significant increases in the quantity of medical care demanded.

The Impact of the Health Care Sector on
Local and Regional Economies

The health care sector makes several potentially important contributions to local and regional economies, as noted in Figure 13.1. This section explores the direct contributions of the health care sector to local and regional economies (right vertical arrow in Figure 13.1) through the salaries and wages paid to employees, through the goods and services that are purchased in the community, and through additional economic spending generated via the multiplier process.

A wide variety of health services are found in rural areas, including physician and dentist practices, pharmacies, health clinics, visiting nurse associations/home health care agencies, and, of course, hospitals. Because of its size, the hospital is perhaps foremost among all health care institutions in its impact on local and regional economies. The health care sector's contribution to the regional economy stems in part from its contribution to the exports of the region in which it is located. By treating patients from outside the area, the rural hospital generates income for the region in which it is located. (It should be noted, however, that rural hospitals that treat only local patients do not contribute to such export activity). In addition, the presence of a rural hospital decreases the necessity for residents to seek care outside of the region, thereby reducing the region's imports. Both the stimulation of exports and the reduction in imports facilitated by the hospital tend to increase regional income.

The health care sector's contribution stems not only from its direct effect of increasing exports and decreasing imports, but also from its indirect effect on local economic activity. This indirect effect occurs through the multiplier process, where an initial direct expenditure (such as an export) becomes income to the region. The recipient of this income will then spend a portion of this income within the region, thereby generating income for another individual, and so on. Each succeeding round of expenditure becomes smaller as each individual either saves or spends some portion of this income. This process continues indefinitely, with the additional expenditure and income streams becoming smaller and smaller. In this way, initial direct expenditures in the form of exports can have a very sizable impact on local economies.

Studies of the Economic Impact of the Health Care Sector

The empirical literature on the local and regional economic impact of the health care sector indicates that: (1) the health care sector has a very sizable impact on local and regional economic activity; and (2) individual hospitals have measurable, although not overwhelming, direct and indirect effects on local and regional economic activity. This section reviews some of the key literature on the local and regional economic impact of the health care sector generally, and of hospitals specifically.

Lichty et al. (1986) reported on the use of a simulation model using an input-output system for assessing the impact of the health care sector on the economy of the Arrowhead Region of Northeast Minnesota. They examined the impact of eliminating the entire health care sector, as well as the impact of closing one hospital. Not surprisingly, eliminating the health care sector had dramatic effects. They estimated that total employment would be reduced by 42 percent over a six-year period, from 121,305 in the status quo baseline case to 70,004 if the medical sector were eliminated. Similarly, regional gross output would decline by 22 percent, from

$4,962,141,000 to $3,866,211,000. In the case of closing a single hospital with 1,200 employees, the effects were estimated to be more modest. Regional gross output by 1990 would decline by 2.1 percent from the baseline estimate, from $4,962,141,000 to $4,855,977,000. Similarly, total employment would decline by 3.9 percent, from 121,305 to 116,553.

In an earlier study, Moore (1974) examined the impact of the Upstate Medical Center on the community of Syracuse, New York. Based on data from the early 1970s, Moore obtained an estimate of the income multiplier of 2.63, indicating that each dollar of direct expenditure by the Upstate Medical Center generated $2.63 of total expenditure. Moore (1974:129) was able to conclude that:

> on balance the operation of Upstate Medical Center has a substantial positive impact on the regional cash flows of both Onondaga County and the City of Syracuse ... The most fundamental conclusion which can be drawn from this study is that large public institutions have the capacity to generate millions of dollars in personal income and employment, through what is, in effect, interregional trade.

Erickson et al. (1986) examined the impact of the hospital sector on a regional economy using 1982 data from the Pittsburgh Metropolitan Statistical Area (MSA). Based on their estimated regional trade multiplier of 2.69, the regional income and jobs generated by the hospitals in the Pittsburgh MSA were $655 million (FY 1982 dollars) and 22,000 jobs, respectively. They conclude that:

> While consumer services have traditionally been regarded as exclusively local-serving industries in most regional economies, many sectors do have an export component and can play a significant role in area income generation ... The participation of hospitals and other service industries in the export base of regions has undoubtedly contributed to the stability and growth of local economies while many of the traditional export sectors have declined (Erickson et al. 1986: 25-26).

Despite their emphases on urban areas, both the Moore (1974) and the Erickson et al. (1986) studies are noteworthy because of their emphasis on how the hospital sector can contribute to both local and regional economies. However, neither paper addresses rural concerns explicitly. By contrast, Christianson and Faulkner (1981) used data for single-hospital rural counties from Idaho, Montana, Nebraska, Nevada, North Dakota, South Dakota, Utah, and Wyoming to measure the contribution of a rural hospital to the income of the community in which it is located. They found that while the salaries paid by the hospitals in their sample generated, on the average, some 1.4 percent of direct benefit to the total county income, the multiplier effect of 1.09 to 1.63 increased this impact to between 1.54 and 2.37 percent. The loss from closing a hospital was only slightly less, ranging from 1.53 to 2.29 percent of total county income.[10] Addressing concerns about rural hospital closure, Christianson and Faulkner (1981: 54) concluded that while:

> *the shock of an income reduction of this magnitude would be considerable . . . the relative importance of hospital spending is not particularly impressive. It appears that the willingness of rural residents to support hospitals through tax subsidies and voluntary contributions . . . must be based on more long-run, less direct considerations, such as the perceived importance of the hospital in attracting or maintaining population, business activity, and community physicians.*

In a more recent study, McDermott et al. (1991) examined the impact of four small rural hospitals in Utah on the their local communities. These hospitals were fairly typical of rural hospitals located in the western United States. After calculating and applying an economic multiplier to the hospitals' local expenditures, the direct and indirect economic impact per bed ranged from $40,000 to over $90,000 per year. These hospitals contributed, directly and indirectly, between 4.0 and 9.0 percent of the average employment in their primary services areas. The authors concluded that, based on these results, rural hospitals do make significant economic contributions to their communities.

Finally, Doeksen and Altobelli (1990) used input-output models to measure the change in local economic activity if sole rural community hospitals closed. Their work examined the Texas communities of Crowell, Breckenridge, and Graham. Assuming closure of each community hospital in 1989, the authors concluded that employment would decrease by 1.1 to 3.0 percent by 1994 when compared to levels that would have occurred without closure. Similarly, both personal income and retail sales would decrease by 0.7 to 1.6 percent under the same circumstances. The authors concluded that, "in all three communities the effects, as expected, were detrimental to the vitality of the local economy" (Doeksen and Altobelli 1990:8).

Cautions About Simple Multiplier Calculations

Although the literature on the economic impact of the health care sector is limited, a clear consensus exists that the health care sector and hospitals, specifically, have a sizable economic impact that goes beyond simply the direct loss of employment and income. As noted in Christianson and Faulkner (1981), however, the direct and indirect economic impact of rural hospital closure may not always be catastrophic.

It is important to note that hospital closures may have impacts that go well beyond the multiplier calculations presented above. As noted by Lichty et al. (1986), elimination of the entire health care sector in the Arrowhead region of Northeast Minnesota would have economically catastrophic results. While such complete elimination is unlikely, the hospital is, in many ways, the linchpin of the rural health care sector. Even in rural areas, many retail businesses sell health care products and services whose demand is directly related to physician and hospital services. Further, many physicians depend upon the hospital for complementary services for their patients (Pauly 1980), and may refuse to practice in areas without a hospital. As a result, hospital closure could lead to sizable economic dislocations as physicians and other health care providers leave the area. Also, the ability of the rural hospital to treat patients is highly dependent on the rural physician. The loss of one or two physicians from a rural area can cripple the viability of a small rural hospital. Such economic losses related specifically to the health care sector are not reflected in the direct and indirect calculations found in much of the literature discussed above. Based on the work by Lichty et al. (1986), further contractions within the health care sector resulting from hospital closure or physician loss could be much more important economically than the initial direct and indirect effects of hospital closure. Such contractions may reflect what Christianson and Faulkner (1981) referred to as the less direct, long-run considerations that move rural communities to show such strong support for their hospitals. Given the present concern over the poor financial condition of many rural hospitals, such far-reaching contractions are especially worrisome.[11]

Part of the strong support that rural communities show for their hospitals may stem from the role that a robust health care sector plays in attracting and keeping new industries and residents. Despite widespread discussion of this role (see, for example, the quote from Christianson and Faulkner (1981) above), as well as much anecdotal evidence, we know of no analytical studies of the role of the health care sector in attracting new industry and population. This lack of research likely reflects the difficulty of quantifying the many determinants of location decisions, rather than the lack of importance of the topic.

There exists some disturbing evidence in the literature that hospitals that are financially weakest also have the largest impact on their local communities. Christianson and Faulkner (1981) used the percentage of hospital revenues obtained from local government and private contributions as a proxy for financial dependency. (Such a measure presumes that those hospitals with the highest levels of such contributions as a percentage of revenue are those that would be most financially threatened if such funds were not available). They found generally positive correlations between financial dependency and the magnitude of the hospital's impact on the local community, leading them to conclude that those hospitals that are more financially dependent have a greater impact on local economies. Along related lines, Doeksen and Altobelli (1990) found evidence that smaller towns suffer a greater percentage impact on retail sales under hospital closure than do larger towns. While both of these findings are limited in their scope and generalizability, they do suggest caution before drawing broad policy conclusions based solely on the simple direct and indirect economic effects gleaned from the multiplier.

When discussing the need for maintaining the rural health care system, an issue arises concerning the relative cost of rural versus urban health care. All other factors constant, are health care services provided at lower cost in rural or urban settings? While it is difficult to answer this question for health care in general, studies have shown that urban hospitals typically have higher costs than rural hospitals, all other factors constant (Grannemann et al. 1986; Hornbrook and Monheit 1985). Of course, controlling for all other factors that affect hospital costs is problematic. It is possible that the statistical significance of the urban variable in such studies merely reflects case-mix or wage differences between urban and rural hospitals that are not captured adequately by other variables used in such studies.

Finally, as noted in passing by Christianson and Faulkner (1981), the time price elasticity of the demand for hospital care has important implications for the economic impact of the health care sector. In addition to an out-of-pocket price for medical care (which may approach zero for the well-insured patient), consumers must also contribute their own time to the consumption of medical care. Under such circumstances, the loss of services in a rural community and the concomitant requirement to travel for needed care may reduce total medical expenditures, thereby, increasing the amount of income available to be spent on other goods and services. Presumably, at least some of this additional income would be spent within the local community. Consequently, the direct economic impact of lost medical services may be less than the direct expenditures of a facility or practice by the amount of this additional local expenditure on non-medical goods and services.

Of course, reductions in health care expenditures may have negative economic repercussions in the long-run. Failure to obtain needed health care in the short-run may increase health expenditures at a later date if existing health problems increase in severity or if new illnesses are left untreated. As noted earlier, health problems reduce labor force participation, labor supply, and wages.

Summary and Policy Implications

This chapter has discussed the effect of health-related human capital and health care on local and regional rural economies. A number of important points have been gleaned from the literature:

1. Contrary to popular opinion, rural populations do not enjoy better health than urban populations. Rural areas have higher crude mortality rates than urban areas. Much of this residential differential can be attributed to the presence of high-risk populations with poor health profiles.
2. Rural residents clearly face more health risk factors, including more poverty, less medical insurance coverage, and higher proportions of the elderly.
3. Rural areas continue to have substantially fewer health care providers per capita than urban areas.
4. Rural hospitals are smaller, more dependent on Medicare, and have lower operating margins than urban hospitals. More rural hospitals are experiencing financial distress, as evidenced in part by twice as many rural as urban hospital closures in 1989.
5. Rural residents have fewer physician contacts than urban residents, and the gap may be widening over time.
6. Poor health decreases labor force participation, labor supply, and labor productivity. These labor findings have been confirmed in studies examining rural populations specifically.
7. The direct and indirect expenditures of the health care sector are vitally important to local and regional economic vitality.
8. While single hospitals make a measurable contribution to local and regional economies, their impact, not surprisingly, is not as great as the entire health care sector. However, to the extent that many rural health care providers depend upon the hospital for viability, the rural hospital makes a greater contribution to local and regional economies than would be suggested by its direct and indirect expenditures.

The picture that emerges from these findings is clear. The importance of the rural health care sector to rural community development and economic well-being is substantial. Not only does the health care sector provide important contributions to local and regional economies, but it also contributes positively to labor force participation, labor supply, and labor productivity through improving the health-related human capital stock. Given that rural populations face more health risks and consume less formal health care than urban populations, the existing contributions of the rural health care sector loom all the larger. Policy-makers and rural community leaders should be aware of these important contributions when formulating both community development policies and financial policies that might affect the vitality and well-being of the rural health care sector.

The above points do not lead, however, to clear and unambiguous policy implications. In particular, the simultaneous relationships between rural poverty, health status, and economic opportunity have not been studied in the literature in sufficient detail to answer many important questions, such as: Are there sufficient gains from health care investments in rural areas to offset the costs? (To our knowledge, no study has performed an explicit cost-benefit analysis of the rural health care sector). Are improvements in health status sufficient to improve wages in the presence of the limited economic opportunities in many rural areas? Should government policies promote the consumption of health care services specifically through providing in-kind subsidies, or should income transfer programs be expanded? Could expanded income transfer programs simultaneously address both adequate health care and rural poverty, or would such programs fail to promote the consumption of merit goods such as health care? Are expanded income transfer programs politically feasible given limited federal and state budgets? Questions such as these remain to be answered before the full implications of alternative policies can be evaluated.

Notes

1. Partial support for this research was provided by the Florida Rural Health Research Center under a grant from the Office of Rural Health Policy (CSR-000001), Health Resources and Services Administration, U.S. Department of Health and Human Services. The opinions expressed here, however, are those of the authors and do not, necessarily, reflect those of the funding agency.

2. Because osteopathic physicians (DOs) have traditionally represented a larger proportion of those individuals who practice medicine in rural areas than in urban areas, we have reported their numbers separate from MDs in Table 13.1.

3. This finding of lower medical service utilization is fairly consistent across a number of studies—with one major exception. In 1986, the Robert Wood Johnson Foundation conducted a telephone survey of a nationally representative sample (Freeman et al. 1987). The results of that survey indicated very similar levels of use of physician services among both nonmetropolitan and metropolitan residents. Freeman et al. (1987) concluded from their results that the goal of closing the residential gap in access to primary care services had been achieved. Few rural health researchers, however, would agree with this conclusion.

4. The crude death rate is the number of deaths per 1,000 population. It does not take into account any differences in the compositional characteristics of the population (e.g., it does not adjust for differences in age distribution, racial make-up or gender composition).

5. The flow of benefits over time can perhaps be thought of most simply as "healthy days."

6. In the Survey of Economic Opportunity, the term disability refers to a long-term health-related impairment (12 months or greater in duration) that limits a person's capacity to function in a job, at school, or while performing housework.

7. Labor market behavior, health, and poverty are best modeled as a system of simultaneous equations. While questions about causality and simultaneity bias arise in the single-equation framework used by Scheffler and Iden (1974), we know of no study that attempts the ambitious task of disentangling these interrelationships.

8. The expected wage was calculated as the predicted value obtained from regressing actual wage against sex, race, age, education, training, and location variables.

9. Women age 16-19 was the only group where the negative coefficient on health impairment failed to achieve statistical significance at the .05 level.

10. The loss from closing a hospital is less than its overall contribution to the local economy, in part, because it is assumed that county revenues and voluntary contributions used to support the hospital would go elsewhere within the community if the hospital were closed.

11. Recent estimates suggest that 600 rural hospitals, or approximately 22 percent of all rural community hospitals, are at serious risk of closure. U.S. Senate Special Committee on Aging, *The Rural Health Care Challenge*, Serial No. 100-N, U.S. Government Printing Office. [(Quoted in Doeksen and Altobelli (1990:1)].

References

Acton, Jan. 1975. "Nonmonetary factors in the demand for medical services: some empirical evidence." *Journal of Political Economy* 83 (3): 595-614.

American Hospital Association 1988. *Profile of small or rural hospitals: 1980-1986*. Chicago, IL.

American Nurses' Association. 1987. *Facts About Nurses 86-87*. Kansas City, MO: American Nurses' Association.

Auster, Richard, Irving Leveson, and Deborah Sarachek. 1969. "The production of health: an exploratory study." *Journal of Human Resources* 4 (4): 411-36.

Bender, L.D., B. L. Green, T.F. Hady, J. A. Kuehn, M. K. Nelson, L. B. Perkinson, and P. J. Ross. 1985. *The Diverse Social and Economic Structure of Nonmetropolitan America*. Washington, DC: U.S. Department of Agriculture, Economic Research Service, Rural Development Report No. 49.

Chirikos, N. Thomas, and Gilbert Nestel. 1985. "Further evidence on the economic effects of poor health." *Review of Economics and Statistics* 67 (February): 61-69.

Christianson, Jon, and Lee Faulkner. 1981. "The contribution of rural hospitals to local economies. *Inquiry* 18 (1): 46-60.

Christianson, Jon, and Colleen M. Grogan. 1990. "Alternative models for the delivery of rural health services." *The Journal of Rural Health* 6 (4): 419-36.

Clarke, Leslie L., and Michael Miller. 1990 "The character and prospects of rural community health and medical care." Pp. 74-105 in A.E. Luloff and Louis E. Swanson (eds.), *American Rural Communities*. Boulder, CO: Westview Press.

Cleverley, W.O. 1989a. *Hospital Industry Performance Report 1984-1988*. Westchester, IL: Healthcare Financial Management Association.

Cleverly, W.O. 1989b. *Hospital Industry Performance Report 1984-1988*. Westchester, IL: Healthcare Financial Management Association.

Clifford, William B., Tim B. Heaton, Paul R. Voss, and Glenn V. Fuguitt. 1985. "The rural elderly in demographic perspective." Pp. 25-55. in Raymond T. Coward and Gary R. Lee (eds.), *The Elderly in Rural Society: Every Fourth Elder*. New York, NY: Springer Publishing Company, Inc.

Cordes, S.M. 1989. "The changing rural environment and the relationship between services and rural development." *Health Services Research* 23 (6): 757-84.

Cordes, Sam M. 1990. "Come on in, the water's just fine." *Academic Medicine* 65 (12, Supplement): S1-S9.

Doeksen, Gerald, and Joyce Altobelli. 1990. *The Economic Impact of Rural Hospital Closure: A Community Simulation*. University of North Dakota Rural Health Research Center.

Erickson, Rodney, Norma Gavin, and Sam Cordes. 1986. "The economic impacts of the hospital sector." *Growth and Change* 17: 17-27.

Farley, P., G. L. Cafferata, and M.C. Berk. 1985. "Who are the underinsured?" *Milbank Memorial Fund Quarterly* 63 (3): 476-503.

Freeman, H.E., R. J. Blendon, L. H. Aiken, S. Sudman, C. F. Millinix, and C. R. Corey. 1987. "Americans report of their access to health care." *Health Affairs* 6: 6-18.

Freeman, H.E., L. H. Aiken, R. J. Blendon, and C. R. Corey. 1990. "Uninsured working-age adults: Characteristics and consequences." *Health Services Research* 24: 811-23.

Friedman, Emily. 1990. "Analysts differ over implications of more hospital closings than openings since 1987." *Journal of the American Medical Association* 264 (3): 310-14.

Grannemann, Thomas W., Randall S. Brown, and Mark V. Pauly. 1986. "Estimating hospital costs: A multiple-output analysis." *Journal of Health Economics* 5 (2): 107-27.

Grossman, Michael. 1972. "On the concept of health capital and the demand for health." *Journal of Political Economy* 80 (2): 223-55.

Hart, L. Gary, Bruce A. Amundson, and Roger A. Rosenblatt. 1990. "Is there a role for the small rural hospital?" *The Journal of Rural Health* 6 (2): 101-18.

Hicks, Lanis L. 1990. "Availability and accessibility of rural health care." *The Journal of Rural Health* 6 (4): 485-505.

Hoppe, R.A. 1985. *Economic Structure and Change in Persistently Low-Income Non-metro Counties*. Washington, DC: U.S. Department of Agriculture, Economic Research Service, Rural Development Report No. 50.

Hornbrook, Mark C., and Alan C. Monheit. 1985. "The contributions of case-mix severity to the hospital cost-output relation." *Inquiry* 22 (3): 259-71.

Kindig, David A., and H. Movassaghi. 1989. "The adequacy of physician supply in small rural counties." *Health Affairs* 8 (2): 99-116.

Kindig, David A., and Thomas C. Ricketts (eds). 1991a. "Issues and trends in availability of health care personnel in rural America." *Journal of Rural Health* 7 (Supplemental Issue): 313-459.

Kindig, David A., and Thomas C. Ricketts. 1991b. "Determining adequacy of physicians and nurses for rural populations: Background and strategy." *Journal of Rural Health* 7 (Supplemental Issue): 313-26.

Kyle, Eleanor H. 1983. "Socioeconomic factors." Pp. 31-43 in William P. Blocker and David Cardus (eds.), *Rehabilitation in Ischemic Heart Disease*. New York, NY: SP Medical and Scientific Books.

Langwell, Kathryn, Shelly Nelson, Daniel Calvin, and John Drabek. 1985. "Characteristics of rural communities and the changing geographic distribution of physicians." *The Journal of Rural Health* 1 (2): 42- 55.

Lichty, Richard, Wayne Jesswein, and David McMillan. 1986. "Estimating medical industry impacts in a regional economy." *Medical Care* 24 (4): 350-62.

Manning, W.G., J. P. Newhouse, N. Duan, E. B. Keeler, A. Leibowitz, and S. Marquis. 1987. "Health insurance and the demand for medical care: Evidence from a randomized experiment." *American Economic Review* 77 (3): 251-77.

McDermott, Richard E., Gary C. Cornia, and Robert J. Parsons. 1991. "The economic impact of hospitals in rural communities." *The Journal of Rural Health* 7 (2): 117-33.

Merlis, M. 1989. *Rural Hospitals*. Washington, DC: U.S. Congressional Research Service.

Mick, Stephen S., and Laura L. Morlock. 1990. "America's rural hospitals: A selective review of 1980s research." *The Journal of Rural Health* 6 (4): 437-66.

Miller, Michael K., C. Shannon Stokes, and William B. Clifford. 1987. "A comparison of the rural-urban mortality differential for deaths from all causes, cardiovascular disease and cancer." *The Journal of Rural Health* 3 (2): 23-34.

Miners, Laurence A., Sandra B. Greene., Eva J. Salber, and Richard M. Scheffler. 1978. "Demand for medical care in a rural setting: racial comparisons." *Health Services Research* 13 (Fall): 261-75.

Moore, Craig. 1974. "The impact of public institutions on regional income: Upstate medical center as a case in point." *Economic Geography* 50: 124-29.

Mushkin, Selma J. 1962. "Health as an investment." *Journal of Political Economy* Supplement: 129-57.

Norton, Catherine H., and Margaret A. McManus. 1989. "Background tables on demographic characteristics, health status, and health services utilization." *Health Services Research* 23 (6): 725-56.

Office of Technology Assessment. 1990. *Health Care in Rural America*. Washington, D.C.: U.S. Government Printing Office, OTA Publication No. OTA-H-434.

Pathman, Donald E. 1991. "Estimating rural health professional requirements: An assessment of current methodologies." *Journal of Rural Health* 7 (Supplemental Issue): 327-46.

Patton, Larry T., Gregory R. Nycz, and John R. Schmelzer. 1990. *Health Insurance Coverage in Early 1987: A Metro-Nonmetro County Chartbook*. Marchfield, WI: Wisconsin Rural Health Research Center.

Pauly, Mark V. 1980. *Doctors and Their Workshops: Economic Models of Physician Behavior*. Chicago, IL: The University of Chicago Press.

Porter, K.H. 1989. *Poverty in Rural America: A National Overview.* Washington, DC: Center on Budget and Policy Priorities.

Rosenblatt, Roger A., and Ira S. Moscovice. 1982. *Rural Health Care.* New York, NY: John Wiley and Sons.

Rural Sociological Society Task Force on Persistent Rural Poverty. 1993. *Persistent Poverty in Rural America.* Boulder, CO: Westview Press.

Scheffler, Richard M., and George Iden. 1974. "The effect of disability on labor supply." *Industrial and Labor Relations Review* 28: 122-32.

Scott, Loren C., Lewis H. Smith, and Brian Rungeling. 1977. "Labor force participation in southern rural labor markets." *American Journal of Agricultural Economics* 59 (May): 266-74.

Smith, Howard L., and Neill F. Piland. 1990. "Strategic adaptations to PPS by rural hospitals: Implications for theory and practice." *The Journal of Rural Health* 6 (2): 140-60.

U.S. Department of Health and Human Services. 1984. *Report to the President and Congress on the Status of Health Personnel in the United States.* Rockville, MD.

Wagenfeld, Morton O. 1990. "Mental health and rural America: A decade review." *The Journal of Rural Health* 6 (4): 507-22.

Walden, D., G. Wilensky, and J. Kasper. 1985. "Changes in health insurance status: Full-year and part-year coverage." *National Center for Health Services Research: Data Preview 21.* Washington, DC: U.S. Government Printing Office, Department of Health and Human Services Publication (PHS) 85-3377.

Wilensky, G., and M. Berk. 1982. "Health care, the poor, and the role of Medicaid." *Health Affairs* (Fall): 93-100.

Wright, J. Stephen, and A. R. Jablonowski. 1987. "The rural-urban distribution of health professionals in Georgia." *The Journal of Rural Health* 3 (1): 53-70.

14

Family and Household Effects on the Educational Attainment of Young Adults

DeeAnn Wenk
Constance L. Hardesty

Introduction

Education is one of the most important human capital resources in our society. While not providing equal monetary returns for all, education nevertheless continues to be a major determining factor of social status. Due to the significance of education as a human capital investment for all individuals, it is essential to explore the various factors that influence educational attainment.

In this chapter, educational attainment is examined primarily in terms of the structural components that provide a context for promoting or inhibiting educational attainment. Specifically, we explore the critical role that the family and household structure play in the educational investment of children while taking into account the effects of individual characteristics. To promote our understanding of education as a resource in rural areas, we explore the differential effects of these family and household variables depending on individuals' residence in rural versus urban environments.

Previous research emphasizes the need to inquire into the variety of family and household factors that influence the educational attainment of children. The effects of family background on the educational attainment of American youth have been extensively examined (McLanahan 1985). Parental characteristics indicate the type of socialization children receive in regards to education, as well as resources available to allocate to education.

But, there is a need, as well, to study the influences of family structure on education. There have been significant changes in family structure in the last 20 years. High divorce rates and high rates of unwed parenthood have substantially increased the risk of spending time in single or step-parent households. Only 27 percent of all black children and 66 percent of all white children lived with biological parents in 1988. Today, approximately one out of every two children can expect to spend some time during childhood with a single parent (Bianchi 1990).

Some recent studies show that the influence of household structure on educational attainment is through socialization and resource availability (Amato 1987; Coleman 1988; Krein and Beller 1988). Living in a single-parent household as a child has a substantial negative impact on the probability of completing high school and college (Mueller and Cooper 1986). Clearly, it is important to examine further how changing family structures are influencing the educational attainment of today's youth.

The present study builds on recent research on educational attainment in several ways. First, we examine the impact of family structure in the year of expected high school completion on finishing high school and on attending at least one year of college. This allows us to examine the effects of family resources immediately available to young adults, and the household presence of parents, at this critical juncture in the youth's educational career.

Second, we measure household structure by whether the youth is living in a two-parent, one-parent or another type of household at the time of expected high school graduation. The effects of living in other types of households including, independent, married-couple, other relative or non-relative, on educational attainment have not been extensively examined. There is a substantial proportion of youth who live in such arrangements at the time they would be expected to graduate from high school or begin attending college (31 percent in the sample used here). Thus, a comprehensive understanding of the process of educational attainment demands that the effects of non-traditional household arrangements be examined.

We also directly measure the availability of resources at the time of expected high school graduation and college attendance by determining family poverty status. Taking into account household structure, we designate youth as either living in households with below or above poverty level income.

Additionally, we examine variation in the relationship between household structure and educational attainment by residence. This allows a test of the effects of additional resources and socialization indicated by one's residence. Specifically, we compare the effects of living in the urban South, urban non-South, rural South, and rural non-South.

Finally, we use a population based sample for analysis. Some studies on educational attainment have utilized school based samples which may be biased because they do not include individuals not attending school (Astone and McLanahan 1991; Coleman 1988). The National Longitudinal Survey of Youth includes an over-sample of disadvantaged youth both enrolled and not enrolled in school. Because this is an annual survey, information on school returnees is also available.

Literature Review

Family Background

Education is one way in which class position is transmitted across generations.[1] Families generally prepare and motivate children to achieve their class level. Parents of different classes use distinct types of discipline and rewards. Lower class parents tend to encourage less independent thought and place less value on education than middle and upper class parents. Kohn (1979) argues that these patterns result from the parent's own socialization and from the parents' views of what is essential to succeed in life.

The research of Luster et al. (1989) provides further support for Kohn's hypothesis focusing on the link between class related parental values, childrearing beliefs, and parental behavior. The authors found that parents with higher levels of education and mothers with higher occupational prestige are less likely to value conformity and more likely to value self-direction. In turn, those parents who value self-direction are more likely to adopt parenting behaviors that have been linked to valued cognitive outcomes in children and that may better prepare children for the classroom setting.

Haveman et al. (1991) discuss parental background characteristics in terms of role model theory positing that parents set examples for children. Parents with more education and higher level occupations act as models to encourage similar behavior in their offspring. In addition to giving stronger encouragement to children, setting examples for children to complete higher education, and adopting parenting behaviors that prepare children for academic success, parents with more education are likely to have more social and economic resources, or human capital, than parents with less education. This means that children of more highly educated parents are likely to grow up expecting and feeling obligated to attend college. They also have greater access to information on receiving higher education. Those who lack this source of capital are more likely to drop out of school (Coleman 1988).

This previous research, specifying the process by which social class influences educational expectations, preparation and attainment, clearly indicates the need to explore parental background characteristics. Here, both mothers' and fathers' educational level and type of occupation are incorporated into the analysis. The inclusion of these variables makes the link between family and education and how they might affect the inter-generational transfer of class related resources. Such analysis has important policy implications. If parental characteristics affect educational attainment, then policies may need to target specific children by focusing on changing attitudes toward education, providing information about opportunities for higher education and stressing the value of education in determining their lives.

Household Structure

Because parents are the major source of social norms and human capital encouraging educational attainment, not having or losing parents may have significant negative effects. Compared to children in two-parent homes, children raised in single-parent homes are significantly less likely to graduate from high school and go on to college (Coleman 1988; Jiang and Wojtkiewicz 1992; Krein and Beller 1988; McLanahan 1985; Mueller and Cooper 1986). This is particularly true for those living in single-mother households. The longer the time not spent in a two-parent home during childhood, the more devastating the effect on school completion (Krein and Beller 1988).

Several hypotheses have been proposed to explain the variations in educational attainment among children of single-parent versus two-parent households. First, single-parent families, particularly those headed by women, tend to be economically disadvantaged relative to two-parent households (Astone and McLanahan 1991; McLanahan 1985; Mueller and Cooper 1986). Due to economic deprivation, less money is available to invest in children.

The remaining factors that have been proposed as differentially influencing children in single-parent versus two-parent families deal not with financial resources, but with variations in family relationships. Time as an available resource is limited when only one parent is present to meet the demands of the family. Because of the large number of responsibilities placed on single parents, they are often forced to decrease their time spent in childrearing (Amato 1987). Related to limitations in time availability, children in single-parent families report lower levels of control and super-vision (Amato 1987; Astone and McLanahan 1991; McLanahan and Bum-pass 1988).

The amount of parental supervision and encouragement has also been shown to be related to academic performance. Astone and McLanahan (1991) found that family relations measured by parental practices such as monitoring child's school progress, having high aspirations for child, and high general supervision, positively influence grades, attendance, attitudes and completion of high school. Furthermore, both parent's and child's expectations and attitudes are significantly lower when there has been a divorce.

Researchers have also explored variations by household structure in the general family environment that may affect child characteristics. Studies have suggested that family life is less cohesive and warm after separations due to tensions and the preoccupation of members with personal problems (see Amato 1988 for review of these studies). However, the findings do not consistently support these conclusions. While single-parent families may offer less supervision, especially during adolescent years (Amato 1987), they may offer more companionship (Astone and McLanahan 1991). Amato's (1987) results indicate that children in single-parent families are just as likely as those from intact families to report that their mothers talked to them often, were interested in them, provided assistance with homework and helped with personal problems.

Coleman (1988) discusses variations in the effects of household structure on family relations in terms of social capital. He argues that the presence of human capital resources could indicate the presence of social capital. In the case of the family, social capital refers to the relations between children and parents. The relationship between the parent and child determines whether or not he or she is able to take advantage of the financial and human capital resources the parents possess. In fact, Coleman (1988: S110) argues "that the human capital itself is irrelevant to the child's educational growth if not complemented by social capital embodied in family relations". The number of parents present in the home is one indicator of social capital.

Clearly, research indicates the need to explore the effects of household structure on the educational attainment of young adults. In this chapter, the effects of living in a single-parent home on high school completion and college attendance are explored. If the negative effects of living in a single-parent home on education attainment are due to economic deprivation, as suggested in many previous studies, then household structure should not have a significant effect when controlling for poverty status. If, however, the effect of household structure is due to variations in human relationships within the family, then the effects of household structure should be significant despite the control for poverty status. The results have important policy implications. If economic deprivation is the main factor hindering the educational attainment of children in single-parent families, then policies must be directed at financial support. If, on the other hand, living in a single-parent family negatively influences education regardless of whether or not financial resources are available, policies must be directed at social rather than financial support. For example, if single-parents have less time for support and supervision of children, we may need to develop policies such as age-specific after-school programs, homework-helping programs, etc. Policies may need to provide social support networks that facilitate the specific needs of single parents.

In the following analysis, two-parent families include both intact and step-parent families. Some previous research suggests that family relationships and their effects on children may be different in single-parent and two-parent households (Astone and McLanahan 1991; Jiang and Wojtkiewicz 1992). Some of these effects may be due to stress and tension related to uncertainty about discipline and affection in step-parent relationships, children's feelings of betrayal toward their non-custodial parent, or feelings of jealousy toward the step-parent (Amato 1987). However, Amato (1987) notes that the addition of step-parents can result in improved family functioning by increasing the standard of living, enhancing the well-being and self-esteem of the divorced parents, and providing compensatory emotional support and companionship for children who have lost touch with the non-custodial parent.

In light of this research, we have combined intact and step-parent families to compare household types in regard to resources (such as time availability) that can be supplied by one versus two parents. The analysis allows us to compare the presence of one versus two parents at the time of expected high school completion to ascertain if the number of parents living in the home determines education attainment of youth. Further, the effects of single versus two-parent households are compared to other non-traditional household forms including independent, married couple, other relative or non-relative households. Little information is presently available regarding the effects of these household types on educational attainment.

Residence

While most studies on educational attainment control for residence, little has been done to directly assess the relative importance of residence versus family background. Willits et al. (1988) examine the process of education attainment within a rural population but do not directly compare differences between metropolitan and nonmetropolitan areas.

The need to focus on educational attainment by residence is indicated by the substantial education gap existing between residents of urban and rural locales. In 1991, among white adults over age 18, 26 percent of those in rural areas had less than a high school education compared to 20 percent of persons living in urban areas. The gap in college education is even greater. Among white adults in rural areas, 13 percent had completed four or more years of college, compared to 23 percent of urban adults. For black adults the figures for four or more years of college are less than one-half of whites, 11 percent in urban areas and 5 percent in rural areas (U.S. Census 1992). In part, the urban/rural differences in educational levels are due to the out-migration of better educated adults from rural areas. However, research has documented that rural residents are less likely to complete high school and when they do complete high school, they are less likely to attend college (O'Hare 1988).

In the following analysis, the effect of residence on high school completion and college attendance is taken into account. The analysis allows an examination of the effects that other variables have on educational attainment within the context of a larger community structure. Two questions are considered. First, the analysis addresses the question of whether there are effects of household structure on educational attainment after controlling for the effects of parent's socioeconomic status. Second, does living in a rural area have an effect on educational attainment, in addition to the influence of individual characteristics, parent's socioeconomic status, and household structure? It is essential to address this question in order to understand the specific development of human resources in rural areas. Through such analysis, it is possible to explore how variation in educational attainment is related to the individual, family or household situations of rural residents or to unique structural characteristics of rural areas.

Data and Methods

The data for this study are drawn from The National Longitudinal Survey of Youth. This annual panel survey of 12,868 men and women aged 14 to 22 in 1979 uses a multistage stratified area probability sample of dwelling units and group quarter units drawn by the Bureau of the Census from the primary sampling units (Center for Human Resource Research 1987). The sample, drawn in 1978, has an over-representation of blacks, Hispanics and economically disadvantaged youth. There was a response rate of 92 percent from 1979 to 1986, the period in which these studies were undertaken.

A subsample that contains 3,854 men and women aged 14 to 18 years in 1979, who had not graduated from high school, is used for analysis. Important features of the data for this analysis include a sufficient number of young men and women for comparing by residence, race, ethnicity and income, detailed information on income and earnings, the availability of data on the place of residence for each year of the survey, the inclusion of family background information and the recency of most data on individual characteristics and household composition.

Logistic regression is used to allow for the analysis of dichotomous dependent variables. The dependent variables in the logistic regression are interpreted as the log-odds of completing high school and the log-odds of attending college by 1986. The beta coefficients indicate the amount of change in the log-odds per unit change in the explanatory variable. The percent change in the probability per unit of the explanatory variable from the overall odds is calculated by using the following formula:

$$\Delta P = \exp(L_1)/[1+\exp(L_1)] - \exp(L_0)/1 + \exp(L_0),$$

where P is the change in the probability, L_0 is the logit before the change and $L_1 = L_0 + B$ is the logit after the unit change (Petersen 1985).

Measures

Educational attainment, the dependent variable, is measured for both high school completion (grade 12 completed) and attendance of at least one year of college (>= 1 year of college).[2]

Individual level independent variables include age, race, ethnicity, sex and self-esteem. All are measured as self reports in 1979. Race and ethnicity are dummy variables coded 1 for black versus 0 for other and 1 for Hispanic versus 0 for other. Sex is coded 1 for male and 2 for female. Self-esteem is measured using an eight-item index and has a range of 10 to 40.[3]

Residential status is measured in the year that the individual typically would be expected to graduate from high school and attend college; 22 percent of the sample have a rural residence. To explore possible variations in the regional influences of southern and non-southern areas, residence is differentiated further by national regions. Residence in the South or non-South at the expected time of high school graduation is designated by state of residence; 37 percent of the sample reside in the South. Non-South urban is the reference category in the logistic regression analysis.[4]

Parent's socioeconomic status is measured by mother and father's education and occupation. Education measures include high school completion (grade 12 completed) and the completion of at least one year of college (> = 1 year of college). Completing less than 12 years is the reference category in the analysis. Mother and father's occupation are coded into broad class categories (professional, clerical/sales, and labor-related occupations) according to the 1980 occupational census classification. No occupation is the reference category in the analysis.[5]

Household structure is measured in the typical year of high school graduation. In each year of the survey, a detailed list of household members was compiled. From this information it was determined whether, in the expected year of high school graduation, each respondent was living in a two-parent household (including step-parents), a single-parent household (including any one parent), or an alternative household form (being a single parent, living with a spouse, living alone, or living in a subfamily). The alternative household form is the reference category in the analysis.[6]

Poverty status ("In poverty"), rather than family income, is selected as the most appropriate variable to assess the influence of monetary resources on educational attainment. Poverty status is used to differentiate those who do or do not have access to basic monetary resources. The analysis examines whether or not the lack of such basic resources impedes educational attainment. Poverty status is measured in the typical year of high school graduation.[7]

The distribution of the sample on the independent variables, for the total

TABLE 14.1. Characteristics of Youth Sample by Residence and Region

		Urban		Rural	
	Total	South	Non-South	South	Non-South
	(3,854)	(1,023)	(1,986)	(471)	(374)
Individual					
Average Age	16.0	16.0	16.0	16.0	16.0
% Female	51.0	54.0	50.0	51.0	47.0
% Black	25.0	44.0	17.0	33.0	5.0
% Hispanic	16.0	16.0	20.0	3.0	12.0
Mean self-esteem score	31.7	31.8	32.0	31.0	31.4
% Grade 12 completed	45.0	43.0	44.0	50.0	45.0
% > = 1 year of college	36.0	38.0	38.0	26.0	36.0
Mother					
% Grade 12 completed	38.0	34.0	40.0	35.0	42.0
% > = 1 year of college	15.0	14.0	17.0	5.0	17.0
% Professional	8.0	9.0	8.0	5.0	12.0
% Clerical/sales	14.0	14.0	16.0	9.0	15.0
% Labor related	29.0	34.0	25.0	36.0	26.0
Father					
% Grade 12 completed	28.0	24.0	32.0	22.0	29.0
% > = 1 year of college	20.0	20.0	23.0	9.0	21.0
% Professional	15.0	15.0	18.0	7.0	16.0
% Clerical/sales	7.0	7.0	8.0	3.0	7.0
% Labor related	45.0	45.0	42.0	52.0	51.0
Household					
% Two-parent	57.0	52.0	59.0	51.0	66.0
% Single-parent	12.0	13.0	12.0	11.0	9.0
% In poverty	38.0	43.0	35.0	48.0	33.0

TABLE 14.2. Logistic Regression Prediciting the Odds of Completing High School by 1986.

	Model 1	Model 2	Model 3	Model 4
Age	-.10**	-.10**	-.08*	-.07
Black	-.16	-.15	.40***	.39**
Hispanic	-.36***	-.41***	.31*	.28*
Sex	.34***	.34***	.43***	.64***
Self-esteem	.14***	.13***	.13***	.13***
South rural		-.40**	.06	.23
South urban		-.03	.03	.13
Non-South rural		-.06	.09	.15
Mother				
Grade 12 completed			.88***	.74***
> = 1 year of college			1.14***	.94***
Professional			.52*	.51*
Clerical/sales			.60***	.49**
Labor related			.31**	.26*
Father				
Grade 12 completed			.72***	.67***
> = 1 year of college			1.29***	1.10***
Professional			.73***	.34
Clerical/sales			1.24***	.81**
Labor related			.25**	-.10
Two-parent				1.00***
Single-parent				.50**
In poverty				-.35***
Intercept	2.66***	2.71***	.77	-3.79***
L²	38.13***	48.29***	500.22***	743.39***
R²	.008	.009	.123	.186

* p<=.05   ** p<=.01   *** p<=.001

sample and by residence, is shown in Table 14.1. One major difference
between the areas is in the percent black and Hispanic. The southern
regions, both urban and rural, report significantly higher proportions of
blacks than other areas. Urban areas, both South and non-South, report
significantly higher percentages of Hispanics. The rural South region
reports the lowest level of high school completion. However, overall there
is little variation in the percent completing high school by region. The

TABLE 14.3. Logistic Regression Prediciting the Odds of Attending 1 or More Years of College by 1986.

	Model 1	Model 2	Model 3	Model 4
Age	-.08**	-.08**	-.07*	-.09**
Black	-.20*	-.22*	.50***	.54***
Hispanic	-.24*	-.31**	.57***	.58***
Sex	.10	.10	.17*	.27***
Self-esteem				.12***
South rural		-.56***	.001	.10
South urban		.06	.11	.18
Non-South rural		-.13	.005	.02
Mother				
Grade 12 completed			.67***	.55***
> = 1 year of college			1.33***	1.17***
Professional			.73***	.75***
Clerical/sales			.18*	.16
Labor related			.40***	.35**
Father				
Grade 12 completed			.60***	.55***
> = 1 year of college			1.27***	1.15***
Professional			.94***	.59***
Clerical/sales			.04	-.33**
Labor related			.48**	.10
Two-parent				.78***
Single-parent				.10
In poverty				-.36***
Intercept	.70	.72	-1.27*	-4.93***
L^2	22.53***	52.09***	874.85***	1122.85***
R^2	.003	.008	.166	.214

* $p<=.05$ ** $p<=.01$ *** $p<=.001$

proportion attending college is significantly lower in the rural South than in the other areas.

Results

The first set of analyses of educational attainment examines the effect of residence relative to the effects of individual, parent's socioeconomic status and household characteristics for the total sample. The equations predicting the odds of completing high school or at least one year of college by 1986 are shown in Tables 14.2 and 14.3. In model 1, the effects of the individual characteristics for each dependent variable are shown. In the second model, the residence variables are entered. Living in the rural South at the expected time of high school graduation has a significant negative effect on completing high school and attending college relative to living in the urban non-South.

In model 3, however, parental characteristics are shown to account for a substantial portion of the effect of residence. Both mother and father's education and occupation are significant predictors of high school completion and college attendance. The negative effect of living in the rural South disappears.

Parental background does not account for all of the difference in the probability of completing high school or attending college. In model 4, measures of household structure and poverty status are entered. Living in a single or two-parent household versus an alternative form at the expected time of high school graduation increases the odds of completing high school. Living in a two-parent household significantly increases the odds of attending college. Living in poverty significantly decreases the odds of both high school completion and college attendance. With the exception of father's occupational status, the family background characteristics remain significant in determining high school completion after controlling for household characteristics. Similarly, except for labor related occupations for mothers and clerical/sales occupations for fathers, the family background characteristics remain significant in determining college attendance.

The second part of our analyses examines the effects of individual characteristics, family background and household structure within each of the residential areas. For these residential subsamples, only the models including all variables are presented (Tables 14.4 and 14.5). Mother's and father's high school completion are significant predictors of the child's odds of completing high school (except rural South). Completion of one or more years of college for mother and father is significant in the non-South and South urban areas. Parental occupation has some significant positive effects mostly in the non-South rural and urban areas. Family background characteristics, especially parents' educational levels, are important in determining college attendance in each of the four areas.

In regard to high school completion, individual characteristics are important in both the rural and urban South. One interesting finding is that being black or Hispanic increases the odds of completing high school in the South and the odds of attending college in all areas except the rural non-South. However, the effects of race and ethnicity are only positive and significant after controlling for family background and household structure

TABLE 14.4. Logistic Regression Predicting the Odds of Completing High School by 1986 by Residence and Region[a].

	Non-South Rural	South Rural	Non-South Urban	South Urban
Age	-.07	-.08	-.08	-.06
	(1.6)	(-1.6)	(-1.8)	(-1.4)
Black	-.29	1.08***	.02	.65**
	(-6.6)	(17.7)	(0.3)	(11.9)
Hispanic	-.56	.44	.04	1.13***
	(-13.3)	(8.4)	(0.8)	(18.2)
Sex	.59***	1.07***	.51***	.69***
	(0.1)	(17.6)	(9.7)	(12.5)
Self-esteem	.11***	.15***	.12*	.14***
	(2.4)	(3.0)	(2.6)	(2.9)
Mother				
Grade 12 completed	.33***	.82**	.86***	.58*
	(6.5)	(14.4)	(15.0)	(10.8)
> = 1 year of college	.23	8.35	.76**	1.48**
	(4.6)	(30.8)	(13.6)	(21.6)
Professional	.42	1.34	.68	.08
	(8.2)	(20.4)	(12.4)	(1.6)
Clerical/sales	.22	.43	.68**	.30
	(4.4)	(8.4)	(12.3)	(6.0)
Labor related	-.16	.36	.22	.29
	(-3.6)	(7.1)	(4.5)	(5.8)
Father				
Grade 12 completed	1.59**	.36	.52**	.89***
	(22.5)	(7.1)	(9.8)	(15.3)
> = 1 year of college	1.74	.72	.98***	1.24**
	(23.6)	(13.4)	(16.5)	(19.4)
Professional	.02	-.17	.64*	-.03
	(0.5)	(-3.7)	(11.9)	(-0.7)
Clerical/sales	6.24	.12	.91*	.75
	(30.8)	(2.5)	(15.7)	(13.5)
Labor related	-.48	-.23	.20	-.53*
	(-11.1)	(-5.2)	(4.2)	(-12.2)
Two-parent	1.73***	1.15***	.79***	1.08***
	(23.5)	(21.1)	(14.1)	(17.6)
Single-parent	1.70*	.34	.24	.66*
	(23.2)	(6.8)	(4.8)	(12.1)
In poverty	-.50	-.33	-.45***	-.18
	(-11.5)	(-7.5)	(-10.2)	(-4.1)
Intercept	-2.92	-4.86*	-2.92	-4.34**
L^2	113.04***	113.86***	113.04***	196.73***
R^2	.213	.149	.213	.162

* $p <= .05$ ** $p <= .01$ *** $p <= .001$
[a]Values reported in the parentheses represent the percent change in the probability of completing high school per unit change in the explanatory variable.

TABLE 14.5. Logistic Regression Predicting the Odds of Attending One or More Years of College by 1986 by Residence and Region[a].

	Non-South Rural	South Rural	Non-South Urban	South Urban
Age	-.24*	-.13	-.10*	-.01
	(-1.8)	(-1.6)	(-1.6)	(-1.5)
Black	.61	1.34***	.42**	.50**
	(15.3)	(25.6)	(9.7)	(11.3)
Hispanic	-.36	1.78*	.52***	.70**
	(-8.8)	(30.6)	(11.7)	(15.3)
Sex	.29	.31	.25*	.33*
	(6.8)	(7.2)	(5.8)	(7.7)
Self-esteem	.15***	.15***	.10***	.14***
	(3.4)	(3.6)	(2.4)	(3.3)
Mother				
Grade 12 completed	.30	.71*	.61***	.51**
	(7.0)	(15.6)	(13.6)	(11.7)
> = 1 year of college	1.02*	2.11**	1.11***	1.37***
	(2.1)	(33.2)	(22.5)	(26.0)
Professional	1.24**	1.07	.78***	.35
	(24.3)	(21.7)	(16.9)	(8.1)
Clerical/sales	1.10**	.40	.37*	.01
	(22.2)	(9.1)	(8.5)	(0.2)
Labor related	.32	.40	.22	-.14
	(7.4)	(9.2)	(5.2)	(-3.5)
Father				
Grade 12 completed	.80*	.98**	.43**	.53**
	(17.2)	(20.4)	(9.8)	(12.0)
> = 1 year of college	1.27**	1.76***	1.02***	1.20***
	(24.6)	(30.3)	(21.6)	(23.7)
Professional	.74	.74	.72***	.28
	(16.2)	(16.2)	(15.8)	(6.5)
Clerical/sales	.36	.13	.18	-.19
	(8.3)	(3.1)	(4.3)	(-4.6)
Labor related	-.46	-.26	-.17	-.58**
	(-11.4)	(-6.3)	(-4.1)	(-14.4)
Two-parent	.72***	1.18***	.70***	.81***
	(15.7)	(23.4)	(15.3)	(17.3)
Single-parent	.13	.69	.11	-.09
	(3.0)	(15.2)	(2.6)	(-8.1)
In poverty	.11	-.78**	-.39**	-.29
	(2.6)	(-19.2)	(-9.7)	(-7.1)
Intercept	-3.87	-6.37**	-4.12***	-6.35***
L^2	144.83***	162.92***	533.68***	308.98***
R^2	.223	.235	.189	.200

* p<=.05   ** p<=.01   *** p<=.001

[a]Values reported in the parentheses represent the percent change in the probability of attending 1 or more years of college per unit change in the explanatory variable.

(not shown). Being female and having high self-esteem consistently have positive effects on educational attainment.

Living in a two-parent family operates as a positive influence on educational attainment for high school and college in each of the geographic areas. Living in a two parent-household at the expected time of high school graduation raises the odds of completing high school and attending college by at least 14 percentage points in all areas. Living in poverty at the expected time of high school graduation significantly decreases the odds of completing high school only in the urban non-South (Table 14.4). Poverty decreases the odds of college attendance in the rural South by 19 percent and urban non-South by nearly 10 percent (Table 14.5).

Conclusions

One important finding from this analysis is that effects of household structure are strong indicators of educational attainment in all regional areas, regardless of parents socioeconomic status. The living situation at the expected time of high school graduation plays a role in determining the resources necessary to continue education, including socialization and income. This indicates that policies to improve human capital resources need to be directed at the social, as well as the financial, disadvantages facing teenagers in single-parent and non-parental households.

The findings from the analysis of each of the regional areas show that there are very few differences in the effects of parents socioeconomic status and household structure between regions. While the effects of parental characteristics on completing high school are not as substantial in the rural areas as they are in urban areas, in all areas, the education of both parents is a powerful predictor of college attendance.

When the effects of family background are controlled, the negative influence of living in the rural South on educational attainment disappears. This suggests that there are family characteristics which are more prevalent in the rural South than other areas which discourage high school completion and college attendance. Because residence is examined at the point of high school graduation, it is evident that this effect is not due to differential out-migration of youth by education.

These results suggest that rural teenagers are just as likely to translate family resources into increased education as are teenagers living in other regions. The problem is that they are more likely to lack family resources. Thus, strategies to increase educational attainment for youth could work through the family in both rural and urban areas. Parents in rural areas need to be made aware of the growing need, opportunity and value of high school completion and college attendance. They also need the means necessary to make this a reality.

These findings do not suggest that the problem of education lies only with the family in the rural South. There are structural causes of the higher proportion of low socioeconomic families in the rural South. It does suggest however, that structural changes intended to improve educational attainment in the rural South must do so, in part, through the family. In particular, difficulties faced by families living in poverty and nontraditional households need to be addressed. Thus, an effective means to increase human educational resources is to attend to difficulties created by family and household circumstances.

Therefore, it is essential that efforts to promote education as a resource, regardless of the area, focus on improving the limited opportunities imposed by household characteristics. This includes measures to increase income for single-parent families so children are not pressured to enter the labor force. Also, strategies to increase child support provide not only economic assistance, but increase the chances of contact between the outside parent and child (Furstenberg et al. 1983). Programs to improve wages and skills of single mothers are needed as well. In general, measures to help teens in nontraditional family arrangements obtain the economic and social resources they need to advance, including student grants and scholarships, are important.

Young adults are facing particularly difficult times today due to the baby boom squeeze in the labor market. Paul Light (1990) argues that young adults today will face greater economic difficulties than their parents and will face them regardless of family background. William O'Hare (1988) argues that rural youth experience even greater difficulties because of the industrial restructuring of many small towns and rural areas. The problem with instituting reforms is that the direct benefits to the providers of support are few. The benefits of helping those who need it most are more long term, and indirect but are, nonetheless, essential for a productive flourishing society.

Notes

1. To remain consistent with the literature being reviewed, the term "class" is used in this paper to refer to socioeconomic status. The term is not being used as a strict Marxian concept.

2. Both were measured in 1986. Cases with missing data for 1986 were either completed from information on earlier years when possible, or deleted from the analysis.

3. It is possible that measuring self-esteem at different ages produces variations in the effects on educational attainment. Self-esteem is significantly and negatively correlated with age. However, 1979 is the only year in which self-esteem was

measured. Moreover, variations in self-esteem by age are similar for those groups who do and do not complete high school or attend college, thereby minimizing the potential for bias.

4. While a measure of the duration of time lived in a rural or urban area before high school graduation would have been preferable, such a variable was not possible because the data lacked complete family residence histories. Therefore, residence during the typical year of expected graduation was considered the most appropriate substitute for determining residential effect on educational attainment by 1986.

Residence for expected year of high school graduation was determined by the question "Do you live in a rural area or on a farm?" Cases with missing data on this variable were eliminated from the analysis.

Southern states included Texas, Oklahoma, Arkansas, Louisiana, Mississippi, Tennessee, Kentucky, Alabama, Georgia, Florida, South Carolina, North Carolina, West Virginia, Maryland and Delaware.

5. If the mother or father was not present, or no data were given, the above variables were coded zero. If mother or father was not employed, was not present or had missing occupational data, occupation was coded 0 and thus, represents the reference category. Because some of the respondents were age fourteen in 1979, they were answering for the current year, while others were providing retrospective data. This measure assumes there was no change in mother or father's status or that such change is not significant to the analysis. Again, the preferred variable would include a comprehensive measure of changing family background. However, the data provided such information for the respondent only at age fourteen.

6. This variable is less than ideal because evidence suggests that living with a step-parent has different effects than living with two natural parents. However, more detailed divisions of household structure were not possible due to resulting limited cell sizes.

Previous studies have occasionally included measures of whether or not a change in household structure occurred during the period prior to high school graduation (Sandefur and McLanahan 1989). Such a strategy, however, poses difficulties because the number of years of information prior to typical high school completion is different for each age group. That is, those aged sixteen at the start of the survey (1979) would have two years of information regarding possible household structure change before the typical high school graduation year. In comparison, those aged fourteen in 1979 would provide four years of household structure information prior to expected high school completion. Given the variation in available information by age groups and the associated potential for bias, the structural change variable was considered inappropriate for the following analysis.

7. A measure of family income would imply that each dollar increment to income would increase the likelihood of educational degree completion. Using poverty status as a measure does present its own problems. The definition of poverty status is relatively arbitrary. For this study, poverty status is measured by whether total family income falls into categories of poverty designated by family size, number of dependent children under age 18 and state of residence. The cut-off levels for poverty status change yearly according to changes in the Consumer Price Index.

Family income includes income from all sources including earnings by all adult family members, AFDC income, and social security income (Center for Human Resource Research 1987; Current Population Report 1979, 1980, 1981). Poverty status is not adjusted for state of residence for 1979, 1980, and 1981.

References

Amato, Paul R. 1987. "Family processes in one-parent, stepparent, and intact families: The child's point of view." *Journal of Marriage and the Family* 49: 327-37.

Astone, Nan Marie, and Sara S. McLanahan. 1991. "Family structure, parental practices and high school completion." *American Sociological Review* 56 (2): 309-21.

Bianchi, Suzanne M. 1990. "American's children: Mixed prospects." *Population Bulletin* 45: 1 Washington, D.C.: Population Reference Bureau, Inc.

Center for Human Resource Research. 1987. *NLS HandBook.* The Ohio State University, Columbus, OH.

Coleman, James S. 1988. "Social capital in the creation of human capital." *American Journal of Sociology* 94 (Supplement): S95-S120.

Current Population Reports. 1979, 1980, 1981. *Characteristics of the Population Below the Poverty Level* Consumer Income, Series Pp. 60, nos. 130, 133, 138. Washington, D.C.: Bureau of the Census.

Furstenberg, Frank F, Jr., Christine Winquist Nord, James L. Peterson, and Nicholas Zill. 1983. "The life course of children of divorce: Marital disruption and parental contact." *American Sociological Review* 48: 656-68.

Haveman, Robert, Barbara Wilfe, and James Spaulding. 1991. "Childhood events and circumstances influencing high school completion." *Demography* 28: 133-57.

Jiang, Hong L., and Roger A. Wojtkiewicz. 1992. "A new look at the effects of family structure on status attainment." *Social Science Quarterly* 73 (3): 581-96.

Kohn, Melvin L. 1979. "The effects of social class on parental values and practices." Pp. 45-68 in David Reiss and Howard A. Goffman (eds.), *The American Family: Dying of Developing.* New York, NY: Plenum Press Publishing Corp.

Krein, S.F., and A.H. Beller. 1988. "Educational attainment of children from single-parent families: Differences by exposure, gender, and race." *Demography* 25: 221-34.

Light, Paul C. 1988. *Baby Boomers.* New York, NY: W.W. Norton & Company, Inc.

Luster, Tom, Kelly Rhoades, and Bruce Haas. 1989. "The relation between parental values and parenting behvior: A test of the Kohn Hypothesis." *Journal of Marriage and the Family* 51: 139-47.

McLanahan, Sara. 1985. "Family structure and the reproduction of poverty." *American Journal of Sociology* 90: 873-901.

Mueller, Daniel P., and Philip W. Cooper. 1986. "Children of single parent families: How they fare as young adults." *Family Relations* 35: 169-76.

O'Hare, William P. 1988. "The rise of poverty in rural America." *Population Trends and Public Policy.* Washington, D.C.: Population Reference Bureau, Inc.

Peterson, Trond. 1985. "A comment on presenting results from logit and probit models." *American Sociological Review* 50 (1):130-31 .

Sandefur, Gary D., Sara McLanahan, and Roger A. Wojtkiewicz. 1989. "Racial and ethnic inequality in earnings and educational attainment." *Special Service Review* 63 (2): 199-222.

U.S. Census Bureau. 1992. *Educational Attainment in the United States: March 1991 and 1990.* Current Population Reports. Series P-20, No. 462. Washington, D.C.: U.S. Government Printing Office.

Willits, Fern K., Donald M. Crider, and Robert C. Bealer. 1988. "Observations on opportunity and change: Data from a two-panel study." *Rural Sociology* 53 (3): 321-33.

15

The Labor Market
and Human Capital Investment

Judith I. Stallmann
Ari Mwachofi
Jan L. Flora
Thomas G. Johnson

Many of the poorest regions of rural America have not benefitted from the national growth that has occurred since the 1960s. Two hundred forty-two (10 percent of) nonmetropolitan counties are classified as persistently poor—they have ranked continuously in the lowest 20 percent of all counties in per capita income since 1950 (Bender et al. 1985). During the 1960s, specific attention was focused on poverty areas in an attempt to raise their standard of living. Even some counties that had rapid job growth did not show a decrease in poverty (Larson and White 1986). Educational achievement was also low. By 1980, only 41 percent of persistent poverty county residents aged 25 and over had completed high school (Bender et al. 1985).

Thus, the long-term impact of past employment creation strategies in rural areas is questionable. The major focus of these strategies has been on attracting jobs to the area, with success being measured by the number, rather than the quality or wage level of jobs. In addition, little attention has been given to the incentives created by the labor market for human capital investment. For example, the demand for highly skilled labor creates incentives for individuals (and communities through their school districts) to invest in human capital, while absence of such a demand may serve as a disincentive to do so.

This chapter will argue that the local labor market creates incentives for human capital investment, particularly education. It contends that, at the individual level, human capital investment is encouraged by the existence of opportunities for better incomes given the required skills. An individual invests in human capital to take advantage of these opportunities to improve his/her income. Because national job information does not flow freely, expectations about returns to human capital investment will be based mainly on the local labor market. Even with information on the larger labor market, the individual may find that the monetary benefits of a move do not outweigh the monetary and nonmonetary costs of such a move.

Human Capital Theory

Human capital theory predicts that an investment will be made when the rate of return on the investment exceeds the rate of return on alternate uses of the capital (and other resources). Schultz (1961) suggested that human capital investment is a specific example of general investment behavior. Schultz defined investment in human capital as any expenditure in education, health, or even internal migration that is aimed at taking advantage of better job opportunities. Becker (1962) stated that investment in human capital is any activity that improves ". . . the physical and mental abilities of people and thereby raises real income prospects." Friedman and Kuznets (1945) implicitly recognized investment in human capital as a determinant of income and wealth.

Thus, the existence of better job opportunities should increase the incentives for human capital investment. Like other investment decisions, if expected returns to human capital investment are higher than the costs incurred, then one would respond positively to that incentive by investing. The costs include the opportunity costs of investing the money in other ways and the income that is lost by attending school or training rather than working. If the costs exceed the returns, there is no incentive for investment and the individual will not invest.

Implicit in the most restrictive versions of this theory is the assumption that labor has perfect knowledge of job opportunities and is mobile. People have an incentive to obtain as much education as would optimize lifetime earnings and to migrate to a place where they can maximize their incomes. That is, the theory assumes the supply of human capital is independent of local demand and instead responds to the national labor market. If an individual can increase his/her income by an amount that exceeds the cost of the move and the increased cost of living (in present value terms), then he/she will make the move.

But people may not behave in this ideal manner for two reasons. Values held by some individuals, particularly those related to family and community, may make such a move emotionally costly. In this case, the monetary gain from making a move—particularly a long distance one—must be substantial before it will be considered. In addition, rural people may lack information about job opportunities elsewhere. In these cases, it is reasonable to expect that the individual responds to job opportunities in the local labor market.

Schultz (1961) found that returns to human capital investment are much higher than returns to investment in physical capital. In general, people with better education earn more money, hold better jobs, and are less likely to be unemployed or poor (Killian and Parker 1991).

But not all returns to human capital investment go to the individual. The public also receives returns to the investment in the form of capacity for technical change, improvement in medical knowledge, higher life expectancy, and economic mobility (Sjaastad 1962; Usher 1978; Welch 1978). When making an investment decision, people generally consider only their returns (increased income). In doing so, they underestimate the total returns to the investment. This causes under-investment in human capital that can result in economic retardation and underdevelopment (Becker 1960; Schultz 1961).

The public good aspect of human capital investment has led many researchers to look at the impact of human capital investment on economic development. The literature on industrial location also assumes that economic development flows from human capital investment (McNamara et al. 1988). The crucial role of human capital in the development process has dominated human capital investment literature and research. The possibilities of causation going in the reverse direction, that is, that economic development may encourage human capital investment, or of the existence of a feedback loop, have been largely ignored. The existence of a feedback loop is suggested in a study by Rosenzweig (1988). Using data from the U.S., Colombia, India, Malaysia, and the Philippines, with models of household behavior, Rosenzweig concluded that population growth and human capital investment reflect the economic circumstances of a country. The observed mix of family size, levels of health, nutrition, and schooling are *symptoms* not *causes* of the economic development level. In another cross-national study, Nuss and Majka (1985) found that the level of economic development (as indicated by per capita GNP) has a positive effect on female education.

Empirical Studies

In this section, we review several studies in which the relationship between human capital and economic development is analyzed. Most of these empirical studies have assumed that the direction of causation flows from the supply of human capital to employment growth. We review each of the studies to determine if there is any evidence that the causality is either in the other direction, or is subject to feedback. As we will see, the human capital perspective often allows a different interpretation of findings.

For example, Rudnicki and Deller (1989) uncovered a positive relationship between high quality stocks and flows of human capital and local economic growth in Maine. This study, using a sample of rural towns, covered a period of high in-migration. Seventy percent of the migrants were employed as professionals, executives, administrators, or managers. It is reasonable to conclude, therefore, that the positive correlation was due to the highly skilled migrants who improved educational levels at the top—a conclusion consistent with the human capital perspective.

Simple correlations are likely to show a relationship between average education and employment growth. The report, *After the Factories*, found that county employment growth increased as levels of education increased. The report noted that, "There were clear associations of some county characteristics with growth, but it is not possible to tell whether those characteristics were causes of growth or results of growth, or whether the relationships are spurious" (Rosenfeld et al. 1985:50). When other characteristics of the local economy are controlled for, there are little or no significant effects of average education (Killian and Parker 1991). For example, DeYoung (1985) found a positive correlation between local investment in education and manufacturing, but when other factors were controlled, this relationship became insignificant.

McNamara et al. (1988) suggest the need to distinguish between stock and flow measures of human capital. While stocks measure the existing human capital, flows measure the marginal changes in the stock of human capital resulting from a variety of human capital investments. While flows of human capital were better predictors of industrial location than were stocks, the study did not address the issue of factors that cause the flow of human capital.

Recent studies indicate that the direction of causality between levels of human capital and employment growth is not as clear as it was assumed to be in the past. Killian and Parker (1991) found that the relationship between education and economic growth is changing over time. Increasing average educational levels does not necessarily cause job growth in local economies. From 1969 to 1979, metropolitan areas with higher levels of average schooling grew faster than those with a lower average. But in the 1980s, average educational levels had little impact on job growth in metropolitan areas. Rather, there was a positive relationship between the percentage of college graduates and local employment growth and between dropout rates and local employment growth. This finding suggests the existence of dual labor markets: one involving well-educated people and the other requiring only low levels of education. Thus, variation in local industrial structure affects the demand for labor. Killian and Parker (1991) found no relation between job growth and education in non-metropolitan areas. John et al. (1988) found that the percentage of the population with a high school education had no significant effect on employment growth rates from 1979 to 1984 in rural Midwestern counties.

McGranahan and Ghelfi (1991) concluded that lack of rural demand for highly skilled labor caused the wage differential between high and low skilled workers to increase more rapidly in urban than in rural areas during the 1980s. Lack of demand resulted in a "substantial out-migration of the better educated rural working age population" (McGranahan and Ghelfi 1991). This is a clear example of the migration that Schultz defined as human capital. It also demonstrates that the individual does respond to labor market demand.

Returns to education are also affected by demographics. The Baby Boom generation had high completion rates for both high school and college. Growth of the educated labor force exceeded the growth in demand. As a result, earnings fell, and fell somewhat more for the better educated young adults than for the less educated (McGranahan 1991). When the supply of college graduates outstripped the demand from 1969 to 1979, college graduates took jobs from high school graduates (Howe 1988; Markey 1988). This could result in a lower rate of return to education for both groups.

While the demand for college graduates has recovered since 1979, the demand for high school graduates has not. Compared with college graduates, high school graduates suffer more unemployment in an economic downturn and their employment rates do not recover as much in an upturn (Howe 1988). With a decline in the returns to a high school education, it is not surprising that high school completion rates have stagnated. In fact, among young men the rate of growth in high school dropouts is higher than the rate of growth in college graduates (McGranahan and Ghelfi 1991). As a result, in 1988, the 25-34 year old cohort had lower educational levels than did the same age cohort in 1980.

A 1977 study of high school dropouts in a three-county area of Missouri showed that students do respond to the local labor market. Fifty-four percent of the dropouts perceived that they would have no difficulty finding jobs and that better jobs would be hard to find even with a high school diploma (University of Missouri 1977). This suggests that students' expectations of the returns to a high school education were not enough of an incentive to keep them in school.

Plunkett and Bowman (1973) suggest that trained personnel migrating into rural Kentucky have higher demands and expectations for educational performance than do locals with similar training. Deaton and McNamara

(1984) stated that the migration of higher-income groups to rural areas in the 1970s resulted in demands for higher quality education.

More generally, Bowles and Gintis (1976) and Collins (1979) argued that character traits and aspirations are heavily influenced by the psychological climate created by management of the dominant local business that reflects its proprietary interests. Management interests may not always be progressive, especially if profitability depends on low-skill immobile labor (Bowles and Gintis 1979). Smith (1989) hypothesized that companies that have a high proportion of trained labor have a stake in the educational system and will push for better quality education. Companies that rely on low-skill workers will not encourage employees to participate in community decisions and actions to increase the supply of educational services. They may even discourage improvement of the schools to avoid paying higher taxes and higher wages.

To alleviate the economically depressed conditions in Appalachia, manufacturing industries were, and are, actively recruited into the region. It is assumed that this creates jobs, raises income levels, stabilizes income and thus reduces poverty in this region. Recent studies have found that manufacturing has not achieved these goals, and that human capital investment still lags far behind that of more prosperous regions. Larson and White (1986) found that as many people entered conditions of poverty in nine Kentucky counties as those who left poverty, leaving poverty levels unchanged. The creation of new jobs through industrialization did not improve human capital investment because the manufacturing jobs created did not require high skills.

Industries in Appalachian Kentucky have very low proportions of workers who are rewarded noticeably for having post-secondary educational qualifications. The replacement of mining jobs with manufacturing jobs resulted in approximately the same ratio of managerial, professional, and technical workers to production workers as previously (Smith 1988). Smith claimed that without a change in job mix, there was no increase in incentives to invest in human capital. DeYoung (1985) found that mining and farming had negative impacts on educational performance in Kentucky while manufacturing had no impact, positive or negative.

These findings raise questions about past approaches to economic development and past assumptions about industrialization as a catalyst for economic development. Rather, the creation of low-skilled jobs merely reshuffles people between unemployment lines, poverty, and low level employment, but does not, in fact, improve the economic or social conditions of the community.

Models of Human Capital Investment
and Labor Demand

A search of the literature revealed few empirical studies that measure the impact of local labor market structure on human capital investment. However, studies that estimated models for other purposes are pertinent.

Hobbs (personal communication, June 22, 1990) specified a preliminary model with the dropout rate of each state in 1988 as a dependent variable. DeYoung (1985) used stepwise regression to select the local economic variables with the most predictive power for individual and community human capital investment in Kentucky counties. Individual investment was measured as the percent of tenth graders with below average reading skills and the percent of ninth graders who graduated from high school. Kraybill et al. (1987) examined the impact of local economic structure on the quality of life in Virginia counties. Several of the dependent variables in this study are also indicators of human capital investment—percentage of the population over age 25 with a college education; dropout rates; and scores on reading, math, and language skills.

In the present study, two models of human capital investment for Virginia counties and independent cities were specified. Following the finding by Killian and Parker (1991) that job growth in metropolitan areas during the 1980s was concentrated in areas with a high percentage of high school dropouts and in areas with a high percentage of college graduates, the dropout rate and the percentage of high school graduates continuing their education were chosen as the dependent variables. High school dropout rates are a negative aggregate indicator of investment in human capital: the lower the dropout rate, the greater the investment in human capital. Dropout rates may be a fairly accurate indication of young people's perceptions or expectations of the returns to formal schooling, an important form of human capital investment. Dropout rates are measured as the annual percent of students who do not continue their high school education (Department of Education 1981). The second measure of human capital investment is the percentage of high school graduates continuing their education (Department of Education 1981). This is a measure of how the returns to higher education are perceived by students.

Various measures of income were used in the above models. In his national study, Hobbs (personal communication, June 22, 1990) found that the percentage of children below poverty increased the dropout rate, but per capita income was not related to the dropout rate. Per capita income was positively related to human capital investment in Virginia, while the incidence of poverty tended to have negative impacts (Kraybill et al. 1987).

Per capita income was positively related to human capital investment in Kentucky (DeYoung 1985).

Real per capita income is expected to be positively related to investment in human capital, because there is less need for students from higher income families to drop out of school to contribute to family income. In addition, higher income families are likely to be aware of the returns to education and more educational opportunities are likely to be made available in the counties with higher incomes.

As unemployment rates increase, the likelihood of finding a job decreases. Although high unemployment rates may reduce the expected short-run returns to education, employers may become more selective in their hiring, choosing the applicant with more education (Howe 1988). Thus, education increases the probability of getting a job. Furthermore, higher unemployment reduces the opportunity cost of remaining in school. Overall, higher unemployment rates are expected to increase human capital investment. High local unemployment rates may also lead some individuals to consider the larger labor market and continue their education in order to compete in that market. Unemployment rates were not significantly related to human capital investment in Kentucky (DeYoung 1985).

Each study cited has used a different measure of the local labor market structure. Kraybill et al. (1987) found that resource dependent counties— defined as counties with at least ten percent of employment in mining, forestry, farming and/or fishing—had a negative impact on human capital investment. Similarly, DeYoung (1985) found mining income was negatively related to human capital investment. Farming income also increased the incidence of below average readers. Manufacturing income was not related to human capital investment.

To test the hypothesis that local labor market structure, particularly the proportions of high and low paying occupations, affects human capital investment, this study includes several measures of local labor market structure.

An area may have high employment growth, but little change in numbers in poverty because many of the new jobs are held by migrants into the area (Larson and White 1986; Smith 1989). Population change, which includes migration into or out of an area, is a proxy for the economic vitality of the area. Because commuting is possible, population growth also reflects the economic vitality of the labor market within commuting distance. Thus, population growth is expected to positively affect human capital investment.

As hypothesized by Smith (1988), individuals will perceive returns to education in areas where there are high percentages of people with jobs who are rewarded for their education. If the majority of available jobs are low-paying and do not reward higher education, investment is expected to be lower. The percentage of occupations that are managerial is expected to positively influence investment as students are able to see the returns to education. The percentage of local jobs that are services is expected to negatively affect human capital investment. The occupations included within each category are presented in the appendix.

McGranahan and Ghelfi (1991) point out that there are differential returns to education between rural and urban areas. A more rural location is expected to negatively affect human capital investment. Location in Appalachia, which is very rural, negatively affects human capital investment in Kentucky (DeYoung 1985). To reflect the differential returns to education in rural and urban areas, a series of bivariate variables based on a nonmetropolitan-metropolitan continuum are introduced. The codes categorize counties according to their proximity to metropolitan areas and population (Butler 1990). The codes range from 0 to 9, with 9 being representative of the most rural areas. Because of the low numbers of counties, categories 0 and 1 and 4 and 5 were grouped. Categories 4 and 5 are nonmetropolitan counties with urban populations of 20,000 or more. Category 4 is adjacent to a metropolitan county and category 5 is not. Only one metropolitan county was classified as "0." This county was grouped with the next category of metropolitan counties. The omitted category is the most urban. A similar classification of counties was used in the report *After the Factories* (Rosenfeld et al. 1985).

Model of Human Capital Investment in Virginia

Two models of human capital investment were specified for Virginia's counties and independent cites. In Virginia, school districts coincide with county and city boundaries, causing less variation in educational opportunities within a county than in most other states. In several cases, counties and cities run a joint school system. In these cases, the counties and cities were combined for the analysis.

The dependent variables for the two models are dropout rates and the percent of high school graduates continuing their education. Independent variables include the percentage of county employment in occupations classified as managerial and services (Center for Public Service 1989),[1] real per capita income (U.S. Department of Commerce 1986), the unemployment rate (U.S. Department of Commerce 1987), the percentage change in population (U.S. Department of Commerce 1972 and 1982), and a measure of rurality (Butler 1990). The means and standard deviations of these variables are presented in Table 15.1. All rates are expressed in percentages

TABLE 15.1. Means and Standard Deviations of Dependent and Independent Variables.

Variable	Mean	Standard Deviation
DEPENDENT VARIABLES		
Annual average dropout rate	5.78[a]	1.91
% continuing education	50.47	12.95
INDEPENDENT VARIABLES		
% managerial occupations	18.50	6.75
% service occupations	12.96	3.18
%unemployment	5.66	1.86
% population change	6.03	8.97
1970-1980 Real per capita income ($1000's)	94.82	27.29
Number of observations = 129		

[a]This is the annual average rate for grades 8 through 12. The cumulative annual rate is approximately five times this rate.

and real per capita income is given in $1000's of dollars. All data are for 1980, unless otherwise specified.

The parameters estimated for the two models are given in Table 15.2. The estimated coefficients indicate the percentage change in the dependent variable associated with a unit change in each of the independent variables. For example, a one percent increase in the employment of managers will reduce the dropout rate by .08 percent.

The data presented in Table 15.2 reveal that an increase in the percentage of managerial occupations in the county reduces the local dropout rate. In addition, it shows that the dropout rate increases as the percentage of service occupations increases. Because service occupations tend to be low-skill, they serve as an option for dropouts. As for unemployment rates, no significant impact on the dropout rate is uncovered. This result is quite plausible if dropouts are entering service employment. Service occupations have realized strong growth in 1980, even while other occupations were experiencing declines in total employment. Growth in population tends to decrease the dropout rate.

Contrary to expectations, counties in the three most rural categories have lower dropout rates than those that are less rural or more metropolitan in nature. It may be that these counties have few job opportunities, so the opportunity cost of students remaining in school may be low. If there are few job opportunities, these counties may also have high out-migration and students may continue in school in response to a non-local labor market.

If we move to an exploration of post-high school education, we find that

TABLE 15.2. Demand for Labor Regressed on Human Capital Investment.

Independent Variables 1980	Dependent Variables	
	Dropout Rate 1980[a]	Percent Continuing Education, 1980[a]
Constant	5.82[b] (4.13)[c]	29.18 (3.46)[c]
% managerial occupations	-.08 (-1.85)[c]	.75 (2.78)[c]
% service occupations	.13 (2.34)[c]	-.10 (.32)
% unemployment	.07 (.61)	.87 (1.37)[c]
% population change 1970-1980	-.05 (-2.26)[c]	-.06 (-.47)
Real per capita income ($1000's)	.01 (.11)	.57 (.97)
Metro 2	.41 (.66)	-5.94 (-1.60)[c]
Metro 3	.07 (.10)	-4.61 (-1.14)
Nonmetro 4, 5	-.77 (-1.13)	3.14 (.77)
Nonmetro 6	.24 (.39)	-6.86 (-1.87)[c]
Nonmetro 7	-.74 (-1.18)[c]	-6.85 (-1.84)[c]
Nonmetro 8	-.91 (-1.38)[c]	-5.47 (-1.38)[c]
Nonmetro 9	-1.08 (-1.55)[c]	-7.96 (-1.92)[c]
$\overline{R}^2$	.18	.35

[a]Numbers in parenthesis are t-values.

[b]The coefficients indicate the percentage change in the dependent variable associated with a unit change in each of the independent variables. For example, a 1 percent increase in employment of managers will reduce the dropout rate by .08 percent.

[c]Statistically significant at .10 or less.

the percentage of high school students who continue their education increases substantially as the percentage of managerial occupations increases. On the other hand, no significant shift is detected when the percentage of service occupations is examined. Services may have little influence on students who decide to continue their education because these students are most likely to graduate. They are not likely to be candidates for the low-wage service jobs that might be available.

As unemployment increases, the percentage of students who continue their education increases. When there is surplus labor, the opportunity cost of remaining in school declines. In addition, better-educated workers take jobs from the less educated so that continuing education increases the future chances of obtaining a job. Population growth has no impact on the percentage of students continuing their education.

Rural counties, in general, have a lower percentage of students who continue their education. One set of urban counties (Metro 2) also has a low percentage of students continuing their education. Nine of the 11 counties in this category border the city of Richmond, a very rapidly growing area that has experienced labor shortages, increasing the opportunity costs of remaining in school.

Overall, the equations support the hypothesis that the local labor market creates incentives for human capital investment. The specific hypothesis that the mix of jobs in the local labor market affect human capital investment is also supported.

Policy Implications and Directions
for Future Research

Although Schultz's original discussion of human capital suggested that the demand for labor creates incentives for human capital investment, this direction of causation has been ignored in research and in practice at the local level. Instead, the emphasis has been on the impact of the levels of local education on economic development and job growth. In practice, this has translated into job recruitment based on existing educational and skill levels in the community. While providing needed short-run jobs, this action reinforces the existing labor market structure and does not increase the incentives for human capital investment.

To break this cycle, communities may need to pursue a variety of long-range strategies. By so doing, employment opportunities for skilled production workers, managers, and professionals should be enhanced. This, in turn, should create the necessary incentives to increase human capital investment.

As an example, communities may wish to develop long-range strategies to recruit firms with more managerial and professional occupations than that currently found in the community. Although such jobs may be filled initially by people drawn from outside the community, this trend may be offset by an aggressive effort to recruit educated former residents back into the community. At the same time, initiatives by communities to upgrade their local labor market should not be restricted to the recruitment of firms found external to the area. Focus also should be directed to the manufacturing sectors that have been a traditional component of the rural employment picture. The rural textile sector, for example, is undergoing major changes that require skills upgrading for both production workers and managers (Dumas and Henneberger 1988). These complementary activities could provide an important signal about the need for higher labor force skills, a message that could lead to an increased level of interest in improving local human capital investments.

Economically, under-developed communities may be reluctant to invest in education. If most of the educated members of the community leave because they are unable to find suitable jobs, the community loses a portion of the return on its investment. If employment in skilled jobs is available, on the other hand, and the majority of educated residents remain or return, then the community is able to realize a full return on its investment. One strategy that has attempted to increase the local return on educational investment was implemented in a small community in Virginia. It created a foundation that provides students with the support to attend college and guarantees them a job in the community upon graduation.

Firms that employ a high proportion of educated workers likely will show interest in improving local education opportunities, and a push on the part of these firms to strengthen education may increase the community's efforts to break out of its steady state of low-wage jobs. For example, some textile firms in conjunction with community colleges are sponsoring skill upgrading programs for both their production workers and managers. Similar programs could be designed for future workers as a part of a high school vocational curricula or as part of a post-secondary vocational training program.

An additional strategy could be directed at improving the amount of information current students have about local job opportunities for educated workers. Such information could increase the number of students completing their high school education. A study of dropouts in Missouri (University of Missouri 1977) suggests that people respond favorably to changes in their information about the local labor market and the returns to education. Job information, combined with educational opportunities for those already in the labor market, may lead to increased investments in human capital.

In conclusion, there is ample evidence that individuals respond to the labor market, especially the local labor market, when making human capital investment decisions. Low wage jobs in the local labor market do not encourage investment in human capital. Carefully crafted information on job opportunities, job training and targeted job creation strategies have the potential to increase incentives for human capital investment.

Notes

1. Alternative models were estimated using percentage of employment by sector rather than occupation, with predictably inferior results.

References

Becker, Gary S. 1960. "Under-investment in education?" *American Economic Review* L (May): 346-54.

Becker, Gary S. 1962. "Investment in human capital: A theoretical analysis." *The Journal of Political Economy* LXX (5): 9-49.

Bender, Lloyd D., Bernal L. Green, Thomas F. Hady, Johna Kuehn, Marlys K. Nelson, Leon B. Perkinson, and Peggy J. Ross. 1985. *The Diverse Social and Economic Structure of Non-Metropolitan America*. Rural Development Research Report No. 49. ERS/USDA.

Bowles, Samuel, and Herbert Gintis. 1976. *Schooling in Capitalist America*. New York, NY: Basic Books.

Butler, Margaret A. 1990. *Rural-Urban Continuum Codes for Metro and Nonmetro Counties*. Staff Report No. 9028, Economic Research Service, USDA (April).

Center for Public Service. 1989. *Virginia Statistical Abstract*. Pp. 508-11. Edited by University of Virginia, Charlottesville, VA.

Collins, R. 1979. *The Credential Society*. New York, NY: Academic Press Inc.

DeYoung, Alan. 1985. "Economic development and educational status in Appalachian Kentucky." *Comparative Education Review* 29 (1): 47-67.

Deaton, Brady J., and Kevin T. McNamara. 1984. *Education in a Changing Environment*. Southern Rural Development Center (February).

Department of Education, Division of Information Services. 1981. *Facing Up-15*. Richmond, VA: Department of Education (January): 28-37.

Dumas, Mark W., and J. Edwin Henneberger. 1988. "Productivity trends in the cotton and synthetic broad woven fabrics industry." *Monthly Labor Review* 11 (4): 34-37.

Flaim, Paul O. 1990. "Population changes, the baby boom, and the unemployment rate. *Monthly Labor Review* 113 (8): 3-10.

Friedman, Milton, and Simon Kuznets. 1945. *Income From Independent Professional Practice*. National Bureau of Economic Research #45. New York, NY.

Hobbs, Daryl. 1990. Personal communication, University of Missouri, Columbia, MI (June 22).

Howe, Wayne J. 1988. "Education and demographics: How do they affect unemployment rates?" *Monthly Labor Review* 111 (1): 3-9.

John, DeWitt, Sandra S. Batie, and Kim Norris. 1988. *A Brighter Future for Rural America?* Washington, DC: National Governors' Association.

Killian, Molly S., and Timothy Parker. 1991. "Higher education no panacea for weak rural economies." *Rural Development Perspectives* 7 (1): 2-7.

Kraybill, David S., Thomas G. Johnson, and Brady J. Deaton. 1987. *Income Uncertainty and the Quality of Life: A Socio-Economic Study of Virginia's Coal Counties.* Virginia Agricultural Experiment Station Bulletin 87-4, Virginia Tech, Blacksburg, VA.

Larson, Donald K., and Claudia K. White. 1986. *Will Employment Growth Benefit All Households? A Case Study in Nine Kentucky Counties.* Rural Development Research Report 55, Washington, DC: Economic Research Service, U.S. Department of Agriculture (January).

Markey, James P. 1988. "The labor market problems of today's high school dropouts." *Monthly Labor Review* 111 (6): 36-43.

McGranahan, David A. 1991. "Introduction." Pp. 1-12 in *Education and Rural Economic Development: Strategies for the 1990s.* ERS Staff Report No. AGES 9153, Agriculture and Rural Economy Division, Economic Research Service, U.S. Department of Agriculture.

McGranahan, David A., and Linda M. Ghelfi. 1991. "The education crisis and rural stagnation in the 1980s." Pp. 40-92 in *Education and Rural Economic Development: Strategies for the 1990s.* ERS Staff Report No. AGES 9153. Agriculture and Rural Economy Division, Economic Research Service, U.S. Department of Agriculture.

McNamara, Kevin T., Warren P. Kriesel, and Brady J. Deaton. 1988. "Manufacturing location: The impact of human capital stocks and flows." *The Review of Regional Studies* 18 (1): 42-48.

Nuss, Shirley, and Lorrain Majka. 1985. "Economic development and education of the female population—a cross-national investigation." *Sociological Perspectives* 28 (3): 361-384.

Plunkett, H. D., and M. J. Bowman. 1973. *Elites and Change in the Kentucky Mountains.* Lexington, KY: University Press of Kentucky.

Rosenfeld, Stuart A., Edward M. Bergmar, and Sarah Rubin. 1985. *After the Factories: Changing Employment Patterns in the Rural South.* Research Triangle Park, NC: Southern Growth Policies Board.

Rosenzweig, Mark R. 1988. "Human capital, population growth, and economic development: Beyond correlations." *Journal of Policy Modeling* 10 (1): 83-111.

Rudnicki, Edward, and Steven C. Deller. 1989. "Investment in human capital as a rural vitalization policy: Some preliminary results." Department of Agricultural and Resource Economics Staff Paper 399, University of Maine, Orono, ME (June).

Schultz, Theodore W. 1961. "Investment in human capital." *The American Economic Review* LI (1): 1-15.

Sjaastad, L. A. 1962. "Costs and returns of human migration." *Journal of Political Economy* 70 (5): 80-93.

Smith, Eldon D. 1988. "Economic and social infrastructure in the strategy of regional economic development: An alternative theoretical perspective relevant to open economies." Staff Paper 250, Department of Agricultural Economics, University of Kentucky, Lexington, KY.

Smith, Eldon D. 1989. "Reflections on human resources in the strategy of rural economic development." *The Review of Regional Studies* 19 (1): 13-22.

University of Missouri. 1977. "Missouri Title V rural development high school dropout project." (March) unpublished.

U.S. Department of Commerce. 1980. *Standard Occupational Classification Manual.* Washington, DC: United States Government Printing Office.

U.S. Department of Commerce, Bureau of Economic Analysis. 1986. *Local Area Personal Income,* Vol. 6, 1979-84: 282-316. Washington, DC: U.S. Government Printing Office (August).

U.S. Department of Commerce, Bureau of the Census. 1987. *County and City Data Book,* 1983: 584-612. Washington, DC: United States Government Printing Office.

U.S. Department of Commerce, Bureau of Census. 1972. *1970 Census of Population, General Social and Economic Characteristics,* Vol. 1. Part 48, Chapter B: 48-11, 48-12. Washington, DC: United States Government Printing Office.

U.S. Department of Commerce, Bureau of the Census. 1982. *1980 Census of Population, General Social and Economic Characteristics,* Vol. 1. Part 48, Chapter B: 48-11, 48-12. Washington, DC: United States Government Printing Office.

Usher, D. 1978. "An imputation to the measure of economic growth for changes in life expectancy." Pp. 193-226 in Milton Ross (ed.), *The Measurement of Economic and Social Performance.* New York, NY: National Bureau of Economic Research.

Welsh, Finis. 1978. "The role of investment in human capital in agriculture." Pp. 259-81 in T. W. Schultz (ed.), *Distortions of Agricultural Incentives.* Bloomington, IN: University of Indiana Press.

Appendix
Rural-Urban Continuum Code

Code

Metropolitan Counties:

0	Central counties of metro areas of 1 million population or more
1	Fringe counties of metro areas of 1 million population or more
2	Counties in metro areas of 250,000 to 1 million population
3	Counties in metro areas of fewer than 250,000 population

Nonmetropolitan Counties:

4	Urban population of 20,000 or more, adjacent to a metro area
5	Urban population of 20,000 or more, not adjacent to a metro area
6	Urban population of 2,500 to 19,999, adjacent to a metro area
7	Urban population of 2,500 to 19,999, not adjacent to a metro area
8	Completely rural or fewer than 2,500 urban population, adjacent to a metro area
9	Completely rural or fewer than 2,500 urban population, not adjacent to a metro area

Source: Butler, Margaret A. *Rural-Urban Continuum Codes for Metro and Non-Metro Counties,* ERS/USDA Staff Report No. 9028. April 1990.

Occupations
Managerial and Professional Specialties

11	Officials and Administrators, Public Administration
12-13	Officials and Administrators, Other
14	Management Related Occupations
16	Engineers
17	Computer Scientists
18	Natural Scientists
19	Social Scientists and Urban Planners
20	Social, Recreation, and Religious Workers
22	Teachers; College, University and Other Post-Secondary Institution
23	Teachers, Except Post-Secondary Institution
24	Vocational and Educational Counselors
25	Librarians, Archivists, and Curators
26	Physicians and Dentists
27	Veterinarians
28	Other Health Diagnosing and Treating Practitioners
29	Registered Nurses
30	Pharmacists, Dietitians, Therapists, and Physician's Assistants
32	Writers, Artists, Performers, and Related Workers
33	Editors, Reporters, Public Relations Specialists, and Announcers
34	Athletes and Related Workers

Service Occupations

50	Private Household Occupations
51	Protective Service Occupations
52	Service Occupations, Except Private Household and Protective
91	Military Occupations

Source: U.S. Department of Commerce. *Standard Occupational Classification Manual.* United States Government Printing Office, 1980.

16

Community Agency and Disaffection: Enhancing Collective Resources[1]

A. E. Luloff
L. E. Swanson

Preface

The importance of the community in the development of both an individual and aggregate worth has been a central feature of the sociological literature. The literature suggests that there are two levels of human agency —the individual and the collective. However, in attempting to isolate those factors most associated with community enhancement researchers have tended to ignore the influence of community agency—the mobilization of collective human resources. We believe this oversight has contributed to the general failure of social policy to meliorate local efforts to address social problems.

In this chapter, we suggest that the community is more a product of participation in local activities than an aggregate of individual characteristics. We emphasize the importance of local activity as a vital resource for successful community development. We also discuss the consequences of ignoring the vital role of such activity, and we describe how this role emerges and can be nourished.

To help accomplish this goal, we introduce and use the notions of community agency and disaffection. Disaffection occurs with the deepening of the degree of fragmentation, anomie, and alienation felt by members of a local society. Its presence among members of a locality is seen to reflect the presence of significant barriers to the limits of creative expression of a community's population.

Introduction

Both the underutilization and low quality of human capacity are often cited as barriers to successful rural development. While part of these barriers is attributable to uneven regional development, including the siphoning off of natural, human, and capital resources from rural areas, more is at work here. Often unassessed is the importance of the quality of community agency—that is, the ability of a community to act in addressing specific locale-oriented needs. To the degree that these activities do not capture the creative and entrepreneurial capacity of a locale's citizens to collectively address local needs, the generalized human capacity of any community development effort will fall below its potential.

Community Agency

What might be termed the macro-structural characteristics of a community, such as labor force structure, demographic profile, economic infrastructure, proximity to centers of economic expansion, and the like, by themselves do not reveal, much less predict, the ability of local societies to effectively mobilize their resources. For example, the presence of a viable economic infrastructure—transportation facilities, industrial base, etc.— does not insure the effective use of a community's resources, just as the lack of a viable economic infrastructure does not preclude the existence (stubborn persistence) of a place. A key for understanding these phenomena can be found in the capacity of people to manage, utilize, and enhance those resources available to them. This ability to act is termed *community agency* —the capacity for collective action. It is one of the important dimensions of a community's social infrastructure.

Our use of this term should not be reduced to the concept of a common collective will or mind, as might be associated with a more romantic usage of the term *community*.[2] Rather it is the coming together of people in a local society to address local needs. These people may have intense conflicts or may be of like mind, but the will to act collectively comes from their shared local needs or conflicts. Collective agency in this case need not assume the existence of shared interests much less a shared understanding of a particular need or conflict. Community agency may be characterized by strong social solidarity and a sense of common purpose, but it is much more likely to be characterized by uninspiring efforts to organize committee meetings that seek to mobilize local capital and human resources to establish a business incubator or develop a plan to bring a small town's water system into compliance with federal regulations.

Community agency should not simply conjure up romantic notions of strong local social solidarity. The collective capacity of volition and choice, however narrowed by structural conditions, makes the notion of community agency important in understanding community well-being. Just like the individuals that compose them, communities make choices and act on them. But communities are much more than the simple sum of their individuals. How they make these choices, how their perceptions of local issues are constructed, and the ability of the members of the community to find and process information are important factors in the utilization of their economic and social resources.

The community development literature utilizes several terms to refer to the social dimension of economic development. *Human capital* is an economic term accepted by economists and sociologists that refers to the importance of *human attributes*. This usage, however, is atomized to a point where individuals are viewed as the unit of analysis. Unwittingly, this reduces viable economic development to the characteristics of individual actors or to their aggregate properties. Communities, in this framework, are simply the aggregation and distribution of such characteristics, especially measures including education, age, income, occupation, marital status, and the like, and are therefore essentially irrelevant. What is missing here is the possibility that communities act, and that such agency is considerably more than the sum of its parts. The Floras (1991) have termed the positive consequences of such agency for business development *community entrepreneurship*. We term all such processes *community agency*.

The term community is itself extraordinarily elusive. It may refer simply to the geographical space of a place or to its institutional structure and networks. It also refers to the notion of a highly focused and shared collective will that is focused on a locality, i.e., *community*. Habitually, the rural development literature has sought and accepted explanations of economic development which fail to include assessments of the quality of social interaction directed toward the enhancement of a locality's well-being. Perhaps this has been due to metatheoretical assumptions which diminish the importance of qualitative social phenomenon that resist efforts to be canonized as laws of behavior. More simply, it might reflect the omission of human agency as a factor shaping human behavior. Regardless, the failure to incorporate community agency into economic development programs has hindered our ability to understand and therefore assist community development efforts.[3]

In this chapter, we address the importance of a community's social interaction in either facilitating or hindering the effective mobilization of human, natural, and economic resources. It is assumed that the lower the quality of community agency, the less likely any mobilization of resources, designed to enhance the general well-being of the community, will be realized.

Traditionally, the community development literature has adopted an optimistic approach to issues associated with community agency. In contrast, we introduce and examine the notion of *disaffection* with local society as a generalized community phenomena and, consequently, as a central factor limiting community agency and thereby local social and economic development. We do not follow this path because we are inherently pessimistic individuals. Rather, we believe that central obstacles for community development include overcoming both the under-utilization of local capacities for effective community agency and the institutionalization of undemocratic and elitist local development decision-making processes. We argue that when community agency is limited to the interests of the local elite, regardless how paternalistic, it is inherently restricted.

The evidence to support our belief that disaffection is widespread is largely anecdotal. However, we suggest that the very nature of the community literature, especially to the extent it is dominated by the *eclipse of community* thesis, implicitly assumes that *community* as a factor governing the social life of most local societies is weak at best. This literature proposes that the decline of *community* is the necessary but unfortunate by-product of modernization and material progress. While we will critique this ubiquitous assumption as a flawed historical perspective of the role of *community* in economic development, we do believe that it may well be accurate in its appraisal of the general quality of social interaction in many of America's local societies.

Disaffection is only one type of social condition influencing community agency. Affection for *community* is prevalent among localities, as it has been in our more romantic reconstruction of community life in times past. Unfortunately, *community* is less dominant as a factor in most reported community development efforts, while disaffection seems to be becoming more prevalent. Therefore, while we emphasize disaffection, we do not discount the existence of more positive expressions of community agency among rural communities. Indeed, our ultimate goal is to underscore the importance of finding ways to remove barriers to effective community agency.

The chapter is organized as follows. First we introduce the notion of the disaffected community and link it to its vital role in studies of human capacity. Emphasis is given to conceptually distancing this notion from the eclipse of community. This is followed by a review of important changes that have contributed to the rise of disaffection. Finally, we provide a perspective on how the incorporation of this concept into ongoing research studies can provide important new insights into the impacts of such changes on communities.

Community Agency and Disaffection

The Shackles of the Eclipse of Community Paradigm

Almost without interruption since industrialization, the media have reported on the foibles of society. Unemployment, poverty, and crime, coupled with the mass exodus to central cities from the rural heartland, helped to rivet attention on, among other things, a decline in the sense of community.

This notion of an eclipse of community, both then and now, carries with it assumptions about community at some previous time. Some of the central features of perceived past community life whose loss is bemoaned include social solidarity, common purpose, and a sense of *community*, all thought to be regularly evidenced in communal activities. This eclipse is said to involve both a decline in local social solidarity and in the importance of local social and economic activities in shaping our lives. The latter point is usually bound up in discussions of the loss of local political and economic autonomy; it's based on the assumption that local societies merely react to the groundswells and currents of macro social and economic forces.

A common perception is that the eclipse of community is the result of modernization, particularly the forces of the "Great Change" (Warren 1978) through which rural communities have been integrated into the mass society. Warren (1978) argues that the *horizontal ties* of interdependency of local society have been transcended by *vertical ties* of dependency upon large-scale private and public bureaucracies, whether national corporations or national (or other extra-local) governments. Moreover, the community eclipse concept is accompanied by the theory of the *massification of society* (Bell 1965). This mid-range theory assumes that the historic cultural diversity associated with ethnicity, region, and family legacy has been steadily consolidated by the influence of the mass media and the standardization of socialization in schools, the military, and other agents of socialization. As we will aver later, this belief in the homogenization of culture not only ignores trends toward greater cultural heterogeneity, it turns attention away from the importance of the individual, and, more importantly for our discussion, community action and volition.

Wilkinson (1974) offers an alternative perspective on the relationship between modernization and *community*. He suggests that the forces of modernization have created an opportunity for the emergence of community. In the presence of enhanced technologies, he argues that improvements in both local technical capacities and in communications and transportation networks should facilitate modern day local interaction. Moreover, some of the barriers to broad-based democratic participation by members of a community have been reduced as women and disenfranchised minorities have struggled to gain the right to vote. Wilkinson essentially turns the question of the weak presence of *community* on its head by asking why *community* has not emerged with modernization. Consequently, he calls into question how some could view community agency as being more viable in times past. Wilkinson also implies that it is not necessary to even consider *community* as a necessary ingredient for effective community agency.

In a similar vein, Bender (1978) contends that social scientists', poets', and philosophers' traditional understanding of community is often based on a romantic vision of solidarity, common purpose, and sense of community which had little basis in the realities of the day. Even the most revered institution of the democratic myth of community, the New England town meeting, was in fact dominated by local elites. In their excellent social history of the Salem witch trials, Boyer and Nissenbaum (1974) show how those dispossessed became the victims of a titanic political economy struggle among competing elites. The one attribute not found in Salem was a strong sense of *community*. We propose that a more accurate appraisal of local society in times past, such as Boyer and Nissenbaum's, informs the persistence of community disaffection today by giving emphasis not to the *eclipse of community* but to the *persistence of disaffection*.

These differences in interpretation can be reconciled by assuming that solidarity, common purpose, and sense of *community* are still present, but that their expression is limited or even subverted. Following this line of thought, a central question for local resource enhancement is not "why (or how) has *community* been eclipsed?" but instead "what are the factors that deter the widespread emergence of modern expressions of effective community agency?"

Issues of Structure and Agency for Understanding the Importance of Community Agency

Current debates in the domain of critical social theory can assist in framing this problem. What is the relationship between structural changes in a political economy and their influences on human volition, whether individual or community-based? The assumptions of both the eclipse of community literature and the mid-range theory of the massification of society are premised on the overriding importance of structural transformations that overpower and even determine individual agency. Not surprisingly, both human agency (i.e., human volition) and culture are relegated to consequences of structural forces rather than a combination of structural and cultural forces mediated through individual biography that are intricately woven dialectically to shape the direction and character of social change.

The reduction of culture to the interests of mass society and of the viability of community agency to extra-local social forces greatly narrows the arenas in which either individuals or communities have volition in the degree to which they act. Rather, both are assumed to be acted upon by the impersonal forces of economic and social structure. Such assumptions effectively eliminate any type of agency—individual or community—as serious factors in models and theories of rural development.

This perspective, which is advocated by structural functionalism, orthodox Marxism, and neoclassical economics, as well as any other theory of social organization that avers the primacy of social structure and natural laws, denies the importance of culture and volition as factors shaping human history and our daily lives. But, community agency as a concept assumes a capacity for individual and community volition—that is, it assumes that people make choices, even though the range of choices may be greatly (but not exclusively) shaped by structural factors. These choices are mediated by individuals' and communities' understanding and interpretation of their social conditions. The vagaries of understanding and interpretation usually reflect the highly individualized processes of socialization. Consequently, such perceptions are intricately bound up in the culture and legacies they receive and articulate.

The more innovative theoretical discussions of our time are directed toward understanding the tension between human agency and the social forces of our society, both structural and cultural (see Archer 1989). We agree with Archer and others (e.g., Boggs 1984; Jessop 1982; Offe 1985; Sassoon 1987) that social processes cannot be reduced to deterministic relationships between social and economic structures and community agency, where the latter is simply a dependent variable. Rather, social processes represent dialectical relationships in which culture and socioeconomic structures act on and are, in turn, acted upon by individuals and communities through the choices they make. This makes any economic development effort an emergent process. Wilkinson's (1974) general question of "why does *community* not emerge?" can be addressed in terms of the tension between structure and community agency that is mediated by cultural factors and individual biography. Community agency as a collective social phenomenon emerges in the context of a locality's people and their talents, skills, and faculties to learn and work together toward common goals.

A Heuristic Community Agency Typology

Figure 16.1 presents a schematic which might assist in visualizing the ways the tension between socioeconomic structure and community agency can be manifested. There are two major axes represented: 1) the *Structural Macro-Local axis* and 2) the *Quality of Local Social Interaction axis*. The first axis draws a distinction between the macro societal relationships and their manifestations at a local level. The second axis differentiates communities with lower quality of interaction from those with higher levels. Where structural impediments restrict the interactive relationship between community activeness and quality of life, disaffection is assumed to occur in both macro and local social settings. Where such impediments do not exist, that is, where there is a high quality of interaction among members of a society, community agency will exhibit an important influence in improving the local quality of life.

These four cells represent two distinct types at two different levels of analysis. The top right is indicative of an effective transition to the massified society at the macro level. Here, substantial amounts of interaction are the norm and there are few structural problems of alienation, anomie, and fragmentation. This cell represents the successful integration of community relationships to extra-local linkages (Warren 1978). The top left cell represents those places where such transitions have been less successful. Structural problems are evidenced here which act to impede the transition process resulting in a lower quality of life.

The local level (bottom two cells) is where the impact of many of these macro forces are experienced. Enhanced local societies are represented in the lower right hand cell. Such localities are marked by fluid interaction among the various sectors and a higher quality of life. These places have been referred to as "Good Communities" (Warren 1970).

Localities positioned in the remaining cell tend to be characterized by lower levels of interaction, higher rigidity in access to resources, and significantly higher levels of disaffection. Such places are more likely to exhibit problems associated with disenfranchisement, unemployment, and

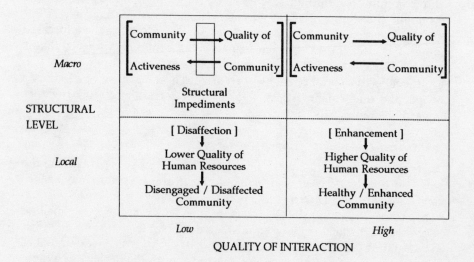

FIGURE 16.1. Conceptual Design for Disaffection.

poverty, all of which contribute to the stifling of the local population's creative expression.

Thus, not only do the prevailing macro trends affect individuals and particular groups, but they impact communities as well. We use the term disaffection to refer to the degree of fragmentation, anomie, and alienation exhibited by members of communities. Such places, in our opinion, are in trouble.

Contrasting Community Agency and the Eclipse of Community and Culture Theses

At this point, we return to our critique of both the eclipse of community and massification of society. It is important to distinguish between our conceptualization of community agency with those assuming the simultaneous eclipse of community and the massification of culture. The latter tends to be overly pessimistic with respect to the capacities of communities to have some control over their destiny; effectively, this literature has purged discussion of community agency from discussions over appropriate rural development strategies. In contradistinction, we assume that community agency is an emergent process that is effective in empowering local societies. This viewpoint contradicts those that assume the insignificance of locality. Rather than bemoaning the loss of community, we should instead spend time examining potential barriers to the viable expression of community agency. We assume that one necessary, though not sufficient, condition for rural development is the enhancement of community agency.

Ignoring Agency and Disaffection

From a sociological standpoint (Castells 1976; Gusfield 1975; Nisbet 1953; Stein 1960), the decline thesis achieved much of its popularity and status as an explanation of the negative consequence associated with the rapid hegemony of urban society. Note that the discussion of the eclipse of community was conducted in the context of "rural versus urban places," not in terms of the emergence of a capitalist political economy within the American cultural experience. Consequently, much of this explanation implicitly rests on a spatial determinism in which rural areas produce fundamentally different types of social relationships. Such a perspective ignores the great transformation in the production relationships of both rural and urban areas. Rather, in the decline thesis, emphasis is given to population density and characteristics of the division of labor.

The eclipse of community and culture theses assert that the complex division of labor in modern society necessarily attenuate communal relationships. Social interaction in such societies tend to be characterized as impersonal, transitory, and segmented and are, therefore, prone to be anomic and alienated (e.g., Wirth 1938). Further, the urban core has been seen as having a pervasive influence on the hinterland, especially in terms of socialization, value orientations, culture, commerce, and trade.

Certainly the character, economic dependency, and integration of small communities within the larger society have undergone profound changes that have removed their relative isolation. In many cases, this has contributed to a de-differentiation as well as a decline in the numbers of key social and economic institutions via consolidation and a restructuring of regional place hierarchies. And, no doubt the culture has been altered and even somewhat homogenized by the mass media. But, these changes have not eliminated the importance of local society to individuals or eliminated residents' attachments to locality.

Again, focusing on "why (or how) was community eclipsed?" begs the more important question "in what ways is community expressed?" One answer is that there are limited opportunities for expression. Forums for community agency may be suppressed or confined to groups with narrow interests. Whatever the form, disaffection is enhanced whenever one's ability to contribute to community activities is retarded.

The Territory-Free View of Community

Another conceptual twist in the community studies literature is to stress the negative aspects of small town life in the past by emphasizing the seemingly positive influences of society's massification. This perspective celebrates the reduced influence of narrow small town values and the power of a majority to force conformity to them. Such an approach might be termed the *territory-free* version of community (Bender 1978; Scherer 1972; Wellman 1979). Rapid developments in transportation and communication technologies, which have greatly reduced the friction of space, provide an ample basis for this perspective.

Indeed, adherents of this framework believe freedom from the domination of small local society ties, which heretofore had helped to encapsulate residents in relatively isolated social worlds, results in a more liberated community environment. Such scholars argue that once freed from the hegemony of local pressures for conformity, previously disenfranchised groups can seek support and organizational strength in the larger community arena (Wilkinson 1990).

This perspective is enticing in its rejection of often suffocating local social relationships, but at the same time it denies the capacity for locality-based action to be an effective economic development strategy. It also hinders the promotion of greater tolerances for new expressions of personal and social activities. The problem with this perspective is its failure to recognize that the very characteristics of small communities that make them suffocating are also barriers to community agency. Rather than identify this as a problem, it is easier to dismiss the importance of locality.

Our concern is that the importance of local society not be rejected, as this massification perspective tends to do, but to recognize the historic barriers to more effective expressions of community agency. These barriers have included undemocratic community decision-making processes that reproduce the class interests of the local elites. It is conceptually possible to place hope in the quasi-emancipatory effects of the reduced influence of small town elites without rejecting the importance of enhancing community agency.

The employment of the massification perspective is not without other difficulties. Those who focus solely on the role of the larger society necessarily miss a constellation of local level social and economic phenomena. And, they contribute to the mistaken notion that social structure can best be identified through an analysis of individual nodes. It is our belief that a framework which measures actions of collectivities of people, rather than an aggregation of individual level measures, is needed.[4]

Evidence Supporting the Importance of the Quality of Community Agency

The quality of community agency in a local society provides valuable information that cannot be reduced to individual characteristics or aggregations of such characteristics. There is indirect empirical evidence of the importance of community agency. Community studies of the adoption of flood insurance, manufacturing development, and the securement of government bonds provide clues to the importance of a place's ability to mobilize local resources (Kuehn et. al 1979; Lloyd and Wilkinson 1985; Luloff and Chittenden 1984; Luloff and Wilkinson 1977; Martin and Wilkinson 1984; Williams et. al 1977). It is possible that the differential success of communities with otherwise shared structural characteristics is due to the relative degree of disaffection toward community activities by their citizens.

Other community studies point to the persistence of communities thought to be candidates for disappearance. One of the more celebrated studies is of Caliente, Nevada (Cottrell 1951). This town was established to serve as a train refueling station during the era of steam locomotives (which had shorter ranges than modern trains). With the advent of diesel locomotives, the economic reason for Caliente's existence disappeared—a casebook example of technological change determining the fate of a social organization. The railroad pulled out most of its people and greatly curtailed operations. Like many other such communities, and apparently against the odds, Caliente did not disappear. Instead, it has remained relatively constant and small in population by actively seeking new forms of employment, usually from the state of Nevada (the most notable being a prison/rehabilitation center).

Why do towns like Caliente persist? Krannich and Luloff (1991) have proposed that a high degree of community activity historically has forestalled the demise of the town. We submit that such communities are examples of places with a high quality of community agency.

Negative examples of disaffection are more numerous. Gaventa's (1980) insightful critique of Middlesboro, Kentucky, in *Power and Powerlessness*, documents how local elites can mobilize power through control of the local economy and political institutions to quell even the appearance of dissent. In this community, both individual and community agency is subjugated to the interests of local elites. Feelings of powerlessness are internalized by the disenfranchised and reproduced one generation to the next. The community literature of the middle of this century is replete with such case studies, including the Lynn's studies of Muncie, Indiana, *Middletown* (1929) and *Middletown in Transition* (1937), Dollard's *Caste and Class in a Southern Town* (1949) and Vidich and Bensman's *Small Town in Mass Society* (1958).

Barriers to Community Agency

The Tension Between Structure, Culture, and Agency

"Community disaffection" has historically dampened and even eliminated community agency. Disaffection is engendered when elites are able to impose their will through the local economy, social structure, and culture. Social historians, such as Boyer and Nissenbaum (1974), have recast preindustrial communities in the U.S. in a less romantic light; it is unlikely our country ever experienced a golden age of community. It may well be that the persistence of disaffection with modernization should take precedence over the eclipse of community.

We propose that expressions of community disaffection were only altered by the emergence of the current capitalist political economy and by the changing character of the U.S.'s highly diverse culture. Consequently, we reject the entrenched traditional explanations based upon rural-urban differences associated with the eclipse of community literature. Critiques of U.S. capitalism have focused on a myriad of structural factors that can disenfranchise individuals and communities while simultaneously empowering economic elites. But the U.S. also has a cultural heritage which values democracy and equality—though legal and de facto realization of these values as rights continues to be a point of political discontent. This heritage creates a dynamic political tension between socioeconomic structures that reproduce capitalist institutions and social relationships on the one hand, and politically powerful cultural frameworks valuing democracy and equality on the other.

Add to this tension the volition of individuals and communities in assessing and making choices and a highly dynamic, even volatile social context for change and conflict at the local level exists. At issue is the management of human agency—individual or community. Culture frames value assumptions for individuals and communities about what is right and wrong and what ought to be, as well as notions on the means for achieving these values. Culture is not determined by socioeconomic structures, but rather interacts with these structures dialectically. Culture mediates individual and community perceptions about social conditions, and consequently influences both the perception of and reasoning process involved in making choices. As Gaventa (1980) notes, culture can reflect the hegemony of elites and produce quiescence among the disenfranchised in a community. Such quiescence is a dimension of community disaffection.

Community agency is repressed when the prevailing cultural norms, coupled to an extant socioeconomic structure that provides for elitist local power configurations to emerge, conspire to promote quiescence among the disenfranchised. Democracy for the few in local society narrows the capacity and quality of community agency in the community field to special interests of entrenched elites. *We hypothesize that both individual and community agency is given its greatest potential for expression when democracy, choice, and information is maximized.*

This does not mean that community agency will lead to successful rural development. Pluralist and democratic political processes, while highly valued in and of themselves, are no assurance of successful community development. To be sure failures will occur, but they will occur in the context of a community's effort to mobilize itself. Wilkinson (1991) argues that the prospects of long-term success may be built upon failed action episodes when these episodes create viable networks and increase the knowledge and information base of the community. Indeed, this phenomenon is recognized by those community development specialists who propose that the first efforts to mobilize a community ought to focus on attainable goals so as to gain the experience of community action.

The Separation of Place of Work From Place of Residence

The industrial revolution swept away once dominant social forms of production based upon the household or guild. As people worked at places other than their homes, new and powerful agents of socialization and culture emerged. The increased separation of place of work from place of residence removed a principal mode for integrating families, schools, neighborhoods, and communities. In their place, multiple new social fields of interaction (production, services, goods, and welfare) were created in various collective arenas (religion, politics, schools, voluntary organizations). The presence of such fields creates opportunities for collective action but neither guarantees, nor necessarily facilitates, the emergence of collective action. Indeed, as proposed earlier, the evidence would suggest that there has been a loss of activity as a result, and that often the actions taken are defensive in tone. Further, the importance of these multiple fields is heightened by the increased presence of other factors which militate against strong local activity.

The Domination of the Authoritarian and Paternalistic Workplace

The structural shift of workplace from the household was often accompanied by the emergence of workplaces with capitalist social relations of production. Place of work became characterized by a separation of labor from ownership, such as in factories or large scale owner-operated businesses. Such firms customarily have been authoritarian in their governance. The rise of government bureaucracies introduced similarly authoritarian relationships—only in this case the "boss" was the agency rather than a private sector employer.

Pateman (1970) effectively argues that authoritarian and paternalistic workplaces represent structural barriers to participatory democracy in the larger society. These workplaces are often purposefully designed to prevent people from acting collectively in their interests. At the same time, they help subvert the socialization process from promoting cooperation and hinder the transfer of collective decision-making skills in any of the major communal institutions, thereby, reinforcing a highly concentrated power structure.

Pateman (1970) proposes that a serious consequence for actual exercise of democratic processes is the absence of the same in the primary institutions in which we spend most of our lives—schools, family, and the workplace. Pateman poses the following question: If democratic processes require skills associated with collective decision-making, and if the primary agents of socialization (family, school, or workplace) do not provide such experiences, then why should we expect to find democratic processes working in the making of local community decisions? Why should we expect skills necessary for pluralistic and democratic decision-making to spontaneously emerge when none of the primary agents of socialization provide an arena for learning such skills?

The consequences of authoritarian and paternalistic workplaces go beyond the barriers they pose to learning collective decision-making processes. The hierarchy of such institutions obviously penetrate the power structure and patterns of local social interaction. If we assume that a community's dominant economic activity and its prevailing social relationships directly influence the well-being of such communities, as most of the community economic development literature claims, then it follows that when such workplaces are authoritarian, paternalistic, and hierarchical in structure, they will exercise similar influences locally. Gaventa (1980) makes this point in his case study of Middlesboro. He attributes the widespread quiescence among the working class directly to the economic and cultural hegemony of the dominant industries. Billings (1990) reaches a similar conclusion in his study of class formation in coalfield and textile-manufacturing communities.

Workplace relationships, then, can be a very important factor in diminishing effective community agency, and thereby can contribute to local disaffection. On the one hand, their influence in the economic field of a community provides a formidable power base, especially in places dependent upon one or two industries. On the other, they directly contribute to normative perspectives on how local decisions ought to be made.

One of the less stressed themes of Goldschmidt's (1978) study of farm and community is the different influences that workplace social relationships can exert on the local society. Those places dominated by family farming, a form of owner-operated business, had impressive evidence of widespread, democratic, local decision making. On the other hand, areas dominated by industrial farming did not. Rodefeld's (1974) study of Wisconsin communities expanded upon this theme by demonstrating empirically that workers from industrial-type operations were far less likely to participate in local decision-making or in any voluntary activities.

Culture as a Barrier to Community Agency

To this point, it may appear that we have targeted structural factors associated with the U.S.'s peculiar expressions of capitalism as the primary and maybe only culprit. But such a conclusion is overly simplistic. Culture also may act as a barrier. Racism, sexism, ageism, uncritical acceptance of authority, and other social prejudices that are reproduced through agents of socialization, create serious barriers to community agency.

Billing's (1990) discussion of the paradoxical role of religion in reproducing stifling and exploitive social relationships, while forming the cultural basis for resistance to entrenched local economic powers offers an example of how culture may facilitate or impede community agency. Utilizing a Gramscian analysis, he compares the different influences of similar Pentecostal sects in a North Carolina textile community and a West Virginia coal mining community.

> *Much as later it would serve black activists in their struggles for civil rights in the South, Protestantism contributed moral, ideological, and leadership resources to the battles for unionization in the coalfields of Appalachia. At the same time, however, it functioned as a bulwark of antiunionism and conservatism in the textile-manufacturing communities of the southern Piedmont* (Billings 1990:1).

Billings (1990: 3) examines "how socially dominant groups attempt to influence the interests and preferences of subordinate groups and how subordinate groups attempt to resist domination and to achieve autonomy." In short, Billings suggests that it is problematic the way culture, particularly expressed locally via a legacy of social relationships, is utilized to maintain the interests of local elites or to resist such interests. The conflict occurs in the community and it directly influences the quality of community agency. Culture, and its myriad expressions, is not a reflection or product of socioeconomic structure. Rather, as in the case of religion in Billings' study, it is a mediating factor in both the emergence and reproduction of socioeconomic structures and of all forms of human agency. As Billings (1990: 27) notes for religion, "it has both a degree of autonomy and material impact." That is, culture is independent of economic and social structures but interacts with such structures and therefore is of great importance in making sense of community development processes.

To the extent that culture provides and reproduces values which degrade and inhibit widespread expressions of human agency, it is a means for the constricting of community agency toward the special interests of local elites. Consequently, for rural development policy to nurture community agency, it must take into account the role of culture in perpetuating inequality and in mediating and facilitating community agency.

What Can Be Done to Improve Community Agency?

We believe that it is incumbent on social analysts studying human capacities of rural and small communities to differentiate between the relative contribution of local and nonlocal influences on such development. This is neither a new nor profound insight; however, the general absence of such concern in the dominant community literature suggests that a reexamination is warranted. Disaffection, as a result of the separation of work from place of residence, the increased geographic mobility and linkage among the population, and the growing dominance of the authoritarian and paternalistic workplace, operates to inhibit the emergence of the full benefits of community to its population.

In order to improve our understanding of community agency, we would suggest that attention needs to be placed on the assessment of disaffection in rural and small communities. The typology presented in this chapter may be a useful framework for helping to guide the selection of sites where such studies could be conducted. As will be recalled, one axis differentiates between macro societal relationships and their manifestations at the local level, while the other focuses on the quality of local interactions. Case study sites which maximally differentiate places on these criteria, will provide insights into the ability of agency to emerge and the conditions which act to impede this emergence. Such research will provide needed insights into the identification and operationalization of measures of human agency that can be used in community studies.

How We Got Where We Are and Why We Need to Go Elsewhere

Buck (Wilkinson 1974) once claimed that the last vestiges of *community* lay in resistance to the influence of powerful extra-local interests; he might also have added the penetration and hegemony of capitalist and State influences. While this pessimism may be justified, and the emphasis on extra local barriers to community agency correctly identified, it may well be extreme. The importance of local society has not and will not recede or be eclipsed by the forces of the larger economy, society, and culture. But there is a great need to enhance the capacity of community agency to perform on behalf of all members of a community. Moreover, the removal or easing of the barriers to greater community agency is not only possible, it is a necessary process for any rural development strategy.

This will not be an easy undertaking. Capitalist influences in the U.S., particularly as expressed in the persistence of authoritarian workplaces, polarized wealth, and beliefs in the primacy of short-term profit margins, are not likely to be eclipsed in even the far future. At the same time, the cultural scourges of racism, ageism, sexism, and other forms of social intolerance are not likely to disappear any time soon. Despite this, the effects of such inhibitors must be addressed if community agency is to fully blossom as a positive factor in rural development.

If a community is to fully utilize its human resource base, barriers to the creative expression of community action must be confronted. By not focusing on the role of community agency and the barriers to its effective expression, social scientists unwittingly contribute to the maintenance of the status quo. As a group, community scholars are responsive to variations in tastes but often cater to the powerful interests of a society. It has not been to their advantage to focus on the barriers to community agency, especially when public and private funding agencies generally have not been supportive of such activity. As a result, students of community have regularly studied structural indicators like poverty, unemployment, levels of educational attainment, and economic opportunities at either an aggregate individual level (using census type data) or at the macro societal level. To date, very limited efforts have been made to study the character and influence of community agency and factors contributing to community disaffection.

The eclipse of community and homogenization of culture themes have been convenient paradigms for dismissing the importance of key *human factors* for formulating rural development strategies. Such a conclusion is not ours alone. Concern is traceable to an often marginal part of the community literature that has long revered the importance of local society as a legitimate arena for inquiry and as a logical starting point for understanding socioeconomic forces shaping societal change (cf. Bernard 1973; Konig 1968; Wilkinson 1979, 1986, 1991). These scholars begin with the domain assumption that the community is the first social grouping outside the family to which each person is exposed. As a result of this exposure, the community continues to be viewed as playing a critical role in the grounding of experience, both individually and collectively, although not much study of the collective effort has occurred.

The relationship between participation, democratic institutions, and the degree to which citizens feel a sense of ownership reflects the degree to which citizens believe they are a part of the process of local decision-making and, thereby, willing to accept and act on local decisions. This does not mean poor decisions will be avoided or that conflict will be eliminated. But disaffection and other forms of alienation will likely be reduced, and a community will have greater access to its human resources. Where exploitative relations (evidenced by structural impediments) exist, local levels of disaffection are seen to be high.

Continued inattention to the identification and development of protocols for removing some of the structural barriers to general participation in the local decision-making process has retarded our ability to create reasonable and sound rural development policy. If, as we have argued, the prevailing system and structure discourages the democratic participation of all members of a locality, then the potentials for effective community action may be subverted. On the other hand, if efforts are made to enfranchise those formerly removed from the decision-making process, then a redistributive effect of community development activities will likely occur.

In part, this reflects the obvious—locations which lack depth and breadth of human resources cannot afford the luxury of ignoring any segments of their population. Further, it is not simply human capital that is at question here, but also what Coleman (1990) has called social capital. This latter concept refers to the "...norms, social networks, relationships between adults and children that are of value for the child's growing up....[S]ocial capital exists within the family, but also outside the family, in the community" (Coleman 1990:334).

Wilkinson's suggestion that the seeming absence of widespread evidence of *community* is not due to the eclipse of community by the forces of modernization but to forces that help deter its emergence, recasts the problem. We propose that disaffection is a worthy focus for this new path of inquiry. Disaffection assumes there is untapped capacities for broad-based and effective community agency. An ancillary assumption is that local society continues to be of importance to rural and urban residents alike. After all, we live out our lives in our local society. The question for those interested in reforming local society so as to foster community agency is "to what extent does a generalized disaffection reduce the opportunities for the emergence of pluralistic and democratic participation by residents in the affairs of their immediate locality?"

Notes

1. This manuscript has benefitted from the reviews of Mark Nord, Myron Schwartz, Kenneth P. Wilkinson, Thomas Greider, Jan L. Flora, and Willis J. Goudy. Assistance from Lionel "Bo" Beaulieu is also acknowledged and appreciated.

2. For the duration of this chapter, we will signify the more romantic notion of community as a highly willful local activity characterized by high social solidarity by italicizing the term. Hopefully, this editing ploy will help the reader to distinguish between the more romantic usage of the term community with the notion of community agency we week to establish in this essay.

3. This ability is no less important but decidedly different from human capital; relatively little is known, however, about the community's adaptive infrastructure which we view as being reflective of its human capacity.

4. The vast majority of the extant community literature has made use of two levels of analysis—either the macro social level or the most micro individual level. In both instances, claims are made about community. However, more limited attention has been focused on the relationships of individuals in collective action at the local level. This absence impedes a more comprehensive analysis of community (Luloff 1990; Luloff and Swanson 1990; Wilkinson 1991; see also Poplin 1972; Bender 1978; and Warren 1978).

References

Archer, Margaret S. 1989. *Culture and Agency*. London: Oxford University Press.
Bell, Daniel. 1956. "The theory of mass society." *Commentary* (July): 75-83.

Bender, Thomas. 1978. *Community and Social Change in America*. New Brunswick, NJ: Rutgers University Press.

Bernard, Jessie. 1973. *The Sociology of Community*. Glenview, IL: Scott, Foresman and Company.

Billings, Dwight B. 1990. "Religion as opposition: A gramscian analysis." *American Journal of Sociology* 96 (July): 1-31.

Boggs, Carl. 1984. *The Two Revolutions: Gramsci and the Dilemma of Western Marxism*. Boston, MA: Southend Press.

Boyer, Paul, and Stephen Missenbaum. 1974. *Salem Possessed*. Cambridge, MA: Harvard University Press.

Castells, Manuel. 1976. *The Urban Question*. London, UK: Edward Arnold.

Coleman, James S. 1990. *Equality and Achievement in Education*. Boulder, CO: Westview Press.

Cottrell, W. F. 1951. "Death dieselization." *American Sociological Review* 16 (4): 358-65.

Dollard, John. 1949. *Caste and Class in a Southern Town*. Garden City, NY: Doubleday Anchor.

Flora, Carnelia Butler, and Jan L. Flora. 1991. "Developing entrepreneurial communities." *Sociological Practice* 8: 197-207.

Gaventa, John. 1980. *Power and Powerlessness: Quiescence and Rebellion in an Appalachian Valley*. Urbana, IL: University of Illinois Press.

Goldschmidt, Walter. 1978. *As You Sow*. Montclair, NJ: Allanheld, Osmun and Company.

Gusfield, Joseph R. 1975. *Community: A Critical Response*. Oxford, UK: Basil Blackwell.

Jessop, Bob. 1982. *The Capitalist State*. New York, NY: NYU Press.

Konig, Rene. 1968. *The Community*. New York, NY: Shocken Books.

Krannich, Richard S., and A.E. Luloff. 1991. "Problems of resource dependency in U.S. rural communities." Pp. 5-18 in Andrew W. Gilg (ed.), *Progress in Rural Policy and Planning*. London, UK: Belhaven Press.

Kuehn, J.A., C. Braschler, and J.S. Shonkwiler. 1979. "Rural industrialization and community action: New plant locations among Missouri small towns." *Journal of the Community Development Society* 10 (Spring): 95-107.

Lloyd, Robert C., and Kenneth P. Wilkinson. 1985. "Communty factors in rural manufacturing development." *Rural Sociology* 50 (Spring): 27-37.

Luloff, A.E., and Kenneth P. Wilkinson. 1977. "Participation in the national flood insurance program: A study of community activeness." *Rural Sociology* 44 (Spring): 137-52.

Luloff, A.E., and Wendy H. Chittenden. 1984. "Rural industrialization: A logit analysis." *Rural Sociology* 49 (Spring): 67-88.

Luloff, A.E., and L. E. Swanson (eds). 1990. *American Rural Communities*. Boulder, CO: Westview Press.

Luloff, A.E. 1990. "Community and social change: How do small communities act?" Pps. 214-27 in A. E. Luloff and L. E. Swanson (eds.), *American Rural Communities*. Boulder, CO: Westview Press.

Lynd, Robert S., and Helen Merrell Lynd. 1929. *Middletown: A Study in Contemporary American Culture*. New York, NY: Harcourt, Brace.

Lynd, Robert S., and Helen Merrell Lynd. 1957. *Middletown in Transition: A Study in Cultural Conflicts*. New York, NY: Harcourt, Brace.

Martin, Kenneth E., and Kenneth P. Wilkinson. 1984. "Local participation in the federal grant system: Effects of community action." *Rural Sociology* 49 (Fall): 374-88.

Nisbet, Robert A. 1953. *The Quest for Community*. New York, NY: Oxford University Press.

Offe, Klaus. 1985. *Disorganized Capitalism*. Cambridge, MA: MIT Press.

Pateman, Carole. 1970. *Participation and Democratic Theory*. Cambridge, UK: Cambridge University Press.

Poplin, Dennis E. 1972. *Communities: A Survey of Theories and Methods of Research*. New York, NY: Macmillan Co.

Rodefeld, Richard D. 1974. *The Changing Organizational and Occupational Structure of Farming and the Implications for Farm Work Force Individuals, Families, and Communities*. Unpublished Doctoral Dissertation. Madison, WI: University of Wisconsin.

Sassoon, Ann. 1987. *Gramsci's Politics*. Minneapolis, MN: University of Minnesota Press.

Scherer, Jacqueline. 1972. *Contemporary Community: Sociological Illusion or Reality?* London, UK: Tavistock.

Stein, Maurice. 1960. *The Eclipse of Community*. Princeton, NJ: Princeton University Press.

Vidich, Arthur J., and Joseph Bensman. 1958. *Small Town in Mass Society: Class, Power and Religion in a Rural Community*. Princeton, NJ: Princeton University Press.

Warren, Roland L. 1970. "The good community—what would it be?" *Journal of the Community Society*. 1 (Spring) 14-24.

Warren, Roland L. 1978. *The Community in America*. Chicago, IL: Rand McNally & Co.

Wellman, Barry. 1979. "The community question: The intimate networks of East Yorkers." *American Journal of Sociology* 84 (March): 1201-31.

Wilkinson, Kenneth P. 1974. "Consequences of decline and social adjustments to it." Pp. 43-53 in Larry R. Whiting (ed.), *Communities Left Behind: Alternatives for Development*. Ames, IA: Iowa State University Press.

Wilkinson, Kenneth P. 1979. "Social well-being and community." *Journal of the Community Development Society* 10 (1): 5-16.

Wilkinson, Kenneth P. 1986. "In search of the community in the changing countryside." *Rural Sociology* 51 (Spring): 1-17.

Wilkinson, Kenneth P. 1990. "Crime and community." Pp. 151-68 in A. E. Luloff and L. E. Swanson (eds.), *American Rural Communities*. Boulder, CO: Westview Press.

Wilkinson, Kenneth P. 1991. *The Community in Rural America*. Westport, CT: Greenwood Press.

Williams, J., A. Sofranko, and B. Root. 1977. "Change agents and industrial development in small towns." *Journal of the Community Development Society* 8 (Spring): 319-29.

Wirth, Louis. 1938. "Urbanism as a way of life." *American Journal of Sociology* 44 (July): 3-24.

17

Human Capital as a Rural Development Strategy: Promise or False Hope?

David Mulkey
Lionel J. Beaulieu

Introduction

The concept of human capital (Becker 1964; Schultz 1961), developed from early attempts to assess the value of human beings and establish the wealth of nations (Kiker 1966), has maintained a prominent place in the social science literature. Even in the policy arena, it has proved important in guiding discussions and shaping policy actions at the national, regional and local levels (chapter by Beaulieu and Mulkey). The logic underlying the human capital approach is, in the words of one author here (Hobbs), "an integral component of American orthodoxy" and "deceptively simple and direct." Investment in human capital is the primary vehicle for individual growth and development, and the aggregate stock of human capital is a major determinant of economic competitiveness and growth at the national and sub-national levels. In the words of Schultz (1961: 1):

Although it is obvious that people acquire useful skills and knowledge, it is not obvious that these skills and knowledge are a form of capital, that this capital is in substantial part a product of deliberate investment, that it has grown in Western societies at a much faster rate than conventional (non-human) capital, and that its growth may well be the most distinctive feature of the economic system. It has been widely observed that increases in national output have been large compared with the increases of land, man-hours, and physical reproducible capital. Investment in human capital is probably the major explanation for this difference.

The human capital model, at its most basic, is one of investment. Individuals, and by extension families and communities, forgo current consumption to invest in human capital (education, training, health care, migration, etc.) in expectation of future returns which, when discounted to the present, exceed the value of the consumption foregone. Individuals benefit through higher life long earnings, and the public gains as more productive citizens make greater contributions and impose fewer costs on society.

However, the process of human capital acquisition and its contribution to individual and societal well being is, in reality, extremely complex. Various criticisms of human capital theory relate to measurement difficulties and the inability to clearly establish causal directions. Alternative approaches have examined the roles of families and communities, the influence of labor demand, the screening hypothesis and job competition models, and the theory of dual labor markets. Still, our understanding of why people invest in human capital, and more importantly, why they choose not to invest, is incomplete. In the aggregate, the link between human capital investment and economic growth and development remains unclear (chapter by Beaulieu and Mulkey).

We do know that the process of human capital development is neither "simple" nor "direct." Clearly, individual decisions with regard to human capital are paramount, but just as clearly, these decisions are subject to factors extending beyond individuals, elements involving individuals' interactions with one another, with families, and with larger social and economic organizations and institutions. This book, its selection of chapters, and its organization, grew out of this complexity; out of the recognition that realizing the potential for human capital development in rural America will require the simultaneous consideration of a broad set of problems.

Chapters in this volume have addressed the treatment of human capital in the literature and considered the main components of human capital investment—education, health care and migration—consistent with the traditional human capital perspective. Chapters treating the broader set of forces shaping rural America—social, economic, and technological—were included as well, as were chapters addressing family considerations, the role of the community, and the impact of local labor markets. Other chapters addressed particular factors or situations which impinge on the acquisition or utilization of human capital skills. In particular, attention was devoted to race, ethnic and gender issues, poverty, and worker displacement.

The intent of the volume was to establish the current state of human capital in rural America, to identify factors which inhibit its further development and utilization, and to suggest avenues for improvement. To that end, individual chapter authors have assessed particular situations, identified issues, and offered policy alternatives for consideration. The remaining challenge in this chapter is to highlight some of the key ideas and issues that have been put forth by these individuals. Hopefully, the common threads contained in this volume will provide a basis for progress in the policy arena and serve to guide further research on the subject of human capital.

Common Ground

Several points discussed in this volume represent areas of general agreement among the various chapter authors. These include a common understanding of changes taking place in rural America, the concept of human capital itself, the existing stock of human capital in rural areas relative to its current utilization, and the role of family and community in the acquisition of human capital.

A Changing Rural America

An oft repeated but important point echoing throughout this volume relates to change in rural America, and associated with this change, the consensus that development policies based on extractive industries and low wage manufacturing are no longer sufficient for most rural communities and rural residents. The skills and abilities of rural residents—the stock of human capital—are increasingly important to individual growth and development and to the success of rural communities. The exact nature of human capital and economic development linkages, as noted above, remains unclear. However, this lack of knowledge does not negate the increased and expanding importance of an educated and skilled labor force to maintain community competitiveness and to allow rural residents to achieve their full potential as productive citizens.

Economically, major forces are at work; most job growth is in the service occupations, the nation's population is aging, small businesses are the primary generator of new jobs, and most industries and businesses are impacted by the global economy. Rural communities are no longer the exception. In fact, due to their dependence on traditional industries and generally more specialized economies, rural localities are more likely to be vulnerable to national and international economic forces. Further, as knowledge-based sectors of the economy become more prominent, this vulnerability is likely to increase (chapter by Pulver).

Sociologically, a similar and related story can be told. Major changes are impinging, not just on the economic vitality of rural communities, but on the very fabric of the community itself, the ability or capacity of residents for collective action on behalf of common problems (chapters by: Luloff and Swanson; Wilkinson).

Technological change, the "information age" and the coming of the information super highway, is equally important to rural residents and communities. Technology offers the potential for dramatic changes in relationships between work place and residential location; rural communities may no longer be isolated from the mainstream of economic and social activity. Yet, technology offers no guarantee of rural success; the eventual impact of technology remains an open question. Forces offering the potential for reduced isolation and inclusion may also portend continued job losses, reduced competitiveness, and weakened community ties.

Modern technologies, across the board, are not being fully exploited in rural areas due to greater profit potentials in urban areas, the lack of a high quality rural infrastructure, and the levels/types of skills and abilities in rural areas. Several authors remind us that without sufficient and committed policy intervention, the potential of technology to bring improvements to rural areas is likely to go unrealized (chapters by: Hyman, Gamm, and Shingler; Pulver; Wilkinson).

The Concept of Human Capital

The traditional view of human capital—skills and abilities residing in people—leads directly to consideration of health care, formal education (elementary, secondary and higher education), occupational training, and job skills learned through experience. However, treatment of the concept here points out other forms of human capital that may be particularly important from a community development viewpoint. Various authors speak of community building skills, specialized leadership and organizations, flexibility and openness to new directions, analytical paradigms for making sound community decisions, economic development literacy, interorganizational exchange, and community problem identification skills (chapters by: Hobbs; Hyman, Gamm, and Shingler; Pulver; Wilkinson). All represent skills or knowledge residing in individuals, and the ability of a community to act—the existence of *community agency* (chapter by Luloff and Swanson)—may well depend on such skills.

Again, the abilities of rural people are increasingly important to individual and community success. However, the set of skills traditionally used to characterize a labor force and usually associated with either rural education or job training programs, is not adequate to describe the stock of human capital necessary for community survival.

Human Capital Stocks in Rural America

Regardless of the latter point above, the traditional aspects of human capital remain important for rural areas. Here, deficiencies have improved in recent years, particularly with regard to high school completion rates.

However, rural areas continue to lag their urban counterparts as reflected in various measures of educational achievement. Gaps in the proportion of adults with less than a high school education are notably larger among rural Blacks, Hispanics, American Indians, displaced workers and those in poverty. Among rural women, the issue is less one of low rates of high school completion and more one of limited investments in education beyond high school. Further, it must be acknowledged that the education problems of rural America are compounded by inadequate access to health care and resulting lower health status among rural populations.

Unfortunately, there is evidence to suggest that rural areas do not currently fully utilize existing human capital, and that individuals may respond to the perceived lack of opportunity by investing less in human capital. That is, large numbers of individuals have education, skills, and experience in excess of requirements of their current job (chapters by: Findeis; Hobbs; Hyman, Gamm and Shingler; Jensen and McLaughlin; Killian and Beaulieu; Lyson; Stallmann, Mwachofi, Flora, and Johnson; Snipp; Swaim; Vogel and Coward; Wilkinson).

More importantly, the findings noted here suggest that human capital investment, in and of itself, may not improve individual or community well-being. For rural areas, this likely means that individuals, in order to better themselves by acquiring additional human capital, will continue to face the prospect of migration to urban areas. In fact, evidence indicates that selective migration continues to reduce the human capital stock of rural areas (chapter by Lichter, McLaughlin, and Cornwell).

The Importance of Family and Community

Evidence and arguments presented here, and the numerous citations which the authors provide to other literature, establish beyond a doubt, the importance of family and community factors to human capital acquisition and utilization. In the education arena, school outcomes are strongly dependent on economic and social attributes of families and communities; the success of schools in educating children is determined to a large extent by factors which are beyond the control of the school.

As with formal education, the same is likely to be true of other types of human capital acquired through formal and informal learning. For example, signals sent by local labor markets will influence perceptions of returns to human capital investments and may influence levels of community support for educational programs. Further, community attitudes towards new ideas, community participation, and receptiveness to change, will influence individual decisions regarding participation in a variety of human capital improvement activities (chapters by: Hobbs; Luloff and

Swanson; Stallmann, Mwachofi, Flora, and Johnson; Wenk and Hardesty; Wilkinson).

Policy Implications

The common threads of agreement noted in the last section hold several general policy implications and highlight continuing research needs relating to human capital investment and individual and community improvements. Clearly, one such implication is simply the range of human capital needs and the types of programs necessary to address those needs. Human capital programs must be broad-based and require sufficient flexibility to address a range of skills which include, but extend beyond, those associated with existing formal education and job training programs. It is necessary to examine the content of current programs in light of increasing requirements for higher levels of cognitive skills. But at the same time, it is critical that attention be focused on the development of additional community problem-solving and organizational skills.

A more troubling implication relates to the apparent current excess of human capital in rural areas based on examination of various measures of educational achievement. Do these findings imply that additional investments in human capital will not increase economic well-being in most rural areas? Alternatively, do these findings simply imply measurement problems? That is, does educational achievement really measure the type or quality of human capital existing in rural communities? Or, does the excess indicate that rural communities have the wrong types of human capital skills?

Which questions are true? A careful reading of the chapters contained in this volume provides no definitive answer, but in the absence of clear answers, giving careful consideration to these questions may be critical to the success of human capital and community development programs. Perhaps, the safest approach is to assume that all are true, to some extent, and considering the degree of rural diversity, in some locations. It also seems reasonable to assume that the role of human capital will likely be more important to the success of rural development efforts in the future. The resulting policy implication is twofold.

First, as noted above, human capital development programs will need sufficient flexibility to respond to the unique needs of specific communities. In some communities, particular types of human capital investment may contribute to increased economic development. In others, however, human capital investment will be successful in addressing rural economic development only if undertaken in concert with programs designed to address both the quantity and quality of available jobs. For example, some communities and community residents may benefit from programs designed to improve workforce skills, while other communities may require attention to family problems or community leadership skills, to structural barriers to personal advancement, or to some other community feature which impinges on the human capital arena.

The latter point above is reinforced by the general consensus over the importance of family and communities to outcomes of education in rural areas and to individual participation in human capital improvement efforts. Again, findings discussed by various authors here suggest that programs which focus narrowly on human capital improvement in the context of existing institutions may not make much difference. For example, efforts which result in marginal increases in financial resources devoted to schools, simplistic reform measures internal to schools, or increases in existing occupational training programs will likely have little lasting effect. Successful programs at the community level will require efforts that begin with and involve local residents in a complete assessment of existing needs and include the flexibility to address those needs.

Future Directions

In summary, it appears that human capital deficiencies persist in rural areas, that such deficiencies are more pronounced in some groups and in some places, and that existing deficiencies describe shortcomings which extend beyond simple measures of educational achievement or labor force skills. Thus, it follows that existing programs of education, job training and health care are not adequate for the task of making significant change in rural areas through human capital investment.

Rural areas need ways to mobilize new and innovative institutional arrangements to attack human capital issues on a number of fronts simultaneously. Efforts must begin with communities and families and address factors such as poverty, inadequate employment opportunities, public services and facilities, and various structural barriers to the full realization of human potential in rural areas.

The approach outlined in the introductory chapter here could provide direction for such a concerted effort to improve human capital in rural areas. Issues were outlined as three related sets of problems: (1) personal or individual characteristics; (2) family and community considerations; and (3) structural barriers which preclude some groups from full participation. Within each of these areas, numerous policy alternatives exist which, individually, can address some aspect of the overall problem. Some which address local issues can be adopted at the community level, and some are likely to require action at the state and/or federal level.

Communities clearly cannot address all human capital problems in the absence of assistance from outside the community, assistance in terms of both policy direction and resources with which to implement human capital improvement programs. Unfortunately, at the federal level, and in most cases, at the state level, there is no clearly articulated rural development policy within which to consider the necessary range of assistance programs. Further, there seems to be little in the way of consensus with respect to a "vision" on which to base such a policy. Perhaps the most significant step at this point is to engage such a debate. The objective would be a concerted rural development effort within a consistent policy context. Without such an effort, the promise of human capital improvement in rural America is likely to remain a false hope.

References

Becker, Gary S. 1964. *Human Capital: A Theoretical and Empirical Analysis, With Special Reference to Education.* New York, NY: Columbia University Press.

Kiker, B. F. 1966. "The historical roots of the concept of human capital." *Journal of Political Economy* 74: 481-99.

Schultz, Theodore W. 1961. "Investment in human capital." *The American Economic Review* 51 (1): 1-17.

Index

American Indian
  education, 17, 139 - 143, 147 -
    152, 154 - 162, 164 - 165, 377
  population, 139, 142 - 144, 148,
    153 - 154, 162 - 163, 165
  reservation, 140, 142 - 147, 151,
    153 - 155, 157 - 158, 163, 165
Black
  educational attainment, 30, 147 -
    148, 177 - 179, 314, 318, 320,
    324
  employment opportunities, 170 -
    176, 179 - 180, 220, 225, 233
  rural, 167 - 169, 171 - 179, 181,
    291, 377
College education, 19, 40, 43 - 46,
    114, 120 - 124, 127, 129 - 130,
    147 - 150, 152, 155 - 161, 163 -
    165, 177, 193, 210, 264 - 265,
    278, 314 - 318, 320, 323 - 324,
    326 - 329, 336 - 337, 339, 347
Community
  agency, 18, 351 - 359, 361 - 363,
    365 - 368
  attributes, 10, 68, 353, 364, 371
  development, 57, 60 - 63, 66, 70,
    74, 77 - 78, 80 - 81, 90, 100, 105,
    135, 272 - 273, 277 - 278, 281 -
    282, 284 - 285, 351 - 354, 363,
    368, 370, 376, 378
  disaffection, 70, 72, 351, 353 - 354,
    356, 358 - 363, 366, 368 - 369
  empowerment, 66, 79, 359
  leadership, 57, 61, 81, 272, 275 - 276,
    307, 364, 379
  solidarity, 355
  structure, 8 - 10, 60, 67, 70, 75 - 76,
    82, 356 - 357, 360 - 361, 363, 365 -
    366, 368
  sustainability, 104 - 105
Displaced workers
  composition, 213 - 222, 225 - 234

incidence, 213 - 222, 225 - 228, 230 -
  231 - 232, 234
Dual economy theory, 13, 19, 21
Economic
  changes, 49, 53, 59, 61, 213, 217
  development, 17, 43, 52, 58 - 59,
    61, 73 - 74, 77, 91, 94, 100, 105,
    135, 137 - 138, 169, 178 - 179, 182,
    204, 209 - 210, 237, 259, 261, 264,
    266 - 267, 269, 271 - 272, 281, 284,
    335, 344, 346, 348, 353 - 354, 360,
    365
  diversity, 50, 57
  forces, 13, 49, 59, 60, 61
  problems, 52, 61, 181
Economy
  farm, 19, 50 - 51, 58, 62, 81, 101
  global, 16, 24, 53, 57 - 60, 94, 179,
    220, 375
  two-tier, 264
Education
  and gender, 189, 193, 197 - 198, 205 -
    208, 210, 316, 320, 325, 326, 327,
    335, 347, 377
  metro, 27, 98, 123
  nonmetro, 98, 123
  performance, 241, 284
  rural, 27, 41, 127, 130 - 131, 136, 138,
    183, 198, 209, 234, 263, 267, 275,
    283, 318, 341
Educational
  aspirations, 6, 8, 19, 131, 277, 283,
    316
  attainment, 3, 7, 9, 11, 18, 25, 27 - 29,
    32, 35, 37 - 38, 42, 112 - 114, 116,
    120 - 121, 127 - 129, 131, 133, 134,
    139, 143, 157 - 158, 176, 193, 207,
    237, 260 - 261, 263 - 266, 275, 313 -
    321, 327, 330 - 331
  performance, 268 - 271, 337
  status, 27 - 28, 243, 245 - 246, 253,
    313

Family
  attributes, 9 - 10, 324, 328 - 330, 377
  background, 6 - 7, 11, 20, 313, 315,
    318, 324, 327 - 329
  characteristics, 3, 7, 18, 117, 315,
    324, 327
  environment, 317, 330
Head Start, 115, 131, 133 - 134, 151,
  178
Health care
  facilities, 52, 96, 285, 289 - 290, 300,
    302, 306, 308, 310 - 311
  impacts, 97, 285, 293, 295 - 296,
    300 - 306, 308 - 310
  maldistribution, 286 - 289, 291, 309 -
    311
  resources, 18, 105, 286, 292, 294
  services, 56, 60 - 61, 95 - 97, 285 -
    286, 288 - 291, 294 - 295, 298 -
    299, 304 - 305, 307 - 308
  use, 289 - 290, 299, 309
High school dropouts, 20 - 21, 30, 42,
  44 - 46, 119 - 122, 131, 133 - 134,
  147, 149, 153, 161, 219, 264, 329,
  337, 340, 342, 345, 347 - 348
Hispanic
  educational attainment, 30, 176 -
    179, 320, 324
  employment opportunities, 170 -
    177, 179 - 180, 220
  rural, 167 - 176, 178 - 179, 181, 377
Household structure, 118, 121, 123 -
  131, 137, 172, 189, 313 - 314,
  316 - 320, 324, 327, 329
Human Capital
  and economic development, 60,
    374 - 375, 378
  and education, 265
  and gender, 183 - 184, 198 - 199,
    204 - 205, 209
  deficits, 17, 24 - 25, 118, 213 - 214,
    219, 222, 225, 227 - 230, 239, 376,
    379
  demand, 26, 31 - 32, 38, 41 - 42
  investments, 4, 6, 9 - 10, 16, 18 - 20,
    24, 38, 40, 43, 112 - 113, 128, 183 -

    184, 189, 199, 204, 206, 225, 259,
    261 - 262, 265, 280, 284, 286, 313,
    333 - 336, 338 - 341, 343, 345 - 347,
    373 - 374, 377 - 378, 380
  mismatch, 35, 38, 41 - 42
  supply, 24, 31, 38, 41
  theory, 4 - 6, 11, 112 - 115, 136, 230,
    262, 265, 334, 374, 380
Information age, 77, 81 - 83, 91, 93 - 94,
  99, 101 - 102, 105 - 106, 376
Job Competition Model, 11 - 12
Jobs
  low-wage, 18, 152, 175, 200, 263, 266,
    284, 344
Labor
  demand, 10, 116, 135, 210, 236, 255,
    333, 337, 339, 343, 374
  queue, 11 - 13, 40
Labor markets
  dual, 14 - 16, 336, 374
  rural, 17, 25, 27, 31, 41, 73, 123, 176,
    184, 189, 193, 198, 200, 207, 210,
    213 - 214, 216, 226, 228, 230 - 231,
    277, 296, 311, 333, 340
  trends, 23, 205, 225 - 230, 233
  urban, 25, 41, 214, 217 - 218, 228, 232,
    234, 255
Manufacturing, 25, 40, 49, 51 - 54, 56,
  57 - 58, 61, 72 - 73, 79, 87, 94, 104,
  105, 173, 180, 193 - 197, 214, 218,
  263, 266, 275 - 276, 283, 336, 338,
  340, 345, 347, 361, 365
Migration
  composition, 235, 238 - 239, 241- 242,
    246 - 253 - 254, 262 - 263
  exchange, 236 - 238, 246, 253 - 254
  rates, 52, 216, 226, 232, 240, 242 - 244,
    247 - 249, 255, 263
  selectivity, 43, 204, 238 - 241, 243 -
    246, 253 - 255
  streams, 27, 72, 210, 236, 238 - 244,
    246 - 249, 256, 259, 334, 338
Occupational
  aspirations, 7, 8, 227
On-the-job training, 4, 13, 18, 20, 113,
  114, 136, 183, 189, 265

Outmigration, 114, 120, 135, 198, 204, 227, 230, 235 - 246, 248, 250 - 251, 253 - 255, 262, 265, 319, 327, 337, 342

Population
aging/elderly, 54, 55, 56

Poverty, 51
and gender, 129 - 130, 137, 189, 204
metropolitan, 111 - 113, 118, 121 - 128
Nonmetropolitan, 69, 72, 87, 111 - 112 - 113, 118, 121 - 124, 127 - 128, 133 - 134, 136 - 137, 208, 270, 291, 296 - 297, 299, 306 - 308, 311, 377

Rural
business, 98, 100 - 101
development, 40, 49, 52 - 53, 59 - 60, 62 - 63, 65 - 66, 73 - 74, 78 - 79 - 83, 86, 90, 104 - 106, 138, 178, 181, 205 - 206, 208, 236, 255, 259, 262, 265 - 267, 271, 277, 282 - 284, 306, 308 - 309, 346 - 347, 351, 353, 357, 359, 363, 367, 373, 380
exploitation, 71, 73, 77, 87, 91, 376
space, 70 - 72, 74, 76, 78, 82, 91, 101 - 102

Schooling, 6
rural, 231, 261, 274 - 275
years, 5, 35, 40, 42, 44 - 46, 118, 148 - 149, 154 - 155, 157, 164, 168, 197, 213, 225, 232, 260, 265

Schools
and community development, 75, 267, 270 - 272, 274 - 281, 283
enrollment, 268 - 270, 284, 315
rural, 18, 59, 98 - 99, 198 - 199, 205, 208, 226, 236, 259, 261, 267 - 272, 274 - 281
urban, 226

Screening Hypothesis, 10 - 11, 20

Small business, 53, 56 - 58, 63, 101, 180 - 181

Social Capital
community, 9, 270 - 271, 273 - 274, 280 - 282
family, 7 - 9, 270 - 271, 317, 369

Status Attainment, 7, 20, 113, 138

Status dropout rates, 151 - 153, 162, 168, 274, 319, 322, 325, 336, 339, 341 - 342

Technology
and communities, 92 - 95, 98 - 105, 265, 278 - 279, 284, 360, 376
high-tech, 20, 53 - 54, 57 - 58, 60 - 63, 85 - 87, 89, 91, 94 - 95, 98, 105 - 106, 181, 220, 282

Teleological society, 89, 90 - 91, 93, 95 - 96, 98, 100 - 101, 103, 105

Work experience, 113 - 115, 118, 120, 189, 200